MW00977171

Disney, Culture, and Curriculum

A presence for decades in individuals' everyday life practices and identity formation, The Walt Disney Company has more recently also become an influential element within the 'big' curriculum of public and private spaces outside of yet in proximity to formal educational institutions. *Disney, Culture, and Curriculum* explores the myriad ways that Disney's curricula and pedagogies manifest in public consciousness, cultural discourses, and the education system. Examining Disney's historical development and contemporary manifestations, this book critiques and deconstructs its products and perspectives while providing insight into Disney's operations within popular culture and everyday life in the United States and beyond.

The contributors engage with Disney's curricula and pedagogies in a variety of ways, through critical analysis of Disney films, theme parks, and planned communities, how Disney has been taught and resisted both in and beyond schools, ways in which fans and consumers develop and negotiate their identities with their engagement with Disney, and how race, class, gender, sexuality, and consumerism are constructed through Disney content. Incisive, comprehensive, and highly interdisciplinary, *Disney, Culture, and Curriculum* extends the discussion of popular culture as curriculum and pedagogy into new avenues by focusing on the affective and ontological aspects of identity development as well as the commodification of social and cultural identities, experiences, and subjectivities.

Jennifer A. Sandlin is Associate Professor in the Justice and Social Inquiry program in the School of Social Transformation at Arizona State University, USA.

Julie C. Garlen is Associate Professor of Education in the Department of Teaching and Learning at Georgia Southern University, USA.

Studies In Curriculum Theory
William F. Pinar, Series Editor

Reynolds/Webber (Eds.)
Expanding Curriculum Theory: Dis/Positions and Lines of Flight, Second Edition

Sandlin/Garlen (Eds.)
Disney, Culture, and Curriculum

Jung-Hoon Jung
The Concept of Care in Curriculum Studies: Juxtaposing *Currere* and *Hakbeolism*

Nohl/Somel
Education and Social Dynamics: A Multilevel Analysis of Curriculum Change in Turkey

Ng-A-Fook/Ibrahim/Reis (Eds.)
Provoking Curriculum Studies: Strong Poetry and the Arts of the Possible in Education

Tröhler/Lenz (Eds.)
Trajectories in the Development of Modern School Systems: Between the National and the Global

Popkewitz (Ed.)
The "Reason" of Schooling: Historicizing Curriculum Studies, Pedagogy, and Teacher Education

Henderson (Ed.)
Reconceptualizing Curriculum Development: Inspiring and Informing Action

Magrini
Social Efficiency and Instrumentalism in Education: Critical Essays in Ontology, Phenomenology, and Philosophical Hermeneutics

Wang
Nonviolence and Education: Cross-Cultural Pathways

Hurren/Hasebe-Ludt (Eds.)
Contemplating Curriculum: Genealogies/Times/Places

Pinar (Ed.)
International Handbook of Curriculum Research, Second Edition

Latta
Curricular Conversations: Play is the (Missing) Thing

Doll
Pragmatism, Post-Modernism, and Complexity Theory: The "Fascinating Imaginative Realm" of William E. Doll, Jr.
Edited by Donna Trueit

Carlson
The Education of Eros: A History of Education and the Problem of Adolescent Sexuality Since 1950

Taubman
Disavowed Knowledge: Psychoanalysis, Education, and Teaching

Pinar
What Is Curriculum Theory? Second Edition

Tröhler
Languages of Education: Protestant Legacies, National Identities, and Global Aspirations

Hendry
Engendering Curriculum History

Handa
What Does Understanding Mathematics Mean for Teachers? Relationship as a Metaphor for Knowing

Joseph (Ed.)
Cultures of Curriculum, Second Edition

Sandlin/Schultz/Burdick (Eds.)
Handbook of Public Pedagogy: Education and Learning Beyond Schooling

Malewski (Ed.)
Curriculum Studies Handbook—The Next Moment

Pinar
The Wordliness of a Cosmopolitan Education: Passionate Lives in Public Service

Taubman
Teaching By Numbers: Deconstructing the Discourse of Standards and Accountability in Education

Appelbaum
Children's Books for Grown-Up Teachers: Reading and Writing Curriculum Theory

Eppert/Wang (Eds.)
Cross-Cultural Studies in Curriculum: Eastern Thought, Educational Insights

Jardine/Friesen/Clifford
Curriculum in Abundance

Autio
Subjectivity, Curriculum, and Society: Between and Beyond German Didaktik and Anglo-American Curriculum Studies

Brantlinger (Ed.)
Who Benefits from Special Education?: Remediating (Fixing) Other People's Children

Pinar/Irwin (Eds.)
Curriculum in a New Key: The Collected Works of Ted T. Aoki

Reynolds/Webber (Eds.)
Expanding Curriculum Theory: Dis/Positions and Lines of Flight

McKnight
Schooling, the Puritan Imperative, and the Molding of an American National Identity: Education's "Errand Into the Wilderness"

Pinar (Ed.)
International Handbook of Curriculum Research

Morris
Curriculum and the Holocaust: Competing Sites of Memory and Representation

Doll
Like Letters in Running Water: A Mythopoetics of Curriculum

Westbury/Hopmann/Riquarts (Eds.)
Teaching as a Reflective Practice: The German Didaktic Tradition

Reid
Curriculum as Institution and Practice: Essays in the Deliberative Tradition

Pinar (Ed.)
Queer Theory in Education

Huebner
The Lure of the Transcendent: Collected Essays by Dwayne E. Huebner.
Edited by Vikki Hillis. Collected and Introduced by William F. Pinar

For additional information on titles in the Studies in Curriculum Theory series visit **www.routledge.com/education**

Disney, Culture, and Curriculum

Edited by
Jennifer A. Sandlin and
Julie C. Garlen

Routledge
Taylor & Francis Group

NEW YORK AND LONDON

First published 2016
by Routledge
711 Third Avenue, New York, NY 10017

and by Routledge
2 Park Square, Milton Park, Abingdon, Oxon, OX14 4RN

Routledge is an imprint of the Taylor & Francis Group, an informa business

© 2016 Taylor & Francis

Library of Congress Cataloging-in-Publication Data
Sandlin, Jennifer A., editor. | Garlen, Julie C., editor.
Title: Disney, culture, and curriculum / edited by Jennifer A. Sandlin
and Julie C. Garlen.
Description: New York : Routledge, 2016. | Series: Studies in curriculum
theory | Includes bibliographical references and index.
Identifiers: LCCN 2015037115| ISBN 9781138957688 (hardback) |
ISBN 9781315661599 (ebook)
Subjects: LCSH: Walt Disney Company. | Popular culture—Study and
teaching—United States. | Motion pictures in education—United States.
| Education—Curricula—United States.
Classification: LCC PN1999.W27 D56 2016 | DDC 384/.80979494—dc23
LC record available at http://lccn.loc.gov/2015037115

ISBN: 978-1-138-95768-8 (hbk)
ISBN: 978-1-315-66159-9 (ebk)

Typeset in Bembo
by Florence Production Ltd, Stoodleigh, Devon, UK

Printed and bound in the United States of America by Publishers Graphics,
LLC on sustainably sourced paper.

For our children
Grant, Taylor, James, and John

Contents

Panning the Field A   xii
Jorge Lucero

Foreword SHIRLEY R. STEINBERG   *xiii*
Preface   *xvii*
Acknowledgements   *xxv*

Panning the Field: Museum Placard   xxviii
Jorge Lucero

Panning the Field B   xxix
Jorge Lucero

1   Introduction: Feeling Disney, Buying Disney, Being Disney   1
JENNIFER A. SANDLIN, JULIE C. GARLEN

Panning the Field C   28
Jorge Lucero

PART I
Feeling Disney: Disney Fears and Fantasies   29

2   waltdisneyconfessions@tumblr: Narrative, Subjectivity,
    and Reading Online Spaces of Confession   31
TASHA AUSMAN, LINDA RADFORD

3   Practical Pigs and Other Instrumental Animals: Public
    Pedagogies of Laborious Pleasure in Disney Productions   47
JAKE BURDICK

4   "This Is No Ordinary Apple!": Learning to Fail Spectacularly
    from the Queer Pedagogies of Disney's Diva Villains   59
MARK HELMSING

5   The Postfeminist Princess: Public Discourse and Disney's
    Curricular Guide to Feminism   73
MICHAEL MACALUSO

6 "The Illusion of Life": Nature in the Animated Disney
   Curriculum   87
   CALEB STEINDAM

   Panning the Field D   102
   Jorge Lucero

PART II
**Buying Disney: Commodified, Caricatured, and
Contested Subjectivities**   **103**

7 I Dream of a Disney World: Exploring Language,
   Curriculum, and Public Pedagogy in Brazil's Middle-Class
   Playground   105
   SANDRO R. BARROS

8 If It Quacks Like a Duck . . .: The Classist Curriculum of
   Disney's Reality Television Shows   120
   ROBIN REDMON WRIGHT

9 Deliriumland: Disney and the Simulation of Utopia   136
   JASON J. WALLIN

10 Camp Disney: Consuming Queer Sensibilities, Commodifying
   the Normative   148
   WILL LETTS

11 Black Feminist Thought and Disney's Paradoxical
   Representation of Black Girlhood in *Doc McStuffins*   161
   RACHEL ALICIA GRIFFIN

   Panning the Field E   176
   Jorge Lucero

PART III
Being Disney: Freedom, Participation, and Control   **177**

12 On the Count of Three: Magic, New Knowledge, and
   Learning at Walt Disney World   179
   GEORGE J. BEY, III

13 Disneyfied/ized Participation in the Art Museum   193
   NADINE M. KALIN

14 The Corseted Curriculum: Four Feminist Readings of a
   Strong Disney Princess   208
   ANNETTE FURO, NICHOLE E. GRANT, PAMELA ROGERS,
   KELSEY CATHERINE SCHMITZ

15 A New Dimension of Disney Magic: MyMagic+ and
Controlled Leisure   220
GABRIEL S. HUDDLESTON, JULIE C. GARLEN,
JENNIFER A. SANDLIN

16 Consuming Innocence: Disney's Corporate Stranglehold on
Youth in the Digital Age   233
HENRY A. GIROUX

Panning the Field F   250
Jorge Lucero

About the Contributors   *251*
Index   *256*

Foreword

Ruining Disney? A Gentle Point of View

Shirley R. Steinberg

How can you suggest that Disney can be a negative influence?

We are a Disney family, there is nothing you say that can change our love for Disney.

We were married at Disneyworld, it is a sacred place for us.

We saved for five years to take our children to Disney. In Brazil, the cost was equivalent to a teacher's salary for one year.

I didn't take your class for you to ruin Disney for me.

Far be it from me to subvert, overthrow, demolish, or become the ruination of the Disney ontology. I beg indulgence for my words, as readers allow me to propose a compromise between lovers of Disney and lucid thought. Inspired by the quotes above (all anonymous, former students), writing this foreword allows me to explore a harmonious and informed way in which Disney can be discussed without tears and agitation. Instead of a raging critique, let this be a benevolent palaver, a harmonious confab, inspired by my desire to contribute to this book, a magnanimous and pedagogic précis on Disney watching.

The work contained in this book is not meant to be vicious or callous, and none of the authors hope to cause children, parents, investors, nor newlyweds harm—nor ruin. To the contrary, these chapters are written by society's historians, academics, and advocates—chapters written to inform and to humbly enlighten, should ruin come to any reader, we must remember that it was not intentional. In *Disney, Culture, and Curriculum,* Sandlin and Garlen have gathered together commentary designed to add to an expanding group of Disney watchers. The book is diverse and unique, blending personal experience and observation with the historical, the academic, and the commercial; none of it directed towards ruining sacred memories, experiences, childhood, or parenting skills. Indeed, let this volume stand as an act of kindness, a cultural and pedagogical intervention created through butterflies, flowers, and fairies tapping readers on the shoulder with sparkling wands. This book will shepherd the angry and the fearful through a discourse of critical theory, radical rationality, and capital sensibility, while hoping that all readers know we meant well, and that when the final page is turned, all will be happier ever after.

Critiques of this book will be concerned that our words will destroy their memories and perceptions of The Happiest Place on Earth, they may balk at suggestions that good parenting would include a way to balance fun with social consciousness, and claim that Disney-spawned television and film extends childhood innocence. Classroom teachers will race out to buy Disney books, bulletin board cutouts, and Epcot curriculum guides, lest our critique cause a global Disney shutdown. With consideration for our critics, we promise reasonable and considerate fair-mindedness. We present different ways in which to understand Disney, with the codicil that a Disney lover/consumer/devotee can still enjoy Disney, but with a socially just, diverse, progressive, and charitable understanding that the giant conglomerate eats its young.

Some of this book's authors may disclose that they live a polarized Disney life. They are consumers, yet they are critics, and the existence of this book stands to their inherent integrity. Self-awareness has, in a sense, ushered in our desire to balance childhood memories, parental guilt, our bank accounts, and societal commitments in search of a Disney discourse. I recall a sunny Orlando day, riding in a little boat on a rail, pen and pad in hand, recording my impressions and thoughts as I rode through *It's a Small World*. Our youngest (of four), Bronwyn, listened with nine-year-old indignation, looked up at me and asked, "Mom, why do you always have to deconstruct everything?" I realized at that moment that my dreams had come true, and I had achieved my ultimate maternal academic goal: I could bring my kids to Disney World and do research.

By balancing these tender scales, I was an inside Disney watcher, a consumer, and a critic—I had to live with this duality. Bronwyn named my discomfort, and admittedly, I am pleased to note her question in my research. Perhaps my admission will soften those who despair that I tread on the sacred.

The watchers in this book span life experiences and positionalities, and all agree that Disney must be watched and understood. Perhaps the plethora of crying students dismayed at *Mickey Mouse Monopoly* has motivated us—was it the alarming amount of adults at Disney properties *sans* children or youth?—maybe we were guided in our watching through Disney's imperialistic machinations these many decades. Our watching includes Baudrillardian analysis, challenging the hyperreal with our own webs of reality. We apply sexual preference, race, ethnicity, the natural, the pure, the royal and the public in our work. Our media literacies have queried evil stepmothers, dead moms, absent fathers, orphaned kids, and silenced females, all contained in the Disney family of desire. There is no better topic than Disney to use in the pursuit of our cultural studies.

There are no denials in this book as to the importance of Disney to global culture, capital, lexicons, and history. In less than a century, Disney has established itself as *the* creator of happiness, dream making, and truth. Readers are given the chance to decide just how these achievements can be interpreted, taught, and, as Bronwyn noted—deconstructed.

Preface

The purpose of this edited volume is to explore The Walt Disney Company and the myriad ways its curricula and pedagogies manifest. As a major multinational entertainment corporation, Disney is represented in almost every media platform (Wasko, 2001), and hundreds of millions of people each year across the globe engage with Disney products in some way. Through its ubiquity, The Walt Disney Company and its products significantly shape individual and group cultural identity (Giroux & Pollock, 2010; Schickel, 1968). Because of its influence on American and global culture, since the 1930s cultural critics and academics within a wide range of disciplines have engaged in cultural analyses of Disney (Budd, 2005), generating thousands of articles and books, including analyses of Disney films focusing on race, class, gender, sexuality, consumerism, colonialism, ethno-centrism, ethnographic analyses of Disney theme parks and planned communities, and critical perspectives on emotional labor and Disney's training programs, to name just a few.

Using a broad range of theoretical lenses, including arts-based and aesthetic inquiry, cultural studies, queer theories, feminist theories, and psychoanalytic approaches, the essays in this current volume take up Disney as curriculum and pedagogy and extend previous analyses into new avenues of exploration by focusing on the affective and ontological aspects of identity development as well as the commodification of social and cultural identities, experiences, and subjectivities. In this volume we embrace a perspective that acknowledges the viewer/consumer as an active, agentic participant in the meaning-making process who can derive pleasure from *and* engage critically with cultural texts and artifacts, such as those produced by The Walt Disney Company. *Disney, Culture, and Curriculum* thus takes seriously the idea that people (including us) are invested in Disney as a source of entertainment and pleasure, but also provides sustained critique of Disney products and perspectives. Unlike the self-proclaimed Disney enthusiasts who have written about the pleasure and entertainment the company provides, the authors in our book take up those themes not only to acknowledge that people engage with Disney in such ways, and to argue that these ways of engagement are important and legitimate, but also to appreciate and understand how the Disney corporation uses these very engagements with pleasure and entertainment to influence education and individual and social identity in the United States and beyond.

Disney, Culture, and Curriculum specifically targets educators, educational researchers, and curriculum theorists, engaging with the curricula and pedagogies of Disney in a variety of ways by critically reading Disney films and theme parks as texts, exploring the ways that Disney has been taught and resisted outside of traditional learning environments, examining the ways in which fans and consumers develop and negotiate their identities through and with their engagements with Disney, and analyzing how race, class, gender, sexuality, and consumerism are constructed through and within Disney discourses. This volume is divided into three sections, each of which explores a different component of Disney's curricula and pedagogies, which are enacted to help shape individual and group identities, culture, education, and society. We call these sections *Feeling Disney* (focusing on the affective turn), *Buying Disney* (focusing on the commodification of social and cultural identities, experiences, and subjectivities), and *Being Disney* (focusing on how Disney shapes our desires for both freedom and control and how we participate in these practices).

Overview

To varying extents, projects within Disney scholarship are always disruptive, especially those that take up Disney in critical ways. Such Disney scholarship disrupts because it bumps up against and punctures what Budd (2005) calls the "distinctive aura" surrounding Disney, which provides a sort of inoculation against critique. Critical scholarship calls into question the classic Disney image of family-friendly fun and nostalgia, and resists taken-for-granted notions that our emotional and consumptive engagements with Disney have no further meaning beyond entertainment. Despite a strong ability to resist critical analysis, however, even the most avid Disney fans have trouble *completely* ignoring Disney's questionable labor practices, relentless promotion of consumerism, profit motives, and stereotypical cultural representations. Fans must thus negotiate what Budd (2005) calls the "return of the repressed" (p. 3)—and critical scholarship can help facilitate those returns. Towards these ends, the book opens with **Jorge Lucero**'s artwork, entitled, *Panning the Field: A, B, C, D, E, and F*, which sets the stage for the various disruptions to come. This piece consists of an initial "Museum Placard" that describes the work as well as six images that are dispersed throughout the book, and seeks to interrupt the ubiquity of Disney imagery that has come to shape our physical and psychic landscapes. The folding collages that constitute the work were made, in Lucero's words, "with the intention of unsettling what is highly recognizable in order to propose open landscapes that are equally (if not more) voluptuous and brimming with energy than the original dynamic Disney forms. The new forms are bodies without organs, if you will." Next, in the Introduction, we (**Jenny** and **Julie**) provide an overview of previous Disney Studies scholarship, presenting some of the major themes and insights that have arisen from this vast scholarship—which have helped disrupt common sense ways of viewing Disney—in order to set the context for this current edited volume. The remainder of the book is divided into three parts, each of which furthers these kinds of disruptions, as they each take up the necessary task of analyzing and problematizing our engagements with Disney in order to advance a critical understanding of the ways that The Walt Disney Company, in all its manifestations, teaches us how to feel, buy, and be through experiences, products, and services that have become an integral part of global popular culture.

In **Part I,** *Feeling Disney: Disney Fears and Fantasies*, contributors explore the meanings and consequences of our emotional investments in Disney. From parks to movies to deluxe cruise line vacations, Disney goes to great lengths to create experiences that defy the realities of our everyday lives and place us in the center of an intricately fabricated fantasy of fulfillment. This dimension of the Disney experience is particularly significant in light of what Clough (2007) has denoted as "the affective turn" in the humanities and social sciences—an increased emphasis on affect across discourses of culture, subjectivity, embodiment, and identity. The essays in this section take up these lines of thought to investigate the shared social and cultural dimensions of fantasies of happiness, hope, and desire—and the fears contained within and repressed or denied by such fantasies—as they are expressed through various Disney discourses, texts, and spaces.

In their chapter on Tumblr as an online Disney confessional, **Tasha Ausman** and **Linda Radford** explore how waltdisneyconfessions@tumblr operates as a curriculum of desire that "pushes us to interrogate the currency of confession and the overall politics of readership". As they explain, the "confessions" thread

> operates as a safe place for adult fans of Disney to reveal their secret desires, wishes, hopes, disappointments and dreams about living, working, and becoming Disney as either cheerful spectators, employees (especially "face characters"), students in the Disney College Program (DCP), or in some cases, adoring devotees who fantasize about becoming 'real' Disney princes and princesses someday.

On the Tumblr site, individual subjectivities are shaped and reshaped within Disney discourses through the act of confession, which occurs via the appropriation and augmentation of familiar Disney images.

Continuing with the exploration of how Disney desires, wishes, hopes, and disappointments are produced and circulated, **Jake Burdick** argues that the early films *Steamboat Willie* and *The Three Little* Pigs can be read as manifestations of Walt Disney's desires for an idyllic childhood, for a Fordist utopian vision, and for the pleasure he associated with labor. Burdick illustrates how these desires still manifest within the recent Disney Pixar film *Inside Out*, demonstrating the durable association between Walt's desires and a romantic notion of the United States' past. Burdick advances a psychoanalytic understanding of these desires as public pedagogies that operate via Disney's seemingly endless intrusion into global life.

Expanding the focus on Disney desires and disappointments to gender identity, **Mark Helmsing** offers a chapter on the "polymorphous perverse curriculum" of queerness enacted through the Disney villains. By thinking queerly about the pedagogies of certain Disney diva villains, Helmsing connects his own experiences at learning to fail at being 'good' (straight, normal) to the spectacular failures of the Disney villains by offering readings of the lessons they provide on self-control, confidence, and love as queer pedagogies that teach us how to question the normalizing, legitimating assumptions and virtues of the fixed, unchanging (and uninteresting) essence of Disney's heroes.

Continuing with Helmsing's focus on gender identity, **Michael Macaluso** examines the popular animated film *Frozen*, which individual moviegoers and film critics alike have heralded as an exemplary feminist fairy tale. Macaluso problematizes the notions of feminism that undergird such praise, arguing that the film instead advances postfeminist characteristics and sensibilities that displace or replace feminist ideals or entangle them with anti-feminist sentiments. Through an analysis of online comments about the film, Macaluso considers how the cultural reception of the film reflects the notion that feminism is no longer needed because of contemporary narratives like *Frozen* that emphasize a progressive view of gender equity. In this way, online media discourse around the film enacts a curriculum of postfeminist cultural production through which the popular media, through the modulation of affect, operates to (re)produce gendered identities and subjectivities.

In the final chapter of this section, **Caleb Steindam** offers a different perspective on the relationship between desire and subjectivity by exploring how portrayals of the natural world in animated Disney films teach us into a particular way of relating to nature. Steindam argues that in spite of, and perhaps because of, being relatively isolated from nature, people are profoundly drawn to the notion of wildness, and animated films capitalize on this attraction. To illustrate how Disney shapes, distorts, and commodifies our concepts of nature, Steindam explores three persistent motifs that Disney uses in its portrayal of nature: *purity*, *wildness*, and *anthropomorphism*. Embedded in idealized animated representations, these motifs shape our emotional investments in animals in nature.

In **Part II**, ***Buying Disney: Commodified, Caricatured, and Contested Subjectivities***, authors explore the relationships between The Walt Disney Company and its consumers, and the particular ways in which those relationships are constructed and concretized. The commodification of Disney-produced characters is one important meaning-making process through which the curriculum of Disney operates. Each of the essays in this section explores how Disney texts appropriate and commodify different aspects of social identity and experience by capitalizing on cultural norms and myths, reinforcing stereotypes, and rewriting subjectivities.

Taking up global issues of class and consumer identity, **Sandro R. Barros** investigates how Brazilian Disney blogs illustrate the ways that the *"viagem para Disney"* (the trip to Disney) has become a middle-class obsession in Brazil. As Barros observes, the trip to Disney "signifies a sense of individual accomplishment, a sense of arrival at a not-so-figurative promised land wherein the meaning of one's success and well-being is oriented by the parks' enactment of societal ideals" that are part of a paradigmatic experience of Americanness. Barros analyzes two randomly selected Brazilian Disney blogs to explore how individuals engage with the Disney trip as an aspiration that is concretized through discursive practices reflective of the neoliberal cultural logic represented by Disney World.

In her chapter on the classist curriculum of Disney's reality television shows, **Robin Redmon Wright** explores the exponential proliferation of reality programs focused on the working-class, such as the Disney-produced programs *Duck Dynasty* and *Swamp People*. Wright analyzes how such programs *stigmatize* poor and working-class people and explains that these shows "not only promote negative stereotypes of lower socio-economic groups, but they also affirm the *naturalness* of the ever-expanding wealth gap. They help curtail dissent and position the victims of inequitable structures of power and capital as culpable for their own oppression." Ultimately, by portraying working-class people in particular ways, these programs operate to recreate the myth of the American dream, reinforce capitalistic meritocracy, and perpetuate class inequalities.

In his chapter, **Jason J. Wallin** explores another kind of myth—that everything is possible through hope—which is commodified and concretized through the "happy curriculum" constituting what he terms a "Disneyish order." He explores how, through simulation, "the Disney experience aims at the realization of dreams bracketed from the encumbrances and indignities of contemporary life." Taking up Disney as an exemplar of what Baudrillard terms "the third order of simulacra," Wallin describes how Disney mechanizes simulation to suspend reality and direct the imagination toward an "infantile nostalgia for happiness, goodness, truth and sincerity." The proliferation of this brand of infinite utopia normalizes the Disneyish dispersion of reality and immerses us in the libidinal economy of capitalism.

Will Letts explores another way that Disney commodifies and caricatures, as he explores camp sensibilities within this libidinal economy as they are expressed through five iconic Disney villains. Reading these villains both with and against the grain, he asserts that they both draw upon and repudiate queer sensibilities. Letts illustrates how a presumed 'normalization' of camp sensibilities actually functions as a pedagogy to commodify heterosexuality and heteropatriarchy, reinscribing the very practices such camp sensibilities seek to militate against.

Another way Disney commodifies subjectivities, as illustrated through the purposely progressive portrayal of female characters highlighted by Macaluso, is through the mobilization of aspirational discourses that capitalize on ideals of social progress. In her chapter on *Doc McStuffins* as progressive empowerment, **Rachel Alicia Griffin** expands that analysis to examine how Disney represents Black girlhood by critically interpreting "the acknowledgement of Disney's corporate, pedagogical influence amid praise, and the intentional portrayal of Doc as a Black girl, as an indication of the company's capitalistic desire to appear inclusive while further tapping into Black children and their parents as a market." Rounding out this group of essays on how Disney capitalizes on cultural norms to rewrite subjectivities, Griffin argues that while *Doc McStuffins* can be read as a significant site of progressive empowerment for Black girls, the show also fuels 'post' logics through deracialization and reinforces racist, sexist stereotypes of Black females as caretakers.

In **Part III**, ***Being Disney: Freedom, Participation, and Control***, authors explore how relationships between consumers and corporations have shifted as digital technologies have expanded and redefined the ways we buy and sell goods and services. With the proliferation of highly interactive online markets, individuals have become active participants in consumption by offering up valuable time and personal information in exchange for the conveniences of customization. Participation presents a significant paradox, as it operates as a process by which users are both empowered *and* controlled, and thus 'taught' into being and acting in ways that serve corporate interests. The chapters in this section explore how Disney operates to control cultural production and intellectual property by exploiting our desires for both freedom *and* control to teach us into action and potentially usurp participation's democratic potential.

In his chapter on magic, new knowledge, and learning at Walt Disney World, **George J. Bey, III** explores participation and control by considering Disney guests as learners who are being taught into a particular understanding of 'Disney Magic.' Taking up the theme park as a learning tool, he examines how Disney Magic operates within Walt Disney World as the ostensible source of all possibilities and positive realities. Drawing on a host of shows, characters, music, foods, places, and moments at Walt Disney World, Bey illustrates how these experiences are designed to help us learn what Disney Magic is, how to use it, and what we learn about the rest of the curriculum and the very idea of being a whole healthy learner by doing so. Through this pedagogical process, Disney Magic becomes the strategic plan or mission statement of the institution used to define and give meaning to all the rest of the curriculum.

Continuing with the themes of participation and pedagogy, **Nadine M. Kalin** explore the Disneyization and Disneyfication of art museum education, specifically in relation to curricular practices that claim enhanced participation and civic engagement for their visitors. To illustrate the myths and constraints at play within a participatory paradigm in art, culture, and education, she uses the case of the Walker Art Center's 2012 symposium, *Discourse and Discord* to suggest that participation, once Disneyfied and Disneyized, functions in the public sphere to perpetuate neoliberal mandates to keep busy and feel self-actualized while constructing a controlled post-political landscape where societal issues are "concealed, neglected, parodied, sanitized, and/or quickly forgotten while continuing on unchallenged and unchanged."

One such societal issue that is often sanitized is gender norms and expectations, which **Annette Furo, Nichole E. Grant, Pamela Rogers**, and **Kelsey Catherine Schmitz** take up in their chapter. In their analysis of Merida, the notably progressive Disney princess featured in the 2012 animated film *Brave,* the authors look to understandings of the gendered body, of curriculum as a lived experience of meaning making, and of the powers of public pedagogy. Through four individual readings, the authors take up these elements to more fully grasp the complex interrelated contexts surrounding the making, telling, displaying, and selling of Merida. In spite of Merida's seemingly progressive characteristics, the authors find that, ultimately, the corset of constricting gender norms inevitably binds Merida to a structured plot that limits her development to a controlled formula.

Expanding on the notion of participation, control, and Disneyfication, we (**Julie** and **Jenny**) join **Gabriel S. Huddleston** in exploring how a new service at Walt Disney World, MyMagic+, operates as both a regulatory device and a mechanism of surveillance that constructs theme park experiences to appeal to the desires of consumers and serve Disney's corporate interests. Drawing on Deleuzian notions of societies of control and post-panoptic surveillance, we explore how Walt Disney World operates as a society of control. Returning to the notion of participatory consumer culture, we examine the role of the "prosumer" (Ritzer, 2015) who willingly participates in the Disney experience and becomes 'productive' in ways that feel empowering but are in fact providing free labor that enables the conditions of surveillance and control.

Widely known for his work in public pedagogy and cultural studies, including Disney studies, **Henry A. Giroux** offers another perspective on the highly disproportionate concentration of control that The Walt Disney Company has over the production, circulation and exchange of information, especially to children. Giroux explores how Disney has aggressively marketed goods and services for infants, toddlers and tweens, many of which are more accessible than ever with the advances of new media that allow for the proliferation of Disney's powerful pedagogies. Through his analyses of Disney's commodification of childhood, Giroux advances the imperative of establishing the pedagogical conditions in which young people can "learn and develop as engaged social actors more alive to their responsibility to future generations than those adults who have presently turned away from the challenge."

References

Budd, M. (2005). Introduction: Private Disney, public Disney. In M. Budd & M. H. Kirsch (Eds.), *Rethinking Disney: Private control, public dimensions* (pp. 1–33). Middletown, CT: Wesleyan University Press.

Clough, P. (2007). *The affective turn: Theorizing the social.* Durham, NC: Duke University Press.

Giroux, H., & Pollock, G. (2010). *The mouse that roared: Disney and the end of innocence* (2nd ed.). Lanham, MD: Rowman and Littlefield.

Ritzer, G. (2015). The "new" world of prosumption: Evolution, "return of the same," or revolution? *Sociological Forum, 30*(1), 1–17. doi: 10.1111/socf.12142

Schickel, R. (1968). *The Disney version: The life, times, art, and commerce of Walt Disney.* New York: Simon and Schuster.

Wasko, J. (2001). *Understanding Disney.* Malden, MA: Polity.

Acknowledgements

This book has been a labor of love and a long time in the making. We want to say a special thank you to our editor and guide at Routledge, Naomi Silverman, for her steadfast encouragement, her unwavering faith in us and in this project, and for her enthusiastic support in helping us see this project to fruition. As always, she has been a pleasure to work with; it is such a great feeling to have someone in our corner cheering us on! We also want to thank the staff at Routledge for their professionalism and care in developing this book. Additionally, we want to thank William Pinar for believing in and supporting the project, and providing a space for the book within his *Studies in Curriculum Theory* series. Special thanks also go to the scholars who reviewed our initial proposal, Belinha DeAbreu of Fairfield University and Douglas Kellner of the University of California, Los Angeles, whose critical feedback and support helped us to refine our thinking and strengthened the project.

We also want to thank all of the terrific authors who are featured in this collection—thank you for all of your hard work and dedication to making your chapters exciting new additions to the Disney studies literature. Special thanks also goes to Shirley Steinberg, who has always been so generously supportive of our work and who graciously contributed the foreword, along with encouraging words and support throughout the entire book process.

We feel especially indebted to the brilliant and talented Jorge Lucero, who has become our 'go-to' person for challenging, amazing, provocative artwork; in this latest endeavor he did not disappoint but, once again, has delighted, as he has brought to this book a fresh, complicated, and provocative perspective. Jorge, you always help us see in ways we haven't before, and because of this any project that includes your vision is stronger and more interesting for it.

Jenny would like to thank the students in her recent *Disney, Culture, and Society* class at Arizona State University, who helped her see and appreciate Disney in new ways. I would also like to thank Mary Margaret Fonow, Daniel Schugurensky, and Bryan Brayboy from ASU's School of Social Transformation for allowing me to take a year sabbatical to work on this and other Disney projects. I also want to thank friends who have supported me in these last few years, both professionally and personally: Jake Burdick, Will Letts, Jory Brass, Sandro Barros, Deb Freedman, Jennie Stearns, Erik Malewski, Cole Reilly, George Bey, Melinda Hollis Thomas, Jeff Johnson, Torie Lynch, Lyndee Kelver, and Christian Payne—I love y'all truly and deeply. :) I also want to give a special thanks to Julie Garlen, for enduring countless hours of work with me on this and so many other exciting projects—your friendship over the years has meant so much to me. An extra special thanks goes to Matt Unger for your constant support and kindness. Finally, I want to thank my parents Richard and Patricia Sandlin and my uncle Marcel Bloch, who always support me even when they don't understand why someone might get paid to study Disney, my sister Cindy Sandlin for her unwavering love and for always accepting me, weirdness and all, and my son, Grant St. Clair, who is a constant source of laughter, love, and life.

Julie would like to thank her former department chair, Dr. Ronnie Sheppard, her current department chair, Dr. Bruce Field, and Dr. Thomas Koballa, Dean of the College of Education at Georgia Southern University, for allowing her to devote an entire semester to this work. She is also appreciative of her Georgia Southern University colleagues for the support and encouragement they have offered, particularly Dr. Ming Fang He, who has spent the last eight years reminding Julie to publish a book, as well as John Weaver and Bill Reynolds, who inspired her to study popular culture. Julie is extremely grateful for the love, patience, and understanding extended by her entire family, who became convinced that her laptop had become a permanent appendage. Her parents, who worked hard to afford many memorable trips to Walt Disney World, have been a vital source of support, and her older sister, Jennifer C. Garlen, a brilliant writer and Disney fan extraordinaire, both inspired and challenged her throughout this process. Finally, there were many friends old and new who contributed to this work by sharing their experience, strength, and hope when it was most needed. You are beloved.

Jorge Lucero
Mexican-American (b. 1976)

Panning the Field: A, B, C, D, E, and F
2015
Six coloring-book collages and educational placard exhibited in a scholarly book

Panning the Field: A, B, C, D, E, and F is a two-part, commissioned artwork by Chicago artist Jorge Lucero. The first part of the artwork is this page. This page was conceptualized and written following the format of a typical museum placard. The museum placard is meant to be informative and mildly educational, while tensely attempting to mask its author's unavoidable subjectivities. Lucero—who also holds a faculty post at a major research institution in the United States—dwells on the institutional placard as an infrequently troubled site that can simultaneously be enacted curricularly and performatively. Lucero has played with the conceptual art potential of the placard in previous notable works such as *Classroom Placards* (2012), *Placard Bomb* (2013) and *THEBARACKOBAMAPRESIDENTIALLIBRARY* (2015).

The second part of this artwork is the series of six collages that this placard describes. The collages were made from a found Peter Pan coloring book and have been strategically placed throughout this book without further commentary. Since 2012 Lucero has been making—what he calls—"folded collages". The folded collage is a quick, minimally contemplated artwork that Lucero repeats in a Sisyphean attempt to discover truth through chance. Lucero has made hundreds of these folded collages following four easy parameters: 1. The folded collage starts with a single preexisting image. 2. That image is then folded unto itself no more than two to three times 3. The image is never cut, pasted, or manipulated beyond the folding gesture. 4. The finished collage is then photographed, scanned, or photocopied flattening it into a new image. After the six images in this book were submitted to the publisher, a request was made to Lucero that the images should be *de-Disney-fied* further since—at first look—the images were still readily identified as being sourced from Disney's version of Peter Pan. The request to obscure the folded collages' source was a near impossible task as is evidenced by the final images themselves. Nevertheless Lucero obliged knowing that the Disney "look" can be suppressed, but never-never eliminated.

1 Introduction

Feeling Disney, Buying Disney, Being Disney

Jennifer A. Sandlin and Julie C. Garlen

As has been noted by many educators who report "special difficulties in getting students to develop critical approaches in the face of the distinctive Disney mystique" (Budd, 2005, p. 3), Disney is in some ways "beyond criticism." Wasko, Phillips, and Meehan (2001), who surveyed 1,250 respondents in 18 countries for their "Global Disney Audiences Project," found that the vast majority have very favorable attitudes towards Disney and consider critiquing Disney to be taboo. One of the reasons Disney is so difficult to critique is the way the company capitalizes on the nostalgia that its fans feel, cultivating an image of family-friendly fun and projecting the idea that our individual and collective engagements with Disney and its products are nothing more than wholesome entertainment. Disney thus purposely facilitates a "close association with and appropriation of childhood innocence as a personal and cultural memory for several generations of parents and children in many countries" (Budd, 2005, p. 2). The power of this personal and cultural memory is exemplified by Julie's early experiences of Walt Disney World, which she visited over two dozen times between the ages of 3 and 33. Having grown up in South Georgia, Julie spent most of her family vacations in Orlando, including one Thanksgiving when her entire extended family (parents, both sets of grandparents, and her aunt and uncle) spent the holiday there. When Julie became a young mother, she continued the tradition, embarking on a winter tour with her 18-month old daughter and a full entourage of family members. Thus, for Julie, Disney is strongly associated with her own memories of familial intimacy and childhood innocence.

These patterns of repeated engagements with Disney that begin for many in infancy create strong emotional and consumptive bonds that complicate critical analysis. In her own teaching, Jenny has found that students resist problematizing Disney because they hold it as a cherished part of their childhoods and an important element of their identities. A few years ago, when Jenny taught a course on Disney to undergraduate students at Arizona State University, she encountered many students who, like Julie, considered themselves as having grown up in 'Disney households.' Their resistance surprised Jenny, who, having had limited interaction with Disney as a child other than one hot, short, and exhausting family vacation to Disney World and occasional exposures to Disney movies and books, had little trouble taking up critical analyses of the company. Inspired by a desire to better understand her students she took her son to Disneyland over Thanksgiving break that semester to experience it with fresh eyes. After having a great time at the park, she returned with a new appreciation for the pleasures of Disney and a realization that successful Disney scholarship must take this pleasure seriously. Quite simply, *people have fun* when they engage with Disney products or spend time in Disney theme parks, and it is precisely this pleasure that makes critique so imperative. Pleasure, we assert, is a profoundly powerful pedagogue.

In this volume, we take up a perspective that positions viewer-consumers as active participants in the meaning-making process who derive pleasure from *and* engage critically with the cultural texts and artifacts produced by The Walt Disney Company. The authors here take seriously the idea that people (including us) are invested in Disney as a source of pleasure, but also provide sustained critique of Disney products and perspectives. Unlike Disney enthusiasts who have written about the pleasures derived from engaging with Disney, we take up pleasure not only to acknowledge that people engage with Disney in such ways—and to argue that these ways of engagement are important and legitimate—but also to appreciate and understand how The Walt Disney Company uses these very pleasurable engagements to influence education and individual and social identity in the United States and beyond.

While we believe that our acknowledgement of Disney's pleasures makes possible a form of critique that recognizes the viewer as an agentic individual who can both appreciate and critically analyze a cultural text, it is critique nonetheless, which might raise eyebrows and ire among devoted Disney fans who do not necessarily want to engage Disney in these critical ways or among academics who do not take the study of Disney seriously. This is a risk we are willing to take. Drawing from Ahmed's (2010) concept of the "feminist killjoy" we claim the role of 'Disney killjoys.' For Ahmed, feminist killjoys expose and critique how emotions such as happiness are used to control, justify, and subjugate—for example how the construction of the "happy housewife" and "happy slave" were used to regulate and normalize gendered and racist institutions and social norms, to construct them as "social goods" that cause happiness. We are enacting similar practices of killing joy in our engagement as Disney killjoys, accepting that our "intensity" about the ways in which Disney's pleasures perpetuate social norms will likely "become tension" (Ahmed, 2010). For us, as for Ahmed, this is an ethical stance, because critique, as an act of cultural activism, necessitates a struggle against happiness and the other emotions that Disney produces, markets, and sells.

For us, this ethical stance begins with the assumption that, despite its efforts to argue to the contrary, The Walt Disney Company's products and experiences constitute much more than wholesome entertainment; its reach is global and its influence is profound. Disney generates over $48 billion dollars per year (Iger, 2014) and continues to expand markets within and beyond the United States through animated and live-action films, theme parks, television and radio stations, publishing, licensed merchandise, schools, museums, sports, music, urban development, a gated community inside Walt Disney World, and myriad other products and entertainment arenas. Disney's 2009 acquisition of Marvel Entertainment, which produces movies based on comic book characters and storylines from the iconic Marvel Universe, further increased the company's share of the lucrative media market and expanded the target audience for Disney films. Meanwhile, in Japan, the new "Tsum Tsum" ("stack stack") franchise, which includes a smartphone game based on a line of stackable stuffed animals by the same name, has quickly become a cultural phenomenon. Since its launch in 2014, the application has been at the top of Apple and Android charts in Japan and has been downloaded more than 14 million times (Graser, 2014). Japanese fans have also purchased millions of the plush toys, which have now found their way into US Disney stores. These various products and experiences are consumed by hundreds of millions of people each year across the globe and have a significant impact on shaping individual and group cultural identity. Schickel (1968) argues that Walt Disney has been "a primary force in the expression and formation of American mass consciousness" (pp. 360–361), while Giroux and Pollock (2010) contend that Disney is a "teaching machine" that "exerts influence over consumers but also wages an aggressive campaign to peddle its political and cultural influence" (p. xiv). Disney is thus a kind of public pedagogy extraordinaire.

We envision Disney not only enacting a broad-reaching [corporate] public pedagogy (Savage, 2010), but also position it as part of a 'big' curriculum (Schubert, 2006; see also Cremin, 1976, and Schubert, 1981) that permeates cultural discourse in myriad ways. This 'big' curriculum of public and private spaces resides in both liminal and distant proximities to formal educational institutions such as schools (Stearns, Sandlin, & Burdick, 2011). As such, we argue that Disney, which is an increasingly salient part of individuals' everyday life practices and identity formation—as well as a major cultural force that helps shape conceptions of family values, gender, sexuality, race, class, ethnicity, 'Americanness,' childhood, pleasure, entertainment, education, and community—must be recognized as an influential element within the big curriculum. Schubert's (2006) perspective on the big curriculum aligns with Pinar's (2004) view of curriculum theory as an "interdisciplinary study of educational experience," with curriculum broadly defined as the educational experiences gained both through and in spite of the structures of formal schooling. We posit that The Walt Disney Company constitutes and enacts just such a curriculum—both inside and outside of schools—that helps to shape the ways we think, learn, and live.

Within the field of education, scholarship on Disney typically critically analyzes how Disney engages with race, ethnicity, and gender in animated films (see, for example, Golden's [2006] or Padurano's [2011] articles on Pocahontas, or Giroux's [2004] examinations of Disney animated films in Steinberg and Kincheloe's [2004] book *Kinderculture*). This work also often focuses on 'princess culture' more generally and how it shapes children's gender identity construction (see, for example, Wohlwend's [2009, 2012a, 2012b] work on boys' and girls' gender identity consumption and production through Disney princess play). While some of this work is outstanding, there is a surprising lack of work on Disney within education, and especially work that takes up analyses of more recent films and other Disney products and that positions Disney within the frameworks of public pedagogy and the big curriculum. That is, education scholars tend to focus on how educators can use Disney in classrooms (critically and otherwise). While that scholarship is important, it tends to underestimate the vast educational import of Disney in the broader public sphere.

One scholar within education who has studied Disney extensively and whose work has been instrumental to our own thinking around public pedagogies in general and Disney as curriculum and pedagogy more specifically is Henry Giroux. Giroux has written prolifically about the relationship between popular culture, schooling, and learning and, since the early 1990s, has critically analyzed the Disney corporation and its products—including both animated and live action films, Disney's town of Celebration, Florida, and Disney marketing and cross promotion—as public pedagogy. Along with Grace Pollock, with whom he wrote the second edition of *The Mouse That Roared: Disney and the End of Innocence* in 2010, Giroux analyzed the Disney Company as a site of public pedagogy where identities are shaped, childhood is created, and nostalgia is crafted; they present a critical analysis of The Walt Disney Company not as a purveyor of wholesome entertainment, but a conglomeration driven by power, politics, and ideology. Our book complements, extends, and updates Giroux and Pollock's work, as authors engage with Disney's curricula and pedagogies by critically reading Disney films and theme parks as texts, exploring how Disney has been taught and resisted outside of traditional learning environments, examining how fans and consumers develop and negotiate their identities through and with their engagement with Disney, and analyzing how race, class, gender, sexuality, and consumerism are constructed through and within Disney discourses. Authors also focus on Disney products and experiences that have been produced in the last five years, including new technologies such as the myMagic+ wristbands used in the parks, and new films such as *Brave*, *Frozen*, and *Maleficent*. The essays herein take discussions of Disney as curriculum and pedagogy into new avenues of exploration—what we are calling "feeling Disney" (focusing on the affective and ontological aspects of identity development), "buying Disney" (focusing on the commodification of social and cultural identities, experiences, and subjectivities), and "being Disney" (focusing on how Disney shapes our desires for both freedom and control and how we participate in these practices). In what follows, we first present a brief overview of previous Disney scholarship before turning to a more extensive discussion of these new avenues of exploration.

A Brief History of Disney Scholarship

This volume follows a long history of the cultural analysis of Disney, which began as early as the late 1930s (Budd, 2005). As Wasko (2001) notes, "since the first Mickey Mouse cartoons were released, Disney films have been analyzed in the popular press by film critics and analysts, who have mostly employed an assortment of aesthetic and art criticism and literary analysis" (p. 109). Wasko (2001) argues that critics in the 1930s and 1940s "were mostly positive about, and typically gushed over" Disney's films, "praising his artistic development" (p. 125); Budd (2005) further argues that critics celebrated the "anarchic energy and carnivalesque rudeness" of Disney's very early Disney films (p. 7). After World War II, however, "more harsh criticism emerged," as critics argued that Disney had "become conventional, static, and less exciting than other studios' animated productions" (Wasko, 2001, p. 125). During the 1940s and 1950s, critics focused on "the mass-cultural blandness and aesthetic banalities" (Budd, 2005, p. 7) that the Disney studios infused into their versions of classic fairy tales. Reminiscent of the elitist 'high culture' critiques of popular culture emerging from some Frankfurt School intellectuals, these critiques focused on the "Disneyfication," or the "sanitization, homogenization, and Americanization" (Budd, 2005, p. 7) of the original source material that Disney turned into popular culture. This criticism was based mainly in aesthetic and moral judgment that sought to maintain cultural hierarchies between high and low culture.

According to Budd (2005), this early period of Disney criticism came to a close with Richard Schickel's (1968) *The Disney Version*, which sat at the threshold between this early criticism and what Budd (2005) calls "Contemporary Disney Studies," which emerged in the late 1980s. Budd (2005) explains that Schickel's influential book "was written at a historical moment when an older tradition of US cultural criticism aspiring to publicness was largely exhausted, while a newer, narrower, and more radical academic cultural studies had yet to develop" (p. 10). Schickel's work rejected the tendency in early Disney criticism to level 'high culture' aesthetic and moral critiques against Disney as 'low culture,' as it extended and updated a tradition of cultural criticism in the US "based in aesthetic and moral judgment but attempting to reach out beyond . . . class snobbery and narrow moralism . . . to create a more inclusive and democratic public culture based in an expanding and educated middle class" (p. 8). Schickel recognized that "older standards of morality and aesthetic discrimination were inadequate if not entirely impossible bases on which to build a critical understanding of Disney" (p. 8). Instead, Schickel attempted to move away from the elitist intellectual critique of Disney and called for cultural critics to understand and engage with popular culture (Budd, 2005). At the same time, during the 1960s and 1970s, strict cultural hierarchies were eroding in the US, as "young people rejected the cultural hierarchy of high and low art, embracing them both with seeming equanimity" (p. 9). Budd (2005) posits that while Disney was often the object of critique during that time as "antithesis to radical social change," (p. 10) those critiques lessened by the late 1970s as the stigma of embracing Disney eroded for the wealthier and more educated classes, and as Disney found new ways to market to more affluent customers.

While early critiques of Disney were written for a general public, university professors began what became known as "Disney Studies" in the academy beginning in the mid-1970s (Doherty, 2006). Academic-based Disney Studies, an interdisciplinary enterprise from the start begun by a "small but growing academic left" who "developed a new interest in mass culture" (Budd, 2005, p. 11) continues to flourish. While some work on popular culture in the 1970s and 1980s under the purview of cultural studies un- critically celebrated popular culture, obscuring the power relations inherent in its production and overemphasizing audience agency, more critical pro- jects during this era focused on the politics of "cultural production, circulation, and reception" (Budd, 2005, p. 11). Disney Studies emerged within this context, as academics began producing work for a smaller (academic, not public) audience, which allowed for more "precise and rigorous" (p. 11) work, with "extended and detailed" (p. 11) analyses. Budd also argues that what made this new work "deeper" and "richer" (p. 12) was the fact that these new Disney academics had grown up with Disney "as both ordinary and alarming, as part of the texture of everyday life at the center of a US-based empire that covered its brutalities at home and abroad with endless pop-cultural distractions. There was little room for polemics" (p. 12); rather, these new Disney academics had to start with the assumption that "We were all Walt's children now" (p. 12). That is, these new Disney academics/cultural critics needed "to understand why people, perhaps including at least part of themselves, actually liked, even needed Disney— without attacking, demonizing, or condescending to those people" (p. 12).

Since the 1980s, Disney Studies scholars have produced a staggering amount of work, and, through this work, have helped contribute to "the reconstruction of a new kind of public criticism of mass culture" (Budd, 2005, p. 13), as they have struggled "to construct theoretically informed academic writing as a limited but generative and critical counterpublic" (p. 12). This work has generated an overwhelming number of articles and books informed by critical theory, critical cultural studies traditions, aesthetic framings, psychoanalytic theories, feminist theories, consumer studies theories of practice and everyday life, and political economy and Marxist class analyses (Budd, 2005; Wasko, 2001). Disney studies work has been grounded in disciplines ranging from "film and television studies, to geography, anthropology, history, and architecture" (Wasko, 2001, p. 109), and methodologically, scholars have typically used qualitative content or textual analysis grounded in literary and film studies, cultural studies, and feminist perspectives, to analyze Disney texts.

To help make sense of this vast scholarship and in order to situate *Disney, Culture, and Curriculum* within it, we provide a brief summary of some of the main themes of this previous Disney scholarship. Here, we focus first on themes emerging from scholarly analyses of Disney films and then turn our attention to scholarship that has focused on theme parks. While some scholars focus on other aspects of Disney—including Disney's business practices (Cheu, 2012); urban planning (Roost, 2005; Siegel, 2005; Warren, 2005); animators and other artists (Peri, 2011); Disney branding (Stein, 2011); biographies/histories of Walt (Gabler, 2006; Susanin, 2011); critiques of Disney's official histories of Walt himself and also of the company's long-touted innovations in film, theme park entertainment, and marketing and business strategies (Budd & Kirsch, 2005; Smoodin, 1994; Wasko, 2001); histories of animation and animation technologies (Lee & Madej, 2012; Pallant, 2011); and explorations of the battles over Disney's role in defining public and private, as citizens attempt to hold Disney publicly accountable for its business practices that very much affect global citizens (Budd & Kirsch, 2005)—the vast majority of work within education and cultural studies, and thus most relevant to this current volume, has focused on Disney's animated films and theme parks. In what follows, we draw upon several recent literature reviews of Disney scholarship (Bryman, 1995; Budd, 2005; Wasko, 2001), as well as our own survey of some notable work produced in the last ten years.

Themes Emerging from Analyses of Disney Films

Many academic studies have analyzed Disney products that have "a common set of characteristics" (Wasko, 2001, p. 109)—what Wasko calls the "Classic Disney" films. The designation 'Classic Disney' refers primarily to animated films and cartoons and the cast of characters associated with those productions, "as well as the consistent set of themes and values that generally represent 'Disney' to the general public and critical analysts" (Wasko, 2001, p. 110). These Classic Disney films "include a specific style, a standard formula of story and characters, as well as a set of common themes and values," which are typically featured in both Disney merchandise and at Disney theme parks (p. 110). While Disney's early cartoons were largely imaginative fantasies without a fixed structure, according to legendary Disney Imagineer Marty Sklar (1980), the narratives became less open ended after 1932, with more "distinct beginnings and usually happy endings" (Wasko, 2001, p. 111). Disney Studies scholarship has helped define a set of characteristics that comprise Classic Disney, including narrative styles, common character traits, and prevailing themes. According to those analyses, Classic Disney is characterized by light entertainment, music, and humor, including especially physical gags and slapstick comedy. The narratives were often revised fairytales or folklore, or followed a classic Hollywood movie model. Characters typically consisted of anthropomorphized, neotenized animal characters; formulaic characters such as hero/heroine, love interests, sidekicks, mentors, villains, and henchman; and stereotyped representations of gender, race, and ethnicity. Finally, the themes and values most prevalent in the films included "mainstream American values" such as individualism and optimism; work ethic, escape, fantasy, magic, imagination; innocence; romance and happiness; and good triumphing over evil (Wasko, 2001, p. 114).

In addition to analyses of Classic Disney texts, Wasko (2001) describes several other aspects of Disney films with which Disney Studies scholarship has engaged, including analyzing Disney texts as aesthetic works. Wasko points out such aesthetic work sometimes problematically attempts "to transcend historical context." (p. 119). Focusing on Disney as art also tends to perpetuate the hierarchy that separates high culture from low culture, a position Budd (2005) suggests was losing validity by the 1960s. Another popular subject of study has been the character of Mickey Mouse. Wasko (2001) argues that Mickey Mouse "represents a fascinating interweaving of culture, politics, and economics: a symbol of just about everything American, as is the Disney company" (p. 123) and has thus been taken up as an object of study for decades by scholars who analyze his evolution, his role in the company, and his cultural importance. Other studies have explored how Disney has interpreted children's literature. Zipes (1995), for example, outlines how Disney has changed the genre of literary fairy tale in a variety of ways. In Disney tales, "technique has precedence over story"; "characters are one-dimensional and serve functions of the film"; "the 'American' fairy tale colonizes other national audiences"; "there is a thematic emphasis on cleanliness, control, and organized industry"; and "the diversion of the Disney fairy tale is geared toward non-reflective viewing" (Wasko, 2001, p. 128; for the full list see Zipes, 1995, pp. 39–40). Such work argues that the ways in which Disney alters traditional folk and fairy tales "have erased much of the potential empowerment once offered by fairy tales in particular and fantasy in general" (Wasko, 2001, p. 128), as Disney has commodified fantasy and thus denuded it of its transformative power.

The area of Disney scholarship that has garnered the most attention (Budd, 2005) includes critical analyses of gender, race, class, and sexuality. Budd (2005) argues that public criticism of how Disney represents African-Americans and other racial and ethnic groups in its animated films is "almost as old as the company's habit of caricaturing such groups," while similar critiques against representations of gender and sexuality have been leveled against the company in the past few decades (p. 20). Wasko (2001) outlines the growth of feminist critique of Disney films in the 1980s that paralleled the rise of feminist theory in the academy. Her overview of feminist analysis highlights an early piece by Stone (1975) that compared the heroines in

Grimm fairy tales to those in the Disney versions. Stone concluded that while the heroines in the Grimm tales are "relatively uninspiring," (Wasko, 2001, p. 133) those in Disney's versions "seem barely alive" (Stone, quoted in Wasko, 2001, p. 133). Wasko's (2001) review also found that *The Little Mermaid* "prompted a flurry of feminist analyses" (p. 133) after its 1989 release. Analyses of the film included a focus on how the film embodied "Disneyfication" of the original story, and examinations of the female characters in the film often viewed Ariel as a "more positive role model" than earlier Disney heroines such as Snow White, although she still embodied "the beauty that characterizes all Disney heroines" (p. 135). Other scholars focused on issues of matriarchy versus patriarchy, examining how the film teaches us "that we can achieve access and mobility in the white male system if we remain silent, and if we sacrifice our connection to 'the feminine'" (Sells, 1995, p. 181). Wasko's review also highlights scholarship that has used psychoanalytic lenses to analyze Disney films, including works such as *Pinnochio*, *The Three Little Pigs*, and *Peter Pan*; this work takes up themes of family roles, fantasy, pleasure, and sexuality. Bell, Haas, and Sells' (1995) classic edited volume *From Mouse to Mermaid: The Politics of Film, Gender, and Culture* expanded this work to include Marxist, poststructuralist, and cultural studies perspectives, as it focused on the politics of gender in Disney films, especially in relation to race, class, sexuality, the family, the nation, science, nature, and technology. Analyses of the politics of femininity, masculinity, and sexuality have continued to be popular in more recent Disney scholarship, seen in Griffin's (2000) *Tinker Belles and Evil Queens*, which examines the long and complex relationship between The Walt Disney Company and LGBTQ communities, focusing on readings of both Disney films and theme parks. Amy Davis' (2006) book, *Good Girls and Wicked Witches: Women in Disney's Feature Animation* and, more recently, *Handsome Heroes and Vile Villians: Masculinity in Disney's Feature Films* (Davis, 2014), also uses feminist film theory and masculinity studies to explore gender in Disney films.

Similarly, studies of race and ethnicity in Disney films exploded in the 1980s and 1990s as scholars took up critical analyses of anti-Semitic representations in *The Three Little Pigs* (see, for example, St. John, 1981), as well as racist representations of African Americans in *Dumbo* and *Song of the South*, Native Americans in *Peter Pan* and *Davy Crockett*, and Arab characters and depictions of Islam in *Aladdin*. *The Lion King* has also been the subject of much scholarship, with the portrayal of the hyenas as "definitely recognizable . . . Black and Hispanic characters lurking about in a jungle version of a ghetto" (Wasko, 2001, p. 141). Other scholars argued that the film "reveals homophobic, racist, and sexist ideologies, reinforcing hierarchical and conservative values" (Wasko, p. 141). Scholars also took up critical analysis of *Pocahontas*, which, despite attempts by Disney studios to be more culturally responsible in their depictions of Native Americans, was still found to be historically inaccurate and to perpetuate many of the themes of Classic Disney films, including the focus on a romantic love story. Furthermore, the film ends with the suggestion that Native Americans and Europeans were "free to coexist peacefully" as "the more profound consequences of institutional racism are never allowed even momentarily to invade the audience's comfort zone" (Edgerton & Jackson, 1996, p. 92).

More recent scholarship has also examined race and ethnicity, including authors in Budd and Kirsch's (2005) edited volume, who, too take up analyses of hierarchies of race, class, gender, and sexuality, focusing on the culture industries' "power to frame and organize social understandings of difference" (p. 20). Jhappan and Stasiulis (2005), for example, through an examination of accents and voice in the films *Pocahontas* and *Pocahontas II*, explore how these films center English and White American superiority and thus reinforce and justify colonialism through what Budd (2005) calls "discursive recolonization" (p. 23). More recently, Brode (2005), in a move that counters most critical analyses of racial representations in Disney films, has argued in *Multiculturalism and the Mouse: Race and Sex in Disney Entertainment* that Disney's representations of difference have been not regressive or racist and sexist but, rather, progressive, and, in fact, paved the way for acceptance of diversity and multiculturalism in the United States. However, two more recent volumes remain insistent that Disney's representations of race and ethnicity remain problematic and should continue to be interrogated as such. Sperb's (2012) *Disney's Most Notorious Film: Race, Convergence, and the Hidden Histories of Song of the South* provides a fresh examination of the film *Song of the South*, tracing its history and the ways in which audiences and Disney have negotiated the controversies surrounding the film over the past seven decades. Finally, Cheu's (2012) *Diversity in Disney Films: Critical Essays on Race, Ethnicity, Gender, Sexuality, and Disability* focuses on the "new multiculturalism" in Disney films. The authors in this edited volume analyze, within Disney films, old and new representations of minority groups and diversity. A common thread throughout the chapters and section is one of "traditions and transformations"—that is, an examination of how Disney representations of race, ethnicity, gender, sexuality, and disability remain 'traditional' and to what extent they actually 'transform' and challenge those traditional (racist, sexist, ableist) representations.

Another area of scholarly work consists of Marxist analyses of class and imperialism in Disney. Dorfman and Mattelart's (1971) *How to Read Donald Duck* did not focus on films but, rather, was a textual analysis of 100 Disney comics that were distributed in Chile in the 1980s. This work analyzed "Disney as global purveyor of capitalist ideology" and became a classic book in a tradition of demystifying popular culture (Budd, 2005). Wasko's (2001) *Understanding Disney* takes up similar themes, as she analyzes The Walt Disney Company as a capitalist enterprise by "concentrating on political economy, how the company works, its classic products and theme parks, as well as audience reception" (Budd, 2005, p. 17). Budd and Kirsch's (2005) edited volume takes up these themes as well, linking cultural studies analyses of race, class, and gender in Disney films, and Broadway productions and theme parks, to political economic analyses, thus seeing Disney "as part of the 'shock troops' of capitalist ideology and commodification" (Budd, 2005, p. 18). Taken as a whole, this work analyzes how the ideologies embedded in Disney's representations of race, class, gender, and sexuality are linked to their "possible economic functions," thus reinforcing Dorfman and Mattelart's argument from the early 1970s that "Disney's representations promote capitalist hegemony and political quiescence" (Budd, 2005, p. 18). These readings of Disney as "prominent in a metastasizing commercial culture" (Budd, 2005, p. 13) extend beyond analyses of film to include analyses of the theme parks, as well as business, labor, marketing, and development practices.

Finally, scholars have taken up analyses of how Disney films have represented animals and nature. As early as the late 1940s, while Disney's anthropomorphized depictions of nature continued to grow in popularity, the company was also producing documentary films that featured explicit descriptions of the natural world and were marketed as educational media. Early on, Schickel (1968) noted the controversy over the inaccurate depictions and staged scenes featured in the *True-Life Adventures* series, but it was not until the 1990s that the rise of radical environmentalism sparked a flurry of scholarly works on Disney's representation of nature, both in animated films and documentaries (see e.g., Johnson & Thomas, 1990; Lutts, 1992; Hastings, 1996; King, 1996). This line of analysis has been taken up more recently by Whitley (2008, updated in 2012), whose *The Idea of Nature in Disney Animation: From Snow White to WALL-E,* specifically examines Disney's animated films and their engagement with the theme of wild nature, and by Tobias (2011) in *Film and the American Moral Vision of Nature: Theodore Roosevelt to Walt Disney*, which examines the "uniquely American moral code" in which Disney images of nature are framed (p. 181).

Themes Emerging from Analyses of Disney Theme Parks

Since the 1960s, a "deluge" of scholarly work on Disney's theme parks has sought to understand both the parks' aesthetics as well as "their meanings and significance as sites of contemporary American culture" (Wasko, 2001, p. 153; see also Budd, 2005). Wilson (1994) argued that, indeed, scholars should pay special attention to Disney's parks, "because they form the landscape against which Disney's visions met the historical and political realities of America" (p. 118). Despite what the company might intend, Disney has created and continues to create, in their parks, a "value-laden environment, which extends and expands Classic Disney into a material or physical existence, as well as providing a strong dose of all-American ideology" (Wasko, 2001, p. 152). The parks thus provide another opportunity for

The Walt Disney Company to commodify, market, and profit from Disney stories and characters. Wasko (2001) argues that the parks "represent a profitable and lucrative business for the Disney company, as well as supporting conservative, corporate, and consumerist ideologies" (p. 157).

Scholars began engaging in analysis and critique of the parks shortly after Disneyland opened in 1955. Julian Halévy (1958) offered one of the first critiques, and is "often cited as an example of the condescending tone of Disney critics" (Wasko, 2001, p. 156). Halévy was followed by Schickel (1968), Schiller (1973), and Real (1977), and in 1981 an entire issue of the *Journal of Popular Culture* was devoted to the parks. During the 1990s scholars such as Eco and Baudrillard set "the pattern for further postmodern musings during the 1990s" (Wasko, 2001, p. 156). During the 1990s (the so-called 'Disney Decade') the company greatly expanded the theme parks and resorts; this expansion "was met with a deluge of academic studies from a variety of disciplines, including anthropology, art, architecture, business, ethnic studies, film and media studies, cultural studies, gender studies, geography, history, marketing, political science, popular culture, rhetoric, and urban planning" (Wasko, 2001, pp. 156–157). Of note within this 1990s scholarship were Stephen Fjellman's (1992) groundbreaking ethnography of Walt Disney World, *Vinyl Leaves,* which focused not only on the pleasures of the park, but also critically examined its social implications, as well as The Project on Disney's (1995) *Inside the Mouse: Work and Play at Disney World,* which used a feminist lens to examine gender and consumption at Disney World, providing an 'alternative ride' through the everyday experience of the park in order to understand how it came to embody American leisure. Such examinations of the relationships between economic aspects and ideological characteristics characterize much of the scholarship on the parks.

One line of inquiry within this economic and ideological framework examines processes and practices of synergy, or how the parks have been cross-promoted and marketed through television shows, starting in the 1950s with the *Disneyland* television show and continuing through a variety of shows featured on the Disney-owned ABC television network (Smoodin, 1994). Davis (1996) analyzed the theme parks as a vital tool for marketing and selling Disney licensed merchandise. Other scholars have focused on how Disney parks commodify entertainment and promote consumption (Bryman, 1999; Fjellman, 1992; Wasko, 2001; Willis, 1993). Not only are the parks themselves objects of consumption, as park tickets alone cost hundreds of dollars, but once inside the parks there are hundreds more opportunities to buy products and experiences (Fjellman, 1992; Wilson, 1994). Indeed, the very cinematic experience of being in the parks—that is, the feeling of being inside a film set as one strolls through the parks—is another marketing strategy that helps immerse visitors in a themed consumptive experience (Wasko, 2001). Budd (2005) explains that being in a Disney park feels like "walking or riding through a narrative space, a theme-in-motion so successful at promoting sales that it has become the model for shopping malls, sports stadiums," etc. (p. 14). Fjellman (1992) calls this experience "commodity zen," as he describes visitors entering a "hyperreal world of sound bites" and product promotion (p. 310). Budd (2005) further explains that this experience of fully immersed consumption "is the strangely distracting and pleasurable new permutation of flânerie" (p. 14). More recently, Knight (2014), in *Power and Paradise in Walt Disney's World* focuses on how Walt Disney World is a place/space that provides themed, immersive experiences that are often (but not solely) centered around consumption. Similarly, scholars have analyzed how commercialization and corporatism are connected to and enacted through the theme parks. For example, Disneyland originally had 32 corporate sponsors that were connected to restaurants and exhibits, including General Electric and Monsanto, and Kodak (Wasko, 2001). Walt Disney World's *The Carousel of Progress*, which was featured at the 1964 World's Fair before moving to Disneyland and later, Walt Disney World, was sponsored by General Electric. Disney World's EPCOT has also featured corporate sponsors such as AT&T, General Motors, and Kraft.

Another area of Disney theme park scholarship explores who goes to the parks and why, focusing not only on demographic analyses of visitors but also on the ways in which Disney parks center on the theme of the family, as advertising and marketing targets mostly middle class families, and families are also depicted in various rides and attractions in the parks (Wasko, 2001). The family—that is, the "heterosexual nuclear family" (Bryman, 1995, p. 88)—is thus seen within this scholarship as both a theme within the parks and the context within which consumption at the parks takes place. Bryman (1995) argues that associating the family unit with consumption is powerful, as it "reinforces the consumerist goals of the parks" (p. 88). Relatedly, scholars have analyzed how Disney theme parks seek to construct a kind of Utopia "that is not only congruent with middle-class values; the Utopia *is* middle-class America" (Bryman, 1995, p. 95). Knight (2014) examines Disney World as pilgrimage center, focusing on how Disney World generates "memorable experiences" (p. 7), and as utopia, focusing on how Walt Disney sought to 'correct' natural landscapes and to create a kind of Garden of Eden, separated far from the everyday, mundane world; this utopia also seeks to "prescribe and reinforce 'proper' behavior, imbuing Disneyworld with utopian—if often unattainable—ambitions" (p. 7). Here, 'pilgrimage' is taken up both in a more general way to mean the "feeling of compulsion to visit a sacred region" (Bryman, 1995, p. 95), and also in a more specific way, examining what constitutes a religious pilgrimage and applying those characteristics to a Disney vacation (Bryman, 1995). Bryman argues that using the metaphor of pilgrimage to describe a visit to Disney is misguided, however. Unlike religious pilgrimages, at Disney there is no carnival and no sense of exuberance. Perhaps most importantly, though, while pilgrims typically head home with a new kind of reality, visitors to Disney parks do not, because the parks "present an essentially conservative image of the world which confirms and reaffirms the conventional and the normal" (Bryman, 1995, p. 98), including traditional images of the family and romantic love. Instead of a new vision of life, it is more likely that "American pilgrims to a Disney park will return with a renewed sense of their roots" (p. 98)—this quest becomes about clinging tight to the past, "to what appears to have been lost to the present, and of reconstituting the past in an idealized and romanticized way" (Reader, 1993, p. 231).

Most prevalent among scholarly studies of Disney theme parks is work that explores how control, the managing of expectations, predictability, and safety, are enacted in the parks, much of which draws upon Bryman (1995), who identified 6 levels at which control operates in and through the parks. First, Disney controls the theme park experience itself, as it controls the movement of visitors within the parks via architecture, queuing designs, and crowd control strategies as well as narratives within the attractions (Borrie, 1999; Shearing & Stenning, 1992). What visitors 'see' and experience on rides, for example, is controlled, as the rides are set up by Disney Imagineers to only allow particular views, thus the experience of visitors on rides is controlled through standardization. Second, Disney theme parks control visitors' imagination, via "the selecting out of undesirable elements from the purview of visitors" (Bryman, 1995, p. 102). Wallace (1985) quotes a Disney Imagineer, who states, "What we create is a 'Disney realism,' sort of Utopian in nature, where we carefully program out all the negative, unwanted elements and program in all the positive elements" (p. 35). This process is explored by Wallace (1996) in his analysis of how Disney parks rewrite and simplify history, removing all controversy, a process Zukin (1991) calls "totalitarian image-making" (p. 220). The highly-scripted entertainment narratives further shape the imagination, as children "lose the capacity for play and spontaneity" (Bryman, 1995, p. 103).

The third way control appears in Disney parks is as a narrative theme in many of the attractions themselves. For example, control of animals, nature, and land features heavily in many of the exhibits at EPCOT; control is also a prevalent theme in both Frontierland and Adventureland, which focus on conquering and controlling the American frontier and its resources and people, and on White colonizers people bringing "civilization to the new world" (Bryman, 1995, p. 106). As Bryman (1995) states, at Disney parks, the theme of control is persuasive because it is "easy to cloak with euphemisms and neutral terms, of science, of progress, and of overcoming wilderness, and by eulogizing the intuition or courage of those who manage to (or seek to) overcome adverse conditions" (p. 107). Highlighting the control over nature and humans as part of the narrative themes of attractions at the park also helps normalize and naturalize the ways in which Disney parks control the immediate environments within and beyond the parks, which is a fourth manifestation of control at the parks. At Walt Disney World in Florida, Walt Disney created "fantasy worlds out of orange groves or swamp lands" (Bryman, 1995, p. 113). The natural environments of the parks continue to be meticulously monitored and controlled, as park employees remove dying and dead plants and unwanted animal populations throughout the park (Borrie, 1999). Additionally, the "backstage magic" of Disney (Wasko, 2001) and strict regulations about what visitors are allowed to see helps create the fantasy that the parks operate by 'magic' (Telotte, 2008). The design of the parks deliberately blocks from view the outside world of highways, shopping malls, and traffic, and the mechanical functioning of the park is also hidden through an underground network of tunnels that mask the movement of employees, power and sewage lines, transportation, electrical wiring, computer cables, and other technologies and processes that would ruin the fantasy (Telotte, 2008).

A fifth aspect of control involves the regulation of park employees and their behavior. Scholarship focusing on this aspect of Disney parks has explored Disney organizational culture and training practices, including how Disney University trains its employees to provide quality customer service, stressing friendliness, cleanliness, and the importance of visitor happiness (Bryman, 1995). Employees—called "cast members," are integrated into Disney's strong corporate culture as they are trained by Disney to speak and enact a Disney customer service model, which includes particular language, behavior, appearance, and values—including being part of the Disney family (Van Maanen & Kunda, 1989). Edwards (1979) and Van Maanen and Kunda (1989) highlighted four forms of control of employee behavior that are enacted through Disney's strong corporate culture: hierarchical control (seen in how employees are supervised), technical control (seen in how rides are mechanized to limit employee movement), bureaucratic control (seen in the many rules of comportment and appearance that control employee behavior), and culture control (seen in how employee emotions about Disney are influenced to create positive feelings about working for Disney and for the company, and to instill loyalty and 'Disney values' into employees). Bryman (1995) posits that this last form of control is the main one used in the parks to control employees, and is important because it "helps to reconcile employees to the other forms of control" (p. 112). Kuenz's (1995) chapter, "Working at the Rat," in The Project on Disney's *Inside the Mouse*, also examines labor at Disney parks, and specifically reveals the contradictions of production that are concealed beneath capitalism's "smooth surface of consumption" (Budd, 2005, p. 13). This essay explores the "contradictory daily reality" that employees navigate and negotiate, including their own "self-surveillance and subversion, enforced familiarity and isolation, [and] enjoyment in the work and dislike of the Disney Company" (Budd, 2005, p. 13). However, despite the contradictions and possible moments of subversion discovered by Kuenz and ethnographers such as Van Maanen, Bryman's (1995) review highlights the high levels of adherence to and cooperation with Disney corporate culture among cast members.

A final aspect of control discussed in Bryman's (1995) review is control over Disney's destiny. Scholars (see Fjellman, 1992, and Ross, 1999, for examples) have traced the history of Walt's establishment of the Reedy Creek Improvement District in Florida, a 40-square-mile area of land in central Florida containing Walt Disney World and Disney's other central Florida theme parks and resorts. In the 1960s, following the success of Disneyland in California, Walt Disney began quietly and cheaply buying up this land. The establishment of the Reedy Creek Improvement District gave The Walt Disney Company "more or less complete autonomy within its domain, so that it became an area of private government" (Bryman, 1995, p. 115). The political autonomy of The Walt Disney Company, like each of the mechanisms of control highlighted in Bryman's (1995) review, create a sense of safety and predictability within the parks, and enable each visitor to have remarkably similar experiences.

Contemporary critiques of Disney theme parks in a wide variety of disciplines drawn heavily on explore Ritzer's (1993, 1999; Ritzer & Liska, 1997) theory of "Disneyfication." Emerging from his concept of McDonaldization, which focuses on how McDonald's practices of efficiency, calculability, predictability, and control, are used to structure economic and social life across the globe, Disneyfication highlights the ways that The Walt Disney Company employs similar practices that shape global consumer culture. Bryman (1999, 2004) outlines a similar process, which he calls "Disneyization," through which the principles of Disney theme parks have come to dominate many sectors of society, leading to the cultural ubiquity of themed environments, hybrid merchandising, expectations of emotional and performative labor, and increased control. These theories have figured prominently in studies exploring how Wasko's (2001) Classic Disney themes are used to (re)present and (re)create the past and the future (Fjellman, 1992; Wallace, 1996). The work of Bryman (1995) in particular has contributed to postmodern critiques of the parks, such as Jackson and West's (2011) *Disneyland and Culture: Essays on the Parks and Their Influence*, which explores the kinds of synthetic experiences visitors engage with there. Such postmodern analyses also explicate the processes of Disneyization and Disneyfication at work in representations of past, cultural present, and future. Most recently, Knight (2014) examined the ways that Disney theme parks teach us "which products, technological revolutions, and social movements point the way towards 'progress' and what kinds of relationships Americans want to foster with their global neighbors" (p. 8).

Feeling, Buying, and Being Disney

Extending this legacy of scholarly work on Disney, this volume explores Disney as a curriculum, a vast and varied totality of experiences that operate as an educational process. Using a broad range of theoretical lenses, including arts-based and aesthetic inquiry, cultural studies, queer theories, feminist theories, and psychoanalytic approaches, the essays in this volume take up many of the themes of previous Disney scholarship while advancing new avenues of exploration by focusing on the affective and ontological aspects of identity development as well as the commodification of social and cultural identities, experiences, and subjectivities. We have organized the book in three parts, each of which addresses a different aspect of Disney's curricula and pedagogies: *Feeling Disney* explores the affective and ontological aspects of identity development; *Buying Disney* analyzes the commodification of social and cultural identities, experiences, and subjectivities; and *Being Disney* explores how Disney shapes our desires for both freedom and control as well as our participation in these practices. Each part of the book questions our engagements with Disney in order to advance a critical understanding of how Disney teaches us how to feel, buy, and be through experiences, products, and services that have become an integral part of global popular culture.

Authors in **Part I, *Feeling Disney: Disney Fears and Fantasies*** extend the work of previous Disney scholars who posited that impactful scholarship on Disney must take into account the emotional investments audiences make in Disney. As Budd (2005) argued, the new generations of Disney scholars rallied around the idea that successful critique could emerge "only from immersion in the Disney experience, including its very real and often valuable pleasures" (p. 12). In *Feeling Disney*, authors take this work into new theoretical areas—influenced by the affective turn in the humanities and social sciences (Clough, 2007)—as they not only take pleasure seriously, but ask questions about what pleasure and other emotional investments in Disney *do*, socially and culturally. Since branding its flagship theme park as "The Happiest Place on Earth" in the 1950s, The Walt Disney Company has marketed itself as a purveyor of good feelings and has created experiences that place consumers inside intricately fabricated fantasies of fulfillment. In fact, Budd (2005) suggests that Disney had learned early on to treat the emotional desires of its audiences "not as demands to be supplied, or human aspirations to be respected and articulated, but as raw materials to be extracted and reconstructed, with the most profitable selected, hyperinflated, packaged, and sold back to the customers in an incomplete but adequately efficient process" (pp. 10–11).

Affect studies turns its attention to just such emotional investments, seeking to understand how affect permeates discourses of culture, subjectivity, embodiment, and identity. Threaded through these interdisciplinary analyses is the notion that human feelings are shaped by physiological and material elements as well as the dynamics of our social interactions. As Smith (2011) notes, "this understanding of affect suggests that what we imagine to be individual and specific—impulses, attitudes, emotions, and feelings—in fact have a social, historical, and therefore shared dimension" (p. 5). Therefore, in this section, authors seek to explore the affective impact of Disney's "shrewdly constructed imaginary personalities, stories, themed fantasy spaces, and merchandise that tap into transcultural myths of magic and childhood innocence" (Budd, 2005, p. 1). The essays investigate the shared social and cultural dimensions of fantasies of happiness, hope, and desire—and the fears contained within and repressed or denied by such fantasies—as they are expressed through various Disney discourses, texts, and spaces. Following this affective line of inquiry, these essays also look to disclose the ways that our emotional investments in Disney's hopeful narratives can be counterproductive to a critical stance. Authors take up the necessary critical task of problematizing our emotional engagements by exploring in a variety of ways the fears and fantasies that circulate through the discourses of Disney.

These questions are explored through analyses of diverse aspects of the Disneyverse such as Ausman and Radford's exploration of waltdisney confessions@tumblr as a digital space that enacts a confessional curriculum of desire helping to reproduce Disney ideologies; Burdick's analysis of the ways that The Walt Disney Company and its products can still be read as extant manifestations of the desires of Walt Disney himself; Helmsing's inquiry into Disney desires and disappointments through a reading of the queer pedagogies of Disney diva villains that reveal how such diva lessons as getting even, gaining power, and becoming "the fairest of them all" can be read as acts that constitute a curriculum of how to succeed in life when one is predestined to fail spectacularly; Macaluso's analysis of the film *Frozen* and online posts and comments about the film that describes how this online media discourse enacts a curriculum of postfeminist cultural production through which the popular media, through the modulation of affect, operates to (re)produce gendered identities and subjectivities; and Steindam's analysis of the relationship between desire and subjectivity through a reading of how Disney films teach us into particular ways of relating to nature, focusing specifically on the curricula of wildness, purity, and anthropomorphism. These chapters thus build upon previous research examining subjectivity, middle-class family pilgrimages, gender and sexuality, and Disney's portrayals of animals and nature, but extend this work through reading these issues through the analytical lenses of curricula of affect and desire. Taken together, these chapters illustrate how emotions, in the context of the Disneyverse, are not simply psychological dispositions but mechanisms that shape subjectivities and mediate relationships between individuals and identities, between people and nature, and between corporations and consumers.

Explorations of the ways in which relationships between The Walt Disney Company and its consumers are constructed and concretized comprise the work of the contributors in **Part II, *Buying Disney: Commodified, Caricatured, and Contested Subjectivities.*** This work builds upon, updates, and extends previous scholarship focused on race, class, gender, and sexuality, and on how Disney packages and sells these subjectivities. The commodification of Disney-produced characters is a meaning-making process through which Disney's curricula and pedagogies operate. In 2001, Ono and Buescher, writing about the process by which Disney's Pocahontas was used to sell a wide variety of products, noted the tendency of American culture to "appropriate, transform, and then (almost obsessively) reproduce figures and forms through the production of commodities" (pp. 24–25). Ono and Buescher argue that in creating a character used to market a vast array of consumer goods, Disney essentially replaced the history of a real Native American with that of her animated counterpart, 'recasting' her through western, capitalist lenses. Of course, Pocahontas was certainly not the first Disney character to be commodified, but her story offers particular insight into the ways that social identities are produced, packaged, and promoted through the appropriation of raced, classed, gendered, and geo-graphically situated subjectivities. The historical Pocahontas, a meaningful figure in Native American culture, was not an empty signifier, but "when Disney *imported* the figure of Pocahontas into mainstream culture and reshaped it, new meanings were ascribed to the figure of Pocahontas, and most older meanings were lost" (Ono & Buescher, 2001, p. 25). Thus, the identity of the original signified 'Pocahontas' is appropriated and resignified for mass consumption, a process that holds significant implications for identity formation. As Ono and Buescher explain, the "recyclable, repro-ducible, and replaceable" products that emerge from this process "tend to collapse race, gender, ethnicity, and class" (p. 26).

Each of the essays in this section, then, explores how Disney texts appropriate and commodify different aspects of social identity and experience by capitalizing on cultural norms and myths, reinforcing stereotypes, and rewriting subjectivities, building on and updating previous critical explora-tions of gender, race, ethnicity, and sexuality (Bell, Haas, and Sells, 1995; Budd & Kirsch, 2005; Cheu, 2012; Davis, 2006, 2014; Griffin, 2000; Jhappan & Stasiulis, 2005; Sperb, 2012; Wasko, 2001). For example, Letts explores how Disney commodifies camp within its libidinal economy, through a reading of four Disney characters who, he asserts, both draw upon and repudiate queer sensibilities, and thus both valorize and offer alternatives to heteronormative masculinities and femininities. And Griffin, in her analysis of *Doc McStuffins* as progressive empowerment, explores how Disney commodifies the subjectivities of Black girlhood through the mobilization of aspirational discourses that capitalize on ideals of social progress. Griffin argues that while *Doc McStuffins* can be read as a significant site of progressive empowerment for Black girls, the show also fuels 'post' logics through deracialization and reinforces racist, sexist stereotypes of Black females as caretakers, while simultaneously expanding its market reach and selling 'progressive' characters. Additionally, while most previous research has focused on troubling representations of race, ethnicity, gender, and sexuality, very little work has been done on Disney's representations of class, other than to focus on how Disney normalizes a middle-class utopia. The work of Barros and Wright thus fills a gaping hole in the literature. Barros' analysis of how Brazilian Disney blogs focuses on the "*viagem para Disney*" (trip to

Disney), illustrates how individuals engage with the middle-class aspirational fantasy and/or reality of a trip to Disney as a form of citizenship pedagogy. Wright's analysis of the classist curriculum of Disney's reality television shows such as *Duck Dynasty* reveals that such programs serve to *stigmatize* poor and working-class people; by portraying working-class people in such ways, these programs perpetuate the myths of the American dream and capitalistic meritocracy, and perpetuate class inequalities. These myths are commodified and concretized through the discourse of hope that is the focus of Wallin's chapter. Wallin describes the "happy curriculum" that produces a "Disney-ish delirium"—an "infantile nostalgia for happiness, goodness, truth and sincerity"— that has spread throughout the West. He also explores how Disney's infinite utopia normalizes the Disneyish dispersion of reality and immerses us in the libidinal economy of capitalism. This work, along with the other pieces in this section, connect Disney's representations of race, class, gender, and sexuality with the "economic functions" they serve (Budd, 2005, p. 18).

Finally, authors in **Part III, *Being Disney: Freedom, Participation, and Control*** build upon previous research that has explored how Disney, through its parks, enacts pedagogies of control and predictability (Bryman 1995, 1999, 2004; Fjellman, 1992; Jackson & West, 2011; Knight, 2014; Ritzer, 1993). The authors here expand discussions of control and predictability into examinations of more recent technologies. In recent years, relationships between consumers and corporations have changed, as digital technologies have expanded and redefined how we buy and sell goods and services. As interactive online markets have expanded, individuals have become active participants in consumption by providing valuable time and personal inform-ation in exchange for the conveniences of customization. These changes are part of what Jenkins (2009) refers to as a participatory culture, which he describes as "a culture with relatively low barriers to artistic expression and civic engagement, strong support for creating and sharing creations, and some type of informal mentorship whereby experienced participants pass along knowledge to novices" (p. xi). Social media, for example, offers an environment where users can freely create and distribute content in the form of text, photo collages, customized videos, personalized cartoon strips, and much more. Aram Sinnreich (2010) uses the term "configurable culture" emphasizing how information is not only consumed by audiences, but actively rearranged in the form of mashups, fan fiction, etc. These interactive digital media seem to suggest a more democratic, 'grassroots' media environment where user-generation could dominate corporate production. However, as Schäfer (2011) observes, the enthusiasm about the participation of users in cultural production "neglects the fact that underlying power structures are not necessarily reconfigured" (pp. 10–11). While the new media practices pose a challenge to some traditional business models, the corporate interests exploiting those models, The Walt Disney Company among them, remain. As Schäfer (2011) explains, "new enterprises emerge and gain control over cultural production and intellectual property in a manner very similar to the monopolistic media corporations of the 20th century. The powerful 'culture industry' is therefore not overturned by a revolution of users" (Schäfer, 2011, p. 11). Participation is thus paradoxical, as users are both empowered *and* controlled, as they are taught into being and acting in ways that serve corporate interests. As contributor Kalin explains "participation no longer denotes subversion of authoritarian bodies, but has become a hallmark of post-industrial economic logics (Bishop, 2012, p. 14) with defanging effects (Wright, 2008)."

Authors in this section thus explore how Disney controls cultural production and intellectual property by exploiting our desires for both freedom *and* control to teach us into action and potentially usurp participation's democratic potential. This theme is taken up in Bey's ethnographic exploration of Walt Disney World, which explores how Disney guests are learners taught into particular understandings of 'Disney Magic' as the ostensible source of all possibilities and positive realities, which helps explain why visitors to theme parks are willing to pay such a high price to participate. Additionally, applying concepts such as Disneyization and Disneyfication to the analysis of other cultural institutions, Kalin draws on the work of Bryman (2004) to analyze art museums and their educational programs, specifically in relation to curricular practices that claim enhanced participation and civic engagement for their visitors. She suggests that participation, once Disneyized and Disneyfied, perpetuates neoliberal mandates to keep busy and feel self-actualized while constructing a controlled post-political landscape where societal issues are "concealed, neglected, parodied, sanitized, and/or quickly forgotten while continuing on unchallenged and unchanged." Expanding on the notion of participation, control, and Disneyfication, we join Huddleston in an exploration of how new 'convenience' technologies used in the parks operate as both regulatory devices and mechanisms of surveillance that construct theme park experiences to appeal to the desires of consumers and serve Disney's corporate interests. Applying these ideas about control in a filmic analysis, Furo, Grant, Rogers, and Schmitz explore the character of Merida, the notably progressive Disney princess featured in the 2012 animated film *Brave,* taking up discussions of the gendered body, of curriculum as a lived experience of meaning making, and of the powers of public pedagogy Their analysis reveals a "corseted curriculum" of constricting gender norms at work in the film that inevitably binds Merida to a structured plot that ultimately limits her development to a controlled formula. Finally, Henry Giroux offers an analysis of the control that The Walt Disney Company has over the production, circulation and exchange of information, especially to children, as he discusses Disney's aggressive marketing campaigns targeting goods and services for infants, toddlers and tweens, many of which are more accessible than ever with the advances of new media that allow for the proliferation of Disney's powerful pedagogies.

Taken together, this collection illustrates Disney's cultural omnipresence as a rich and important source for critique. Yet, the authors in this collection do not seek only to critique and/or deconstruct Disney products and perspectives but also to appreciate and understand the ways that The Walt Disney Company operates to influence education and popular culture in the United States and beyond. In a recent volume on Disney, Giroux and Pollock (2010) encourage citizens to ask themselves, "How does the power of a corporation like Disney affect my life and shape my values as a citizen, consumer, parent, and individual?" (p. xv). While acknowledging Disney's ubiquitous potential to craft social and cultural norms and influence identities, we also recognize our own investments in Disney as a source of entertainment and pleasure. That is, we posit that Disney can also provide "opportunities to venture beyond mundane, everyday experience while laying claim to unrealized dreams and hopes" (Giroux & Pollock, p. 7). Thus, we hope that this collection of essays will present readers, both Disney fans and critics alike, with compelling questions about the ways that Disney operates as a cultural curriculum and new possibilities for exploring the ways that we are taught into particular ways of being through our investments in and engagements with Disney discourses.

References

Ahmed, S. (2010). *The promise of happiness*. Durham, NC: Duke University Press.

Bell, E., Haas, L., & Sells, L. (Eds.). (1995). *From mouse to mermaid: The politics of film, gender, and culture*. Bloomington: Indiana University Press.

Borrie, W. T. (1999). Disneyland and Disney World: Constructing the environment, designing the visitor experience. *Loisir et Société, 22*(1), 71–82.

Brode, D. (2005). *Multiculturalism and the mouse: Race and sex in Disney entertainment*. Austin: University of Texas Press.

Bryman, A. (1995). *Disney and his worlds*. New York: Routledge.

Bryman, A. (1999). The Disneyization of society. *The Sociological Review, 47*(1), 25–47.

Bryman, A. (2004). *The Disneyization of society*. Thousand Oaks, CA: SAGE.

Budd, M. (2005). Introduction: Private Disney, public Disney. In M. Budd & M. H. Kirsch (Eds.), *Rethinking Disney: Private control, public dimensions* (pp. 1–33). Middletown, CT: Wesleyan University Press.

Budd, M., & Kirsch, M. H. (Eds.). (2005). *Rethinking Disney: Private control, public dimensions* Middletown, CT: Wesleyan University Press.

Cheu, J. (2012). *Diversity in Disney films: Critical essays on race, ethnicity, gender, sexuality, and disability*. Jefferson, NC: McFarland.

Clough, P. (2007). *The affective turn: Theorizing the social*. Durham, NC: Duke University Press.

Cremin, L. A. (1976). *Public education*. New York: Basic Books.

Davis, A. (2006). *Good girls and wicked witches: Women in Disney's feature animation*. London: John Libbey Publishing.

Davis, A. (2014). *Handsome heroes and vile villains: Masculinity in Disney's feature films*. Bloomington: Indiana University Press.

Davis, S. (1996). Theme park: Global industry and cultural form. *Media, Culture & Society, 18*(3), 399–422.

Doherty, T. (2006). The wonderful world of Disney studies. *Chronicle of Higher Education, 52*(46), B10.

Dorfman, A., & Mattelart, A. (1971). *Para leer El Pato Donald*. Valparaiso, Chile: Ediciones Universidad.

Edgerton, G., & Jackson, K. M. (1996). Redesigning Pocahontas: Disney, the "White man's Indian," and the marketing of dreams. *Journal of Popular Film and Television, 24*(2), 90–98.

Edwards, R. (1979). *Contested terrain: The transformation of the workplace in the twentieth century*. New York: Basic Books.

Fjellman, S. J. (1992). *Vinyl leaves: Walt Disney World and America*. Boulder, CO: Westview Press.

Gabler, N. (2006). *Walt Disney*. New York: Alfred A. Knopf.

Giroux, H. A. (2004). Are Disney movies good for your kids? In S. R. Steinberg & J. L. Kincheloe (Eds.), *Kinderculture: The corporate construction of childhood* (2nd ed.) (pp. 164–180). Boulder, CO: Westview Press.

Giroux, H., & Pollock, G. (2010). *The mouse that roared: Disney and the end of innocence* (2nd ed.). Lanham, MD: Rowman & Littlefield.

Golden, M. (2006). Pocahontas: Comparing the Disney image with historical evidence. *Social Studies and the Young Learner, 18*(4), 19–24.

Graser, M. (2014). Will Japan's 'Tsum Tsum' characters translate in the U.S. for Disney? *Variety*. Retrieved from: http://variety.com/2014/biz/asia/will-japans-tsum-tsum-characters-translate-in-the-u-s-for-disney-1201256414/

Griffin, S. (2000). *Tinker belles and evil queens*. New York: NYU Press.

Halévy, J. (1958, June 7). Disneyland and Las Vegas. *The Nation*.

Hastings, A.W. (1996). Bambi and the hunting ethos. *Journal of Popular Film and Television, 24*(2), 53–60.

Iger, R. (2014). The Walt Disney Company fiscal year 2014 annual financial report and shareholder letter. Anaheim, CA: The Walt Disney Company. Retrieved from: http://thewaltdisneycompany.com/sites/default/files/reports/10k-wrap-2014_1.pdf

Jackson, K. M., & West, J. I. (2011). *Disneyland and culture: Essays on the parks and their influence*. Jefferson, NC: McFarland Press.

Jenkins, H. (with K. Clinton, R. Purushotma, A. Robison, & M. Weigel). (2009). *Confronting the challenges of a participatory culture: Media education for the 21st century*. Cambridge, MA: MIT Press.

Jhappan, R., & Stasiulis, D. (2005). Anglophilia and the discreet charm of the English voice in Disney's *Pocahontas* films. In M. Budd & M. H. Kirsch (Eds.), *Rethinking Disney: Private control, public dimensions* Middletown, CT: Wesleyan University Press.

Johnson, O., & Thomas, F. (1990). *Walt Disney's Bambi: The story and the film*. New York: Stewart, Tobori, and Chang.

King, M. (1996). The audience in the wilderness: The Disney nature films. *Journal of Popular Film and Television, 24*(2), 60–69.

Knight, C. K. (2014). *Power and paradise in Walt Disney's world*. Gainesville: University Press of Florida.

Kuenz, J. (1995). Working at the rat. In The Project on Disney (Ed.), *Inside the mouse: Work and play at Disney World* (pp. 110–162). Durham, NC: Duke University Press.

Lee, N., & Madej, K. (2012). *Disney stories: Getting to digital*. New York: Springer.

Lutts, R. (1992). The trouble with *Bambi*: Walt Disney's *Bambi* and the American vision of nature. *Forest and Conservation History, 36*(October), 160–171.

Ono, K. A., & Buescher, D. T. (2001). Deciphering Pocahontas: Unpackaging the commodification of a native American woman. *Critical Studies In Media Communication, 18*(1), 23–43.

Padurano, D. (2011). "Isn't that a dude?": Using images to teach gender and ethnic diversity in the U.S. history classroom—Pocahontas: A case study. *History Teacher, 44*(2), 191–208.

Pallant, C. (2011). *Demystifying Disney: A history of Disney feature animation.* London: Continuum.

Peri, D. (2011). *Working with Disney: Interviews with animators, producers, and artists.* Jackson: University Press of Mississippi.

Pinar, W. (2004). *What is curriculum theory?* Mahwah, NJ: Erlbaum.

Reader, I. (1993). Conclusions. In I. Reader & T. Walter (Eds.), *Pilgrimage in popular culture.* London: MacMillan.

Real, M. R. (1977). *Mass-mediated culture.* Upper River Saddle, NJ: Prentice Hall.

Ritzer, G. (1993). *The McDonaldization of society: An investigation into the changing character of contemporary social life.* Newbury Park, CA: Pine Forge Press.

Ritzer, G. (1999). *Enchanting a disenchanted world: Revolutionizing the means of consumption.* Newbury Park, CA: Pine Forge Press.

Ritzer, G., & Liska, A. (1997). McDisneyization and post-tourism: Complementary perspectives on contemporary tourism. In C. Rojek & J. Urry (Eds.), *Touring cultures: Transformations of travel and theory* (pp. 96–109). London: Routledge.

Roost, F. (2005) Synergy city: How Times Square and Celebration are integrated into Disney's marketing cycle. In M. Budd & M. H. Kirsch (Eds.), *Rethinking Disney: Private control, public dimensions* (pp. 261–298). Middletown, CT: Wesleyan University Press.

Ross, A. (1999). *The Celebration chronicles: Life, liberty, and the pursuit of property value in Disney's new town.* New York: Ballantine.

Savage, G. C. (2010). Problematizing "public pedagogy" in educational research. In J. A. Sandlin, B. D. Schultz, & J. Burdick (Eds.), *Handbook of Public Pedagogy* (pp. 103–115). New York: Routledge.

Schäfer, M. T. (2011). *Bastard culture! How user participation transforms cultural production.* Amsterdam: Amsterdam University Press.

Schickel, R. (1968). *The Disney version: The life, times, art, and commerce of Walt Disney.* New York: Simon and Schuster.

Schiller, H. (1973). *The mind managers.* Boston: Beacon Press.

Schubert, W. H. (1981). Knowledge about out-of-school curriculum. *Educational Forum, 45*, 185–199.

Schubert, W. H. (2006). Focus on the big curriculum. *Journal of Curriculum and Pedagogy, 3*(1), 100–103.

Sells, L. (1995). "Where do the mermaids stand?": Voice and body in *The Little Mermaid.* In E. Bell, L. Hass, & L. Sells (Eds.), *From mouse to mermaid: The politics of film, gender and culture* (pp. 175–192). Bloomington: Indiana University Press.

Shearing, C. D., & Stenning, P. C. (1992). From the panopticon to Disney World: The development of discipline. In R. V. G. Clarke (Ed.), *Situational crime prevention: Successful case studies* (pp. 300–304). New York: Harrow and Heston Publishers.

Siegel, G. (2005). Disneyfication, the stadium, and the politics of ambiance. In M. Budd & M. H. Kirsch (Eds.), *Rethinking Disney: Private control, public dimensions* (pp. 299–323). Middletown, CT: Wesleyan University Press.

Sinnreich, A. (2010). *Mashed up: Music, technology, and the rise of configurable culture.* Amherst: University of Massachusetts Press.

Sklar, R. (1980). The making of cultural myths—Walt Disney. In D. Peary & G. Peary (Eds.), *The American animated cartoon: A critical anthology* (pp. 58–65). New York: E. P. Dutton.

Smith, R. (2011). Postmodernism and the affective turn. *Twentieth Century Literature, 57*(3/4), 423–446.

Smoodin, E. (1994). *Disney discourse: Producing the Magic Kingdom.* New York: Routledge.

Sperb, J. (2012). *Disney's most notorious film: Race, convergence, and the hidden histories of Song of the South.* Austin: University of Texas Press.

Stearns, J., Sandlin, J. A., & Burdick, J. (2011). Resistance on aisle three? Exploring the big curriculum of consumption and the (im)possibility of resistance in John Updike's "A&P". *Curriculum Inquiry, 41*(3), 394–415.

Stein, A. (2011). *Why we love Disney: The power of the Disney brand.* New York: Peter Lang Press.

Steinberg, S. R., & Kincheloe, J. L. (Eds.). (2004). *Kinderculture: The corporate construction of childhood* (2nd ed.). Boulder, CO: Westview Press.

St. John, T. (1981). Walter Elias Disney: The cartoon as race fantasy. *Ball State University Forum, June 1981,* 64.

Stone, K. (1975). Things Walt Disney never told us. *Journal of American Folklore, 88,* 42–50.

Susanin, T. S. (2011). *Walt before Mickey: Disney's early years, 1919–1928.* Jackson: University Press of Mississippi.

Telotte, J. P. (2008). *The Mouse machine: Disney and technology.* Chicago: University of Illinois Press.

The Project on Disney (Ed.). (1995). *Inside the mouse: Work and play at Disney World.* Durham, NC: Duke University Press.

Tobias, R. B. (2011). *Film and the American moral vision of nature: Theodore Roosevelt to Walt Disney.* East Lansing: Michigan State University Press.

Van Maanen, J., & Kunda, G. (1989). "Real feelings": Emotional expression and organizational culture. *Research in Organizational Behavior, 11,* 43–103.

Wallace, M. (1985). Mickey Mouse history: Portraying the past at Disney World. *Radical History Review, 32*: 33–57.

Wallace, M. (1996). *Mickey Mouse history: Portraying the past at Disney World.* Philadelphia: Temple University Press.

Warren, S. (2005). Saying no to Disney: Disney's demise in four American cities. In M. Budd & M. H. Kirsch (Eds.), *Rethinking Disney: Private control, public dimensions* (pp. 231–260). Middletown, CT: Wesleyan University Press.

Wasko, J. (2001). *Understanding Disney.* Malden, MA: Polity.

Wasko, J., Phillips, M., & Meehan E. (Eds.). (2001). *Dazzled by Disney? The Global Disney Audiences Project.* Leicester, UK: University of Leicester Press.

Whitley, D. (2012). *The idea of nature in Disney animation: From Snow White to WALL-E* (2nd ed.). Farnham, UK: Ashgate.

Willis, S. (1993). Disney World: Public use/private state. *Southern Atlantic Quarterly, 92*(1), 119–137.

Wilson, A. (1994). The betrayal of the future: Walt Disney's EPCOT center. In E. Smoodin (Ed.), *Disney discourse: Producing the Magic Kingdom* (pp. 118–130). New York: Routledge.

Wohlwend, K. R. (2009). Damsels in discourse: Girls consuming and producing identity texts through Disney princess play. *Reading Research Quarterly, 44*(1), 57–83.

Wohlwend, K. E. (2012a). "Are you guys girls?": Boys, identity texts, and Disney princess play. *Journal of Early Childhood Literacy, 12*(1), 3–23.

Wohlwend, K. E. (2012b). The boys who would be princesses: Playing with gender identity intertexts in Disney princess transmedia. *Gender and Education, 24*(6), 593–610.

Zipes, J. (1995). Breaking the Disney spell. In E. Bell, L. Hass, & L. Sells (Eds.), *From mouse to mermaid: The politics of film, gender and culture* (pp. 21–42). Bloomington: Indiana University Press.

Zukin, S. (1991). *Landscapes of power: From Detroit to Disney World.* Berkeley: University of California Press.

Part I

Feeling Disney

Disney Fears and Fantasies

2 waltdisneyconfessions @tumblr

Narrative, Subjectivity, and Reading Online Spaces of Confession

Tasha Ausman and Linda Radford

When we scroll down the threads on our tumblr.com dashboard, we get tangled in the murky (cyber)space lingering underneath conventional social media sites. Tumblr is different from Twitter and Facebook, where individuals write their lives for all to see through personal pictures and status updates. Tumblr is a social media website where people upload and reblog millions of posts each day. As of October 2014, there were 93.9 billion independent posts on Tumblr feeds in 13 languages, and over 207 million blogs all over the world. Tumblr boasts being a space where "you can customize anything, from colors to your theme's HTML." Its logo, reminiscent of a school uniform crest, brands users as "the world's creators." Each user has a dashboard that becomes the platform from where posts are launched, and where members spend time modifying, captioning, and animating GIFS to make each post unique. The vast majority of users reblog content from other Tumblr feeds, creating 'genres' often around specific themes like people's hobbies, areas of study, sports, and also personal fascinations and revelations about controversial topics such as "pro-anorexia." Users choose this space to reveal what they want others to see, provoking audiences to respond or re-post or even up the ante with more provocative or sometimes disturbing images, GIFS, taglines, and comments. Users are totally anonymous, identifying themselves with screen names; there is nothing tying together Tumblr's users except common 'threads.'

One high profile blog, with its daily posts and bright images, is waltdisneyconfessions@tumblr.[1] The "confessions" thread operates as a safe place for adult fans of Disney to reveal their secret desires, wishes, hopes, disappointments and dreams about living, working, and becoming Disney as either cheerful spectators, employees (especially "face characters"), students in the Disney College Program (DCP), or in some cases, adoring devotees who fantasize about becoming 'real' Disney princes and princesses someday. This blog is so popular that the blog moderator recently declared that the "queue has been turned up to 15 times per day . . . for now, because we've just made so many confessions! <3" (Walt Disney Confessions Blog Owner, 2014b). On this thread, which we joined and continue to follow, we can view images and read captioned confessions uploaded daily by anonymous users who recycle images from Disney movies, history, and theme parks as a means to express their very beings.

Navigating the complex web of Tumblr posts, we ask ourselves, what is this 'place' where stories are told and recycled? We note that different social media sites have different cultures. Tumblr is a fluid (cyber)space while also being the property of the major multinational tech corporation Yahoo, which bought Tumblr to increase its appeal and profitability by re-entering the youth market (Cringely, 2013). Facebook is highly regulated with a prescribed format for each user's homepage, monitoring of content (photos and content deemed inappropriate are removed by site administrators), and clearly framed spaces into which personal information and photos can be entered or uploaded. Tumblr, by contrast, is free to be edited in format and content, even at the level of HTML. These differences in and among sites tell us that using the single category of 'social media' to describe a sweeping array of potential ways people create and represent identities online might not be fitting. In looking at Tumblr as a particular cultural hub, we are taken back to the work of Williams (1983), who reminds us that the concept of culture takes on an anthropological dimension. Cultural artifacts are central to defining a group of people, and material production is at the forefront. In cultural studies and the humanities, by contrast, the concept of culture revolves more around signifying and symbolic systems.

Given these dual but complementary definitions of culture, we take note of Tumblr as a bounded-yet-unbounded social media space. We see the website as an ethnographic location where posts become digital artifacts open for analysis and are also representative of a cultural group, a community of online practices and practitioners (who upload, comment, and 'like' others' posts). Drawing upon a poststructuralist view of culture, we also recall that the signifier's arbitrariness and instability determines signification. In other words, each re-written, re-blogged, re-posted, and re-cycled submission on Tumblr leads to another page and another theme in a seemingly unending semiotic chain. The compelling ideas and places (virtual or real) being signified draw readers like us in, only to become caught up in the web, the threads that lead us to new places on the site. Taking up Tumblr as a complex cultural artifact, we consider what it means to 'confess' in a place of in-betweens: between real identities and virtual ones, anonymity and recognition, and Disney-as-text and confession-as-stylized-Disney-screen-capture. We propose that waltdisneyconfessions@tumblr might be thought of as a curriculum of desire embedded in the conflicts of identity that pushes us to interrogate the currency of confession and the overall politics of readership. In this chapter, we employ rhetorical analysis (Felman, 1982), which is part of a psychoanalytic stylistic (Radford, 2008), to examine the structures of reading effects in several confessions posted on the Tumblr thread in

Fall 2014. The Tumblr confessions illustrate Disney's discursive and ideological power and offer insight into how meaning is made in digital spaces. Our analysis reveals how this Tumblr is both the repository for new cultural artifacts and an articulation of the psychic power Disney has to force confession.

Conceptual Framework: Peeking Out from Behind the Curtain

The necessity of an addressee—in this case, the wider world of Tumblr thread followers—has a critical role to play in creating, even forcing utterances. As Brooks (1984) notes about the circularity of literary confession that Paul de Man describes, confessions need a confessor and a confessant—a structure that helps to manufacture the guilt that confessions require. In this sense, the public space of confession acts in contradistinction to historically institutionalized (i.e., the Catholic Church) confessions, which are necessarily private. Yet spaces like Tumblr become the dark places—the virtual rabbit holes and seedy undergrounds of the amusement parks and bright cartoon movie premieres—where users play hide and seek with their confessions, simultaneously seeking readership while at the same time hiding their real life identities from scrutiny. Tumblr is seedy precisely because it becomes a place where people go but don't want to be known or recognized—like a shady strip club where people avoid making public who they really are—allowing the masquerade of Disney to take control of their lives.

Though users are free to submit their 'confessions' to the hidden and anonymous blog owner, their requests sitting in the inbox "queue will remain in the queue" (Walt Disney Confessions Blog Owner, 2014a) if they do not meet certain requirements. For example, the unnamed blog owner of waltdisneyconfessions, frustrated by "a buttload of Frozen confessions," instructed users to reconsider the kinds of submissions they put forth, because "Walt Disney Confessions is not a place for you to rant or vent about your hatred or defense of Frozen. It's a place to share personal experiences that you have with Disney movies, parks, shows, music, etc. and the way that Disney has affected you" (Walt Disney Confessions Blog Owner, 2014a). Furthermore, posters are reminded that "When you submit a confession, think to yourself; Is this sharing a personal experience with Disney and how it has affected me/someone? Or is this just ranting/venting? If it's the latter, don't submit it. It will get deleted."

Each blog owner can morally regulate the content, and publicly address his or her following. Like the colonial master, the blog owner sits at the metropole, relegating unworthy followers to the marginalized periphery should their requests not meet the system grounding the discursive space of the blog's intended ideology. Like the huddled masses, the desperate "digital natives" (Prensky, 2001) seek to be validated and heard. Their messages move from inbox request to colorful "acceptance letter" for all to see—a real waltdisneyconfession complete with screenshot and stylized font. Since not all requests make it to the main page, each accepted post is like winning an admission ticket into the virtual theme park of preferred Disney confessions.

Suspended between the real, sometimes troubled realities lived by the followers of waltdisneyconfessions and the fantasyland of the blog, individuals are caught in time and digital space waiting to be heard and for their identities to take public shape. Some never do. This liminal space of identification can be thought of as a quantum (third) space (Ausman, 2011, 2012; Ng-A-Fook, Radford, & Ausman, 2014). Bhabha (1994) explains that Third Spaces are spaces of identification,

> a process of identifying with and through another object, an object of otherness, at which point the agency of identification—the subject—is itself always ambivalent, because of the intervention of that otherness. . . . [T]he importance of hybridity is that it bears the traces of those feelings and practice which inform it, just like a translation, so that hybridity puts together the traces of certain other meanings or discourses.
>
> (p. 211)

This explanation, in Bhabha's words, removes the idea of a "sovereign self" that can exist outside culture. Bhabha also proposes that hybridity helps eradicate cultural binarism at the level of the subject, and the result is that we "emerge as the others of ourselves" (p. 39). This concept is abstract. Our understanding of Bhabha is that the space in-between and along the way between subject and its other is the space of *translation*. It is an identity (a hybrid one), which is a space (a third space). Furthering this theory to incorporate what we term a 'quantum' dimension of (third) spaces, we consider the existence of several spaces at the same time, in varying dimensions. This allows us to think of third spaces as both places and the spaces between places. On waltdisneyconfessions, several spaces e/merge: users write from all over the world in and from their lived realities, clustered around a common theme. Identities become hybrid on account of the transformation *into* Disney (animated and captioned), and the process of applying for, and being accepted as a worthy confessant.

Methodology: A Curriculum of Desire and the Politics of Readership

While reading the posts on the waltdisneyconfessions@tumblr blog, we are aware of our role in consuming others' deepest fears and fantasies about becoming Disney. Readers can either respond to the thread or, like us, act as witnesses or even casual flâneurs of its unfolding. The psychoanalytic stylistic method (Radford, 2008) we use to analyze the aesthetic form/modes of address in the text allows us to read these dynamically against and with the forces of desire in reading, paying attention to power struggles that unfold through the psychic and social uses of texts by viewers/confessants. A psychoanalytic stylistic is attentive to the psychic structures mobilized in reading such as transference and also to the dynamics of form and the provocation of aesthetic structure. This method is derived from Brooks' (1984) concept of narrative. Interested in the conjunction between literature and psychoanalysis, and what we can understand about identity and reading practices through this connection, Brooks combines a structuralist approach to narrative and Lacan's poststructuralist psychoanalytic theory to explain the play of desire in time in a text. After Aristotle, Brooks (1984) asserts how plot is the most important element, and why psychoanalysis, as a theory and a practice, presents a model of psychic processes salient to the dynamics (emplotments) of texts. Insisting that attention must be paid to how the form of a story acts as a place where we may return to the implications of our own identifications and better understand our reading practices, Brooks (1984) illustrates why psychoanalysis matters to literary critics and why we can also interpret it as something that should matter to the educator. He takes us step by step through how the dynamic of transference, a psychoanalytic concept that describes a compulsive, unconscious recalling of the past, functions in literary experience (Radford, 2008).

Using Freud's phantasy model of the text to illustrate his conviction that the structure of literature is in some sense the structure of the mind, Brooks (1987) begins with the dynamics of an intertextual relation, where Freud's articulation of the "revised editions of old texts" or "new editions of old conflicts" operates (cited in Brooks 1987, p. 9). The conflicting issues of identity become transference, a present reprint of the past as one reads a piece of literature, or in this case as one watches/reads/consumes Disney. Taking our relationship to the viewers of Disney into account, we note in our examination of Tumblr that we read the confessants as desiring subjects (Sarup, 1996). Reading through a psychoanalytic framework, identification with the Disney characters onscreen evoke projective, transferential, and narcissistic responses in the form of confessions that demand to be published. Freud came to see identification as "not simply one psychical mechanism among others, but the operation itself whereby the human subject is constituted" (Laplanche & Pontalis, 1973, p. 206). Thus, the Tumblr site exists as the place whereby viewers of Disney cannot only reconstitute their subjectivities, formed on account of, and through Disney, but do so in a digital world designed to enable them to come into being, engendered as fully formed, albeit fictional subjects.

Below, we show how confessants' readings of Disney are manifestations of unconscious desire where "the affects from the past are projected in the present through the inter-textual signifying operation of transference which functions not only in therapeutic communication, but also in reading" (Robertson, 1994, p. 167). Thus, desire performs in language. Because of the dynamic nature of the unconscious, what it means is never fully knowable and the process of discovery of such is interminable. But how it means (desire), or how it is mapped, is revealed through the repetition of the effects that the reading has on the reader. The reading effect thus names the unresolved tensions or historical contradictions animated and produced within language through the experience of reading (Felman, 1985). The transference effect is a concept and practice through which movements of desire may be registered and interpreted through language by marking the ambivalences and exhilarations.

Snow White

Figure 2.1 Snow White

We begin our reading of these confessions, constructed like beautiful postcards, with Snow White (Disney, et al., 1937; see Figure 2.1), fittingly peeking out from behind the curtain, but still deeply involved and perhaps oblivious to those who see her. Safe inside the home, like the user who has confessed that she needs to "just pause," Snow White is frozen in a moment of bliss, ignorant that her 'evil stepmother' is envious of her being the 'fairest in the land' and plots to kill her. She stands in for all the princesses in imminent danger, all the way up to the recent film *Frozen* (Del Vecho, Buck, & Lee, 2013) with "Elsa and Anna" and "everyone in between [sic]". The user posting the confession, like Snow White, peers out from behind her own curtain. The curtain might be thought of metaphorically in relation to quantum (third) spaces. The confessant is propelled forth by desire to gaze at herself from the outside of her lived reality—seeing the 'other of herself' in the image of a fantasy character. If translation is a matter of understanding subjectivity's multiple locales—in the home, making a private confession behind the computer screen (a digital curtain) while seeking the reward of rescue and redemption from her fears—then we might consider Tumblr to be the space that helps her awaken from the long slumber of pain and anxiety. After all, she readily identifies with the princesses who always survive and are rewarded with a happy ending. They become her role models for overcoming trauma, danger, and death. Brooks (1984) calls this "reading for the plot," which is "a form of desire that carries us forward, onward, through the text" (p. 37). The woman makes meaning of her own anxiety through the trope of *every* Disney-princess-as-survivor through a confession that is, as Brooks explains, "a structuring operation elicited in the reader trying to make sense of those meanings that develop only through textual and temporal succession" (p. 37).

Quasimodo

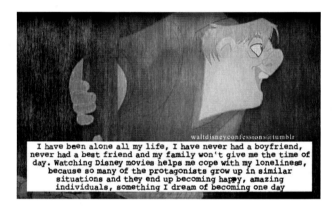

I have been alone all my life, I have never had a boyfriend, never had a best friend and my family won't give me the time of day. Watching Disney movies helps me cope with my loneliness, because so many of the protagonists grow up in similar situations and they end up becoming happy, amazing individuals, something I dream of becoming one day

Figure 2.2 Quasimodo

The Disney rendition of *The Hunchback of Notre Dame* (Hahn, Trousdale, & Wise, 1996; see Figure 2.2) provides the backdrop for examining the shared fantasies of desire, happiness, and hope fostered by certain Disney characters. Quasimodo, a character reviled and feared, never gets the princess at the end of this Disney movie, yet the citizens hail him as a hero. This alternate plot to the conventional ending provides a space on the margins of the plotline for viewers of Disney who cannot identify with typically beautiful princes and princesses, who might feel unaccepted by their own communities, families, and peers. Instead of dying as he does in the original Victor Hugo story, Disney rewrites Quasimodo as the hero who accepts both his place in the Notre Dame tower and the fact that he is not entitled to have his love reciprocated. He is happy nonetheless, singing along with his anthropomorphic gargoyle friends from the façade of the cathedral. We bear in mind that "[n]arrative operates as metaphor in its affirmation of resemblance, in that it brings into relation different actions, combines them through perceived similarities, . . . appropriates them to a common plot, which implies the rejection of merely contingent (or unassimilable) incident or action" (Brooks, 1984, p. 91). The person confessing, in writing himself or herself as a kind of Quasimodo figure, who has "been alone all [his or her] life," writes the plot of similarity between reality and animated story. The story of the confessant's life and that of the poor Disney hunchback become one and the same, and the provision of becoming a "happy, amazing individual" is not only a possibility, but is inevitable. In the affective milieu of joy and resolution that washes over all characters, even the most marginalized characters are redeemed and brought center-stage. The person confessing, who has "never had a boyfriend, never had a best friend, [and whose] family won't give [him or her] the time of day" can dream to be seen, recognized and loved "one day."

Belle

I always wanted to be a face character at Disneyland and I know I would be perfect for it if only I didn't have a big Italian nose

Figure 2.3 Belle

Belle, the bookworm and free-spirited protagonist in Disney's *Beauty and the Beast* (Hahn, Trousdale, & Wise, 1991; see Figure 2.3), is the exact opposite of Quasimodo. She is beautiful and rejects the conventionally handsome, hyper-masculine suitor named Gaston who attempts to seduce and marry her at the beginning of the story. Living in the castle, Belle grows to love the Beast despite his judgmental and aggressive nature. Like Belle, who eventually realizes that her charm and beauty in taming the Beast are more valuable than her intelligence, the women who wish to become face characters must endure the process of the Disney Parks talent casting auditions (Disney Auditions, 2014). In a sample job posting for "Female Disney Character Look-alikes" closing November 3, 2014, the site describes how only certain physical requirements meet Disney's needs:

> Females, 4′11″–5′7″, are needed to portray Disney princesses and heroines from the following Disney animated features: *Alice in Wonderland, Beauty and the Beast, Cinderella, Frozen, The Little Mermaid, Sleeping Beauty, Snow White and the Seven Dwarfs*, and *Tinker Bell*.

On the same page, Disneyland Paris (Disney Auditions, 2014) seeks "Disneyland Character, Parade and Character Look-alike Performers" and groups prospective performers by type of princess in the audition call ending November 5, 2014:

Mulan (5'2"–5'6"/157–168cm)

Princess Tiana (5'5"–5'8"/165–173cm)

Rapunzel, Ariel (5'4"–5'7"/163–170cm)

Sleeping Beauty, Belle, Cinderella, Snow White, Anna, Elsa (5'3"–5'7"/160–170cm)

Merida, Jasmine (5'4"–5'6"/163–168cm)

Furthermore, "All look-alike performers must have . . . the distinguishing characteristics to portray these animated characters." What these audition requirements make clear without calling for particular racial or cultural characteristics outright (using the euphemism "distinguishing characteristics" instead) is that certain female bodies fall into the acceptable imagination of what a princess should look like. The different categories tell us that Disney hires a particular type of racialized and physical body for each character. The confessant in this postcard names what we already presume about Disney—that her "big Italian nose" won't do. The confession is doubly narrated: a confession that reveals her knowledge that Disney's family-friendly stories are not actually for everyone, and a story about her private pain about having a dream foiled by her ethnicity. If we consider Disney to be what Brooks (1984) describes as a "fully achieved plot" (p. 114), these longings to define the self through the paragons of culture that Disney animates,

are most clearly dramatized in narratives of an autobiographical cast since these cannot evade an explicit concern with problems of closure, authority and narratability . . . autobiographical narration must necessarily . . . show margins outside the narratable, leftover spaces which allow the narrating *I* to objectify and look back at the narrated *I* and to see the plotted middle as shaped by and as shaping its margins.

(p. 114)

The "margins outside the narratable" implicate Disney in that which cannot be uttered against its Equal Opportunity hiring motto of "Drawing Creativity from Diversity," namely, that Disney does indeed hire people who look like its characters, rather than 'draw creative' characters that look like real people. As the narrator of her own confession, the woman who wants to be the Belle face character speaks about a narrative *I* that can only exist as a fantasy, not even as a fictional character in a job that requires dress-up. She is relegated to the margins by the corporate colonial metropole—a hegemonic machine of normalizing practices that dictate what childhood dreams and adult fantasies to become Disney ought to be about. The boundaries are very clear. If you do not meet the bodily regulations, you "need not apply." The confessant is aware of her place in this corporate hegemony: Disney is all-powerful. Reading through quantum (third) spaces, the confessant's cognizance that her body is inadequate collides with her identity as a Disney fan who "always wanted to be a face character." She is not delusional or wildly hopeful, but nonetheless holds onto the dream of acting the role, authorized by the officials of the Disney 'world.'

Aurora

There is this one girl who I cannot stand. She's just so rude and full of
herself and learning that she dresses up as a Disney Princess and goes
around to children's parties acting like one makes me cringe on the
inside. Even the fact that she and I both love Princess Aurora makes my
insides crawl with disdain for her. I don't think she deserves to wear
the crown or dress for these children at all.
                                              waltdisneyconfessions@tumblr

Figure 2.4 Sleeping Beauty

While the face characters who want to play Belle at the theme parks are regulated by the Disney corporation's hiring policies, the gatekeeper here regarding who has the right to dress as a princess is another Disney fan. This confession (see Figure 2.4) is angry; the woman confessing feels betrayed by another "girl" who "dresses up as a Disney princess and goes around to children's parties acting like one." The repressed layers of this confession, revealed in one frustrated rant, are not about repentance or conventional notions of personal pain. Instead, the confessant feels entitled: some women deserve to dress up while others do not meet certain criteria to be just like Princess Aurora (Sleeping Beauty). The plot of *Sleeping Beauty* (Disney, Geronimi, Clark, Larson, & Reitherman, 1959) is also about possession: Aurora, having fallen asleep after being pricked by a spinning wheel on her sixteenth birthday will only awaken if she is kissed by the man to whom she was betrothed at birth, Prince Phillip. No other man is deserving of her beauty, and conversely, she is not fated to be awakened by anyone else— condemned to a life of slumber unless the right man comes along. We can read Brooks (1984) again to understand better what compels the confessant's investment in, even ownership over, the 'correct' narrative emplotment for herself:

If plots seem frequently to be about investments of desire and the effort to bind and master intensive levels of energy, this corresponds on the one hand to narratives thematically oriented toward ambition, possession, mastery of the erotic object and of the world, and on the other hand to a certain experience of reading narrative, itself a process of reaching for possession and mastery. Speaking reductively, without nuance, one might say that on the one hand narrative tends toward a thematics of the desired, potentially possessable body, and on the other toward a readerly experience of consuming.

(p. 143)

The woman in the confession sees only one 'true' princess—reading herself alongside the fairy tale itself. That is, there is only one true Sleeping Beauty that can be awakened, can dress the part, and who deserves the role. The confessant wishes to right the wrong, and does so by re-mastering the image of the imposter behind the text in the postcard, blurring out her eyes. Symbolically, this woman cannot 'see' that she has no right to "wear the crown or dress for these children at all" because she is "rude." But we, as readers of the confession, can gaze from outside the storyline, presumably from the vantage of the confessant as well, to imagine that this person has no business being in the plot. The 'proper' Sleepy Beauty story with the right princess should be the only one that children learn about at their parties. The confessant is disturbed that another reader of the Sleeping Beauty story could get it so wrong, to the point where the fact that they "both love Princess Aurora" is enough to make her "insides crawl with disdain."

Peter Pan

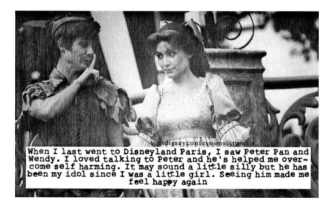

When I last went to Disneyland Paris, I saw Peter Pan and Wendy. I loved talking to Peter and he's helped me overcome self harming. It may sound a little silly but he has been my idol since I was a little girl. Seeing him made me feel happy again

Figure 2.5 Peter Pan

We saw how the woman in the previous Tumblr post cannot bear that the wrong kind of "girl" lives between Disney-world and our lived one. This confessant steps through the wardrobe into the psychic world of the theme parks to meet Peter Pan (Disney, Geronimi, Jackson, Luske, & Kinney, 1953; see Figure 2.5), who has helped her "overcome self harming." If we return for a moment to Bhabha (1994), we can imagine the spaces that Disney makes available, not just between the real and fantastical, but also at the level of the psychic. Identity in quantum (third) spaces is not merely a space, that which lies between the self and the other-of-itself, but is able to become so on account of the multiple effects of culture, language, family, and genealogy, that continue to shape and reshape identificatory practices along the way. The space here between childhood and adulthood is recursive. The digital space opened up on this Tumblr wall is a space where people need to perform their dilemmas of identity-making. Their narrative plottings of self are re-shaped, re-posted, and revised, and importantly in this post, Peter Pan not only exists physically in the theme park when you buy a ticket to "Disneyland Paris" but is there to comfort, guide, and return to the Neverland which is Tumblr. Peter Pan, who reminds Wendy in the picture to keep quiet, represents the private pain associated with self-harming. His reassurance reminds us that the woman's secret stays in the theme park, where it is safe to be yourself until you step out of the gates. The effect is doubled by the availability of Tumblr as the place to admit that Peter is the confessant's "idol" and confidant: Tumblr keeps her secret in the form of the anonymous confession to which she can return and re-read as a reminder of Peter's support, frozen in time like his character in Neverland. Her identity as a 'freeze frame' in-the-moment of being helped and comforted by Peter is preserved in pixels and fonts, an interesting effect if we consider quantum (third) spaces to be fluid, multi-dimensional, moving, and re-imagined self-identifications. Insomuch as we are shaped and changed on account of our many cultural encounters, and considering that the process of fixing an identity is neither possible nor desirable in conventional readings of third spaces, one might ask how the digital space of Tumblr affords everyday people the opportunity to latch onto a moment of identification and perform their identities by stylizing the confessions graphically, and returning to the annals of cyberspace whenever they choose. The cyclic nature of re-identification with the same moment reminds us that recursivity and fixity can be part of the ever-evolving concept of hybridity—in this case, made possible by Tumblr's digital theme park where readers and writers of waltdisneyconfessions can enter the space freely, and scroll through the threads to read them time and again.

Caught in the Web

The Tumblr confessions illustrate the powerful ideology Disney conveys through its storytelling. Its discursive power unfolds as children grow up with and through Disney, and as they feel guilt and desire with and against it. This is enabled by the melodramatic structure of the victim heroes—those that face fantastic challenges and always overcome them to arrive at a happy ending (Radford, 2009). The confessants, we argue, read themselves against these plots, often returning to the stories to make sense of their own lives. Brooks (1984) gives us insight about these kinds of happy endings:

> Ends, it seems, have become difficult to achieve. In their absence, or their permanent deferral, one is condemned to playing: to concocting endgames, playing in anticipation of a terminal structuring moment of revelation that never comes, creating the space of an as-if, a fiction of finality.
>
> (p. 313)

Disney movies are not entirely about permanent deferrals since each story has a happy ending. But they are about the "fiction of finality," that there is a happily ever after that promises a world beyond tribulation and strife once the characters become princesses and princes in their rightful places. The imaginary life after the story promises redemption, closure, and finality and confessants, seemingly unaware of the impossibility of happy endings in real life, nevertheless read their own potential in the imaginary but often unrealized space of Tumblr.

Tumblr compels viewers of Disney to work with and note their deeply felt moments in the films—not in the pedagogic space of the classroom, but still in a way that compels the writers to reflect. As Brooks (1984) reminds us, the space of confession in some ways helps to structure the need to reveal—to tell all. Not unlike the Catholic Church confession booth, the digital space is the place where it becomes necessary to speak, to divulge a secret. The person seeking redemption in the writing might not be looking for judgment and its attendant punishments so much as safety in numbers by divulging adult attachments to the world of Disney so many feel is reserved for children. The confessants here are bound and compelled to confess in certain ways by the blog rules and its moderator, and the structure of permissibility about what is acceptable to confess, since only some confessions make it out of the queue onto the main page.

Reading through quantum (third) spaces, the confessants reveal how their recurrent encounters with Disney, films that they find safe and comforting, ground them and enable them to read their own lives. The formation of subjectivities alongside and with(in) the discourse of Disney is recurrent. In a quantum (third) spaces framework, subjectivities are (re)formed anew with each cultural encounter; they become identities 'out there' in the world. And we can see the power of Disney as the place where these encounters occur: to gain the courage to stop self harming, to offset the effects of loneliness, to remind individuals that their cultural attributes leave them at the margins, to provoke anger about those who are 'imposters' of Disney.

Conceiving of identities *as* a space of (re)negotiation, as Bhabha (1994) does, and we continue to do, allows us to play on the concept of Tumblr as the place where we fall down the rabbit hole of identities and subjectivities to a new Wonderland where people write themselves anew through the act of confessing.

The narrative structure of these online confessions necessarily defers endings (Brooks, 1984). We note that the blog posts on Tumblr continue to appear, day after day, seemingly without an end in sight. The thread, just like the Internet as a whole, continues to expand. There seems to be an unending number of people in the "queue" wanting and waiting to confess. For us as researchers, the texts of Disney and the confessions act both as the object of analysis, and that which has a degree of textual mastery to speak back to the readers (Felman, 1982). We do our own identity work through this piece and we have our own confessions. On the one hand, we are confessors of sorts—those who hold the power to redeem through our writing about this blog, to academically critique the posts in our attempts to engage them as non-mainstream forms of writing. We are also, however, confessants of culture through analysis. Our turn towards a psychoanalytic stylistic and quantum (third) spaces framework allows us the freedom to work through the same things facing the confessants on Tumblr—our own desires, attachments, or even horror at the kinds of things we read on the blog. In asking about our own resistances as 'highbrow' readers and writers of official academic discourses, we confess: we find the space alluring, one we feel compelled to return to and read for its plots and to understand the digital as a valuable cultural space. Tumblr is the third space of cultural translation where the meanings behind acts of confession are carried forth by both the confessants and their readers rather than in the anonymous, redemptive space of the church confession booth. These viewers, compelled to confess, remind us of the currency of confession even in the digital age. However, we are cognizant that the narratability of the self is inextricable from large multinational corporations: Disney is the subject of the confessions, and Yahoo owns the space where they are put forth. Those seeking catharsis through confession find those confessions corporatized as they become linked to the consumption of Disney and Tumblr. To that end, the digital world is quite literally a space where confessions are bought and sold. The huddled masses seek more than redemption, they seek *recognition*. waltdisneyconfessions@tumblr, then, expands our understanding of what it means to narrate the private self in public, to call forth memory. Through this cathartic process participants read themselves with and against highly recognizable plots of childhood fantasy.

Note

1   Since the time of initial authorship of this paper in September, 2014, the waltdisney confessions@tumblr URL has also been directed to waltdisneyconfessions.tumblr. com. Both URLs are valid as of the date of publication.

References

Ausman, T. (2011). A curriculum of cultural translation: Desi identities in *American Chai.* *Transnational Curriculum Inquiry, 8*(2), 23–40.

Ausman, T. (2012). Indian diasporic films as quantum (third) spaces: A curriculum of cultural translation. *Master's Thesis.* University of Ottawa: Ottawa, Ontario.

Bhabha, H. (1994). *The location of culture.* New York: Routledge.

Brooks, P. (1984). *Reading for the plot: Design and intention in narrative.* New York: Knopf.

Brooks, P. (1987). The idea of psychoanalytic literary criticism. In S. Rimmon-Kenan (Ed.), *Discourse in psychoanalysis and literature* (pp. 1–18). New York: Methuen.

Cringely, R. X. (2013, May 20). Now that Yahoo owns Tumblr, where will all the cool kids hang out? *InfoWorld.* Retrieved from: http://www.infoworld.com/article/2614667/cringely/now-that-yahoo-owns-tumblr—where-will-all-the-cool-kids-hang-out-.html

Del Vecho, P. (Producer), Buck, C., & Lee, J. (Directors). (2013). *Frozen* [Motion Picture]. United States: Walt Disney Pictures.

Disney, W. (Producer), Cottrell, W., Hand, D., Jackson, W., Morey, L., Pearce, P., & Sharpsteen, B. (Directors). (1937). *Snow White and the seven dwarfs* [Motion Picture]. United States: Walt Disney Productions.

Disney, W. (Producer), Geronimi, C., Clark, L., Larson, E. & Reitherman, W. (Directors). (1959). *Sleeping beauty* [Motion Picture]. United States: Walt Disney Productions.

Disney, W. (Producer), Geronimi, C., Jackson, W., Luske, H., & Kinney, J. (Directors). (1953). *Peter Pan* [Motion Picture]. United States: Walt Disney Productions.

Disney Auditions. (2014). *Audition calendar and casting calls.* Retrieved from: http://disneyauditions.com/audition-calendar/

Felman, S. (Ed.). (1982). *Literature and psychoanalysis: The question of reading, otherwise.* Baltimore, MD: Johns Hopkins University Press.

Felman. S. (1985). *Writing and madness.* Ithaca, NY: Cornell University Press.

Hahn, D. (Producer), Trousdale, G., & Wise, K. (Directors). (1991). *Beauty and the beast* [Motion Picture]. United States: Walt Disney Pictures.

Hahn. D. (Producer), Trousdale, G., & Wise, K. (Directors). (1996). *The hunchback of Notre Dame* [Motion Picture]. United States: Walt Disney Pictures.

Laplanche, J., & Pontalis, J. (1973). *The language of psychoanalysis.* New York: Norton.

Ng-A-Fook, N., Radford, L., & Ausman, T. (2014). Living hyph-e-nations: Marginalized youth, social networking, and third spaces. In A. Ibrahim & S. Steinberg (Eds.), *The critical youth studies reader* (pp. 240–254). New York: Peter Lang.

Prensky, M. (2001). Digital natives, digital immigrants. *On the Horizon, 9*(5), 1–6.

Radford, L. (2008). *The mirror theatre of reading: Explorations of the teacher's apprentice and juvenile historical fiction.* Unpublished Doctoral Dissertation. University of Ottawa: Ottawa, Ontario.

Radford, L. (2009). Apprenticing teachers' reading: The cultural significance of juvenile melodrama. *Journal of the Canadian Association of Curriculum Studies, 7*(1), 58–84.

Robertson, J. P. (1994). *Cinema and the politics of desire in teacher education.* Unpublished Doctoral Dissertation. University of Toronto: Toronto, Ontario.

Sarup, M. (1996). *Identity, culture and the postmodern world.* Edinburgh: Edinburgh University Press.

Walt Disney Confessions Blog Owner. (2014a, October 17). A "chilling" announcement about Frozen and other things (shoot me) [Tumblr]. Retrieved from: http://waltdisneyconfessions.tumblr.com/

Walt Disney Confessions Blog Owner. (2014b, October 26). Queue has been turned up to 15 times per day [Tumblr]. Retrieved from: http://waltdisneyconfessions. tumblr.com/

Williams, R. (1983). *Keywords: A vocabulary of culture and society*. New York: Oxford University Press.

3   Practical Pigs and Other Instrumental Animals

Public Pedagogies of Laborious Pleasure in Disney Productions

Jake Burdick

Disney's most prominent productions and performances of culture evidence a fixation on the past, on a particular moment of American history that, as with any construct of nostalgia (Anijar, 1996), likely never existed. From the conceptualization of Celebration, Florida, a suburban space draped in the symbology and social politics of the 1950s, to the theme park concept of Tomorrowland, a site still fixed into the space travel motifs of the 1960s, to the constant resurrection of older Disney films from what their marketing script calls "the vault," the Disney fantasy is one of reminiscence and/or regression. The iconic statue of Walt Disney and Mickey Mouse in Anaheim, California's Disneyland, turns away from the entrance to Sleeping Beauty's castle, perhaps not signifying that portal as a gateway to fantasy, but rather that the *fantasy is the gateway itself*, to a seemingly utopic time before.[1] But when and what is this past, and what can we say about the repeated pedagogical resurrection and reinvention of a fanstasmic history? Here, I am taking up fanstasmic as a psychoanalytic construct, one that involves the production of fantasy spaces as a means to facilitate both the production of a desired identity and the repression of other elements of the psyche. Moreover, keeping with the purposes of this collection, what might we say about the pedagogical implications of the ways in which the past is articulated and mobilized via Disney?

In this chapter, I work these questions via a psychoanalytic take on the concept of public pedagogy (Sandlin, O'Malley, & Burdick, 2011), starting with the short films that are credited with Disney's rise as an entertainment leviathan and considering these films' lingering remnants in the contemporary Disney ethos and topography. Taking up understandings of Disney as a distinct, durable, and knowable cultural edifice (Giroux, 1999), as well as public pedagogy work that describes cultural and corporate entities' capacities and performances as educational agents (Giroux, 2005, 2015; Sandlin & Milam, 2008), my chapter argues from two foundational bases: first, that despite Walt Disney's death in 1966, The Walt Disney Company and its products can still be read as extant manifestations of the desire behind its creation and structuration; and second, that this underlying desire forms the basis of Disney's pedagogical form and content as it re/produces cultural meanings (Giroux, 1999). Accordingly, I forward an understanding of Disney as a psychoanalytic text, one whose primal scenes of trauma—largely echoes of Walt Disney's own demanding childhood (Berland, 1982; Harrington, 2015)—manifest symptomatically within its cultural products. Further, Walt Disney, the company he founded, and the historical moment in which this founding occurred exist in a kind of knotted tension, overlapping but never subsuming wholesale, together producing what Harrington[2] conceptualizes as a homunculus—a mythic creature produced via the alchemical synthesis of other beings. My interest, then, is creating a preliminary psychoanalytic understanding of this intersected entity and its pedagogical imperatives.

To meet these ends, the chapter is divided into two sections. The first addresses the historical moment of Disney's inception via a careful reading of two of its most influential early films: *Steamboat Willie* (Disney, Disney, & Iwerks, 1928) and *The Three Little Pigs* (Disney & Gillett, 1933). Both of these films have become iconographic pieces within the Disney library, and both situate Depression Era logics and values at the heart of the Disney enterprise. More importantly, both are laden with a kind of moral overtone that is suggestive of Walt Disney's early life and of his vision of a utopic American life. In the second section, I argue that the fantasies implicit in these early films remain intact in the contemporary Disney/Pixar landscape, with the recent film *Inside Out* (Docter & Del Carmen, 2015) still evincing values that cohere with the logics of productivity and the industrious self, as well as a fixation on childhood as a traumatically, but necessarily, lost object within the world of work. Despite these later films' seeming 'affective turn,' I suggest that they can be understood as reinventions of Fordist fantasies for contemporary sensibilities. Responding to these analyses, I pose questions about the embedded nature of these pedagogical works and suggest how psychoanalytic forms of 'teaching' might allow for a more nuanced, culturally productive reading of Disney's filmic library. Whereas Disney's ubiquity in the global marketspace should be read as a species of capitalistic colonialism (see, for example Nooshin, 2004), I argue that in this rise to prominence, the corporation has also been unprecedentedly successful in producing images that can be taken up by uncannily diverse populations of people. And, this appeal to a kind of fundamental fantasmic space within the human experience is where critical educators might locate their own counter-hegemonic practice.

On Boats and Behind Bricks: Labor as Pleasure

Steamboat Willie and *The Three Little Pigs* are the two films that are consistently mentioned in Disney's early rise in the late 1920s and early 1930s (Harrington, 2015; Watts, 1995, 1997). Both evidenced tremendous innovation in terms of animation quality, and both employed soundtracks that synchronized visual performance to melody and song, an attribute that was both novel and immediately celebrated by audiences. *Steamboat Willie*, by virtue of its introduction of Mickey Mouse, now enjoys iconic status within the mythology of Disney, with Mickey's whistling image affixed as a branding image that precedes most Disney films. And, whereas *The Three Little Pigs* has not enjoyed similar status, its central song, "Who's Afraid of the Big Bad Wolf?", and its reinvention of the folklore it drew upon became emblematic symbols of the American Depression and the general populist response to that period's overwhelming despair. Shortsleeve (2004) argues that under the aegis of the Depression, "The Big Bad Wolf could represent any of the fears of the day: a landlord, the threat of war, or hunger" (p. 7). The image of the wolf, relentlessly pursuing and nearly capturing the two leisure-loving pig brothers, became a populist icon, and "in 1933, after nearly four years of economic disaster, the blustering fanged predator could hardly be seen as anything other than a symbol of the Depression" (Watts, 1997, cited in Shortsleeve, 2004, p. 7). Given these films' centrality to Disney's genesis into a cultural empire and their primacy in the Disney mythology, psychoanalytic interpretation offers three critical inroads for viewing the films: as Walt Disney's own fantasmic wish fulfillment and symptomatic structures, as a social psychodrama that shores up the economic and identifactory anxiety inherent in early twentieth-century American life, and as a site of representation in which personal and sociological traumas become sutured via near-mythic narrative constructs.

Music, Labor, and the Instrumentalization of the World

Both Berland (1982) and Harrington (2015) comment heavily on the associative relationship between Mickey Mouse and his creator, Walt Disney, suggesting the ways in which Mickey—and later, the greater pantheon of Disney characters—serves as Walt's attempt to reframe his own problematic childhood and early adult life. These authors both cite biographical work that illustrates Walt's struggles with "a complex adolescence that was riddled with ambiguity and inconsistent emotional feedback from his father" (Harrington, 2015, p. 42). Within a psychoanalytic construct, Mickey serves as a fantasmic form of Freudian wish fulfillment, a production/performance of an identity construct that enacts and inhabits a way of living desirous to its creator and enables that creator a certain modicum of libidinal pleasure (as Freud's original term frequently cohered to sexuality). Thus, via the realization of *Steamboat Willie* across celluloid frame, Walt effectively attempted to redraw the childhood he felt he had lost, as well as perform the identity he desired—the development of an ego ideal (Berland, 1982) in the public forum of American cinema. Structurally speaking, Mickey Mouse serves as a symptom, a means of shoring up and making bearable

Disney's desire for an inaccessible past and present. Harrington (2015) continues this Freudian analogic-analytic reading by illustrating the id-like qualities inherent in Donald Duck, including the infantilization suggested by his sailor cap and coat, his difficulty in speech, the libidinal suggestion in his lack of pants, and the radically emotive and irrational ways in which the character behaves. All of these qualities are foiled by Mickey's calm, directive, and divisive persona, traits that are hinted at in *Steamboat Willie* but become more prevalent with each film (Harrington, 2015).

Taking *Steamboat Willie* as the ontogenesis of ego-ideal-Mickey—and in many ways of the very persona of The Walt Disney Company, as another extension of Walt's desire into social space—the entirety of the short can be read as an expression of this egoic construct and the simultaneous actualization/denial of the wish it attempts to fulfill. Fundamentally, *Steamboat Willie* reveals a scene in which pleasure is derived via industrious practices and performances, in which music and rhythm are collocated with labor, and in which the entire corpus of the surrounding world can be used as a technology towards the human end of labor-pleasure. A large part of *Steamboat Willie's* iconography is the simple, anthemic tune that Mickey whistles in the opening moments of the short. He whistles while he steers the steamboat, weaving both the mechanics of the tugboat—the physical steering of the ship and ringing of the ship's warning bell—and the mechanics of his body—whistling the tune and bending his knees in synchrony—into a rhythmic totality, one that simultaneously illustrates the inherent gratification of music as well as music's ability to produce efficacious, machinic bodies. This knotting of music, pleasure, and labor would become a motif of sorts for Disney, occurring most famously in *Snow White* with the seven dwarves' numerous work-songs proving a sort of score for the realities faced by the labor class, particularly in Fordist, depressed US history. Mickey, as such, might not simply be a psychic projection of an idealized past; instead, I suggest that he can be read as Walt's desirous production of an idealized subjectivity in the present, one that manifests as both reflexive and ontological wish. Mickey is the ideal Walt, living in a world that expresses its libidinal gratification via Taylorian cadence.

The short's climactic moments come in the form of a larger musical number, one that, while not directly tied to the ongoing work of the steamboat, involves its livestock cargo. Mickey has been displaced from his captainship of the steamboat by his intimidating, cat-like boss. Along their journey, they have collected a small group of animals, as well as Minnie Mouse, whose sheet music provides the catalyst for the final performance when it, in regurgitated form, is made sonorous by a goat. As he joins the goat—whose tail is now being cranked via Minnie—Mickey produces his accompaniment via the objects around him on the boat's deck, including a wash bucket and board, pots and a spoon, and a trash bin. As he proceeds, however, Mickey incorporates the animals on the boat as well, largely against their will, and in a manner that embodies no small modicum of violence.

First, perhaps as an act of retribution to the cat-boss who had just removed him from the ship's wheel, Mickey pulls a cat's tail while stepping on its body to make it mewl in time with the song, moving rapidly to swinging the cat around his head. Mickey then stretches a duck's neck to create a brass-type sound, much to the duck's evident dismay. He pulls the tails of suckling piglets and transforms a cow's teeth into a makeshift xylophone, all while maintaining the same pumping knees and vacant smile he evidenced in the short's opening. In essence, Mickey is able to transform the natural world around him into the cultural product of music, and his desire to enact this transmogrification overwrites (over-rights) any claim to autonomy that these animals possessed. Living things become literally instrumental in relation to Walt's egoic construct, repurposed so they might contribute to Mickey/Walt's musical wishes.

A simple psychoanalytic read of this appropriation of (non-anthropo-morphized) animal life can attribute Mickey's actions as a retelling of the Freudian (Freud, 1990) ego's triumph over the id or the symbolic castration enacted by a Lacanian (Lacan, 2006; see also Fink, 1995) father. These ontogenetic analyses each illustrate a sort of intrapsychic *taming* of one's drives to better cohere with a social order; thus, the entire scene on the steamboat might serve as a staging of psychic development, complete with the violence that characterizes this splitting of one's subjectivity (Lacan, 2006; Fink, 1995). However, in light of Disney's radically social scope and project, I find that a more historically grounded psychoanalytic interpretation might be of more use. For this interpretation, it is useful to locate *Steamboat Willie* within the historical moment of still-surging expansionist and capitalist ideology, logics that wholly locate the natural world as a technology for human advancement, rather than a world unto itself. Following a posthuman critique of this instrumentalizing of the natural world (Kahn, 2010; Snaza et al., 2014), it is the logic of capitalism and the Fordist reconceptualization of labor that reinvents the world as resource, as a Cartesian plane inhabited only by humans and the objects they utilize and consume. Mickey's consumption of animals as instruments, as tools to be used despite their reluctance and suffering, follows this logic, as it not only entreats the cultural production of music, but a music that Disney consistently links to the cadence of labor. Walt's creation of Mickey as a sort of savant illustrates his desires for his own capacities as a labor leader, as an ego ideal within the rising tide of industrialists, a reading that bears fruit, given Walt's espoused political and economic disposition.

A Bigger, Badder Wolf

Almost as central to the development of the Disney brand as *Steamboat Willie*, *The Three Little Pigs* clearly continued the theme of industriousness as pleasure, but further qualified that pleasure via illustrating its 'perversion' and that perversion's ultimate punishment. Adapting the classic fairy tale of the same name, Disney's *The Three Little Pigs* centers on the same cautionary fable of a wolf's gambit to eat the pigs and the pigs' differing degrees of success in keeping the wolf at bay via the construction and materials of their individual houses. The changes made by Disney, however, illustrate a similar set of values as those discussed within *Steamboat Willie,* as well as a revelation regarding Disney's own ideological values. In the Disney short, the pigs who have created houses out of straw and sticks, Fifer Pig and Fiddler Pig, respectively, are both depicted as hurrying their construction in order to enjoy a leisure time that is accompanied by playing musical instruments. The two pigs wear the same sailor hat and shirt as Donald Duck, and they share in both his infantalization as well as his symbolic castration, as neither pig wears any clothing on the bottom half of his body. By contrast, Practical Pig has built his house from brick, sacrificing leisure time for the integrity of the structure. Practical Pig admonishes the two others, laboring while they entertain surpluses of joy, and in contrast to their childish, unfinished dress, Practical Pig wears workman's overalls, indicating not only his removal from the others' infantile nature but also his affiliation with populist labor.

The majority of the story progresses without meaningful changes to the original tale—the wolf huffs, puffs, and blows down the straw and stick houses, using disguises to maintain close proximity to the pigs. Yet, as he reaches Practical's brick house, he takes up the disguise of a brush salesman, with caricature-like Jewish features (an aquiline nose, long black beard, and beady black eyes) and accent (the voiceover would eventually be re-recorded). Whereas Disney's anti-Semitism has been widely documented by a variety of biographers (Berland, 1982; Harrington, 2015), the popularity of this sentiment in the Depression- and pre-Depression-United States has been largely obfuscated by the Manichean narrative (US as monolithically noble, Axis forces as wholly monstrous) that emerged following World War II. In the early 1920s Henry Ford reprinted *The Protocols of the Elders of Zion,* a book that was purported to be evidence of a Jewish conspiracy for world hegemony. Žižek (1992) has described the sort of mastermind of conspiracy theory as "the Big Jew," a term that signifies the centrality of anti-Semitism to Western notions of clandestine power and manipulations. Of significance here is the shared admiration and friendship between Ford and Disney. According to Shortsleeve (2004),

> Watts calls Henry Ford "Disney's greatest hero" (157). Eric Smoodin correctly suggests that "Disney might be better understood in relation to another type of American cultural icon, the systems builder" (3). Eliot writes, "Ford admired both Mickey Mouse and his creator. Walt held Ford in equally high esteem, and the two men developed a lasting friendship" (135). As Disney once said, the process of creating a cartoon was "much as an automobile goes through an assembly plant" (qtd. in Watts 169).
>
> (p. 9)

Shortsleeve continues this line of analogy between the two men, describing their alleged affability with the Nazi party, their parallel practices in assembly line work, and their shared hatred of unionization. These elements of Walt Disney's ideological standing, despite their manifestation in characters like the Big Bad Wolf, have been largely repressed by the force of his iconoclastic stature. Disney has been mythologized within US culture, deified as an iconographer of US culture and (re)creator of childhood dreaming (Shortsleeve, 2004; Watts, 1995) Further, the popularity of these ideas throughout US culture during the Depression—evidenced at least in part by the widespread success of *The Three Little Pigs*—has also been lost to history to some extent, particularly the anti-Semitic undertones that marked the 1930s. The United States' entry into World War II and the monstrous revelation of The Holocaust potentially provoked a repression of the persistent scapegoating of Jewish peoples. Disney produced films that supported the war effort (Harrington, 2015), as standing against the German Other necessitated a suppression of common interests across the two nations.

The success of *The Three Little Pigs* and several other Disney shorts (collectively called *Silly Symphonies*) marked the 1930s as the golden age of the company. However, as Shortsleeve (2004) notes, the era's end was not related to the war, but to the struggles within Disney's own walls: "In 1941, a financial crisis and a bitter labor dispute threatened every good thing that had happened to Walt. As every biographer of Walt Disney has noted, the Disney Studio strike of 1941 was a turning point" (p. 11). The strike of 1941 effectively collapsed the harmonious labor dream enjoyed by Walt, culminating in his claims that it was the darkest point of his life, his involvement in a fistfight with a worker, and his open weeping at the workplace (Shortsleeve, 2004). Walt Disney himself responded publically to the debacle, claiming "To me, the entire situation is a catastrophe . . . The spirit that played such an important part in the building of the cartoon medium has been destroyed" (quoted in Watts, 1997, cited in Shortsleeve, p. 12). The Disney strike evidences a psychic break between the fantasmic, musical world of Walt's ideal ego and the Real ethical consequences of instrumentalist logics as applied to human life. The Fordist factory of Disney production could not find its analogue within Mickey's steamboat orchestra, nor could Disney locate his ego as overlapping with either Mickey or Practical Pig, conductors whose music charmed the world into rhythmic, moral labor. This break, both within Walt—and by virtue of his colocation with the company he built—within the identity of Disney as an entity, might be read as a restaging and performance of Lacanian alienation and exile from the jouissance of fully inhabiting the fantasmic world (Fink, 1995). The strike itself might be read as an irruption of the Law, a rupture of fantasy due to its untenable effects in actual life, effectively castrating Disney and denying the pleasure inherent in actualizing the fantasy promised in *Steamboat Willie* and *The Three Little Pigs*.

The strike and its radical denial would establish the 1930s as a sort of nostalgic primal fantasy of The Walt Disney Company, a state of grace from which all of Disney's future fantasies would emerge. The evidence of this lasting psychic landscape emerges in the words of former Disney CEO Michael Eisner, who wrote, "'For some reason I've always found drama in assembly lines' (402). Eisner was reminiscing about childhood tours of the Hershey factory and the Corning Glass Works. 'Those experiences,' he wrote, '[are] paying off in my adult life' (402)" (cited in Shortsleeve, 2004, p. 9). The utopic fantasy inherent in Disney production and iconography is desirously affixed to a mode of production that, despite the strike of 1941's overwhelming sentiment, is construed as a sort of portal to a more pleasurable world. Walt and Mickey's statue at Disneyland—in-between the fantasmic recasting of Main Street and the Magic Kingdom's gates—is another, a portal that restores the capacity to restore the nostalgic primal scene and the access to that fantasy without the intrusion of waking life. Following the lines that Berland (1982) and Harrington (2015) have produced, these are pathways to both a shared, wholly manufactured fantasy of the US past, and to the childhood and adulthood denied to Walt Disney himself.

The Spectre of Desire in *Inside Out*

To put these suggestions to work, I provide a brief analysis of the latest Disney production, *Inside Out* (Docter & Del Carmen, 2015), suggesting that despite what Nooshin (2004) describes as an ideological invisibility, the film still promotes the relationship between normative, economically rational subjectivities and access to pleasure. Although this film is a production of Pixar's Brain Trust, rather than Disney proper, the shift in creative production and media has not resulted in any kind of drastic shift in the Disney brand's ideological claims. Just as the same swooping signature and Mickey's whistling serenade from *Steamboat Willie* still adorn each film, the commitment to the ideological world of Walt Disney remains. *Inside Out* is a film that takes up psychoanalytic content in a relatively direct way, personifying five emotional states (named *Joy*, *Sadness*, *Fear*, *Disgust*, and *Anger*) as workers within a psychic landscape that overtly resembles a manufacturing plant, one that is in the business of producing memories. The central conflict in the film internally, even metaphysically, involves Joy and Sadness being accidentally expelled from Riley's (the host of these emotions) "control room" and undergoing a series of near-disastrous adventures to return. Depicted in parallel, Riley's external conflict centers on her inability to cope with her family's relocation from Minnesota to San Francisco and her decision to run away due to her growing resentment at the situation. The resolution of these dual conflicts centers on Riley's maturation: on her ability to let go of certain psychic artifacts—most notably her imaginary friend Bing Bong, the realization by Joy that she must allow other emotions to intersect with her functioning, and her resulting decision to return home to her family instead of taking a bus to her former home. What unifies these storylines is a thematic centered on the bittersweet transition from the almost-pure joy of childhood to the emotionally complicated and ultimately painful adult world. The circumstances of Riley's life—move and loss of home, her parents' seeming detachment, and her difficulty in establishing herself in San Francisco—all serve as significations of the emergence into more complex psychic and social relations. The film's conclusion sees Riley's reunification with her parents, as well as an expanded partnership between Riley's psychic laborers, with the emotions' control room gaining a more robust, multi-user interface.

The simple metaphoric throughline between this film and my analysis of early Disney work is apparent: recasting affect as industry overtly links production and emotion, with Joy as the central agent and most invested laborer of the five personifications. As harmoniousness is achieved within the psychic factory-scape, all of the emotions become more productive and—in a state of seeming parallax (do our emotions have emotions?)—themselves become more joyful and contented in their work. More subtly, Riley's change in emotional state illustrates a shift from demand for love to desire for love (Fink, 1995), signifying the kind of displacement of id-based structuration to the complicated negotiation of the ego (Freud, 1990). Thus, Riley undergoes the same kind of loss of a primal access to jouissance that I have described in terms of both Walt and his corporation. However, rather than producing fantasy as a means of shoring up the lack produced by her transition to adult affective responses, the fantasy space already exists as an element of the film's espoused metaphysics. Thus, Riley's maturation and likely future pleasure is wholly linked to the sustained and happy functioning of her emotive laborers. Despite his death nearly 50 years before this film's release, Walt's fatherly eidolon (Burdick & Sandlin, 2014) still looms over his production company, in search of the happy workers that will allow him to reinvent and reclaim his lost childhood.

Conclusions: Repression, Fantasy, and Pedagogy

Feldstein (1996) writes that the "visibility required by a discourse in the field of representation is directly proportional to the invisibility of what the discourse is intended to exclude from that field"; he further posits that "showing more in order to hide better is the principle of what the discourse of a political promise requires of visibility in the field of representation" (p. xxiv). Reading this quote from an educational standpoint, I argue that both curriculum and pedagogy are equally interested in this practice of hiding while showing, particularly in terms of history and identity. With Disney pedagogies emanating from a place of repression and idealization, the corporation's attempts to rewrite historical memory via a performance of a fantasmic past obscure the Real of its origins. And, if we are to take seriously Disney's ubiquitous and democratizing claim, "it makes no difference who you are," which seems to conflict deeply with Walt's anti-Semitic and anti-union beliefs, then these pedagogies take on the character of a symptom, as they both pursue and deny their own cause (Fink, 1995; Lacan, 2006; Žižek, 1989). Nooshin (2004), discussing the musical colonialism embedded in Disneyland's *It's a Small World* ride, describes "music's role in simultaneously articulating the Disney message and enabling Disney to render the ideological invisible: to wave its magic wand and transform the political into a seemingly neutral universal 'truth'" (p. 247). The *magic* in the Magic Kingdom is the same species of spellcraft as ideology's symptomatic and ironic system of denying what it affirms. *It's a Small World* celebrates global diversity via a colonizing musical landscape. *Inside Out* promotes the cultivation of a wide range of emotional dispositions via the heroic narrative of Joy. *The Three Little Pigs*, developed by a growingly disgruntled factory line of animators, celebrates the pleasure that emanates from difficult labor. Pedagogy's work here is the double move of enhancing the egoic ethos of its heroic, hopeful narratives while denying the Real conditions and suffering that these narratives entail. The hydraulics and motors of Disneyland's rides are secreted behind plaster-made facades. The recreated Main Street USA is staffed with customer servants who live in houses both geographically and historically distant from Walt's fantasy of home.

A critical, psychoanalytic response, then, might not be the wholesale refusal of these images as simply and uniformly capitalistic, colonialist, or any of the other claims that have been leveled at Disney via critical culture work. Rather, Lacan's later work refigures the symptom as sinthome, claiming that the repressed object or idea exists itself within the symptomatic response (Verhaeghe & Declercq, 2002). In other words, the symptom contains its treatment as a necessary element of its metaphysical life, so that the commonplace practice of finding ways to cease symptomatic behaviors becomes an enhancement, rather than an enervation of desirous energies. Agreeing with this reconfiguration, my questions around rethinking a critical pedagogy of Disney via psychoanalysis center on what it might mean to teach the symptom *as symptom*. What responses might we raise when we simultaneously celebrate the triumph of Joy in *Inside Out* while asking questions about the privilege inherent in Riley's "dire" situation or the productivity of anger, particularly the anger that has been denied to non-Whites and women via the normalizing presence of White rationality? Can we use the figure of the Wolf in *The Three Little Pigs* and the later World War II Disney propaganda pieces as a complicated historical knot that allows us to understand history as contradictory and complicated, rather than Manichean? Finally, can we look at the archetype of Mickey-Walt as fantasy—as a site of refuge from the problematics of the past—and create conversations about the everyday practice of fantasmal identifactory work, the commonplace production of ego ideals, and the potential ontological arrogances that these ideals might harbor? These questions situate pedagogy at the liminal space between desire, repression, and cause, asking us not to give up our fantasies, but to simply enjoy them differently, critically, and with the full awareness of their illusory promise. Thus, when we stand with Walt and Mickey's statue in Disneyland, we know it as a signpost to a litany of imagined worlds, a signpost to a repressed and overly wrought history, and a signpost to the park's exit and the irruption of the Real of daily life, including the misery that these fantasies have produced. If we were to simply tear it down, would these paths still be as clear?

Notes

1   It should be noted that the positioning of the statue has it facing away from the arched entrance to Sleeping Beauty's castle and towards "Main Street," a conflagration of shops and attractions modeled to resemble a sort of archetypical American small town's main thoroughfare. In my reading, then, Walt Disney is leading Mickey Mouse out of the fantasmic space of the "Magical Kingdom," and instead into an area that is purportedly modeled after a reality—however tinged by the Disneyfication of the past. The fantasy, then, or at least its imaginary epicenter embodied by Mickey Mouse, moves towards and gazes on the mythic American past, transmogrifying it along the lines and logics of the fantasy. In this way, the scene produced by the statue offers an interpretation of the complex pedagogy of memory—a reconstruction of the past via the fantasies and desires of the present, all of which serve in part to obviate the past's role in the traumas that have contributed to this desirous state of being. It is a narrative that effaces its own storyteller as well as any trace of its own constructed nature.
2   Much of my work in this chapter owes its conceptual underpinnings as a psycho-analytic take on The Walt Disney Company to Harrington's (2015) *The Disney Fetish*, as this text represents a sustained and foundational Lacanian reading of Disney as a total enterprise. Accordingly, readers interested in this chapter are strongly encouraged to take up Harrington's work.

References

Anijar, K. (1996). Star Trek the ideological frontier: A social curriculum in three acts. *Taboo, 1*, 165–204.

Berland, D. I. (1982). Disney and Freud: Walt meets the id. *Journal of Popular Culture, XV*(4), 93–104.

Burdick, J., & Sandlin, J. A. (2014). Turning down the dead father: Eidolons in public pedagogy research and theorizing. In J. Burdick, J. A. Sandlin & M. P. O'Malley (Eds.), *Problematizing public pedagogy* (pp. 105–116). New York: Routledge.

Disney, R. O. (Producer), Disney, W. (Producer/Director), & Iwerks, U. (Director). (1928). *Steamboat Willie* [Motion picture]. United States: Walt Disney Productions.

Disney, W. (Producer), & Gillett, B. (Director). (1933). *The three little pigs* [Motion picture]. United States: Walt Disney Productions.

Docter, P., & Del Carmen, R. (2015). *Inside out* [Motion picture]. Emeryville, CA: Pixar Animation Studios and Walt Disney Pictures.

Feldstein, R. (1996). Introduction I. In W. Apollon & R. Feldstein (Eds.), *Lacan, politics, aesthetics* (pp. xi–xix). Albany, NY: SUNY Press.

Fink, B. (1995). *The Lacanian subject: Between language and jouissance.* Princeton, NJ: Princeton Paperbacks.

Freud, S. (1990). *The ego and the id* (The standard edition of the complete psychological works of Sigmund Freud). New York: W. W. Norton.

Giroux, H. A. (1999). *The mouse that roared.* Lanham, MD: Rowman & Littlefield.

Giroux, H. A. (2005). Cultural studies in dark times: Public pedagogy and the challenge of neoliberalism. *Fast Capitalism, 1*(2). Retrieved from: http://www.henryagiroux.com/online_articles/DarkTimes.htm

Giroux, H. A. (2015). Totalitarian paranoia in the post-Orwellian surveillance state. *Cultural Studies, 29*(2), 108–140.

Harrington, S. J. (2015). *The Disney fetish.* Bloomington: Indiana University Press.

Kahn, R. (2010). *Critical pedagogy, ecoliteracy, and planetary crisis: The ecopedagogy movement.* New York: Peter Lang.

Lacan, J. (2006). *Écrits.* (trans. B. Fink). New York: W.W. Norton.

Nooshin, L. (2004). Circumnavigation with a difference? Music, representation, and the Disney experience: "It's a small, small world". *British Forum for Ethnomusicology, 13*(2), 236–251.

Sandlin, J. A., & Milam, J. (2008). "Mixing pop [culture] and politics": Cultural resistance, culture jamming, and anti-consumption activism as critical public pedagogy. *Curriculum Inquiry, 38*(3), 323–350.

Sandlin, J. A., O'Malley, M. P., & Burdick, J. (2011). Mapping the complexity of public pedagogy scholarship: 1894–2010. *Review of Educational Research, 81*(3), 338–375.

Shortsleeve, K. (2004). The wonderful world of the Depression: Disney, despotism, and the 1930s. Or, why Disney scares us. *The Lion and the Unicorn, 28*(1), 1–30.

Snaza, N., Applebaum, P., Bayne, S., Carlson, D., Morris, M., Rotas, N., Sandlin, J., Wallin, J., & Weaver, J. (2014). Toward a posthumanist education. *JCT: Journal of Curriculum Theorizing, 30*(2). Retrieved from: http://journal.jctonline.org/index.php/jct/article/view/501/snaza%20etal.pdf

Verhaeghe, P., & Declercq, F. (2002). Lacan's analytical goal: "Le Sinthome" or the feminine way. In L. Thurston (Ed.), *Essays on the final Lacan. Re-inventing the symptom* (pp. 59–83). New York: The Other Press.

Watts, S. (1995). Walt Disney: Art and politics in the 20th century. *Journal of American History, 82*(1), 84–110.

Watts, S. (1997). *The Magic Kingdom: Walt Disney and the American way of life.* Columbia: University of Missouri Press.

Žižek, S. (1989). *The sublime object of ideology.* New York, Verso.

Žižek, S. (1992). *Looking awry: An introduction to Jacques Lacan through popular culture.* Cambridge, MA: MIT Press.

4 "This Is No Ordinary Apple!"

Learning to Fail Spectacularly from the Queer Pedagogies of Disney's Diva Villains

Mark Helmsing

In a post titled "Why I'd rather be a Disney villain" (mikee013, 2011), blogger "mikee013" recounts how she and some of her friends had recently been discussing which Disney princesses they would wish to be in real life. Her friends chose the usual suspects: Snow White, Cinderella, Jasmine from *Aladdin*, and Ariel from *The Little Mermaid*. The friend group paused to consider whether Pocahontas from her eponymous film and Nala from *The Lion King* "count" as Disney princesses. The assembled friends reached an impasse, which ended when mikee013 rendered the conversation moot by suggesting she would rather be Ursula from *The Little Mermaid*. The remainder of her delightfully witty and well-reasoned blog post is devoted to explaining why she would rather be a Disney villain. mikee013 argues that unlike "those silly princesses who are subversive mainly because they're after love, the villains revel in their subversion. Some may call them evil, but I call them fabulous."

This fabulousness that mikee013 identifies with the Disney villains is a powerful element of the Disney diva villain. These characters not only were (and are) my favorite characters from the Disney films, they lingered with me long after the films ended. They were whom I desired amongst the action figures at toy stores and whom I coveted when swapping Disney collectable stickers or trading cards. A simplistic explanation for this is that, as a young gay man, it was my destiny to be enamored with these characters and turn these villains into my own anti-heroes to worship. Like the presence of Judy Garland in gay generations before my time, Lady Tremaine, the severe evil stepmother from *Cinderella*, and Ursula, the gorgonesque evil sea witch from *The Little Mermaid*, were the appointed 'hags' in my formative childhood (in both the colloquial sense of the controversial gay figure of the fag hag and the literal sense of being haggard females or haggish in appearance and deportment). If one can reason upon the surprisingly high number of viral videos on YouTube that remix and re-imagine the diva villain in contemporary tropes—from Todrick Hall's (2014) "Spell Block

Tango" to Oh My Disney's (2014), "Counting Scars," their villainous version of OneRepublic's "Counting Stars"—my fellow Millennials and I appear to have a thing for these cultural icons that queer the moral purpose driving Disney animated films. There is something about these characters that demands critical attention.

A curious query of the popularity of Disney villains may be surprising, as Byrne and McQuillan (1999) contend that the "reactionary ideology of Disney . . . is predicated on an opposition to a pre-existing and fixed set of 'leftist' values which [Disney] opposes" (p. 3). In this chapter I queer the 'leftist' values that Byrne and McQuillan position as the real villain in the Disney empire within the very space in which these ideologies operate pedagogically as moral lessons or modeled virtues for film viewers. If one identifies with or cheers for the villains, then in part Disney's intended ideological lessons have failed. This is the ultimate act of 'failure' that Disney's diva villains teach us, and this lesson forms the context within which I investigate my own nostalgic recollections of their affective pedagogical qualities. From the sophisticated and cultured queerness Ursula teaches Ariel to the corset-tight discipline Cinderella's 'stepmommy dearest' dishes out, the diva villains consistently lend themselves to queer appropriations and pleasures, opening up scenes of affective engagement with the (presumably heterosexual) family-friendly fare Disney sells.

In this chapter I travel with four of the more canonical Disney diva villains who enact a perverse curriculum of queerness, divadom, transgression, and willfulness. These villains teach viewers through these four affective engagements in order to do what Sedgwick (1994) identified as a central move of all queer texts: to "make invisible possibilities and desires visible; to make tacit things explicit; to smuggle queer representation in where it must be smuggled" (p. 3). As a good queer kid, I learned to invest my own fascination and dutiful learning in these animated teachers who performed model lessons in what Halberstam (2011) identifies as the queer art of failure—lessons teaching me how to embrace failure fabulously and how to not relinquish my abjection (of being queer, frail, and weird) that was seemingly keeping me from succeeding in the straight, normal world of Prince Charming and Aladdin.

By thinking queerly about the pedagogy of four Disney diva villains— Grimhilde, the evil queen from *Snow White and the Seven Dwarfs* (Disney et al., 1937); Lady Tremaine, the evil stepmother from *Cinderella* (Disney, Geronimi, Jackson, & Luske, 1950); Maleficent, the evil fairy from *Sleeping Beauty* (Disney, Geronimi, Clark, Larson, & Reitherman, 1959); and Ursula, the evil sea witch from *The Little Mermaid* (Musker, Ashman, & Clements, 1989)—I read some of the signature lessons from the Disney diva villains— how to get even, how to gain power, and how to become the fairest of them all—less as destructive outcomes and more as a curriculum of how to thrive and survive queerly in a straight fantasy world. In order to read this curriculum as a queer text, I identify queer elements of the diva villains and explore what precisely constitutes a diva, before concluding with the lessons of transgression and willfulness the Disney diva villains teach us.

Queer Pedagogues

Disney diva villains are, as a subset of all possible Disney villains, unabashedly queer. The word queer derives from the Old English word 'twerk' translating as 'to twist or turn' and is related to 'thwart,' to transverse or cross (Sedgwick, 1994). To be queer, then, is to err or stray from the path, and the errors of the Disney diva villains are often attributed to this irregular queerness. They cross paths with the (straight) natural order of things in the worlds they inhabit and with communities of characters who uphold civic virtues of honesty, courage, and strength.

Queer theorists studying at the intersection of cultural studies and gay cultural life have followed this trope in many works; they show in their writing how queer audiences resist, deviate, or 'thwart' intended narrative functions. Farmer (2000) convincingly argues that gay male audiences frequently identify with the tortured and doomed young man (think here of James Dean and Montgomery Clift), not because gay male audiences see themselves as fundamentally doomed or tragic, but because they recognize in that particular figure the *social forces* that have resulted in his particular victimized status. In a similar fashion, I argue, queer viewers see in the Disney villain not simply an unadulterated and incomprehensible evil, as the films themselves would have us believe, but instead a character who is, like the queer viewer, the victim of social oppression. This viewing-as-learning is rarely on the surface and having conversations about these ideas and possible readings with friends and colleagues feels like a repeated coming out, not caring if others regard liking and identifying with the Disney villains as weird, unnatural, or messed up. Thus, this kind of queer(ed) viewing, Farmer (2000) suggests, "often results in an alienating preclusion from the public components of film reception, an enforced retreat into a privatized space of difference" (p. 31). The Disney diva villains continue to work pedagogically long after the films end as they help gay male audiences overcome these alienating identifications.

There is something of a binary opposition operative in the four canonical Disney diva villains and the movies in which they star. Their status as diva can be predicated upon their operation as a foil to the four Disney princesses, the namesakes for their respective films. Snow White, Cinderella, Aurora, and Ariel are all princesses by virtue of birth, with the three 'classic' princesses—Snow White, Cinderella, and Aurora—spending most of their screen time in the films as royalty denied, as the lives of love and happiness destined to them are thwarted by the diva villains. Both Grimhilde and Lady Tremaine are stepmothers, respectively, to Snow White and Cinderella. We learn these young heroines' fathers married the cold, cruel women and died not long after. On the surface the princesses' misery is blamed on the beloved fathers' unfortunate marriages to these wicked women. But at the risk of invoking a problematic psycho-cultural construct of the absent father in the lives of gay men, I approach the deaths of the fathers as the catalyst for these princesses' fate. Having distant, unresponsive dads (who may be 'dead' to we queer boys) is not an unknown concept. The queer child knows he is in a childhood that grows sideways—that is, his relations, motions, and futures are always unfolding in ways that are not straight forward (Stockton, 2009). A feeling of dire and immediate consequence for Cinderella, who should be living the happy childhood that was robbed from her, is less compelling for "any child who feels out of sync with the children around her or feels repelled by the future being mapped for her" (Stockton, 2009, p. 52). Through the grief and the anguish the four princesses express in their films (all of whom leave home and family out of choice or necessity), viewers begin forming attachments to the princess protagonists: they must win, they must defeat the oppressive hardships inflicted by the wicked women in their lives. Also, lest we forget, they must find happiness ever after.

But the queer viewer has learned these outcomes are futile. Our attachments are queered. We cannot identify with the recuperation of the lost father in the form of the handsome prince (from Prince Charming to Prince Phillip), even if we secretly desire to push Ariel aside and run our fingers through Prince Eric's dark, black hair. In the closeted worlds of our childhoods, we have learned early on that attaining the prince is not in our cards—society will not allow it to happen—and so we must forge other, queered attachments. Luciano (2011) contends that an "attachment marks a site between the psychic and the social, invested in both but proper to neither . . . both within and beyond the individual" (p. 126). For Luciano, articulating attachments is more productive than articulating affects or feelings because attachments are born out of relationality. I relate much more to Ursula, who lives alone and isolated in her drag queen boudoir under the sea, likely reviled for her visible body fat and unsexy appearance (I feel you, gurl).

If Berlant (2011) is correct in her critical analysis of the productive and "cruel" failure of optimism in our lives, then the attachments viewers create for the princesses become "a cluster of promises we want someone or something to make to us and make possible for us" (p. 23). Otherwise how else would so many viewers over the past half-century feel pangs of identification when Cinderella instructs them that "a dream is a wish your heart makes" and to "have faith in your dreams, and someday your rainbow will come smiling through" because "the dream that you wish will come true." If only. A queer(ed) attachment finds this wanting because the queer viewer cannot have his happiness or wishes fulfilled in a heterosexual society. When the diva villain brings the princesses back to reality through a shout or a sneer, that is a reality closer to a queer lived experience. The pedagogical promises in the diva villains' lessons form and bond my queer attachment to their storylines through their actions and dialogue. Better to be fabulous and have gone out big (as a dragon or a witch) than a dowdy, boring scullery maid or servile housemother to ungrateful dwarfs.

Diva Pedagogues

My queer attachments turn towards forms of identification I associate with queerness in the diva villains' pedagogy: vanity in the evil queen, cruelty in the evil stepmother, sarcasm in the evil fairy, and self-preservation in the evil sea witch. These are four 'master classes' in being a diva the villains teach for viewers both queer and straight. Such characteristics underscore what Doty (2007) claims makes the figure of the diva "a force to be reckoned with" when "dominant cultures and narratives" punish the diva for "not being a conforming good girl" (pp. 2–3). The diva's force is especially educative and liberating for marginalized minority groups because such groups learn from divas "the costs and the rewards that can come when you decide both to live a conspicuous public life within white patriarchy and to try and live that life on your own terms" (p. 2). Living within the White patriarchal world of Disney, the diva villains are well aware of their public role (denying Maleficent her public role is the slight that motivates her villainous acts in *Sleeping Beauty*). Their vainglorious quests for beauty and power are no different from the conforming public desires in the dominant culture, but the diva villains pursue them on their own terms, so much so that Ursula even has Ariel sign a contract for their Faustian bargain in which Ursula's terms are quite steep. The divas' DNA predisposes them to make their queerness legible through vanity, cruelty, sarcasm, and self-preservation, all of which are employed to make the diva villains seen and spectacular, as they harness the power of spectacle. As for the diva villains, in their overt fabulousness, coded through elaborate costumes and punchy dialogue, the allegedly 'evil' diva villains offer themselves up to the queer viewer as a source of divadom, or camp pleasure, in that gay viewers take pleasure in the artifice and the catty cruelty that these characters so often exhibit. It is not that we do not like Ariel and Eric, or Jasmine and Aladdin; rather, it is that their heterosexual romance does not offer the same pleasure as that given to us by the characters that exist transgressively outside of these heterosexual circuits and the dialogue this affords them.

One can certainly imagine the Disney diva villains when Abowitz and Rousmaniere (2004) suggest that a diva "cultivates a personality that befits such attention: a magisterial and confident pose, elegant diction, graceful movement, and a studied indifference to the mundane and tedious elements of daily life" (pp. 4–5). The Disney diva villains strike all of these poses because they "move and speak with enormous style and panache—so much so that they often 'steal' the scenes from the supposed leading characters in the stories" (Griffin, 2000, p. 74). In articulating the visual elements that make Maleficent's appearances in *Sleeping Beauty* so spectacular, Griffin

(2000) notes how she "moves with grand sweeps of her cape and long-flowing gown, and strikes magnificent 'diva'-like poses" (p. 74). Abowitz and Rousmaniere (2004) note the reliance divas have upon their physical appearance as an effect of being spectacular, as "divas twist the feminine into a commanding source of authority through their performance as powerful people" (p. 10).

When the diva villains are on screen, they steal the scene—literally. Their bodies take up the full display of the shot and the colors and lighting change drastically to highlight their disruptive arrival in the film. Part of their pedagogical power comes from their commanding presence. Queer pedagogues make their presence known, lighting up a classroom or other space of learning, creating a vacuum of attention. It is no coincidence that Grimhilde, the evil queen in *Snow White and the Seven Dwarfs*, occupies a significant amount of time in the film, taking center stage in the opening scene during the film's first five minutes as she interrogates her dutiful pupil in the Magic Mirror. One could soundly argue, as do Disney animators Johnston and Thomas (1993) in their intimate book on the creation of Disney villains, that *Snow White and the Seven Dwarfs* is the queen's film and a story of her own rise and fall; Snow White is an accidental heroine. As a dutiful pupil, I sit up and take notice when the divas demand our attention. They have something to say and we best listen to their admonishments.

The visual and speaking roles of the diva villains occupy what Warner (2002) terms a counterpublic, a world made through "embodied sociability, affect, and play" as opposed to "rational-critical dialogue" (p. 122). Because "dominant publics are by definition those that can take their discourse pragmatics and their lifeworlds for granted," the spaces of counterpublics are, oppositionally, "spaces of circulation in which it is hoped that the poesis of scene making will be transformative, not replicative merely" (Warner, 2002, p. 122). The Disney princesses replicate heteronormative lessons in the normalizing public sphere of Disney lifeworlds whereas the diva villains engage viewers (especially queer viewers) transformatively through the scene making Warner identifies.

Upon first consideration this may not make sense. The princesses and other Disney protagonists are often the characters who undergo specific transformations—Cinderella turns *into* a princess, Ariel turns *into* a human. The straight viewer learns, however, that such transformations are unnecessary to a life lived happily ever after. Straight children do not need to learn lessons in transformation because they are always already endowed internally with all that is needed for happiness. It is the twisted, out of joint queer kids who need a transformation, a process perniciously taken to its horrific extreme in gay conversion therapies. But the diva villains do not transform, at least not morally or ethically; they do not sell out. Grimhilde transforms into a witch, alternately billed as "the old crone" or "the hag" in references to her climactic transformation in *Snow White and the Seven Dwarfs*. Maleficent memorably turns into a fire-breathing dragon as a last resort to thwart Prince Phillip's enactment of masculine heterosexual conquering. Ursula transforms into the human Vanessa in order to right her wrong from King Triton. These transformations are seen as necessary evils, not wish fulfillment as is the case when Cinderella received a sparkling blue gown from her fairy godmother. When Grimhilde visits Snow White in the disfigured guise of an old crone, her transformation results in a marked shift of diction and speech. Giving up her gorgeous beauty for the haggard image and persona of the old crone, Grimhilde pushes through her change in body and speech in order to teach Snow White a morbid lesson:

GRIMHILDE: And because you've been so good to poor old Granny, I'll share a secret with you. This is no ordinary apple. It's a magic wishing apple.
SNOW WHITE: A wishing apple?
GRIMHILDE: Yes! One bite and all your dreams will come true.
SNOW WHITE: Really?
GRIMHILDE: Yes, girlie. Now, make a wish, and take a bite.

The straight viewer knows Grimhilde is lying and cannot be trusted. No, Snow White, your dreams will not come true; do not eat the apple! The queer viewer also knows this is a lie, but a necessary one. The queer child often must deceive and fib in order to survive and outlast the crushing disapproval and social scorn from the heterosexual society. My queerness was a protection against the naive, gullible world my straight peers lived within earnestly. The only thing I could offer in terms of a forbidden desire was no ordinary affection, no ordinary apple. The queer kid learns that to eat from the wishing apple, to bite into the longings of same-sex lust, may indeed make all of our closeted, protected dreams come true, but at a high cost: not the physical death that will befall Snow White until a heterosexual kiss rescues her, but a social death that could only be reversed through a heterosexual kiss—made in public—to reaffirm our legitimacy in a kind of heterosexual salvation. Grimhilde's 'hag' is dangerous, a preternatural pedophile preying upon the innocent Snow White whom she wants to consume, figuratively, in order to remain the "fairest of them all." But to the queer viewer, Grimhilde as a (fag) hag is familiar, relatable, through a shared understanding of having to stake a claim to exist when the straight heroines steal our essence, and girls steal our secret crushes while being praised for being "the fairest of them all" in a world where they do not have to hide or change their identity to live. Divas fight just to survive and be recognized.

The straight salvation is kept untarnished in the films' endings when the diva villains perish, physically or otherwise. Unlike horror movies, the villains in Disney films never have the 'last laugh' nor are they seen plotting a return. They have, in the phrasing Edelman (2004) notoriously uses, "no future" insofar as the villains use their diva qualities to resist the heteronormative structures of happy endings and making wishes and finding one's true love.

In doing so the diva villains teach the queer viewer how to "refuse the insistence of hope itself as affirmation" even if in the process such actions, with villainy and queerness as taboo, "register as unthinkable, irresponsible, inhumane" (Edelman, 2004, p. 4). The divas' actions are a type of death drive as the logic of the Disney universe means they have no future other than to lose, to fail, to die. Growing disenchantment with the untenable and unrealistic expectations of happiness the Disney canon has long instilled as the social norm may be one reason for a recuperative valorization of the Disney villains in contemporary culture. Crashing markets, dismal employment outlooks, ceaseless violence, and warfare make it hard to keep wearing fragile glass slippers or wave ineffective fairy wands. Being down and out is the new normal for post-9/11 life. Who, then, could be better to relate to than the down and out diva villains who demand to survive and outlast to their final exit? The diva villains' desires are both transgressive and willful, much like Judy Garland and Joan Crawford in the same era in which Maleficent and Lady Tremaine held their own against the reproductive hope for the happy ending Princess Aurora and Cinderella desired (Brode, 2005).

Transgressive Pedagogues

Mothers are supposed to nurture and support daughters, helping them navigate life in order to "keep on believing" and "lose your heartaches" as Cinderella sings in her 1950 animated film. But Cinderella's mother is dead and her father married Lady Tremaine sometime before his own death. Lady Tremaine's cruelty is performed through her transgressive take on maternal care and love. When Cinderella cautiously asks Lady Tremaine for permission to attend the prince's royal ball, her stepmother searchingly wonders aloud, "I see no reason why you can't go . . . if you get all your work done." Good parenting requires children put in some work before having leisure. Cinderella, overcome with surprise at her stepmother's acquiescence, promises she will get all of her work done. As a prim and proper mother figure, Lady Tremaine also insists Cinderella must find something suitable to wear, a mother-daughter trope long enacted from petticoats to corsets to leggings and midriffs. Again, Cinderella promises she will do so and thanks her seemingly beneficent stepmother before rushing off to begin her Sisyphean chores. Lady Tremaine's daughters from a previous marriage— Drizella and Anastasia—are aghast that their mother would dare allow Cinderella to go to a royal affair. "Mother, do you realize what you just said!" Drizella shouts. Taking the slow, methodical pause in her speech actor Eleanor Audley made so memorable in her performance, Lady Tremaine sarcastically remarks, "Of course. I said, 'If.'" Mother and daughters toxically bond in a fit of cackling laughter. It is a supremely cruel and amazing scene of base, transgressive motherhood.

In a long meditation on the politics and aesthetics of transgression, Wolfreys (2008) argues that transgression means, "to step over or beyond a limit or boundary, to cross a threshold, to move beyond the commonly determined bounds (of law, decency, or whatever)" (p. 3). In departing from the straight and narrow, the Disney diva villains queerly disrupt the normal order of things in the Disney universe. They teach us the limits of Disney's stifling social logic by unveiling the mechanisms by which these 'evil' characters are forced to survive in a world of social inflexibility. From a psychological standpoint akin to one Bettleheim (1976) might have endorsed with his *Uses of Enchantment*, or, more recently, by Zipes (2006) in *Fairy Tales and the Art of Subversion*, the Disney diva villains allow viewers to take their own pleasure in transgressive acts without harm or punishment, for every villain takes the fall by receiving a punishment in the end for any transgressive acts. Wolfreys makes this more nuanced, however, in his suggestion that we are formed and informed by a kind of otherness produced through "a constant, if discontinuous negotiation" with transgressive acts (p. 1). Transgression constitutes our identities, our subjectivities, no matter how hard Disney wants us to believe otherwise.

Part of the transgressive queerness in Disney's diva villains comes across through a hallmark of diva pedagogy: teaching us to be sassy. Through sarcasm, a diva (and queer) can cut through artifice, phoniness, and insincerity by turning insincerity back upon itself and amplifying it through a cutting remark or, to use the colloquial phrase, by 'throwing shade' upon a lesser person in an act of self-preservation (Eribon, 2004). This is a signature feature of Maleficent's pedagogical style. My queerness was informed as a child by her devastating lines, defenses against the forces of King Stefan's kingdom that render her abject. Maleficent condenses the entire curriculum of a painful queer childhood in her reaction to being uninvited to Princess Aurora's christening. After making a fiery entrance with her glowing green flames, Maleficent struts down the catwalk of King Stefan's palace eyeing all of those who were deemed suitable to invite for a place at the table. "Well," Maleficent slowly begins, "quite a glittering assemblage, King Stefan. Royalty, nobility, the gentry, and—" laying eyes upon the three 'good' fairies, "—oh how quaint, even the rabble." Such shade, indeed. When it appears her scorned feelings are ignored or invalidated, Maleficent, with the snap and turn of the most seasoned drag queen, clangs her scepter on the palace floor and demands, in the most serious of tones, "listen well, all of you! The princess shall indeed grow in grace and beauty, beloved by all who know her. But, before the sun sets on her sixteenth birthday, she shall prick her finger—on the spindle of a spinning wheel—and die!" The teacher's lesson has been delivered just as she laughs and disappears into the same burst of green fire whence she entered, laughingly shouting "stand back, you fools!" It is all quite arch and bordering on camp, qualities few divas can do without. She has ruined a joyous occasion and just cursed an innocent, beautiful child all because she was not invited to the party. The queer viewer may have a lifetime of moments of being ridiculed, unwanted, and uninvited to partake in the normal events of a heteronormative public and can only wish to lay it out for the "fools" in their lives in the same shocking manner as Maleficent does. The lessons of transgression taught by Disney's diva villains are not about being violent or excessive, but of being upsetting and outrageous, turning over the apple cart, so to speak, demanding to be seen and to be heard. The Disney diva villains teach queer viewers how to hold their own; they say things they can get away with that I so very much want to say, but know I cannot.

What makes the pedagogical style of the Disney diva villains unique is how the divas depart from, or transgress, the mundane typical curricula of villainy. Unlike straight Disney villains, such as Gaston in *Beauty and the Beast*, the diva villains do not want love or their own charming prince. Love and happiness are childish things. Normal, 'straight' villains often have a moment in which they 'snap' or lapse into evil. The diva villains, however, have a personal life history that positions them to be transgressive. For all we know they were born this way (hint: queer). They are always already on the side of transgression before their films begin. The movement and passage of their transgressions is not a result of a botched science experiment or a victimized childhood.

The queer viewer learns from the diva villains how to make a queerly 'happy' life out of dejection and abandonment. Ursula lives in a dark grotto, still "under the sea" with the annoyingly happy singing fish and crustaceans, but in her own private space. Maleficent has her own gothic castle with requisite thunder and lightning, whereas Grimhilde and Lady Tremaine carve out an existence in the homes they inherited from their deceased husbands, palatial homes made dark and foreboding by the divas' inhabitance, as seen in the expository scene in *Cinderella* where the heroine enters Lady Tremaine's bedroom that is enshrouded in darkness from closed curtains. The lives, livelihoods, and inhabited locations of Disney heroes are in places Wolfreys (2008) would describe as "always on the side of the law . . . standard, acceptable, decent, proper, correct, approved, or authorized" (p. 3). This is "the wonderful world of Disney" produced through reading unending narratives of fantasy and wish fulfillment created out of a world of rules connected to the natural or normal state of affairs. But queer viewers are always wondering about the limits of these places, and the geography lessons we learn from the diva villains are about how queer children can measure themselves against such fantasylands in order to see "how they might belong, to what extent they are excluded or can never belong" (Wolfreys, 2008, p. 4).

In *The Little Mermaid*, Ursula suggestively persuades Ariel to come into the sea witch's lair, a moment of pedagogical seduction par excellence in the Disney canon. Eyeing Ariel's polite reticence, Ursula turns the polite manner in on itself by exclaiming to Ariel, "come in, come in my child. We mustn't lurk in doorways. It's rude. One might question your up-bringing." Ursula has already questioned Ariel's upbringing by her father King Triton as part of Ursula's reasoning to exact revenge for the way she has been mistreated and outcast by the ruler of the sea. Ursula has already decided that Ariel is a far-too-easy pupil, naive and unaware of how the world works. In scenes of queer public life, from drag bars to gay clubs, older and more experienced queer mentor figures tend to see younger, inexperienced queer youth with the jaded type of pity and condolence Ursula has for Ariel. "Oh, no, no, no. I can't stand it! It's too easy!" Ursula admits to her two eel companions. "The child is in love with a human. And not just any human. A prince! Her daddy will love that. King Triton's headstrong, lovesick girl would make a charming addition to my little garden [of lost souls]." The innocence queer children lose, or never have to begin with, is easily read upon Ariel's precocious, endearing wish to be "part of that world" in which humans reside. As a mermaid, her desire is already queer. This is perhaps what makes Ursula a suitable, though transgressive, teacher. Both Ursula and I are all too familiar with the folly of heartache and pining after that which one cannot have (a human prince). Taking on the pedagogical role of the 'fag hag,' Ursula lays out some simple truth (or 'tea/t' in gay parlance):

URSULA: Well, angelfish, the solution to your problem is simple. The only way to get what you want is to become a human yourself.
ARIEL: Can you do that?
URSULA: My dear, sweet child! That's what I do! It's what I live for, to help unfortunate merfolk, like yourself, poor souls with no one else to turn to.

After Ariel reflects on the ramifications of choosing to contract with Ursula her voice in exchange to become a human, Ariel lands upon the startling reality of such a transgressive decision:

ARIEL: If I become human, I'll never be with my fathers or sisters again.
URSULA: That's right. But you'll have your man. Life's full of tough choices, isn't it?

Indeed, life is full of tough choices and tough lessons. The sarcasm dripping in Ursula's framing is all too familiar to the queer viewer who, though a lifetime of transgressive desire, has had to learn how to both recognize and reverse the object of our queer desires. Often for 'baby gays' (young men in the process of coming out and finding their own place in the gay community), an older, knowledgeable person does the instructing and the mentoring (either another gay man or the 'fag hag'). Such pedagogical travels are through valences of sarcasm and tough love, brutal honesty and gentle support. Ursula is just doing her job, enacting the *quid pro quo* queers have learned to barter for survival. Everything comes with a price. Coming out, is, after all, one of life's toughest choices, isn't it (said in my best Ursula impersonation)?

Towards Unhappy Endings: Concluding Thoughts

Each Disney diva villain makes a grand exit. Narratively speaking, the diva villain's demise signals the arrival of the animated film's conclusion. A straight reading of these endings suggests strong moral lessons are transmitted to viewers: evil never wins, good always prevails, and happiness comes to those who are virtuous and worthy. A queer reading of these endings, however, suggests Disney's way of ordering human experience and distributing moral worth can have a different resonance. When these villains fail at gaining power under the sea or becoming the fairest of them all, they succeed through outlasting how other (straight) characters might have misunderstood or misrecognized the villains all along. Some viewers, especially through a queer sensibility, may come to see the Disney heroes as misrecognizing the failure of diva villains. The villains' demise and final exit from the straight world may not signal the championing of good over evil, but instead a recognition of how the straight world has failed to allow the villains to live and co-exist. The queer pedagogies of the Disney diva villains deconstruct and reconstruct dominant messages in the Disney films as cultural texts. The feeling of utter disempowerment and exclusion Disney may urge us to learn as the outcome of a villainous life is rerouted as a different feeling.

This kind of feeling is transgressive, as it stands to be unthinkable that one would root for or support a villain. But the Disney diva villains refuse to acquiesce in the face of contempt or disgust from the straight world. In *Sleeping Beauty,* Fauna, one of the 'good' fairies, remarks aloud, "Maleficent doesn't know anything about love, or kindness, or the joy of helping others. You know, sometimes I don't think she's really very happy." If so, it is because Maleficent sees through the happiness of a straight world as a failed charade, a cruel optimism that can never be accessible for the queer viewer. She knows *too much* about love and joy and how fleeting and ephemeral they are. Thus, for queer viewers, Maleficent's drive to be heard and seen through a demanding diva presence outlasts her physical demise when she falls off a cliff in her dragon form. The queer viewer identifies with Maleficent's willful taunting of Prince Phillip, whom she imprisoned to keep away from Princess Aurora, the now-sleeping beauty: "Oh come now, Prince Phillip. Why so melancholy? A wondrous future lies before you— you, the destined hero of a charming fairy tale come true!" She describes aloud his fantasy, in which Prince Phillip ages into an old man while Aurora never ages. When he is finally released to kiss her, haggardly approaching his own mortality at any time, Prince Phillip is to wake Aurora with "love's first kiss and prove that 'true love' conquers all," which Maleficent sarcastically laughs away in forcing home the futility and wasted life Prince Phillip faces. The straight curriculum with which Maleficent attempts to disidentify and discredit in her pedagogical relationship with Prince Phillip (and, by proxy, all straight viewers) is built upon a knowledge of failure. The queer viewer knows the grammar of the Disney film cannot allow for

Maleficent's contempt for Prince Phllip's valorous heterosexuality to remain unpunished, but the queer viewer also knows the promise that true love conquers all is also a fantasy. Maleficent's queer teaching, as with the teaching of all of the villains, cannot be tolerated and she will fail in her plans to thwart the straight romance from unfolding. Disney's diva villains refuse to apologize, neither recanting their actions nor rescinding their lessons to viewers. These divas would rather perish than disavow their transgressive curriculum. As mikee013 affirmed in her blog post about being a Disney villain, "whether it's by the phallic prow of a ship or being thrown out the window to dissolve into nothingness, the villain's story ends. I'll have none of that ambiguous '[t]hey lived happily every after' crap." These are endings that teach queer viewers to outwit, outlast, and outshine those who wish them dead.

References

Abowitz, K. K., & Rousmaniere, K. (2004). Diva citizenship: A case study of Margaret Haley as feminist citizen-leader. *The Initiative Anthology: An Electronic Publication about Leadership, Culture, and Schooling*, 1–27. Retrieved from: http://www.units.miamioh.edu/eduleadership/anthology/OA/OA04001.pdf

Berlant, L. (2011). *Cruel optimism*. Durham, NC: Duke University Press.

Bettleheim, B. (1976). *The uses of enchantment: The meaning and importance of fairy tales*. New York: Vintage.

Brode, D. (2005). *Multiculturalism and the mouse: Race and sex in Disney entertainment*. Austin, TX: University of Texas Press.

Byrne, E., & McQuillan, M. (1999). *Deconstructing Disney*. London, UK: Pluto Press.

Disney, W. (Producer), Cottrell, W., Hand, D., Jackson, W., Morey, L., Pearce, P., & Sharpsteen, B. (Directors). (1937). *Snow White and the seven dwarfs* [Motion Picture]. United States: Walt Disney Productions.

Disney, W. (Producer), Geronimi, C., Clark, L., Larson, E., & Reitherman, W. (Directors). (1959). *Sleeping beauty* [Motion Picture]. United States: Walt Disney Productions.

Disney, W. (Producer), Geronimi, C., Jackson, W., & Luske, H. (Directors). (1950). *Cinderella* [Motion picture]. United States: Walt Disney Productions.

Doty, A. (2007). Introduction: There's something about Mary. *Camera Obscura, 22*(2), 1–8.

Edelman, L. (2004). *No future: Queer theory and the death drive*. Durham, NC: Duke University Press.

Eribon, D. (2004). *Insult and the making of the gay self*. Durham, NC: Duke University Press.

Farmer, B. (2000). *Spectacular passions: Cinema, fantasy, gay male spectatorships*. Durham, NC: Duke University Press.

Griffin, S. (2000). *Tinker belles and evil queens: The Walt Disney Company from the inside out*. New York: NYU Press.

Halberstam, J. (2011). *The queer art of failure*. Durham, NC: Duke University Press.

Johnston, O., & Thomas, F. (1993). *The Disney villain*. New York: Hyperion.

Luciano, D. (2011). Nostalgia for an age yet to come: *Velvet Goldmine's* queer archive. In E. L. McCallum & M. Tuhkanen (Eds.), *Queer times, queer becomings* (pp. 121–155). Albany, NY: SUNY Press.

mikee013. (2011, September 9). Why I'd rather be a Disney villain. Retrieved from https://everythingisqueer.wordpress.com/2011/09/09/why-id-rather-be-a-disney-villain/

Musker, J. (Producer/Director), Ashman, H. (Producer), & Clements, R. (Director). (1989). *The little mermaid* [Motion picture]. United States: Walt Disney Pictures.

Oh My Disney. (2014, October 27). *Counting scars featuring Disney villains* [Video file]. Retrieved from https://www.youtube.com/watch?v=VqrBsMFRaLA

Sedgwick, E. (1994). *Tendencies.* Durham, NC: Duke University Press.

Stockton, K. B. (2009). *The queer child: Or growing sideways in the twentieth century.* Durham, NC: Duke University Press.

Hall, T. [todrickhall]. (2013, October 28). *Spell Block Tango* [Video file]. Retrieved from https://www.youtube.com/watch?v=GAUZIw95ueM

Warner, M. (2002). *Publics and counterpublics.* New York: Zone Books.

Wolfreys, J. (2008). *Transgression: Identity, space, time.* London: Palgrave Macmillan.

Zipes, J. (2006). *Fairy tales and the art of subversion* (2nd ed.). London: Routledge.

5 The Postfeminist Princess

Public Discourse and Disney's Curricular Guide to Feminism

Michael Macaluso

Disney's animated film *Frozen* (Del Vecho, Buck, & Lee, 2013) has enjoyed enormous popularity and success. In addition to being praised for its endearing characters, catchy music, stunning visuals, and heartfelt storyline, moviegoers and film critics have used online popular media (social media websites and blogs) to also suggest that *Frozen*'s success lies with its updated, *feminist* spin on a traditional fairy tale (e.g., Joyce, 2013; Rosten, 2013; White, 2013). Even some self-proclaimed feminists have gone so far as to call the film "flawlessly feminist" (Joyce, 2013). This understanding of the film marks an important shift in thinking about Disney films: whereas Disney has usually been criticized for reinforcing traditional or even damaging gender norms (e.g., Bell, Haas, & Sells, 1995; Giroux & Pollock, 2010), *Frozen* is being celebrated for its feminist qualities of sisterhood, strong female protagonists, and the relegation of romantic love and the "someday-my-prince-will-come" trope to a side-storyline (Rosten, 2013). With these qualities in mind, participants of popular media have discussed *Frozen* in a way that suggests feminism's goals and objectives have been achieved, accomplished, or idealized, as evidenced by *Frozen*'s story and characters.

Upon further analysis, however, many of the reviews of the film rely on misguided or narrow notions of feminism, and, as such, popular online media has become a platform for debating the feminist nature of the film. In this chapter, I provide a different perspective of and for this debate by problematizing these notions of feminism, arguing that the film instead advances *postfeminist* characteristics and sensibilities that displace or replace feminist ideals or entangle them with anti-feminist sentiments (Butler, 2013; Gill, 2007). With this in mind, I also incorporate into my analysis the postfeminist curricula that come into being through the cultural reception of *Frozen* via online popular media—comments, reviews, and discussions about *Frozen* from participants on public social networks like Reddit, film sites, and feminist-oriented blogs—and I use these media to complicate the postfeminist reception of the film. This analysis of the film and its related popular media allows me to argue for the cultural reception of *Frozen* as a form of postfeminist cultural production; I argue that popular media may serve as a rich mediator for the re/production of identities and subjectivities that inform and are informed by post/feminism.[1]

Postfeminism: The General Idea(l)

The term 'postfeminism' (e.g., McRobbie, 2007; Tasker & Negra, 2007) refers to "a range of cultural discourses" (Butler, 2013, p. 41) regarding a belief that the construct of feminism is no longer needed, that its politics are a "thing of the past" in light of the many "celebratory narratives proclaiming feminism's 'success' in bringing about gender equity in education, work, and the home" (Butler, 2013, p. 43). This sensibility regarding the 'pastness' of feminism undermines—and to a certain extent replaces—earlier feminist goals (e.g., gender equality, equal rights, and collective action) for the neoliberal auspices of individualism, empowerment, and choice. As such, it promotes and naturalizes a limited and normative notion of feminism that essentially renders it a diluted, apolitical "slogan or generalized 'brand'" (Banet-Weiser, 2007, p. 208).

One strand of postfeminist discourse involves an automatic backlash against the term and label of 'feminism' or 'feminist' because of associations with those terms "as extreme, difficult, and unpleasurable" (Tasker & Negra, 2007, p. 4). In this case, feminism is brushed aside and resisted—indeed 'othered'—in favor of a *postfeminist* stance that is less grounded in feminist critique and politics (a popular strand with young celebrities who misrepresent and/or shun feminism). A second strand involves less backlash and envisions the purposes, agenda, and politics of feminism unnecessary in contemporary culture because they are positioned as having already been achieved and actualized. This stance argues that because feminism has been integrated into mainstream culture and has achieved successes toward equal rights, there is a perceived need to "let it go" because the critique is no longer necessary.

Within both strands of postfeminism, there are certain characteristics that perpetuate the image of feminism as irrelevant, extreme, or out of touch. For example, in her article, *For White Girls Only?: Postfeminism and the Politics of Inclusion*, Jess Butler (2013) delineates six postfeminist characteristics or discourses: the achievement of gender equality, the conflation of feminism and femininity, sexual subjectification, the makeover model, empowerment, and the maintenance of whiteness. While other postfeminist scholars (Munford & Waters, 2014; Tasker & Negra, 2007) may offer variations of these characteristics, all of them target popular culture as the site of postfeminist mediation. This chapter contributes to an established conversation that explores postfeminism as a phenomenon through media and cultural practices (Tasker & Negra, 2007) by analyzing a Disney film *and online spaces*—social media, online communities such as Reddit, and feminist-oriented blogs and the discussion/response sections associated with them—

devoted to or about that film. My analysis of *Frozen*, organized around the postfeminist discourses most salient to the film, includes comments from online spaces—from public forums and discussions dedicated to feminist purposes (e.g., Joyce, 2013; Rosten, 2013; White, 2013[2])—to highlight the conflicts, tensions, or interactions between feminism and postfeminism, or to show how participants position or negotiate their post/feminist identities.

Femininity and the Makeover Model

Postfeminist discourses conflate feminism with femininity and the maintenance of feminine beauty culture. As such, the recurrent trope of the female makeover positions beauty and appearance, or essentialized femininity, as a solution to or pathway for feminist concerns of freedom and confidence (McRobbie, 2007; Tasker & Negra, 2007).

In Disney's attempt to portray a strong female protagonist, Elsa is developed, animated, and written in a way that aptly captures a postfeminist sensibility, particularly during her 'transformation' sequence midway through the movie. This 'transformation,' the result of her secret powers being outed at her coronation party and her subsequent flight to an isolated mountaintop, however, does not fit the mold of other Disney transformations, like Ariel exchanging her fins for human legs or Maleficent literally embodying her draconic personality. These are actual transformations, whereas Elsa's transformation simply represents a glamorous makeover (Moseley, 2002), a new production of self. She sheds her dark dress, cape, and tight bun for a sleekly cool, glittery dress with a slit halfway up her leg, a whimsical cape, loosely braided hair, and, of course, high heels.

Part of the appeal of this makeover is that it comes with Elsa's perceived liberation, a key feminist feature. While she can let go of her fear, inhibition, and repression, her liberation is also tied to a postfeminist vision of femininity and sexuality, as depicted by her new wardrobe and hairdo. For example, in her online review of the film, Luttrell (2014) calls this scene Elsa's "self-empowerment" moment and argues,

> [Elsa] is finally on her own, she finds beauty in herself . . . she is good enough for herself, and that's all that really matters . . . her freedom and ability to be herself without compromise are more important to her than anything . . . even when it means isolation, confidence is a worthwhile goal—and it's sexy.
>
> (para. 7)

Luttrell's comment ties Elsa's confidence and independence to her sexuality, as instantiated by the makeover. This makeover is "sexy" and as such, it suggests that Elsa's femininity—here, her sex appeal and sexual empowerment—results from her newfound confidence, isolation, and freedom.

In this way, both the film and Luttrell conflate the qualities of feminism—liberation, confidence, independence—with postfeminist sensibilities, notably femininity and sexuality.

Registered members of the social media website Reddit have repeatedly discussed this makeover scene on its various themed pages or interest-categories, called "subreddits." Each of these pages, which are created and moderated by Reddit users, acts as a type of bulletin board where users can post any kind of media they want: pictures, videos, text, memes, hyperlinks, etc., and subreddits have been created for "frozen," "feminism," and "Disney." These pages have served as sites of rich discussion about the film and its many themes since the film's release. In regard to this makeover scene, one user, named "The_lady_is_trouble" (2013), commented in her post, "I found the near thigh-high slit on her dress to be a bit more than it needed to be, given the target audience. However, I was so floored that the main plot line was about sisters loving each other that I'll let it slide" (n.p.). In this case, this Reddit user recognizes the sexualization of Elsa in the makeover scene (the unnecessarily high dress slit), but is willing to "let it slide" because of her perception of the movie's feminist themes (sisterhood).

Herein lies the postfeminist problem of the makeover trope. Despite Elsa's makeover being heralded as one of *the* feminist moments of the film (i.e., Luttrell, 2013), the makeover reinscribes a certain type of femininity. According to Tasker and Negra (2007), "the postfeminist heroine is vital, youthful, and playful while her opposite number, the 'bad' female professional, is repressive, deceptive, and deadly" (p. 9). Elsa's story nicely overlays this theoretical concept: before the makeover, she is repressed, stoic, and distant. Her tight, dark clothes (a black corset buttoned to her neck) mirror her personality, and once her powers are outed, she is depicted as a deadly sorceress, hell bent upon freezing her citizens to death (as is the opinion of the village people upon initially seeing her powers). But after her makeover and eventual control of her powers, Elsa is fun (she creates an ice rink for everyone in the middle of summer), fresh, and has taken on glittery garb as she faces the dawn head on. Now, her femininity can be expressed through her powers in a grand and awesome way that was not possible before.

Moseley (2002) has also argued that the conflation of femininity, youth, and magic, as is the case with Elsa, is problematic and specifically tied to the postfeminist project. For her, the idea of the glamorous witch (and, similarly, the glamorous makeover that accompanies the witch's transformation) serves as another postfeminist trope through which "appropriate feminine identities are constructed and reinforced" (p. 406)—for example, the gothic, alternative, or conservative look is replaced with superficial glamor that ties together femininity with power. The glamorous power of the witch allows her to remain "sexy" but keep her body under control and powers in check, maintain a feminine sparkle (the substantiation of her magic or dress), and "inscribe and validate a respectable white hegemonic glamour" (p. 121), offering a way for the witch to be both powerful yet conventional, glamorous yet ordered—something that the non-witch (e.g., the average woman) would be unable to accomplish unless she submits to consumerist and capitalist demands that reinforce quick-and-easy aesthetic transformations.

Postfeminist Empowerment

Closely tied to the makeover mentality is the idea of female empowerment. This celebratory discourse contributes to the idea that feminist politics are no long needed because it centers on young, vital, beautiful, and empowered women who easily transcend societal problems (such as those connected to patriarchy) through an essentialized femininity, a production of their own selves, or through a plethora of choices in their professional, domestic, physical, and sexual lives.

When considering the history of Disney's animated princesses, it's clear that it's good to be a man in the Disney megaverse—dashing heroes regularly save the princess (*Sleeping Beauty* [Disney, Geronimi, Clark, Larson, & Reitherman, 1959], *Snow White* [Disney et al., 1937], *Aladdin* [Clements & Musker, 1992], *Hercules* [Dewey, Musker, & Clements, 1997]), girls sacrifice their whole lives and worlds for men they have barely met (*The Little Mermaid* [Musker, Ashman, & Clements, 1989], *Beauty and the Beast* [Hahn, Trousdale, & Wise, 1991]), and of course, characters maintain certain idealized images or body types (unless they are an animal, a hunchback, or Peter Pan). While, *Frozen*'s Elsa and Anna maintain an idealized feminine body, they are positioned as empowered against the traditional Disney backdrop of masculine heroes: they succeed at their goals, they are agentive and exercise power, and they save each other and everyone else while the men act as supporting characters. However, according to Tasker and Negra (2007), "One of postfeminism's signature discursive formulations couches the celebration of female achievement (whether on the playing field, in the concert arena, or in the boardroom) within traditional [and masculinist] ideological rubrics" (p. 7). One may consider a traditional Disney film as one of these ideological rubrics, where men have been the heroes and saviors or where female achievement is measured in relation to heteronormative notions of success (e.g., physical strength, cunning, dominating personality). In other words, if a female 'succeeds' of her own accord in a Disney film, then surely feminism has succeeded in penetrating a traditionally male-dominated field.

Because *Frozen* depicts two women who take on roles that have been traditionally assigned to male characters in Disney films, such as the hero, the savior, or the protagonist, celebratory discourse around *Frozen* and feminism pervades online social media. For example, Joyce (2013) commends the depiction of princess Anna as "vibrant, laughing, and playful" (para. 11) as opposed to her being docile and submissive, and Rosten (2013), in her review, "Disney's 'Frozen': The Feminist Fairy Tale We've Been Waiting For", praised the film for its "complete reversal and subversion of the Disney Princess conventions" (para. 2). Comments like these portray feminism as actualized, as indicated by the empowered female characters of *Frozen*.

Similarly, Elsa's retreat and subsequent makeover signal her empowerment and freedom from the oppression she endures throughout her childhood and early adult life. In this moment, she accepts and owns her unique powers and rebrands herself, transitioning from the weak, anxious, and restricted woman to an independent, empowered woman, ready to take initiative, make her own decisions, and be her own person. Her flight to the isolated, icy mountainside is purposeful because her new self relies on her *choice* to flee the public world and retreat into physical and emotional isolation, following her father's advice that if she is to rule effectively one day, she must "conceal, don't feel." As with her makeover, the new and empowered Elsa personifies postfeminism's quandary: a tension between feminism and femininity—"a perceived conflict between feeling protected and having the approval of visible femininity, on the one hand, and being self-determining and active, on the other" (Mukherjea, 2011, p. 3). In this case, Elsa's physical and emotional isolation results in her empowerment, reinforcing the postfeminist notion that women must control their emotions or must keep their emotions at bay if they are to be independent, successful, or powerful.

Along these lines, postfeminism "generates and draws strength . . . from a rhetorical field that produces buzzwords and slogans to express visions of energetic personal empowerment" (Tasker & Negra, 2007, p. 3), such as "you go, girl" or "girl power". For Elsa, and indeed for millions of fans and moviegoers since, "let it go" has become her (and our) own firebrand slogan for independence and empowerment—she's not just talking about her hair as she belts her anthem. For Elsa, this moment (similar to the postfeminist brand of "girl power") replaces feminism for the optimistic but individualized and insurgent female perspective (Munford & Waters, 2014). Posting on the subreddit "feminism," Reddit user momoxdear (2014) writes about this scene: "I do agree that the main theme of that scene was not embracing sexual prowess but instead becoming who she really was inside and allowing herself confidence that she had deprived herself of her entire life. All in all, the movie made the feminist in me pleasantly surprised" (n.p.). Here, momoxdear recognizes Elsa's empowerment and fierce independence, and she overlooks the sexualization and emotional isolation of Elsa in order to see what she wants—a confident, empowered, feminist character.

Considering Whiteness

Postfeminism also operates "as a subtle mechanism of racial exclusion" (Butler, 2013, p. 47) by "reinstituting (Western) whiteness as a dominant cultural norm" (p. 47). By reinvigorating White femininity, postfeminism invokes "'pre-feminist' cultural productions . . . [and] 'forgets' the work of both the civil rights movement and the women's liberation movement" (Munford & Waters, 2014, p. 11). As such, power is produced in the form of White hetero-supremacy (Butler, 2013) and considerations of race are minimized.

Just as Disney has been criticized for its gender depictions, so too has it been criticized for its failure to portray diverse characters across its films and media (e.g., Bell et al., 1995; Giroux & Pollock, 2010; Hurley, 2005). *Frozen* has come under particular scrutiny for its all-White cast of characters, and some have argued that the characters look nothing like the indigenous people of Norway, the actual place that inspired the town Arendelle in the film (Feminist Disney, 2014[3]). While there is no one else to blame but Disney filmmakers for this lack of racial representation, users of popular media re/produce postfeminist sensibilities when they defend or rationalize the omission of characters from traditionally marginalized populations because postfeminism works to not only exclude racial diversity, but to actually affirm the White, female, heterosexual subject (Butler, 2013).

For example, in her online review of the film, titled "Why the Feminist Controversy Over *Frozen* Misses the Point," blogger Cindy White (2013) writes,

> When we get incensed that Disney princesses are too pretty or too white or look too much like the last Disney princess, aren't we really saying that aesthetics are more worthy of concern than *any other aspect* of a character? . . . To focus solely on appearance without considering what's beneath the polished exterior isn't just shallow, it's hypocritical.
>
> (para. 16)

In her comments, White draws on a familiar postfeminist trope when she dismisses the racial discourse around the film in favor of an idealized subject or heroine depicted as a White, Western woman who embraces femininity, independence, and empowerment. For her, concerns about aesthetics trump concerns about racial diversity, and while she writes her article with feminist intent (praising the movie for its presumed feminism), her comments evoke a postfeminist disposition.

What makes White's review so interesting, however, is the comments that follow the review in the discussion section of the blog. Here, reviewers hash out their own post/feminist identities in response to White's review. For example, several users—and presumably, these participants are frequent consumers of this website—actually challenge and call out White for her implied racial bias. One user, lauren, writes, "Feminism is worthless if it doesn't speak for all women, and that includes Women of Colour" (White, 2013), staking her claim on what feminism is or should be: representative of all women. Others respond to White's review in similarly harsh tones:

LIZ: i think YOU'RE missing the point. the problem isn't that she's a pretty princess, it's that she's (ANOTHER) white princess. the problem is that young girls of color aren't getting to see themselves reflected back on screen, and are still (STILL) only getting to see strong female white characters.

COREY: . . . But by mentioning the "too white" criticism in your final paragraph—however casually—you implicitly dismiss discussions of race along with discussions of "prettiness," "aesthetics," and "appearance." And this is my problem with your article.

Here, Liz and Corey push back against White's opinion about race in an attempt to position themselves and each other around race and gender. Liz takes a stand about the prevalence of White female characters in Disney films while Corey, similarly, challenges White for her dismissal of the racial implications of the film. While there are plenty of comments that support White's point of view (and White even uses the discussion section to further explain her points in light of this criticism), lauren, Liz, and Corey's comments together link race and gender in a way that attempts to resist postfeminist sensibilities: in this case, the postfeminist ideal that affirms the White heterosexual subject.

This online conversation about race, waged in the discussion section, is different from those online comments previously included in this chapter. Specifically, it shows that some Disney consumers, presumed feminists, and/or social media participants are not 'dupes' of postfeminist cultural production. Rather, Liz, lauren, and Corey attempt to resist or counter-produce the post/feminist ideals White advances, and they illustrate how participants of online social media use these spaces to negotiate or debate cultural tensions. Further, their reception—of both the film and White's comments—underscores the important role popular media plays in bringing together the film and commentary about it. Social media affords a public space where participants may accept or resist the curriculum of long-standing Disney associations with race—that it is invisible or subservient to the plot and characters or, on the other hand, that Whiteness represents innocence, goodness, and pristine character and beauty.

Postfeminist Masculinity

As a consequence of female agency, power, and independence, postfeminism also carries with it a certain type or depiction of masculinity that usually pokes fun at or critiques the straight, White male in order to further distinguish him from the strong female characters around him (Tasker & Negra, 2007). These men are characterized as foolish or immature and unable to do things on their own while the women around them are portrayed as strong, confident, and demanding.

In *Frozen*, much of the "fixer-upper" sequence gently ridicules Kristoff (he's "grumpy," "smelly," "socially impaired," and "likes to tinkle in the woods," etc.) while Anna asserts her own authority and commands him to bring her up the north mountain to find Elsa. Kristoff also provides moments of subtle humor like when he stumbles over his words in asking to kiss Anna or, of course, when he claims that "all men . . . pick their nose . . . and eat it!" At the same time, Hans fulfills the trope of the dashing prince—including winning over the girl and displaying his bravado on multiple occasions—only to have it completely disregarded once his evil intentions are revealed. He ends up dumbfounded, punched in the face by Anna, thrown in prison, and left to deal with his (presumably suggested) more masculine older brothers at the movie's close. A deleted Reddit user (2014) from the subreddit "TwoXChromosomes"[4] picked up on these postfeminist themes (like those participants in the previous section on Whiteness), noting that while "the princess" is Disney's "brand", Disney "seem[s] to have gone from the princess needing rescuing to princess saving the day. Which is a nice direction, tho [sic] I just hope they don't continue to make the men in their movies well like buffoons really and that always make male characters weak idiots" (n.p.).

In addition to the deployment of these postfeminist masculinities, and despite feminist claims otherwise, much of the latter half of the film revolves around the machinations of Hans—the still dashing, but now evil villain of the film—and their effects on the other characters: both Anna and Elsa at some point fulfill the role of the damsel-in-distress and Kristoff is (still) positioned as the hero ("riding across the Fjords like some valiant, pungent Reindeer King!") and as 'Mr. Right' who gets the girl at the movie's end. Finally, whereas Anna has been lauded for her heroism and bravery, her role throughout most of the movie functions to save Elsa. Like Belle before her, Anna's agency—and purpose—is limited to the whims of the mis-understood, misrepresented, and emotionally and physically abusive 'beast' (Elsa) she is there to save. Though her act of selfless love eventually saves everyone, this trope is a familiar one in Disney films (e.g., *Pocahontas* [Pentecost, Gabriel, & Goldberg, 1995]).

Rethinking Cultural Production and Cultural Reception

The postfeminist themes I have explored here contribute to a public framing of the film that is decidedly postfeminist. But why does it matter, and why should we care that the film and its public reception advance postfeminist notions? In his influential book, *The Mouse That Roared*, Henry Giroux (1999) argued that Disney is a major cultural and corporate player in both American life and popular culture, and, more specifically, that because of Disney's ties to children's culture and consumerism, "we need to pay attention to how pedagogical practices produced and circulated by Disney . . . organize and control a circuit of power that extends from producing cultural texts to shaping the contexts in which they will be taken up by children and others" (p. 167). Since then, scholars, educators, and cultural critics and theorists have taken up that call to examine Disney as a cultural force and the ways in which it commodifies both adults' and children's innocence, dreams, and desires. For example, in the context of *Frozen*, Disney is certainly intentional in marketing the film to and for feminist audiences for its own economic and ideological gains.

At no other time is this call more necessary, as Americans continue to reel from the global impact of *Frozen*. In grossing over a billion dollars in ticket sales, it financially surpassed every other animated movie, and thus has been named the number one animated film of all time. Additionally, the song "Let It Go" won both Best Animated Film and Best Song at the Academy Awards; the soundtrack, the top-performing album of 2014, enjoyed an unprecedented 13-week reign at the top of the Billboard charts; and its DVD sales totaled 3.2 million on its first day of release alone and has since sold 7.6 million DVDs and another 6.5 million Blu-Ray DVDs (Hare, 2014; Stelter, 2014). Needless to say, *Frozen* has captured audiences and reinstated Disney as an animation—and cultural and corporate—powerhouse. As such, spin-offs, sequels, increased TV presence, a Broadway play, increased merchandise production, and a new theme park attraction are already planned or in the works to cash in on its popularity. The public success of *Frozen* further illustrates Disney's pedagogical potential and establishes *Frozen* as a cultural artifact.

However, Giroux (1999) only advocates for the critical analysis of *Disney as a cultural producer*—for an exploration of the ways in which Disney's corporate pedagogies act on us, inscribe onto us cultural ideals and values, shape certain values and identities within us, and "attempt to influence experience and subjectivity" (Segall, 2004, p. 494). I argue, instead, that in today's proliferate internet "participatory culture" (Jenkins, Clinton, Purushotma, Robison, & Weigel, 2009), where opportunities abound through social media and web 2.0 features to access and express each other's thoughts, opinions, and musings, the average theater-goer has become a cultural critic and as such, cultural *reception* has also become a form of cultural *production*. Thus, social network websites act as a form of public pedagogy (Schubert, 2010), as a space useful for understanding "the developments of identities and social formations" (Sandlin, Schultz, & Burdick, 2010, p. 1). While movies, television, music and other forms of popular culture serve as the impetus for debate, analysis, and critique, participants in online social media negotiate their own identities and subjectivities through their own reception of the these media. In the case explored in this chapter, the curriculum involves the ways in which feminism is positioned as a cultural construct and the ways in which postfeminism is used and deployed.

This type of cultural production has become even more apparent when one analyzes *Frozen* in conjunction with reviews and opinions from participants with/in online popular culture who take up, redefine, and use popular culture texts—like the film *Frozen*—for post/feminist purposes. This kind of mass participation highlights the ways in which these opportunities re/produce cultural values and personal identities, as explored in the postfeminist analysis above. Indeed, the pedagogical implications of these user-based sites and comments are clear as they uncover the post/feminist "curricula of our lives" (Schubert, 2010, p. 15). While the same type of analysis can be applied using other theoretical lenses, postfeminism allows me to see the role online participants play in producing and reimagining their post/feminist identities and the identities of others. With *Frozen*, Disney the corporation offered no *explicit* curricula on the gendered elements of the film; instead, participants of popular social media sites picked up on the *null* and *implicit* curricula of and around the film and used them to advance certain notions of their own post/feminist identities. For some participants, their emotional attachments to Disney and to past Disney films resulted in counterproductive talk; as if watching the movie uncritically, they could not see postfeminist sensibilities operating on them (e.g., bloggers White and Luttrell). Others, however, use these sites as important spaces for remixing Disney's gendered dimensions and for resisting postfeminist ideologies (e.g., Liz, lauren, Corey, and the Reddit user who wrote about the depiction of men in the film). This critical aspect could be lost if we were to view Disney as *the sole* cultural producer and ignore the cultural reception occurring via these public spaces.

This reception offers a more complex, nuanced picture of cultural production, and the implications of this type of public pedagogy are quite clear. While there is no doubt that scholars and educators have long been critical of Disney's gender representations and portrayals on film, the relationship between Disney (as a larger institution) and feminism has become even more complicated in an age characterized by the internet, social media, and the heteroglossic proliferation of Disney fans' voices. No longer can critical educators point solely to Disney for the authoritative perpetuation of certain norms, ideologies, and opinions of gender in its on-screen portrayals. Instead, we must look to ourselves for the ways in which we understand, mediate, and remediate our post/feminist notions of the Disney megaverse, asking such a question as "How have we become as we are?" (Schubert, 2010, p. 15). Certainly the task becomes challenging because it involves Disney and all of our emotional attachments to it as a hopeful, happily-ever-after harbinger of things to come or a mirror of our own modern sensibilities. Indeed, these attachments can mask, or even blind, our critical capabilities to view and analyze Disney as a cultural force, but we can be hopeful in the creative, critical capacities that seem possible via social media.

Conclusion

Giroux (1999) has long argued that "Disney needs to be engaged as a public discourse" (p. 10) such that "How audiences interpret Disney texts may not be as significant as how some ideas, meanings, and messages under certain political conditions become more highly valued as representations of reality than others" (p. 8). While I agree that Disney needs to continue to be engaged as a public discourse, I believe that, in this era of proliferate social media, this public discourse need to be engaged *as public discourse*—that is, it needs to be analyzed in terms of what it says and how it positions us pedagogically and as a site of cultural production. If the internet has opened up possibilities and avenues for the everyday critic or the public intellectual, then perhaps audience reactions to and interpretations of Disney texts have now become incredibly significant, more so than ever before, because they reveal *to* us something *about* us, and reinscribe our notions of some ordered reality. Tyson (2011) argues that any form of popular culture—be it a (Disney) song, story, or film—reveals something about the culture that creates it. This chapter, through an analysis of *Frozen* and its associated cultural reception through online commentaries, illuminates that point, and, as such, this analysis should *not* be taken as another jab to criticize Disney for once again failing to live up to the expectations we may have of it (Bell et al., 1995; Giroux & Pollock, 2010), but as an effort to point out how *our own* post/feminist sensibilities have become the cultural work this movie performs, produces, and reinforces.

Notes

1   While postfeminism is always linked to feminism, I will use this notation at some points in this chapter to capture their dialectical relationship, as is especially evident in online spaces when they are debated or when postfeminist sensibilities are reified under feminist pretenses.

2   In fact, these three websites are perfectly indicative of the laudatory feminist praise the film has received, and it is with these websites in mind that I mention the praise the film has received. For an overview as to how self-proclaimed feminists *positively* review the film, see any of these sites.

3   This website provides an excellent discussion of feminist issues and concerns across Disney films and media. The entry on *Frozen* is particularly generative as it catalogs and summarizes several discussions across online popular media regarding the gender, race, and indigenous criticisms of the film. See here for these detailed conversations and critique.

4   Though the comment can still be seen on the Reddit page, this user's name/account has since been deleted.

References

Banet-Weiser, S. (2007). What's your flava? In Y. Tasker & D. Negra (Eds.), *Interrogating postfeminism: Gender and the politics of popular culture* (pp. 201–223). Durham, NC: Duke University Press.

Bell, E., Haas, L., & Sells, L. (Eds.). (1995). *From mouse to mermaid: The politics of film, gender, and culture*. Bloomington: Indiana University Press.

Butler, J. (2013). For White girls only?: Postfeminism and the politics of inclusion. *Feminist Formations*, *25*(1), 35–58.

Clements, R., & Musker, J. (Producers/Directors). (1992). *Aladdin* [Motion picture]. United States: Walt Disney Pictures.

Del Vecho, P. (Producer), Buck, C., & Lee, J. (Directors). (2013). *Frozen* [Motion picture]. United States: Walt Disney Pictures.

Deleted Reddit user (2014). Disney's Frozen is genuinely feminist in the best way: It is about women while also being about women while treating both things as utterly normal. [Reddit Comment]. Retrieved from http://www.reddit.com/r/TwoX Chromosomes/comments/1rpn5q/disneys_frozen_is_genuinely_feminist_in_the_best/

Dewey, A. (Producer), Musker, J., & Clements, R. (Producers/Directors). (1997). *Hercules* [Motion picture]. United States: Walt Disney Pictures.

Disney, W. (Producer), Cottrell, W., Hand, D., Jackson, W., Morey, L., Pearce, P., & Sharpsteen, B. (Directors). (1937). *Snow White and the seven dwarfs* [Motion Picture]. United States: Walt Disney Productions.

Disney, W. (Producer), Geronimi, C., Clark, L., Larson, E. & Reitherman, W. (Directors). (1959). *Sleeping beauty* [Motion picture]. United States: Walt Disney Pictures.

Feminist Disney. (November, 2014). Is Disney frozen in time, or moving forward? [Tumblr]. Retrieved from: http://feministdisney.tumblr.com/post/72728984022/is-disney-frozen-in-time-or-moving-forward

Gill, R. (2007). Postfeminist media culture: Elements of a sensibility. *European Journal of Cultural Studies*, *10*(2), 147–66.

Giroux, H. A. (1999). *The mouse that roared: Disney and the end of innocence*. New York: Rowan & Littlefield.

Giroux, H. A., & Pollock, G. (2010). *The mouse that roared: Disney and the end of innocence*. New York: Rowman & Littlefield.

Hahn, D. (Producer), Trousdale, G., & Wise, K. (Directors). (1991). *Beauty and the beast* [Motion picture]. United States: Walt Disney Pictures.

Hare, B. (2014, October 20). Platinum albums? Not this year. *CNN Entertainment*. Retrieved from: http://www.cnn.com/2014/10/20/showbiz/music/frozen-beyonce-no-platinum-albums/index.html

Hurley, D. L. (2005). Seeing White: Children of color and the Disney fairy tale princess. *The Journal of Negro Education*, *74*(3), 221–232.

Jenkins, H., Clinton, K., Purushotma, R., Robison, A. J., & Weigel, M. (2009). *Confronting the challenges of participatory culture: Media education for the 21st century*. Cambridge, MA and London: MIT Press.

Joyce, M. A. (2013, October 26). Advance perspective: Disney's frozen defies expectations. *Feminist Advisory*. Retrieved from http://feministadvisory.com/2013/10/26/advance-perspective-disneys-frozen-defies-expectations/

Luttrell, G. (2014, January 20). 7 moments that made frozen the most progressive Disney movie ever. *Mic*. Retrieved from http://mic.com/articles/79455/7-moments-that-made-frozen the-most-progressive-disney-movie-ever

McRobbie, A. (2007). Postfeminism and popular culture: Bridget Jones and the new gender regime. In Y. Tasker & D. Negra (Eds.), *Interrogating postfeminism: Gender and the politics of popular culture* (pp. 27–39). Durham, NC: Duke University Press.

Momoxdear. (2014). Feminism and sexuality in "Frozen" [Reddit comment]. Retrieved from: http://www.reddit.com/r/Feminism/comments/22xa6p/feminism_and_sexuality_in_frozen/

Moseley, R. (2002). Glamorous witchcraft: Gender and magic in teen film and television. *Screen, 43*(4), 403–422.

Mukherjea, A. (2011). My vampire boyfriend: Postfeminism, "perfect" masculinity, and the contemporary appeal of paranormal romance. *Studies in Popular Culture*, 33(2), 1–20.

Munford, R., & Waters, M. (2014). *Feminism and popular culture: Investigating the postfeminist mystique.* London: I.B. Tauris.

Musker, J. (Producer/Director), Ashman, H. (Producer), & Clements, R. (Director). (1989). *The little mermaid* [Motion picture]. United States: Walt Disney Pictures.

Pentecost, J. (Producer), Gabriel, M., & Goldberg, E. (Directors) (1995). *Pocahontas* [Motion picture]. United States: Walt Disney Pictures.

Rosten, S. (2013, December 2). Disney's "Frozen": The feminist fairy tale we've been waiting for (with no prince charming). *Feminspire.* Retrieved from: http://feminspire.com/disneys-frozen-the-feminist-fairy-tale-weve-been-waiting-for-with no-prince-charming/

Sandlin, J. A., Schultz, B. D., & Burdick, J. (2010). Understanding, mapping, and exploring the terrain of public pedagogy. In J. A. Sandlin, B. D. Schultz, & J. Burdick (Eds.), *Handbook of public pedagogy: Education and learning beyond schooling* (pp. 1–6). New York: Routledge.

Schubert, W. H. (2010). Outside curricula and public pedagogy. In J. A. Sandlin, B. D. Schultz, & J. Burdick (Eds.), *Handbook of public pedagogy: Education and learning beyond schooling* (pp. 10–19). New York: Routledge.

Segall, A. (2004). Revisiting pedagogical content knowledge: The pedagogy of content/the content of pedagogy. *Teaching and teacher education, 20*(5), 489–504.

Stelter, B. (2014, April 1). Frozen is cash machine for Disney. *The Buzz Investment and Stock Market News RSS.* Retrieved from: http://buzz.money.cnn.com/2014/04/01/disney frozen/?hpt=hp_t3

Tasker, Y., & Negra, D. (2007). Feminist politics and postfeminist culture. In *Interrogating postfeminism: Gender and the politics of popular culture* (pp. 1–25). Durham, NC: Duke University Press.

The_lady_is_trouble. (2013). Disney's Frozen is genuinely feminist in the best way: It is about women while also being about women while treating both things as utterly normal [Reddit comment]. Retrieved from: http://www.reddit.com/r/TwoXChromosomes/comments/1rpn5q/disneys_frozen_is_genuinely_feminist_in_the_best/

Tyson, L. (2011). *Using critical theory: How to read and write about literature* (2nd Ed.). New York: Routledge.

White, C. (2013, November 23). Why the feminist controversy over Frozen misses the point [Web log post]. Retrieved from: http://geekmom.com

6 "The Illusion of Life"

Nature in the Animated Disney Curriculum

Caleb Steindam

Disney films forge the childhood fantasies that shape our "roles, values, and ideals" (Giroux, 1999, p. 84). I grew up captivated by the story of Mowgli the man-cub, raised in the jungle by a panther, bear, and family of wolves. I frequently fantasized a life spent foraging for food, sleeping in trees, avoiding hungry pythons and fleeing from tigers. Informed by Disney's caricatured distortions, the jungle of my imagination bore little resemblance to reality. Still, *The Jungle Book* (Disney & Reitherman, 1967) seemed to rouse my yearning for the "forgotten freedom we must all once have shared with other wild things" (Reben, 1991, p. 133).

Nature is a thematic and aesthetic element of nearly all animated Disney films, evoking romance (e.g., *Snow White* [Disney et al., 1937]; *Sleeping Beauty* [Disney, Geronimi, Clark, Larson, & Reitherman, 1959]), spirituality (e.g., *Pocahontas* [Pentecost, Gabriel, & Goldberg, 1995]; *Brother Bear* [Williams, Blaise, & Walker, 2003]), adventure (e.g., *Robin Hood* [Reitherman, 1973]; *Tarzan* [Arnold, Buck, & Lima, 1999]), fun (e.g., *Peter Pan* [Disney, Geronimi, Jackson, Luske, & Kinney, 1953]; *The Princess and the Frog* [Del Vecho, Lasseter, Clements, & Musker, 2009]), and absurdist fantasy (e.g., *Dumbo* [Disney & Sharpsteen, 1941]; *Alice in Wonderland* [Estrella, Geronimi, Jackson, & Luske, 1951]). On the surface, these films depict nature in a positive light. The Disney Corporation has crafted an Earth-friendly image through their marketing of some of these films (Bruckner, 2010), and also through "edu-tainment" (King, 1996) products like the True Life Adventure series, the Animal Kingdom theme park, Disneynature's documentary films, and the Disney Channel's "Friends for Change" campaign. Yet generations shaped by Disney's "teaching machines" (Giroux, 1999, p. 84) have had an uneasy relationship with the natural world and its inhabitants, characterized both by destruction of our environment and estrangement from it. Thus it is important to consider the influence of these films on our ideas of nature and our relationship to it.

Nature is a "leaky" concept (Haraway, 1991, p. 152), for there is no true border separating the natural from the human. We are all part of nature, existing within it and dependent upon it. At the same time, there is no nature left in the strictest sense of the word, for no part of Earth remains unaffected by humans' impact on the climate. Still, I maintain that there is a meaningful distinction, intuitively sensed if not precisely defined, between that which occurs 'naturally' and that which humans have deliberately altered or manufactured. For the purposes of this chapter I accept Selhub and Logan's (2012) definition of nature as "the nonbuilt, nonsynthetic environment— sights, sounds, aromas, rivers, oceans, plants, animals, and light in as close a form as possible to that from which we evolved" (p. 2). I argue here that humans are drawn to nature even in our present-day isolation from it, and that Disney's animated films capitalize on this innate attraction. I present examples of three persistent motifs that Disney uses in its portrayals of nature: *purity*, *wildness*, and *anthropomorphism*. These motifs are significant in helping us understand how Disney shapes, distorts, and commodifies our conceptions of nature. I close with a brief commentary on the implications of these films' substitution of synthetic representations for authentic experiences of the natural world.

The Allure of Nature

By the time Disney released its first animated feature film, *Snow White*, industrial capitalism had led to extraordinary changes in people's relationship to the natural world. There was not yet widespread awareness of humans' capacity for ecological destruction, but we were advancing unknowingly toward the present-day catastrophe that has caused mass extinction of species across the globe and threatens countless species including our own (Klein, 2014). More immediate was the impact of industrialization on our environments and lifestyles.

Contemporary human lifestyles represent an unprecedented anomaly in the context of *Homo sapiens'* 200,000-year history. Humans spent 95 percent of this history as nomadic hunter-gatherers, as wholly immersed in the natural world as every other creature. Our ancestors started settling into agrarian lifestyles some 10,000 years ago, remaining ineluctably attuned to the cycles and seasons of nature. Even as industrialization began to spread, the majority of people continued to work on the land. It was not until the nineteenth century that people's everyday experiences began to become significantly isolated from the natural world, in a progression that has been accelerating ever since. Today, we humans increasingly surround ourselves with manufactured environments remarkably dissimilar from the living and nonliving forms of which the earth is composed in its natural state. More and more, our experience of the world derives from manufactured rather than natural contexts. No longer the essence of our lived reality, we have come to perceive nature as *other*, yet we remain bound to nature even in our perceived separation from it, for we share an evolutionary heritage with all beings on Earth: "They are the matrix in which the human mind originated and is permanently rooted" (Wilson, 1984, p. 139). As we isolate ourselves from our earthly heritage, we maintain a powerful if indistinct yearning to engage with the living beings and systems that comprise our world.

Wilson (1984) coined the term 'biophilia' to signify people's "urge to affiliate with other forms of life" (p. 85), a trait he characterizes as innate and universal:

> It unfolds in the predictable fantasies and responses of individuals from early childhood onward. It cascades into repetitive patterns of culture across most or all societies, a consistency often noted in the literature of anthropology. These processes appear to be part of the programs of the brain. They are marked by the quickness and decisiveness with which we learn particular things about certain kinds of plants and animals. They are too consistent to be dismissed as the result of purely historical events working on a mental blank slate.
>
> (p. 85)

A considerable body of research substantiates Wilson's claim. Various studies indicate that children's identification with animals occurs independently of social influences (Hyun, 2005; Kahn & Kellert, 2002; Melson, 2001), although their appreciation of animals appears to increase with greater exposure (Bjerke, Kaltenborn, & Ødegårdstuen, 2001). If anything, Wilson's (1984) conception of *biophilia* understates the extent of humans' identification with nature by limiting the construct to living things. Stefanovic's (2004) phenomenological research and literature review suggest an affiliation with nature not limited to living organisms, but inclusive of the earth itself: "Children appear to have a sensual attachment to earth—squeezing it, rolling it, and even tasting it—that may perhaps enlighten us to the hidden dimensions of a belonging that, with age, we often forget" (p. 66).

Our attraction to nature is embedded within and among countless intertangled, socially constructed subjectivities, but to some degree it is rooted in our biological heritage. This may challenge social theorists who find "discomfort" in those "elements of our subjectivity [that] may not be totally socially constructed" (Braidotti, 2013, pp. 82–83). But its implications are substantial and should not be ignored. The Disney Corporation appears to be keenly aware of nature's allure. Its films capitalize masterfully on our yearning for nature while reshaping our understandings through distorted representations, as I discuss in the following section.

Depictions of Nature in Disney Animation

Disney's animated films warrant close examination in order to understand how they may influence our ideas and actions in relation to nature. In this section, I organize my analysis of these depictions into three broad categories. First I examine Disney's representations of nature as *purity*, symbolic of virtue, harmony, and perfection. I then explore depictions that evoke a sense of *wildness* through nature. Finally I discuss the ubiquitous *anthropomorphism* of Disney's animal depictions that personify human qualities.

Purity

Disney frequently presents nature as a state of purity. These depictions often contain moral or spiritual implications, distinguishing good from evil within a dichotomized worldview (see, for example, Booker, 2010; Miller & Rode, 1995; and Pike, 2012). This conception of purity is usually presented as a feminine trait and often used to endear characters to the audience by virtue of their association with nature. From *Snow White*, and *Sleeping Beauty* to *The Little Mermaid* (Musker, Ashman, & Clements, 1989) and *Pocahontas*, princesses demonstrate unassailable virtue when they sing with wild animals. This association occasionally arises with male characters as well. For example, Quasimodo of *The Hunchback of Notre Dame* (Hahn, Trousdale, & Wise, 1996) and Cody of *The Rescuers Down Under* (Schumacher, Butoy, & Gabriel, 1990) both gently assist wild birds in the scenes where they are first introduced. Purity is also demonstrated in Disney's pristine landscapes, from the ambrosial forest of *Bambi* (Disney & Hand, 1942) to *The Lion King*'s sweeping Pride Lands (Hahn, Allers, & Minkoff, 1994). Music is used to evoke a reverence for nature, evidenced in lyrics lauding a beauty "far too much to take in" (*The Lion King*'s "Circle of Life" [John & Rice, 1994]) and "a paradise untouched by man" (*Tarzan*'s "Two Worlds" [Collins, 1999]). Cuddly animals contribute to a sense of nature's innocence, from the bunnies, birds, and squirrels that surround Snow White to Pocahontas's raccoon and hummingbird friends.

Of course, the realities of the natural world do not conform to Disney's conceptions of purity. Members of the insect and arachnid classes rarely appear, for though they constitute the majority of animals on land, they do not conform to the aesthetic of Disney's idealized versions of nature. This omission is part of a broader tendency to portray nature as unequivocally accommodating and comfortable for characters deemed worthy of its graces. Given the deficit of many viewers' actual exposure to nature, this distortion could have negative consequences. Unlike Disney's anesthetized portrayals, real-life nature has hazards, discomforts, and inconveniences. We grow accustomed to nature's discomforts through exposure to them. But for those accustomed to viewing idealized versions of nature from predictable indoor settings, the idea of actual nature may become more intimidating, making them less inclined to enter its ungoverned spaces. Evidence of this effect emerges in a study commissioned by The Nature Conservancy (2011), which found that the most common reason for not spending more time in nature, cited by 80 percent of the youth participants, was that they believed "It's uncomfortable, because of things like bugs, heat, etc." (p. 3). Yet nature was considered "uncomfortable" by only 14 percent of those youth who had actually spent substantial time in nature (p. 7).

Even more consequentially, Disney's idealized depictions of nature almost uniformly overlook animals' consumption of one another. With the notable exception of *The Lion King*, these films either treat carnivorism as a character flaw or omit it completely. In *The Jungle Book*, there is no indication that Mowgli's panther and wolf friends—and, presumably, Mowgli himself—prey on other animals for survival. *Brother Bear* depicts only the hunting of salmon, which, unlike all other animals in the film, are given no personality. Shere Khan, the antagonistic tiger in *The Jungle Book*, and Sabor, the villainous leopard in *Tarzan*, are motivated by hatred, not biological need or instinct, and betray no intention of actually eating the protagonists. *Bambi*'s only predators are the faceless human hunters and their ferocious dogs, which, as Bruckner (2010) observes, "oddly [implies] that predation between animals is man-made" (p. 193). This omission and villainization of carnivorism in Disney's depictions of nature has likely contributed to a "hierarchy among attitudes toward animals" (Bart, 1972, p. 4) in the American public that favors herbivores and domesticated animals over carnivores. Despite their negative portrayals, predators are ecologically essential. Because the public's financial and political support is imperative for conservation efforts (Eisenberg, 2014), Disney's portrayals impact real animals and ecosystems, and by extension, all of us.

Bambi, Disney's first nature-centered film, warrants a closer examination, for it offers an acute portrayal of nature as purity by means of a stark and impenetrable human-nature divide. The forest setting is idyllic (see Bruckner, 2010, and Whitley, 2013, for excellent analyses of the aesthetics of *Bambi*'s nature imagery), and the animal protagonists are uniformly virtuous, from Bambi's mother's nurturing love and his father's majestic stoicism to his mate Faline's cherubic femininity and his rabbit friend Thumper's childlike charm. In contrast, the categorically wicked antagonists to nature are unseen humans, known to the animals as "Man," who kill Bambi's mother with their guns and cause a forest fire that threatens all the forest's innocent creatures.

Bambi's juxtaposition of nature's sublimity and humans' heinousness made for deeply affective entertainment, prompting an immediate and controversial response when the film debuted. Hunters labeled it "the worst insult ever offered in any form to American sportsmen" (Brown, 1942, quoted in Cartmill, 1993, p. 11), while the Audubon Society lauded *Bambi* for compelling viewers to "[put] themselves into the place of the hunted, just as *Uncle Tom's Cabin* put the unimaginative in the place of the slaves" (Peattie, 1942, quoted in Hastings, 1996, p. 54). By some accounts it was the most influential film of all time with respect to our perceptions of nature. Whitley (2013) credits *Bambi* with "[inspiring] conservation awareness and [laying] the emotional groundwork for environmental activism" (p. 4), Cartmill (1993) calls it "probably the most effective piece of antihunting propaganda ever made" (p. 7), and King (1996) asserts that *Bambi*'s impact on environmental awareness was greater than Carson's (1962/2002) *Silent*

Spring. Hastings (1996) suggests that assertions of the film's environmental impact are overblown, but it had an undeniable effect on at least some viewers' behavior.

Specific examples of *Bambi*'s influence are illustrative. In at least two cases, the film seems to have inspired an overzealous protectiveness of deer that proved counterproductive. The year after *Bambi's* release, public opposition prevented the conservationist Aldo Leopold from introducing a deer-hunting season that would have promoted ecological balance by curbing overpopulation (Lutts, 1992). The following year, the US Forest Service instituted an ill-advised no-burn policy that sought to eliminate even naturally occurring forest fires necessary for ecological health—a policy believed to have been directly influenced by the public's response to *Bambi*'s terrifying forest fire scene (Cartmill, 1993). A more positive example of the film's influence comes from the musician Paul McCartney. When he watched *Bambi* as a child, McCartney felt a strong sense of empathy for the animals and revulsion at the humans' cruelty, an experience he now identifies as foundational to his development as an activist for animal rights and conservation (Former Beatle "Inspired by Bambi," 2005).

There is a crucial difference between the case of McCartney, for whom *Bambi* prompted positive action, and the protesters who reflexively obstructed healthy forest fires and sustainable hunting. The well-intentioned but ecologically illiterate protesters seem to have based their actions exclusively on the film itself, while for McCartney *Bambi* was only the spark. McCartney's case substantiates the thoughtful conclusion of Bruckner's (2010) analysis, which states that despite the misleading and detrimental messages they often present, animated films like *Bambi* have the potential to "produce a limited environmental sensitivity that is only a *starting point* for the necessary ecological discussions" (p. 202, my italics). There seems to be some educational value, then, in the potential of idealized representations to elicit emotional investment in animals and nature. On their own, though, they are more likely to be miseducative due to their gross misrepresentations of ecological realities. And despite their positive portrayals of the natural world, Pike (2012) argues that these films may ultimately turn us away from nature by presenting a "faulty syllogism: Nature is good. Humans are not Nature. Humans are not good" (p. 56), which leaves no room for positive engagement with nature.

Wildness

In a classic scene in *The Jungle Book*, Baloo the bear, having decided to take Mowgli under his wing, teaches the man-cub the art of the "big bear growl." The image of boy and bear alternately roaring at one another is a classic celebration of wildness, or "the animal in us" (Thoreau, 1852/2011, p. 390). The definitive manifesto of wildness remains Thoreau's essay "Walking," (1862/1981), which famously declares that "in Wildness is the preservation of the World" (p. 390). Thoreau's conception of wildness "regard[s] man [*sic*] as an inhabitant, or a part and parcel of Nature" (p. 371), thus it relates to the concept of *biophilia* (Wilson, 1984) discussed above. Wildness is a quality we perceive in nature and can also find in ourselves. In Thoreau's understanding, wildness emerges in actions performed with absolute freedom, without regard for society's expectations. For example, the playing of a bugle once reminded him "of the cries emitted by wild beasts in their native language" (p. 400). Berry (1987) clarifies the concept of wildness as the antithesis of *domestication*. Though we are highly domesticated animals, there will always be some wildness within us, just as any pet-owner knows no animal can be so fully tamed as to lose all its wild animal qualities.

Wildness, like purity, is a gendered construct in Disney's cinematic world—this time, a predominately male one, as epitomized by characters like Tarzan, *The Jungle Book*'s Mowgli, *The Aristocats'* Thomas O'Malley (Hibler & Reitherman, 1970), and *Brother Bear*'s Kenai. Some female characters also demonstrate wildness, like *Tarzan*'s Jane and *The Lion King*'s Nala, but these examples emerge almost exclusively in the more recent films. Disney films through the 1980s left little room for female manifestations of wildness because, as Miller and Rode (1995) note, they present a "binary pole of experience" (p. 102) that "divides the world of Nature and Nurture" (p. 101), juxtaposing the predominately male trait of *wildness*, with the female trait of *domesticity* (Booker, 2010).

The thematic framework of earlier animated Disney films, as characterized by Miller and Rode (1995) and Booker (2010), recalls Berry's (1987) juxtaposition of wildness with domestication. However, lacking Berry's subtlety, the Disney framework eschews the possibility of harmony between wildness and domesticity, always (until the late 1990s) following a narrative arc that favors domesticity (Nurture) over wildness (Nature). Mowgli abandons his jungle friends for the "man-village" (*The Jungle Book*). Snow White teaches the dwarfs to keep a clean house. Wendy and her brothers come home from Neverland (*Peter Pan*, 1953). Pinocchio flees Pleasure Island and becomes a well-behaved boy (Disney, Sharpsteen, & Luske, 1940). Alice escapes the anarchy of Wonderland (1959). Dumbo kicks the booze and pink elephant hallucinations to enjoy a predictable life in the circus with his mother (1941).

In recent films—most notably *Tarzan* and *Brother Bear*—this trend has reversed, with wildness presented as an ideal to pursue rather than a temptation to overcome. *Tarzan* tells a similar story to *The Jungle Book* but takes a very different approach. Like Mowgli the "man-cub," Tarzan the "ape-man" is a human raised by animals in the jungle. However, unlike Mowgli who walks and talks like a 'civilized' human boy, Tarzan's movements are distinctly gorilla-like, representing what Wells (2009) calls the *hybrid humanimal* as he simultaneously embodies both human and animal qualities. At first Tarzan believes he is a gorilla, but he gradually becomes aware of his difference. Tarzan's most significant moment of self-realization arrives through nonverbal communication with his gorilla mother, Kala. As described by Hooks (2005), "Tarzan places his hands against Kala's. That is when it hits him that, without any doubt, he is of a different kind than his 'mother'" (p. 164). Unlike Mowgli, however, and unlike the Tarzan of the original books (Vernon, 2008), Tarzan ultimately chooses the jungle over human civilization, as do Jane and her father who join him to live out their lives in the jungle. In a marked departure from the traditional Disney formula, the film closes with an exuberant celebration of wildness as Tarzan's animalistic holler resounds through the jungle after vine-swinging with his human and animal friends.

Brother Bear also conflates human with animal in its celebration of wildness. After Kenai, the young Inuit protagonist, kills a bear to avenge his brother's death, the spirits transform Kenai into a bear himself so he can atone for his wrongful act. As a bear, Kenai becomes a big brother to a younger bear, Koda, whom Kenai later discovers to be the son of the bear he killed. At the end of the film, when Kenai has the opportunity to return to human form, he chooses to remain a bear. The Disney tradition of unambiguously happy endings remains intact as the human and bear characters frolic together in the company of the spirits of Kenai's brother and Koda's mother. The resolutions of *Brother Bear* and *Tarzan* are thus remarkably similar. In both cases the protagonist has a choice between living as a civilized human or as an animal. Both choose the animal life. Disney also applied this thematic shift retroactively to *The Jungle Book* as it revised Mowgli's story for the made-for-DVD sequel *The Jungle Book 2* (Chase, Thorne, & Trenbirth, 2003), which finds Mowgli coexisting in both the "man village" and "jungle" with no apparent conflict.

How do we interpret Disney's recent trend of privileging wildness over domesticity? The repudiation of traditional plot structures seems to coincide with a broader infiltration of postmodern sensibilities into pop culture, but there seems to be a larger explanation. Disney's business has always been the peddling of fantasy. With today's unprecedented isolation from nature, back-to-nature tales offer a potent form of escapist fantasy. However, these films remain merely fantasy. They are so far outside viewers' range of experience or possibility that they are unlikely to positively impact their audiences' relationship with nature. Set among an Inuit tribe from centuries past, *Brother Bear*'s context is so removed from twenty-first century perspectives that its depiction of a world where "man and nature lived side by side" (Collins, 2003) is unlikely to feel plausible or relevant to audiences' lives. Meanwhile, *Tarzan* seems to imply that to leave the jungle would be to cut off all ties to nature, while its viewers do not have the option of abandoning civilization for the jungle. Neither film indicates our potential to interact with nature from within human society. Thus, while these films successfully commodify our desire for nature's wildness, they offer not a substantial connection to nature but a passive and unfulfilling substitute.

Anthropomorphism

Anthropomorphism, or the attribution of human characteristics (e.g., language, behaviors, expressions, and anatomical features) to nonhuman beings, is ubiquitous in Disney films. With some rather unremarkable exceptions (the aforementioned salmon in *Brother Bear*, for example), Disney offers few animated portrayals of wildlife that are not anthropomorphized. Degrees of anthropomorphism, however, vary considerably, from a character like *Pinocchio's* Jiminy Cricket (1940), who appears essentially human with no discernable cricket characteristics, to the gorillas of *Tarzan* who are rendered with remarkable anatomical accuracy. Aside from their use of language—which, admittedly, is no small aside—the gorilla characters are no more physically altered to appear human than Tarzan is physically altered to appear gorilla. Despite the inherent inaccuracies of anthropomorphism, Disney animation achieves "the illusion of life" (Thomas & Johnston, 1981, p. 9) in its animal characters in surprisingly effective ways.

There is a range of controversy around the anthromorphism in Disney films. Some argue that anthropomorphic representations impede our understanding and concern for animals by distorting animals' natures (e.g., Bruckner, 2010; Grauerholz, 2007; Orr, 1992). It has also been attacked for precisely the opposite reason, with accusations of manipulating viewers into undue empathy for animals, as when *Field and Stream* magazine attacked *Bambi's* "outright anthropomorphism" as "brainwashing" (quoted in Cartmill, 1993, p. 6). This attack implies that anthropomorphism is inherently deceptive, a perspective that emerges to some degree in other critiques of Disney films (e.g., Byrne & McQuillan, 1999; Miller & Rode, 1995). Yet to reject anthropomorphism outright is to dismiss a schema that has existed across cultures for thousands of years and is widespread in art, storytelling, religion, and even science (Epley, Waytz, & Cacioppo, 2007; Mitchell, Thompson, & Miles, 1997).

As "a process of inductive inference" (Epley, Waytz, & Cacioppo, 2007, p. 865), there seems to be at least some degree of reason and evidence underlying the anthropomorphic approach. For example, Jane Goodall's research (Van Lawick & Goodall, 1963) is indisputable evidence of at least some overlap between humans' and other species' social and emotional expressions. Disney animators Frank Thomas and Ollie Johnston (1981) confirm that they looked to Goodall's findings, including the ways chimpanzees "fling their arms around each other for reassurance, throw things in anger, steal objects furtively, and scream wildly with excitement" (p. 17), to inform their representation of nonverbal communication in human and animal characters alike. Disney artists also conducted their own in-depth studies of animals to learn how they "communicate their feelings in body attitudes" (p. 18). Judging from the animators' accounts, they established intimate familiarity with animals as they prepared to draw them:

> If Disney artists were going to animate a fox, they would try to get a
> real fox to study and photograph, and, if possible, feel. Nothing matches
> the learning that comes from feeling an animal's bones and muscles and
> joints, to discover how they are put together and how far they can
> move in any direction; it is always surprising.
>
> (Thomas & Johnston, 1981, p. 332)

From the way they describe it, Disney animation aims for the common
ground between human and animal personalities through characters that
bridge that separation. In creating the Bambi character, for example, they
began with naturalistic forms, and then exaggerated certain features that
would allow the deer to "emote as broadly as animators require" until
arriving at an image of "what people imagined a deer to look like" (Thomas
& Johnston, 1981, p. 332). They were not aiming for accurate representations
of deer, but neither did they merely insert the personality of a human into
the body of a deer (as some might mistakenly assume about anthropomorphic
animation). Bambi has a distinctly deerlike personality, while anthropomorphism allows for increased communication and identification with the
human audience.

At the very least, anthropomorphism is preferable to the antithetic
approach of "[consigning] animals to never feeling anything as we do, and
therefore never feeling anything at all" (Jacobson, 1997, p. 4). Still, "the
concession favors us; the measure of all things is still consciousness as we
understand it" (Jacobson, 1997, p. 4). This is the most substantive critique
of anthropomorphism: that it is anthropocentric, meaning it "establishes
humanity as the barometer for normative values and affirms the centrality
of human life" (Bruckner, 2010, p. 188). Or, as King (1996) describes it,
Disney's version of nature is "not an ecosystem, but an ego-system—one
viewed through a self-referential human lens" (p. 62). Furthermore, the
anthropocentric viewpoint, according to Berry (1987), can lead to "gross
and dangerous" human behavior (p. 148). Yet Berry believes that "some
version of self-centeredness" is unavoidable: "An earthworm, I think, is living
in an earthworm-centered world; the thrush who eats the earthworm is
living in a thrush-centered world; the hawk who eats the thrush is living
in a hawk-centered world" (p. 148). Clearly, it is only through our human
lens that we can identify with animals, so our perception of them is
necessarily anthropocentric. As research suggests (Hyun, 2005; Kahn &
Kellert, 2002; Melson, 2001) and anyone who has spent time with children
and animals can confirm, we naturally identify with animals, without the
need for anthropomorphism. In some cases (as with McCartney, as discussed
above), anthropomorphism may offer a shortcut to cross-species empathy,
but this empathy remains shallow and incomplete in the absence of authentic
experience with animals.

Discussion

Semblances of truth shine through the many distortions in Disney's representations of nature. In the portrayals of *purity* we may find a faint suggestion of Earth's splendor that inspires awe and hope in something greater than us. The sense of *wildness* can remind us that we are inhabitants of Nature before Civilization (Thoreau, 1862/1981), and perhaps embolden us to defy the mechanistic oppression of modernity. And through *anthropomorphism* we may examine our identification with other creatures and, by extension, our union with all of Earth's life.

The non-manufactured world still speaks to us, if we allow it. Interaction with nature—which includes walking, gardening, sketching or writing in natural spaces, as well as indoor time with plants and pets (Selhub & Logan, 2012)—appears to have a positive effect on health, outlook, and academic achievement (Kellert, 1998; Louv, 2005; MacGregor, 2010; Sternberg, 2009). More crucially, experiencing nature leads us to "value nature, engage with it, and feel empowered to do something about it" (The Nature Conservancy, 2011, p. 3; see also MacGregor, 2010, and Selhub & Logan, 2012). Disney's animated worlds, however, are no match for the majesty of the world we inhabit. But nor are they as troubling as the real world. It is harrowing to confront the fact that there are no more Javan tigers alive in our world and the probability that there soon will be no more Javan rhinoceroses. How unthinkably devastating, then, is the reality of human-induced mass extinction. The appeal of Disney films is not hard to understand: in their world, only villains are responsible for environmental destruction, and the villains are always defeated in the end. But in this crucial moment we cannot afford to distract and console ourselves with fantasy in lieu of dealing with our reality.

The changes needed, if we are to end the ecological annihilation of which we are both perpetrators and victims, cannot occur on a merely individual level (Klein, 2014). We need cooperation and consensus to dismantle all systems that allow the ravaging of earth and life for money, and we need courage and community to overcome the collective complicity of our compulsively consumptive culture. We are in "a cosmic struggle for the triumph of the motley and the various and the beautiful" (Foltz, 2006, p. 125) and must engage with more than images on screens if we are to find our place within the beauty and the struggle.

References

Arnold, B. (Producer), Buck, C., & Lima, K. (Directors). (1999). *Tarzan* [Motion picture]. United States: Walt Disney Productions.

Bart, W. M. (1972). A hierarchy among attitudes toward animals. *The Journal of Environmental Education, 3*(4), 4–6.

Berry, W. (1987). *Home economics.* New York: North Point Press.

Bjerke, T., Kaltenborn, B. P., & Ødegårdstuen, T. S. (2001). Animal-related activities and appreciation of animals among children and adolescents. *Anthrozoos: A Multidisciplinary Journal of the Interactions of People & Animals, 14*(2), 86–94.

Booker, M. K. (2010). *Disney, Pixar, and the hidden messages of children's films.* Santa Barbara, CA: Praeger.

Braidotti, R. (2013). *The posthuman.* Cambridge, UK: John Wiley & Sons.

Bruckner, L. D. (2010). *Bambi* and *Finding Nemo*: A sense of wonder in the wonderful world of Disney? In P. Willoquet-Maricondi (Ed.), *Framing the world: Explorations in ecocriticism and film* (pp. 187–205). Charlottesville, VA: University of Virginia Press.

Byrne, E., & McQuillan, M. (1999). *Deconstructing Disney.* London: Pluto Press.

Carson, R. (2002). *Silent spring.* New York: Mariner. (Original work published in 1962.)

Cartmill, M. (1993). The Bambi syndrome. *Natural History, 102*(6), 6–13.

Chase, C., Thorne, M. (Producers), & Trenbirth, S. (Director). (2003). *The jungle book 2* [Motion picture]. United States: Walt Disney Pictures.

Collins, P. (1999). Two worlds. On *Tarzan: An original Walt Disney Records soundtrack* (CD). Burbank, CA: Walt Disney Records.

Collins, P. (2003). Great spirits [Recorded by T. Turner]. On *Brother bear: An original Walt Disney Records soundtrack* (CD). Burbank, CA: Walt Disney Records.

Del Vecho, P., Lasseter, J. (Producers), Clements, R., & Musker, J. (Directors). (2009). *The princess and the frog* [Motion picture]. United States: Walt Disney Pictures.

Disney, W. (Producer), Geronimi, C., Clark, L., Larson, E., & Reitherman, W. (Directors). (1959). *Sleeping beauty* [Motion picture]. United States: Walt Disney Productions.

Disney, W. (Producer), Geronimi, C., Jackson, W., Luske, H., & Kinney, J. (Directors). (1953). *Peter Pan* [Motion picture]. United States: Walt Disney Productions.

Disney, W. (Producer), Cottrell, W., Hand, D., Jackson, W., Morey, L., Pearce, P., & Sharpsteen, B. (Directors). (1937). *Snow White and the seven dwarfs* [Motion picture]. United States: Walt Disney Productions.

Disney, W. (Producer), & Hand, D. (Director). (1942). *Bambi* [Motion picture]. United States: Walt Disney Productions.

Disney, W. (Producer), & Reitherman, W. (Director). (1967). *The jungle book* [Motion picture]. United States: Walt Disney Productions.

Disney, W. (Producer), & Sharpsteen, B. (Director). (1941). *Dumbo* [Motion picture]. United States: Walt Disney Productions.

Disney, W. (Producer), Sharpsteen, B., & Luske, H. (Directors). (1940). *Pinocchio* [Motion picture]. United States: Walt Disney Productions.

Eisenberg, C. (2014). *The carnivore way: Coexisting with and conserving North America's predators.* Washington, DC: Island Press.

Epley, N., Waytz, A., & Cacioppo, J. T. (2007). On seeing human: A three-factor theory of anthropomorphism. *Psychological Review, 114*(4), 864.

Estrella, R. (Producer), Geronimi, C., Jackson, W., & Luske, H. (Directors). (1951). *Alice in Wonderland* [Motion picture]. United States: Walt Disney Productions.

Foltz, B. V. (2006). The resurrection of nature: Environmental metaphysics in Sergei Bulgakov's *Philosophy of economy. Philosophy and Theology, 18*(1), 121–142.

Former Beatle "inspired by Bambi." (2005, December). *BBC News.* Retrieved from http://news.bbc.co.uk/2/hi/entertainment/4520658.stm

Giroux, H. A. (1999). *The mouse that roared: Disney and the end of innocence.* New York: Rowman & Littlefield.

Grauerholz, L. (2007). Cute enough to eat: The transformation of animals into meat for human consumption in commercialized images. *Humanity & Society, 31*(4), 334–354.

Hahn, D. (Producer), Allers, R., & Minkoff, R. (Directors). (1994). *The lion king* [Motion picture]. United States: Walt Disney Pictures.

Hahn, D. (Producer), Trousdale, G., & Wise, K. (Directors). (1996). *The hunchback of Notre Dame* [Motion picture]. United States: Walt Disney Pictures.

Haraway, D. (1991). *Simians, cyborgs, and women*. New York: Routledge.

Hastings, A. W. (1996). Bambi and the hunting ethos. *Journal of Popular Film and Television, 24*(2), 53–59.

Hibler, W. (Producer), & Reitherman, W. (Producer/Director). (1970). *The Aristocats* [Motion picture]. United States: Walt Disney Productions.

Hooks, E. (2005). *Acting in animation: A look at 12 films*. Portsmouth, NH: Heinemann.

Hyun, E. (2005). How is young children's intellectual culture of perceiving nature different from adults? *Environmental Education Research 11*(2), 199–214.

Jacobson, H. (1997). *Seriously funny: From the ridiculous to the sublime*. London: Viking.

John, E., & Rice, T. (1994). Circle of life [Recorded by E. John]. On *The Lion King: Original Motion Picture Soundtrack* (CD). Santa Monica, CA: BOP Recording Studios.

Kahn, P. H., & Kellert, S. R. (Eds.) (2002). *Children and nature: Psychological, sociocultural, and evolutionary investigations*. Cambridge, MA: MIT Press.

Kellert, S. R. (1998). *A national study of outdoor wilderness experience*. New Haven, CT: School of Forestry and Environmental Studies, Yale University. Retrieved from: http://www.childrenandnature.org/uploads/kellert.complete.text.pdf

King, M. J. (1996). The audience in the wilderness: The Disney nature films. *Journal of Popular Film and Television, 24*(2), 60–68.

Klein, N. (2014). *This changes everything: Capitalism vs. the climate*. Simon and Schuster.

Louv, R. (2005). *Last child in the woods: Saving our children from nature-deficit disorder*. Chapel Hill, NC: Algonquin Books of Chapel Hill.

Lutts, R. (1992). The trouble with *Bambi*: Walt Disney's *Bambi* and the American vision of nature. *Forest and Conservation History, 26*, 160–171.

MacGregor, C. (2010). *Partnering with nature: The wild path to reconnecting with the earth*. New York: Atria Books.

Melson, G. F. (2001). *Why the wild things are: Animals in the lives of children*. Cambridge, MA: Harvard University Press.

Miller, S., & Rode, G. (1995). The movie you see, the movie you don't: How Disney do's that old time derision. In L. Haas, E. Bell, & L. Sells (Eds.), *From Mouse to Mermaid* (pp. 86–104). Bloomington: Indiana University Press.

Mitchell, R. W., Thompson, N. S., & Miles, H. L. (Eds.). (1997). *Anthropomorphism, anecdotes, and animals*. Albany, NY: SUNY Press.

Musker, J. (Producer/Director), Ashman, H. (Producer), & Clements, R. (Director). (1989). *The little mermaid* [Motion picture]. United States: Walt Disney Pictures.

Nature Conservancy. (2011). Connecting America's youth to nature. Retrieved from http://www.nature.org/newsfeatures/kids-in-nature/youth-and-nature-poll-results.pdf

Orr, D. (1992). *Ecological literacy: Education and the transition to a postmodern world*. Albany, NY: SUNY Press.

Pentecost, J. (Producer), Gabriel, M., & Goldberg, E. (Directors). (1995). *Pocahontas* [Motion picture]. United States: Walt Disney Pictures.

Pike, D. M. (2012). *Enviro-toons: Green themes in animated cinema and television.* Jefferson, NC: McFarland.

Reben, M. (1991). Night song. In L. Anderson (Ed.), *Sisters of the earth* (pp. 132–133). New York: Random House.

Reitherman, W. (Producer/Director). (1973). *Robin Hood* [Motion picture]. United States: Walt Disney Productions.

Schumacher, T. (Producer), Butoy, H., & Gabriel, M. (Directors). (1990). *The rescuers down under* [Motion picture]. United States: Walt Disney Pictures.

Selhub, E. M., & Logan, A. C. (2012). *Your brain on nature: The science of nature's influence on your health, happiness and vitality.* Toronto, Canada: John Wiley & Sons.

Stefanovic, I. L. (2004). Children and the ethics of place. In B. V. Foltz & R. Frodeman (Eds.), *Rethinking nature* (pp. 55–76). Bloomington: Indiana University Press.

Sternberg, E. H. (2009). *Healing spaces: The science and health of well-being.* Cambridge, MA: Harvard University Press.

Thomas, F., & Johnston, O. (1981). *Disney animation: The illusion of life.* New York: Abbeville Press.

Thoreau, H. D. (1981). *Walking.* In L. Owens (Ed.), *Works of Henry David Thoreau.* New York: Avenel Books. (Original work published in 1862.)

Thoreau, H. D. (2011). The animal in us. In J. S. Cramer (Ed.), *The quotable Thoreau* (p. 390). Princeton, NJ: Princeton University Press. (Original work published in 1852.)

Van Lawick, H. (Director/Producer), & Goodall, J. (1963). *Miss Goodall and the wild chimpanzees* [Documentary]. United States: National Geographic Society.

Vernon, A. (2008). *On Tarzan.* Athens, GA: University of Georgia Press.

Wells, P. (2009). *The animated bestiary: Animals, cartoons, and culture.* New Brunswick, NJ: Rutgers University Press.

Whitley, D. (2013). *The idea of nature in Disney animation: From Snow White to WALL-E.* Farnham, UK: Ashgate.

Williams, C. (Producer), Blaise, A., & Walker, R. (Directors). (2003). *Brother bear* [Motion picture]. United States: Walt Disney Productions.

Wilson, E. O. (1984). *Biophilia.* Cambridge, MA: Harvard University Press.

Part II

Buying Disney

Commodified, Caricatured, and
Contested Subjectivities

7 I Dream of a Disney World

Exploring Language, Curriculum, and Public Pedagogy in Brazil's Middle-Class Playground

Sandro R. Barros

In many ways, the levels of income disparity that characterize Brazil as the seventh largest world economy are counterintuitive. In spite of great progress in the recent decade in the form of direct financial assistance programs (Nobrega, 2013), wealth concentration still represents a serious challenge in a nation of 200.4 million citizens aspiring to class mobility (OECD, 2014). Still, when examining the characteristics of Brazil's income disparities, we encounter peculiar economic data. This nation's tourist sector occupies one of the leading positions in the number of international visitors to Walt Disney World (Stratton & Fernandez, 2014). In fact, Brazilian tourists who traveled abroad in 2014 outspent most nations of the globe, averaging a total of US $2,956 (Mebane, 2014). But in a country where the average minimum wage in 2013 was approximately US $350 a month (Ministério do Trabalho e Emprego), the popular *viagem à Disney* (Disney trip) constitutes a notable personal sacrifice, particularly considering the lack of disposable income of the average middle class.

It is precisely within the idiosyncrasies present in Brazil's concentration of wealth that the Disney trip emerges as a social narrative worth exploring. How individuals engage with the Disney trip as a life goal allows for a nuanced understanding of how less affluent middle classes are able to concretize their 'dream of Disney' through discursive practices that pedagogically reify the cultural logic of neoliberalism represented by Disney World. As Clavé (2007) remarks, theme parks do not merely represent "a system of escape from the daily routine" (p. 5); they are places with a didactic vocation. Thus, sketching those instances in which the Disney trip becomes normalized as an identifiable discourse, attached to specific social realities and productively becoming culture through language—as I do in this chapter—can reveal how consumption patterns naturalize the Disney theme park experience as ideology. The ways Brazilians express themselves publicly in relationship to Disney World reveal a form of citizenship pedagogy that underwrites the Disney trip as part of a curriculum for class membership. This pedagogy, instituted through 'ready-made' language, is part of a broader acquisitional discourse carrying ideological parameters that define semantic fields (Bourdieu, 1991) for the negotiation of the meaning of citizenship in relation to consumption.

Mapping the Location of the Disney Trip Discourse

While various studies have deconstructed the meaning of Disney's products in relationship to the specificity of their reception in Latin America, particularly in regards to the Good Neighbor Policy years and Disney (e.g., Parker, 1991; Smoodin, 2013), fewer studies have been concerned with the ways the company's 'magic' is manifested in the middle class's Disney trip as ideology. I supplement this analytical lacuna by examining how the theme park experience is constructed through public discourse in Brazil. I argue that the ways Brazilians talk about the Disney trip advance models for citizenship identification that discursively articulate the 'dream of Disney' as a linguistic ritual. This ritual comprises embodied language inasmuch as it introduces speech acts that are yet to be embodied by subjects who aspire to engage with what characterizes the middle class's "linguistic market" (Bourdieu, 1991). By describing the linguistic ritualization of the 'dream of Disney,' I hope to verify the degree to which individuals produce and reproduce language in response to Disney's broader marketing appeal.

While consumption as a form of 'reproductive being-ness' rooted in materialism can be argued as the apogee of neoliberalism's control over the individuality of experiences, i.e., companies attempt to manage consumers' experiences, what epitomizes Disney's successful 'pedagogy' is the fact that it cuts across cultural contexts. Disney's public pedagogy—the company's incitement of desire, needs and modes of consent among its consumers (Giroux, 2003)—works well precisely because the company anchors its products in the immateriality of broad signifiers such as 'dreams,' 'hopes,' 'childhood,' 'freedom,' etc. As Arvidsson (2005) notes, the means of consumption offered by many of today's companies "rely on the active involvement of the consumers to produce the desired experience" (p. 246). This is to say companies rely on consumers' immaterial labor by providing consumers with the "contours of and raw material for the exercise of their productive agency [while] consumers are free to themselves produce a set of social relations and shared meanings—a common" (p. 247).

Brazilians' trip to Disney, whether as desire or realization, creates a virtual space akin to what Arvidsson (2005) defines as a "common," a space where consumers construct social relations and craft shared meanings. The middle class's sense of pertinence to this common, which can appear, for instance, in the form of social media platforms, invites Brazilian subjects to embody consumption values espoused by the richer 'successful' Other—in this case, Disney, which functions as a synecdoche of the United States. This embodiment of US models of capitalism is implicit in the discourses that individuals produce at the encounter with the theme park or while preparing for the Disney World trip experience.

Yet, consumers' potential to make meaning—their "productive agency" (Arvidsson, 2005)—is restricted by how Disney manages the order and immateriality of signs around its products. These signs, which are part of the company's broad marketing strategy, underscore individualism above all things. In other words, the only collaborative aspects implicit in the consumption of the Disney theme park experience are those that the company sets as policies within its corporatized domains, within which visitors must, of course, operate and to which they must conform as a price to be paid for admission into the Magic Kingdom and all it represents.

In order to illustrate the complex manifestation of what I call "the Disney trip discourse" in Brazil, I randomly selected two blogs among the millions available online. My choice for a randomized selection of textual material obeys a few particular principles concerning how one epistemologically approaches data. I believe, siding with Fairclough (2001), that the study of any text, when one accounts for the social conditions of production and interpretation, can reveal much about: (1) the order of discourse itself, i.e., the institutional sanctioning of spaces and mechanisms that allow individuals access to a voice *per se* (Foucault, 2002); and (2) the exposition of common-sensical assumptions that "are ideologically shaped by relations of power" through language practiced socially (Fairclough, 2001).

My choice of the blog medium as a representative sample for analysis presents advantages not only in terms of ease of access to the validation of subjects' lives in their own public words, but also in terms of how the medium allows for the observation of dialogical interventions in social phenomena as an ongoing process through blog posts' responses. The archived nature of blogs makes them "amenable to examining social processes over time," which is in itself conducive to an interpretative cohesion when approaching research texts dynamically (Hookway, 2008, p. 91).

Brazilian Disney blogs are incredibly similar in how they display a linguistic arsenal expressing the 'consumption/inclusion' dyad as a cultural rationality. In many blogs, subjects express the impetus to help others *chegar lá* ("to arrive there," a much repeated expression) in a way that appears not only pedagogical, in the traditional sense of the word, but also declarative of an operating cultural curriculum materialized by the ways subjects talk about Disney. Tips on financial planning, the dissection of the ins and outs of Disney parks, as well as opinions about the nature of the Disney experience as a dream of consumption suggest not only the Disney trip as a form of social practice within the Brazilian context, but also as a type of acquired language. Following Foucault (2002), we could argue that subjects who partake in the Disney trip establish themselves as discourse inasmuch as they are established by the discourses they have at their disposal. These discourses, acting as if they had a life of their own, communicate ideology *through*

Disney-goers, even if Disney-goers themselves may superficially alter the direction of discussions on the significance of the theme park experience by reproducing acquired language about the company *with difference*.

"I Bring My Own Cooler to Disney": Challenging Consumption within Middle-Class Normativity

Among the roughly one million entries yielded from a Google search of the key terms "Brazilian, Blogs, and Disney," one finds Patricia Vargas's blog *www.bempaticinha.com*, which the author has maintained since January 2013. The site could be best characterized as an autobiographical lifestyle magazine whereby Patricia documents, through videologs and written posts, frequent visits to malls and fashion fairs. The site often blends what appears to be a direct marketing sales pitch on feminine beauty products with intimate snapshots of the blogger's family life. The videos and images that populate *www.bempatricinha.com* are stylistically edited, as are Patricia's appearances in front of the camera. The term '*bem Patricinha*' (very Patty), which gives the blog its title, alludes to the diminutive form of Patricia in Portuguese. It functions both as a signifier for the blogger's name and as the designation of the Brazilian version of the stereotypical US 'valley-girl' from the 1980s. Indeed, Patricia's public image addresses viewers through a type of com-moditized self-fashioned imagery whose message, in essence, remains cognizant of the fact that in the virtual world one is what one desires to appear.

Yet, what stands out as noteworthy about *www.bempatricinha.com* is how the blog functions as a vehicle for the expression of a bourgeois consumer sensitivity that pedagogically legitimizes neoliberalism's zeitgeist to viewers. It also underscores how Disney, as a commons, enables Brazilian visitors to engage their understanding of cosmopolitanism through the status represented by the Disney park as a specific cultural practice. In one of Patricia's video entries titled "Pobreza de brasileiro na Disney," the blogger recounts a family visit to Disney World in which several Brazilian tourists are reported to have regarded her with utmost disdain after noticing that she had brought a cooler filled with snacks into the park (April 26, 2014). As Patricia describes this episode, other nearby Brazilians stared at her as if she were "the world's poorest person" (*como se eu fosse a maior pobre do mundo*). The entry further develops into a diatribe in which the author continuously defends herself against the disparaging looks of her compatriots. Patricia makes no mention in her post of any dialogue exchange that explains why she felt judged to be a poor person; she merely reacts with repulsion to what she perceives to be an unfair class-based assessment based on her act of bringing a cooler into the park.

Indeed, within traditional Brazilian bourgeoisie demeanor, bringing food into public parks or corporate spaces constitutes what is commonly referred to as *uma falta de classe*, literally "a lack of class." This gesture, however, represents not only a symbolic transgression on the public space as a culture, as de Certeau (2011) contends, but also a transgression of a societal norm underwritten by the Brazilian middle class. In this sense, Patricia's "I am not poor" reaction is striking because it defies the middle-class order of discourse by contesting, through new forms of identification, what it means for Brazilian foreign visitors to behave like the poor. Put differently, the ways in which one chooses to consume goods as a public performance are tied to how individuals envision their social location and the status afforded by one's presence in restricted public spaces.

It is well to note that at no point in "Pobreza de brasileiro" does Patricia denounce Disney's pricing practices as unjust, which may have led her to bring a cooler filled with snacks from home. Nor does the blogger argue that one should forgo shopping while in the park. Rather, Patricia clarifies to viewers that the act of bringing a cooler and choosing to refuse purchasing overpriced goods at Disney constitutes a personal choice. Hence, the emphasis is on the self's empowerment within capitalism. As Patricia didactically argues throughout her blog's entries, we are individually responsible for making informed decisions not only about *what* to consume but also *how*. Thus, www.bempatricinha.com could be read as a manual of sorts whose discursive action connotes, denotes, and legitimizes what constitutes the dos and don'ts of a responsible global consumer.

There is, indeed, a liturgical quality to Patricia's didacticism concerning what it means to behave like a poor person. For example, the excessive repetition of the personal pronoun "I" when the blogger defends herself against the disparaging looks of her compatriots underscores to readers the 'self-made wo/man' mythology that rejects poverty on the grounds of how hard one works. In various occasions Patricia states that because she earns her own money, she can therefore consume as she pleases. These statements are certainly consistent with neoliberal ideology, particularly in reference to self-determination, economic agency, and choice. Yet, Patricia's statement of "I work hard not to be poor" fundamentally reveals a type of self-defensive articulation that frames poverty as an insult. In the commentary sections of "Pobreza de brasileiro," Patricia's readers similarly adopt the same orientation that she gives to the terms 'poverty' and 'poor' by reproducing these terms in their responses. What eventually emerges from the "dialogues" between Patricia and her audience is a discursive rationale that attributes new forms of citizenship to the middle class that now can access the Disney park. In this context, the "I am not poor" (*eu não sou pobre*) statement is evoked as a defense against any judgment on the ways one chooses to consume at the amusement park. In reaction to this judgment, Patricia is keen on providing her own lessons on how one should determine appropriateness and value through how one chooses to consume a given product. This is to say, when being looked down as if she "were the world's poorest person," Patricia claims that "hard work" trumps traditional views on how individuals should perform consumption. Put differently, hard work affords individuals the right to consume Disney as they please. Poverty no longer exclusively signifies scarcity of resources. It means an attitude, a way in which individuals choose to react amidst the many choices they have to consume a product. As one of Patricia's readers, Franciele, reflects in reaction to the cooler episode: "*Ay!* *It's something typical of Brazilians*, really, *but of Brazilians who are spiritually poor.* I super agree with your attitude, girl. *I myself* when *I travel I bring my own* snacks. Even when I go to work *I bring my own* lunch. *We know* where our $$ comes from and *how much we struggle to earn it*" (April 26, 2014, my italics).

In the aforementioned entry, we notice how Franciele's commentary displaces the signifier 'poverty' to the realms of the immaterial. She redescribes poverty as a spiritual condition, which should be attributed to those workers who identify themselves as industrious members of a hardworking class. Her comments suggest that hard work, more so than tradition, affords individuals their right to consume goods and publicly perform this consumption as they see fit. Nevertheless, there are still proper ways to consume at Disney. But rather than propriety being defined within what traditional bourgeois logic sets as normativity, the 'spiritually rich' middle-class consumer places a greater emphasis on the recognition of his or her knowledge and power to spend his or her hard-earned money responsibly.

Within this socio-cultural rationale, what characterizes one's moral deficiency—read exclusion—is a type of consumption performed without cognition of one's 'hard-earned money.' Put in another way, as Franciele's comments articulate, those who judge an individual bringing a cooler into Disney as a behavior attributed to the poor are, in fact, the ones who are 'spiritually poor.' This rationale, of course, is devoid of any consideration of what fundamentally characterizes poverty: income inequality across social classes, which restricts access to goods and services. Franciele's discourse, like Patricia's, frames poverty as an insult. The anaphoric "I" that Franciele restates from Patricia's original post is also particularly telling of the neoliberal subject's urgency to link hard work to freedom to consume as one chooses to. In this sense, both Patricia and Franciele's exchanges confirm what many critics of neoliberalism have underscored. Culture has become implicated as a set of practices in which consumption is the only viably pragmatic form of citizenship (Gammon, 2012; Giroux, 2014). As a determinant logic of our times, neoliberalism's zeitgeist, according to Giroux (2014), is "steeped in the language of self-help, individual responsibility and is purposely blind to inequalities in power, wealth and income and how they bear down on the fate of individuals and groups."

If we follow Giroux's assertion, we notice that the exchanges between Patricia and her readers do not elicit any form of consciousness regarding inequality and availability of work at a superstructural level. This is to say, as Franciele centers her commentaries on the culture of spending money according to one's means, she disregards the fact that not all individuals are able to work and have their work valued equally in society. The fact that an increasing number of Brazilians from lower sections of the middle class are now able to afford the Disney trip, and challenge consumption practices based on the limits of their income, does indeed defy exclusionary practices characteristic of capitalism. Yet, as Brazilian consumers defy tradition through the ways they choose to consume Disney, they do so in a way that remains unaware of the consequences of discursively—and quite aggressively— conflating spiritual richness with work ethics and consumption. For the value of labor is not a choice; it is a function of an economic system that depends on the exploitation of workers to produce "surplus value" (Marx, 1867/ 1977), regardless of the status afforded by the Disney trip.

Lessons in their own right, Patricia's posts ultimately publicly reinscribe a curriculum for wellbeing through the testimony of what she experiences as a Disney consumer. As the entry "Pobreza de brasileiro" illustrates, consumption is an "active and emotional process" through which the self's performance serves as evidence of the efficacy of current neoliberal paradigms of living (Miles, 2012, p. 228). For many Brazilian tourists, testimonies such as Patricia's legitimize those ideals of success that are represented by what the Disney trip means as a public curriculum symbolic of personal success and achievement for the Brazilian middle class. If followed and properly 'studied,' this curriculum can lead middle-class identified subjects to a sense of inclusion, even if participating in its discourse through virtual fora, such as social media platforms. For speaking about Disney also means tapping into a culture that is powerfully imagined by a multiform global community. Thus, it necessarily involves a common imagination around shared texts (Anderson, 1991). Whether or not the concretization of the *viagem a Disney* for many Brazilians represents sign of status, speaking about Disney World and acquiring the many discourses generated by individuals' adoption of neoliberal ideology in terms of personal effort, consumer power and the illusion of choice can equally signify one's entrance into the Magic Kingdom. I develop this particular hypothesis further in the next section of this chapter.

Loucos por Disney: Dreaming as Commodity

If the trip to Disney represents a tangible reality for many Brazilians identified with the middle class like Patricia, for others Disney constitutes an aspiration, an objective of consumption yet to be acquired. This object of consumption is framed by many bloggers as an experience akin to overcoming arduous obstacles, the theme park as the 'conquest' of a commonly shared ideal. The term 'conquest' (*conquista*) is meaningful in the sense that this lexical choice advances the notion of the dream of the Disney trip not only as a 'thing' residing outside individuals, but also as a struggle to possess, reflecting, in fact, a colonial odyssey. In other words, one struggles to conquer the dream that inherently belongs to one's self; making this dream real implies reintroducing it within one's *lebenswelt* as a product for identification as well as for consumption.

Lexical choices that frame dreaming as a process of acquisition appear throughout many Disney blogs; one dreams to *have* the dream in a physical sense. Among these blogs one finds Cristiane Araújo's *Loucos por Disney* (http://loucospordisney-cristianearaujo.blogspot.com.br). Cristiane, a self-confessed Disney fanatic, has maintained her blog sporadically since 2007 (she has recently deleted pages before 2015). Cristiane's profile describes her as a university student, "in search of a dream" (*Eu estou em busca de um sonho*). Like millions of children, Cristiane's introduction to the world of Disney came through television cartoons, which she reports watching transfixed as a child. Cristiane's blog photos display a myriad of advertising pictures with models smiling and posing for pictures in conventional Disney World tour sites. Cristiane emulates these pictures by posing and dressing herself as a high fashion model and by photoshopping her image into the park. This articulation of Cristiane's public persona, which resembles supermodel photographs in editorial fashion magazines, clashes against the childlike quality that is apparent both in the design of her homepage and throughout the content of entries. The color pink, the tiled background filled with Disney princess representations, and the logotype *Loucos por Disney* in the shape of a butterfly, correspond to signs that cue to readers how to perceive the author's public persona. Cristiane asserts unabashedly that the "little girl inside . . . grew up but never stopped dreaming." The articulation of Cristiane's public self leaves room for ambiguity, as one wonders whether the blogger is a grown woman or a teenager. Frequently, Cristiane bids readers farewell with the customary interjectional kisses to the imagined and hoped for an audience: "*Mil beijos a todos vocês*" (a thousand kisses to you all). The page's counter indicates that Cristiane has no subscribed followers.

Throughout several posts, Cristiane's rhetoric style showing enthusiasm for all things Disney evokes a type of authenticity that is essential to autobiographical writings' credibility. It is precisely through this articulation of a relatable public self that Cristiane discloses how deeply Disney is entrenched in her personality. She does so not only by referencing common cultural identifications, but also by framing Disney's multiple signifiers as part of her essence as a dreamer. Pictures wherein Cristiane inserts herself playing the role of a park visitor abound throughout her blog entries, as if the blogger attempts to live the dream of Disney to the extent technology enables her to. These pictures do not make the simulacrum, the hyperrealism of this —for now—impossible encounter between Disney World and Cristiane less truthful in terms of the emotional impact on the account of the virtual effect (c.f. Baudrillard, 1994). The predominance of these images in her blog pedagogically frames to others the possibility of living a pseudo-reality, one through which Cristiane's personal life, in fact anyone's life, can be re-imagined and fused into a 'concrete,' visualizable life project in the present. In this sense, Cristiane's blog functions as a proxy for Disney values that she re-imagines and reproduces as her own, consciously positioning herself as Walt Disney's teacher apprentice. She is, confessedly, a consumer who is taught how to dream by the company. As Cristiane notes using the third person in reference to herself, "With Disney's magic she learned to believe even more in her dreams."

Throughout Cristiane's entries, the 'magic' of the Disney park, Disney's own discourse of consumption, and the company's own organization of signs for consumers' identification not only reveal the existence of a pedagogy for dreaming, but also implicate how dreaming of Disney affects individuals in a fundamental level. In a Happy Father's Day message on her Facebook page, Cristiane writes:

> Today I want to say Happy Fathers Day *to the father of all this magic*, even though this guy (Walt Disney) is no longer with us on Earth, he continues to enchant us with his stories that *teach us how to dream*, and to believe that everything is possible! And to fathers everywhere, I wish you all a Happy Father's Day. LOL.

Two things are worth noting in this entry besides the characteristic tenderness with which Cristiane refers to Walt Disney. First, Cristiane's discourse shifts between the first and third person, implying a divorce between her adult self and the imagined personality of childhood that she cultivates. As Cristiane explains, she has been insistently re-drafting an old drawing since early childhood. This drawing shows an older girl taking a younger one by the hand to the gates of Walt Disney World, suggested as a type of heavenly gate. Second, embedded within this subjectivity split, which is marked by the self-reference in the third person, Cristiane invokes Disney as a sliding signifier for the father figure whom she admits never knowing. The artist is acknowledged both as the father she never had and as the pedagogue who actually "teaches us how to dream." Cristiane furthermore reflects upon her own self and role as the teacher of "the little girl inside." As the blogger writes, "I will show to this little girl that exists inside of me the kind of Disney that she always dreamed of knowing, the Disney *that was worth dreaming of*, and believe that dreams can come true!" [my italics].

Within what can be considered a truly perverse logic, Cristiane, representing the neoliberal subject-dreamer, ultimately divulges her own dream as a form of dispossession. The blogger sees Disney as a dream that she imagines, but that nevertheless does not truly belong to her, for she still needs to afford it. While personal, Cristiane's framing of the Disney dream is not restricted to the intimate. As she frames it, dreaming of Disney, the experience of the theme park can only be made meaningful at this stage in her life if tapped into a community, imagined as a collective saga. As Cristiane writes,

I thank you all for following me on my Facebook page and my blog. Thank you so much you guys!! I am very happy for you being with me and accompanying me in this dream of mine, *and dreaming it with me*, I know that soon, soon *we will all make our dreams come true*!!! Kisses!! °o° [my italics]

One notices here how Cristiane frames herself as a point of reference for an imagined community *to* and *for* whom she writes. In other words, she imagines the audience as the object-learners of what her blog has to teach. The urgency to express the trip to Disney as a collective endeavor, besides being supported by the royal 'we,' is also characterized by how Cristiane qualifies the dream of Disney as "saga." This word choice, arguably heroic, captures what middle-class travelers undergo in order to actualize their dream of Disney inasmuch as it underscores the "immaterial labor" produced for Disney in the process of preparing for the dream (Hardt & Negri, 2000). For beyond facing common financial exigencies, Brazilians wishing to go to Disney are subjected to complex visa bureaucracies, to which they must prove ownership of property, ties to Brazil through letters from employers, etc. Surpassing these obstacles requires, indeed, a great deal of sacrifice.

Cristiane represents the millions of Brazilians who do not have the means to travel abroad. The blogger does invoke, however, those common tropes that are part of Disney travelers' discursive imagination as if she were able to travel. Cristiane proves herself to be extremely knowledgeable of Disney's history in her entries inasmuch as she demonstrates knowledge of the geography of Disney parks' attractions and tourist tips. Through the performance of this knowledge, Cristiane illustrates how Disney language has become ritualized among those travelers wishing to visit Disney World. "Come with me," "dream with me," "let us conquer this together" are phrases that she commonly repeats, as do other Disney bloggers. This ritualized speech identifies subjects as a community and conjures a communal sense of Disney. The repetition of advertising expressions such as "come travel with me" and "come share my dream" become a cohesive force of identification that has the power to unite individuals as an "imagined community" (Anderson, 1991). Membership to this consumer "commons" (Arvidsson, 2005), besides revealing the proclaimed subjects' love for what Disney represents, inevitably entails consuming the park and its various attachments. This consumption requires, nevertheless, intricate and multiple displays of symbolic affections, not only as simple as acquiring a t-shirt or watching a Disney movie. In fact, the consumption of the Brazilian dream of Disney requires, in particular, that Disney-goers adopt language that both enables and embodies a common understanding of the significance of Disney signs and rituals to the community members' lives at large. This ultimately affords members distinction through knowledge of what constitutes a 'tasteful' consumption of the Disney trip and the specific rituals associated with it in the Brazilian context (c.f. Bourdieu, 1991). Moreover, the 'Disney language' present in many blogs injects the sort of repetitious resonance that is necessary to reinforce the notion that, through the alignment of one's goals with that of others, one actually belongs to a larger project than oneself, albeit still rooted in a neoliberal consumption-existence dyad.

Much like the repetition observed in liturgical texts, Cristiane's 'Disney discourse' materializes language that conflates the sacred and the profane in relation to Disney as a communitarian act that linguistically performs dreaming as consumption. Cristiane infuses her writings and video logs with "God willing" ("*Se Deus quiser*") expressions and religious optimism, underscoring the eerie similarity between Disney's slogans—e.g., "when you wish upon a star," "where dreams come true," etc. Surely, expressions that evoke "God" are not uncommon in colloquial Brazilian Portuguese, especially within discourses that are adopted to convey optimism for the future, greetings, farewells, etc., independently at times from one's actual belief in God. Yet, when Cristiane states on several of her entries that "Christ wants you to win," and "God willing *we will* achieve it," one cannot help but notice that the tenor of her utterances resembles the devotion of Pentecostal expressions, which in themselves are a perfect blend of the spiritualism represented by the desire for happiness in an afterlife, and the material pleasure present within the physical realm of lived experiences. Cristiane's adoption of this blended form of sacred and profane rhetoric is not altogether strange, as the growth of Pentecostalism in Latin America coincides with the rise of neoliberalism as a cultural phenomenon infusing every aspect of life as a justification for capitalism's "immoral morality" (Dean, 2012).

Dreaming, as faith, is therefore posited throughout *Loucos por Disney*'s entries as an acquisitional item, much in the way indulgences were previous to the Reformation. Yet, the subject's attachment to the immaterial, to God, requires that one anchors one's faithfulness and expressed desire through totems as a means of belonging, as well as embodying that which exists exclusively in the imaginary. In this sense, Disney operates very much in parallel to traditional religious systems, wherein totems are used to center and root meaning that is expressed through immaterial signifiers such as love, happiness or faith. Indeed, what one could judge as fanaticism concerning Cristiane's "dreaming of Disney," the blogger herself considers "spiritual endurance," a need to prove her worth to gain entry into the Disney Magic Kingdom as a kind of heaven. The small Mickey Mouse tattoo that Cristiane wears behind her left ear serves as a stimulus, very much like the sign of the cross or any totem in which one would deposit, according to Jung (1964), one's faith in order to anchor a sense of identity in a momentary lapse of conscious control of what an experience means. As Cristiane states, her financial circumstances require she fights against all odds in order to achieve something that for her is a greater life, the Disney trip as a "saga." The task at hand might be quixotic, given economic exigencies. But for Cristiane, as Disney's motto suggests, "all dreams can be made real."

This statement is eerily similar to the biblical verses found in Philippians 4:13, which state, "I can do all things through Christ who strengthens me." Moreover, Cristiane's expression of a Disney dream manifested liturgically through *Loucos por Disney* affirms a type of identification in relationship to an existing social structure—religion—wherein the spectacle represented by the subject's performance of creed is, as Debord (1994) suggests, "the outcome and the goal of the dominant mode of production" (p. 5). The symbolic affiliation to the "Church of the Mouse" is, as it is for those who proclaim their faith in Christ, what ultimately affords citizenship, independently from differences in denominations, differences in ways of understanding the premised experience. Entering the Disney kingdom, in this sense, constitutes merely a rite of passage, like a journey to Mecca or Jerusalem, or receiving a sacrament.

Yet, the dream of Disney that is evoked throughout Cristiane's blog posts signifies the delusion of a dream inasmuch as it represents the dream itself. For the blogger's affirmation of her love for Disney, as complicated as it may be, does not constitute a mere passive consumption of the company's principles. When the blogger professes affections for Disney, she also unavoidably participates in a complex process of intervening in the Disney-as-ideology discourse as "a place where dreams come true." The blogger testifies to the company's benefits, to one's sense of wellbeing, through participating in the public perception of Disney as a producer-agent, thus adding surplus value to the Disney trip by talking about it even if in the conditional tense. The power of the discourse that derives from one's testimony of Disney, nevertheless, is obtained from the pleasure that the company enables consumers to feel in their quasi-religious experiences when arriving at the park. Subjects who locate themselves within Disney's pluralistic narrative structures personalize their experiences and feelings as conquerors of a dream. However, as Cristiane's blogs suggests, Disney's creation of a semantic, transterritorial multidimensional space wherein symbols operate within a characteristic logic (Disneyization), requires that the individuality of dreams become commercialized experiences whose pleasure can be attained only if the dream resides outside individuals' minds, consumed and acquiring meaning as 'experience' in the embodiment of Disney's signs. As Voloshinov, Matejka, and Titunik (1973) explain, there is "no experience outside of embodiment in signs . . . It is not experience that organizes expression, but the other way around—expression organizes experience. Expression is what first gives experience its form and specificity" (p. 85). In this sense, we are left to wonder, how much agency does the individual really have in creatively determining how he or she consumes ideas as products?

The answer, if we take into account Cristiane's and other Disney bloggers, appears pessimistically akin to an Orwellian neoliberal nightmare in which the control of language in relation to citizenship in a global society appears destined to confirm the grammatical corporatization of everyday life, those basic instances in which individuals are led to speak about their dreams as something to be acquired and conquered outside one's mind. Such is the process through which neoliberalism's ideology has come to colonize postmodern subjectivity; neoliberalism posits the essence of democracy as consumption. Disney bloggers confirm this particular viewpoint, as dreams imagine the Disney trip within pedagogically systematized ready-made experiences. In the context of these experiences, the act of choosing is merely an illusion, "a point in history [in] which nothing is true . . . history . . . vanishes into the microscopics or the stereophonics of news" (Baudrillard, 1995, p. 6). Alienated from truly agential reality, individuals become, as Baudrillard (1995) posits, "lost in space" (p. 2).

Concluding Remarks

As Cristiane notes in one of her video logs, "if you don't have a dream, you don't have a reason to live . . . and Disney teaches you how to dream." These words are particularly telling of how individuals find in Disney's premises not only a reason for living, but also a set of material principles that enable living itself. The trip to Disney that many Brazilians cultivate since childhood underscores The Walt Disney Company as the producer of a powerful public curriculum inasmuch as the company's marketing campaign embeds in individuals' cultures concrete linguistic practices at the pedagogical level. These practices confer attributes to Disney that characterize the company's existence as a slippery signifier that constantly 'breeds' speech acts endowed with what Dorfman and Mattelart (1986) term "auto-magic antibodies." These 'antibodies' constitute the immediate dismissal of any harsh criticism of the company and its products as an attack on individuals' ability to dream and aspire to universal values such as purity, childhood, and family life. As Dorfman and Mattelart (1986) observe, Disney discourse in fact neutralizes criticism because it culturally appeals and mobilizes association with values that are instilled into people in their early processes of socialization, "in the tastes, reflexes and attitudes which inform everyday experience at all levels" (p. 29).

Thus, when Cristiane asks her readers, "Pray for me . . . because there is a dream behind all of this," and Patricia reports on the ways that smart individuals consume Disney, one cannot be exactly sure if the "dream" and the choice of consuming Disney represents freedom or subjugation to what has already been decided in the sphere of mass production—the individual's 'infection' by Disney's "auto-magic antibodies." Still, for many Brazilians adept to Disney cultures, speaking publicly about the theme park ultimately means reifying a particular social rationale that insists upon the 'dream of Disney' as a form of heuristics for the very act of dreaming. It is apparent, however, that the costs of dreaming and 'speaking Disney' are unwittingly high in spaces wherein grave social inequalities persist as the norm, and broad access to the realization of the Disney trip as a dream continues to be restricted to a relatively small sector of the population.

References

Anderson, B. (1991). *Imagined communities: Reflections on the origin and spread of nationalism*. London: Verso.

Arvidsson, A. (2005). Brands: A critical perspective. *Journal of Consumer Culture, 5*(2), 235–258.

Baudrillard, J. (1994). *Simulacra and simulation*. Ann Arbor: University of Michigan Press.

Baudrillard, J. (1995). *The illusion of the end* (trans. C. Turner). Cambridge, UK: Polity Press.

Bourdieu, P. (1991). *Language and symbolic power*. Cambridge, MA: Harvard University Press.

Clavé, S. A. (2007). *The global theme park industry*. New York: CABI.

Dean, M. (2012). *The growth of Pentecostalism in Brazil*. Western Oregon History Department Working Papers. Retrieved from: http://digitalcommons.wou.edu/his/14

de Certeau, M. (2011). *The practice of everyday life*. Oakland: University of California Press.

Debord, G. (1994). *The society of the spectacle*. New York: Zone Books.

Dorfman, A., & Mattelart, A. (1986). *How to read Donald Duck: Imperialist ideology in the Disney comic*. New York: I. G. Editions.

Fairclough, N. (2001). *Language and power*. New York: Longman.

Foucault, M. (2002). *The order of things*. New York: Taylor & Francis.

Gammon, E. (2012). The psycho- and sociogenesis of neoliberalism. *Critical Sociology, 39*(4), 511–528. http://doi.org/10.1177/0896920512444634

Giroux, H. A. (2003). Public pedagogy and the politics of resistance: Notes on a critical theory of educational struggle. *Educational Philosophy and Theory, 35*(1), 5–16.

Giroux, H. A. (2004). Public pedagogy and the politics of neo-liberalism: Making the political more pedagogical. *Policy Futures in Education, 2*(3), 494–503.

Hardt, M., & Negri, A. (2000). *Empire*. Cambridge, MA: Harvard University Press.

Hookway, N. (2008). Entering the blogosphere: Some strategies for using blogs in social research. *Qualitative Research, 8*(1), 91–113.

Jung, C. G., & Franz, M.-L. von. (1964). *Man and his symbols*. Garden City, NY: Doubleday.

Marx, K. (1977). *Capital: A critique of political economy* (trans. B. Fowkes). New York: Vintage Books. (Original work published in 1867.)

Mebane, P. B. W. (2014, May 2). Where Brazilians go to splurge. *The New York Times*. Retrieved from: http://www.nytimes.com/2014/05/04/magazine/where-brazilians-go-to-splurge.html

Miles, S. (2012). The neoliberal city and the pro-active complicity of the citizen consumer. *Journal of Consumer Culture, 12*(2), 216–230.

Ministério do Trabalho e Emprego. (n.d.). Salário mínimo. Retrieved from: http://portal.mte.gov.br/sal_min/

Nobrega, C. (2013, November 5). Bolsa-Família: Template for poverty reduction or recipe for dependency? *The Guardian*. Retrieved from: http://www.theguardian.com/global-development-professionals-network/2013/nov/05/bolsa-familia-brazil-cash-transfer-system

OECD. (2014). *Better life index.* Retrieved from: http://www.oecdbetterlifeindex. org/countries/brazil

Parker, A. (1991). *Nationalisms and sexualities.* New York: Routledge.

Smoodin, E. (2013). *Disney discourse: Producing the Magic Kingdom.* New York: Routledge.

Stratton, J., & Fernandez, A. (2014). Brazilian visitors to Orlando now outnumber visitors from England. *Orlando Sentinel.* Retrieved from: http://articles.orlandosentinel.com/ 2014–06–29/business/os-brazil-tourists-now-tops-20140629_1_visit-orlando-universal-orlando-brazilian-tourism

Voloshinov, V. N., Matejka, L., & Titunik, I. R. (1973). *Marxism and the philosophy of language.* New York: Seminar Press.

8   If It Quacks Like a Duck . . .

The Classist Curriculum of Disney's Reality Television Shows

Robin Redmon Wright

A memory from my childhood has recently begun to haunt me. Sometime during my sixth grade year, my little sister and I arrived home from school, as we routinely did, before my mother got home from her job at the nearby shirt factory. Inevitably, we would occupy ourselves by watching television. At that time, television reception in rural East Tennessee was limited, and we received only two channels, NBC and CBS. One of the stations broadcast reruns of *The Beverly Hillbillies*. It was one of our favorites. Growing up in a poverty stricken offshoot of the Appalachian Mountains called the Cumberland Bowl, we found the characters of Granny, Pa, Jethro, and Elly May to be vaguely familiar, as was much of their vocabulary and accent. Of course, we recognized the absurdity of their reactions to the situations they encountered, but there was something oddly reminiscent of people we knew. The memory that haunts me is of my mother coming home one day to find us watching the show. My mother, who was forced in ninth grade to drop out of school to work, immediately turned off the television and told us we were not to watch *The Beverly Hillbillies*. She explained that she had watched it a few times when it had originally aired and was offended—insulted. A child of the depression, with 13 living brothers and sisters, of whom 11 were younger than she, my mother was an intelligent, wise, dignified woman, and she recognized the portrayal of negative stereotypes about her lived culture and the people who called the mountains around us home. She strongly objected. She said, "Robin, they're just making fun of people like us." Her words now resonate with me.

Whenever I am browsing television channels and pause on reality shows, I am reminded of that moment from my childhood and of my mother's admonition. Today, negative stereotypes about poor and working-class people are perpetuated on television in a much more insidious way—through the proliferation of 'reality' television (RTV). Programs like *Honey Boo Boo*, *Dirty Jobs*, and even *COPS* depict people who often conform to middle-class viewers' assumptions about the working class. Unlike situation comedies, these shows represent scripted scenarios as 'reality,' thus confirming assumptions and prejudices *as fact*. Such programs not only promote negative stereotypes of lower socio-economic groups, but they also affirm the *naturalness* of the ever-expanding wealth gap. They help curtail dissent and position the victims of inequitable structures of power and capital as culpable for their own oppression. Many may be surprised to learn that the media corporation responsible for the greatest proliferation of RTV programming is The Walt Disney Company. With programs like *Duck Dynasty*, *Swamp People*, and the many versions of *Storage Wars* proliferating Disney's many cable networks, it is important for educators and activists to analyze the cultural curriculum inherit in RTV.

In this chapter, I provide an analysis of a selection of Disney's RTV with respect to these questions: (1) What do they represent? (2) Why can they be viewed quite literally 24/7 on Disney-owned networks? and (3) What is Disney's agenda when producing RTV that targets adult audiences? The neoliberal response is that Disney is merely recognizing a demand and meeting it (Mirrlees, 2013). Miller (2010) suggests such programming is cheap to produce and "suffused with deregulatory *nostra* of avarice, possessive individualism, hyper-competitiveness, and commodification, played out in the domestic sphere rather than the public world" (pp. 160–162). In other words, they yield more bang for the buck, promote consumption, and advance a capitalistic worldview. These are certainly part of the impetus for such programming. Yet an analysis of these programs indicates a more surreptitious agenda behind their promotion, especially during an era when income and wealth disparity in the US is growing at record rates. I posit that these scripted programs serve to *stigmatize* poor and working-class people as deserving of their lower socioeconomic status. By depicting the working class and the poor as (1) content, even happy, to be poor; (2) proud of their ignorance and lack of social capital; and (3) undeserving of socialistic government programs that might provide opportunities for advancement, authentic education, and a robust social safety net, they provide viewers with a "stigma-theory, an ideology . . . [for] rationalizing an animosity based on . . . social class" (Goffman, 1963, p. 5). And it seems to be working.

Disney's Reality

According to Giroux (2010), "Disney has transformed culture into a pivotal educational force," a force that "offers no language for defining vital social institutions as a public good, links all dreams to the logic of the market, and harnesses the imagination to forces of unfettered consumerism" (p. 415). He points out that Disney has "ample funds to hire a battalion of highly educated and specialized experts to infiltrate the most intimate spaces" of peoples' lives (p. 415). These experts use state-of-the-art research techniques and cutting-edge ethnographic models to uncover ways to indoctrinate consumers, creating loyalty to the Disney brands, and turning that loyalty and consumers into commodities themselves. The practices described by Giroux make it evident that Disney has "disengaged itself from either moral considerations or the social good" (p. 414). And while much of Giroux's numerous critiques of Disney focus on the infiltration of childhood, I argue that critical educators also need to focus on its overarching curriculum aimed at adults that naturalizes a neoliberal capitalist doctrine.

Despite Disney's carefully crafted image as a wholesome, family-friendly entity, it is a vast and expanding corporate empire with annual revenues totalling $48 billion dollars (Iger, 2014), and like any other corporation, the goal of media giants like Disney is "profit maximization" (Mirrlees, 2013, p. 60). Although many people may not immediately associate RTV with The Walt Disney Company, the reality is (pun intended) that through its cable properties like the History Channel(s), the Biography Channel(s), the Lifetime Network, the ABC Network, ESPN Networks, and A&E, Disney produces a plethora of popular RTV programs. Gary Hoppenstand (2010) laments the loss of *history* on the History Channel: "If I wanted to watch some mindless reality program, I would turn to MTV" (p. 670). Many RTV programs depict individuals and/or groups with low socio-economic status, often located in the southeastern United States. In effect, these are programs *about* White working class and poor people.[1] Bourdieu and Passeron (1977) describe class as one's position in a hierarchy relative to economic, cultural, social, and symbolic capital—the gateways to healthcare, life quality, education, information, opportunity, and overall well-being. Beginning with the recent economic downturn, and especially since the recession of 2007, there has been an exponential proliferation of reality programs focused on the working class and working poor. No longer content to transform "childhood dreams into potential profits" (Giroux, 2000, p. 109), Disney now saturates cable television with RTV programs like *Duck Dynasty*, *Swamp People*, *Lady Hoggers*, and *Appalachian Outlaws*. To insure the widest possible audience in this age of mobile media consumption, Disney-ABC TV Group collaborated with Amazon.com and Netflix to stream Disney's digital TV content, and purchased equity interest in *Hulu* and *Fusion* (Mirrlees, 2013). Moreover, like their children's programing, some of these RTV shows have massive merchandising campaigns that include DVDs, bobble-heads, tee-shirts, coffee mugs, caps, key chains, videogames and, of course, lunch boxes.

The list of RTV programs on Disney networks is both long and expanding. Many are being shown in reruns, and new ones are added periodically. Figure 8.1 provides a partial list, and represents a selection of the Disney programs that feature primarily working-class people, their jobs, and their interactions around money and consumption, with special attention paid to the participants' cultural milieus, as well as the 'reality stars' themselves. As Giroux (2000) points out, Disney has mastered the art of infiltrating personal spaces with

Alaska Off Road Warriors	*Flipping Boston*
American Daredevils	*Flipping San Diego*
American Hoggers	*Flipping Vegas*
American Jungle	*Fix This Yard*
American Pickers	*Gods, Guns, and Automobiles*
American Restoration	*Great Lake Warriors*
Appalachian Outlaws	*Hardcore Pawn*
Ax Men	*Hatfields & McCoys*
Bad Ink	*Heavy*
Bamazon	*Hoarders*
Barry'd Treasure	*Ice Road Truckers*
Barter Kings	*Lady Hoggers*
Big Rig Bounty Hunters	*Mountain Men*
Big Shrimpers	*Mudcats*
Biker Battleground	*No Man's Land*
Billy the Exterminator	*Nor'easter Men*
Brandi & Jarrod: Married to the Job	*Obsessed*
Breaking Boston	*Parking Wars*
Cash Cowboys	*Pawn Stars*
Cajun Pawn Stars	*Rodeo Girls*
Cement Heads	*Shipping Wars*
Chasing Tail	*Sold!*
Counting Cars	*Storage Wars*
Country Buck$	*Storage Wars: New York*
Dark Horse Nation	*Storage Wars: Texas*
Dog, the Bounty Hunter	*Storage Wars: Vegas*
Down East Dickering	*Swamp People*
Duck Dynasty	*The Great Santini Brothers*
Extreme Makeover Home Edition	*The Legend of Shelby the Swamp Man*
Flip this House	*We're the Fugawis*

Figure 8.1 A Sampling of Disney-Owned Reality TV Programming

Information gathered from The Walt Disney Company (n.d.), and author's analysis of programs airing on Disney-owned networks.

its products and its ideals. With RTV, they haven't simply infiltrated personal space but have also inverted the concepts of the public and private spheres, making the private lives of the working-class public—and putting them on a t-shirt.

The Corporate Agenda of Constructed Reality

According to Miller (2010), reality television has its origins in "the activities of the Propaganda Ministry of the Nazi Party in the 1930s" with their popular program *Die Kriminalpolizei Warnt!* [The Criminal Investigation Department Warns!] (p. 162). Like today's catch-a-crook shows, it featured a host interviewing police about "unsolved cases and invited audiences to cooperate in catching opponents of the state" (p. 162). Boggs (2010) certainly makes a clear case for entertainment media as corporate ideological propaganda that perpetuates an imperial system of neoliberal state-corporate order.

He argues that corporate entertainment as a "propaganda apparatus" legitimates war-for-profit in a way that "surpasses any such apparatus in history" (p. 28). Miller (2010) points out that RTV programs are scripted, and the dialogue and drama are also scripted, just as in other genres. In 2005, a Cornell University study of US cable networks "found that reality shows accounted for 39 percent of writing jobs" (Miller, 2010, p. 161). Moreover, even when no script is mandated, Cooke-Jackson and Hansen (2008) found that

> the creators of reality television shows film hours of material and then edit those hours to create 30-, 60-, 90-, or 120-minute programs. By selecting or rejecting materials for the show, the content producer is indeed imposing his/her own definitions or stereotypes on the individuals included in the production.
>
> (p. 191)

Moore (2007) argues that RTV has "absorbed the popular demand to see and hear from regular people. . . . But these are more accurately described as simulations of democratic participation . . . neither 'real' nor entirely 'fake'" (p. 467). Citing Baudrillard, he describes RTV as a space of "hyperreality" where 'real' people perform scripts as "amateur actors" (p. 468). In a study of RTV viewers, Rose and Wood (2005) found that consumers, indeed, "blend fantastic elements of programming with indexical elements connected to their lived experiences to create a form of self-referential hyper-authenticity" (p. 284), and argue that RTV "contributes significantly to [viewers'] construction of social reality" (p. 295). Clearly, these shows do not represent 'mindless entertainment,' nor do they represent 'reality.'

Wood and Skeggs (2011) argue that reality shows mediate definitions of class, normalizing middle- and upper-class performance (the performative normative) by highlighting working-class deficits and promoting the myth of upward mobility. They posit that "it is important to discuss television's intervention in class formations, particularly at a time when political rhetoric is diverting the blame for structural inequality onto personal, individualized failure" (p. 2). The neoliberal agenda of blaming the poor for being poor is affirmed by showcasing poor and working-class 'ordinary' people enacting scripts that emphasize their 'difference' from middle-class viewers. If a number of them have achieved financial security, like the rags-to-riches backstory of the Robertson family in *Duck Dynasty*, their exaggerated lack of cultural capital (Bourdieu & Passeron, 1977) becomes the centerpiece of the show. They are depicted as struggling to stay true to their working-class roots (together with its crude and stereotypical views and practices) in spite of their new-found wealth—a veritable modern day *Beverly Hillbillies*.

Journalists in the popular press recognize the corporate agenda behind RTV. In a 2009 piece in *Vanity Fair*, James Wolcott announced, "Reality TV wages class warfare and promotes proletarian exploitation" (quoted in

Wood & Skeggs, 2011, p. 1). While there have been numerous studies exposing RTV's positioning of middle and upper-class lifestyles as normative and universal (Wood & Skeggs, 2011), that is only one subtext of RTV's message. Wood and Skeggs (2011) argue that RTV about 'ordinary' people is always about class and "espouses mobility and choice at precisely the same time as the gap between rich and poor widens and social mobility rates remain stagnant" (p. 2). In the rapidly shifting global economy the "new capitalist modes of production only reorganize those that cannot mobilize themselves around the shifting job market, leaving many . . . related to the mode of production by their very alienation from it, discarded (literally and metaphorically) as the 'waste' of the 'system'" (Wood & Skeggs, 2011, p. 4). RTV's focus on those alienated groups confirms in consumers' collective cultural psyche the neoliberal trope that the poor and working classes are deficient individuals from deficit cultures, not worthy of the opportunities inherit in the mythical American Dream.

Finally, the tactics used by corporations for reaffirming this modern myth are remarkably similar to the ways the image of the 'happy darkey' was propagated in popular culture around the turn of the twentieth century to justify the inequitable treatment of African Americans (Mellinger, 1992). Images that portrayed African Americans as content to serve Whites were crucial to composing the discourse of racism in a post-slavery world. In addition to my analysis of how RTV stigmatizes working-class cultures, I will also draw parallels between popular culture's positioning of African Americans in the post-Civil War South "as racial inferiors to justify and legitimate the apartheid power structures of America" (Mellinger, 1992, p. 18), and contemporary RTV depictions of a White working class that are used to justify and legitimate corporate abuse of working-class laborers and widening economic disparity. For the purposes of this chapter, I will structure my analysis around the three most common types of RTV foci: (1) people who work in low wage, difficult, dangerous, and/or disgusting occupations; (2) people who make, buy, repair, sell and/or barter *things* for profit; and (3) people who have rejected traditional employment altogether.

It's a Dirty Job: Working-Class Heroes

The first group of programs features jobs many viewers would not want to do. Programs like *Ice Road Truckers*, *Ax Men*, *Big Rig Bounty Hunters*, and *Great Lake Warriors* abound on Disney-owned networks. These programs idealize difficult, dangerous, working-class occupations and the men who do them. It is important to note at the outset that "none of these reality TV shows mention unions and organizing labor—instead, they focus on the eccentricities of the job, and the drama of personality wars among cast members" (Leistyna, 2008, p. 153). These shows promote the neoliberal individualism that has drained power from collective groups and shifted it to corporate headquarters. Corporate America has been systematically undermining organized labor for decades and media corporations are major players in efforts to shift public opinion away from support for unions and toward an ethos of 'personal responsibility.' Despite the fact that union members earn 30 percent more than non-union workers and receive far better benefits, the number of labor unions and their memberships are steadily declining (Leistyna, 2008). No mention of working-class struggles or issues slips into the RTV scripts.

These 'working-class hero' programs feature primarily White, working-class men and are scripted for a White, working-class male audience (Leistyna, 2008; Skeggs, 2009). Workers are portrayed as heroic for doing essential jobs most middle-class people would never consider. They are hard-working icons of the struggle for the American Dream. The jobs are physically intense, demanding, and typically pay low wages, while requiring enormous personal sacrifice (long hours, time away from home and family, frequent injuries, etc.). Yet the stylized, edited, scored versions of these men's lives minimize those issues while focusing on what amounts to right-wing rhetoric common in political ads: 'family values,' boot-strap ideology, strong work ethic, and the efficacy of 'trickle-down,' economic policies.

Ice Road Truckers is typical of the 'working-class hero' theme. For example, season three opens with Aerosmith's "Living on the Edge" pulsing to harrowing scenes from previous episodes. As the volume decreases, the narrator, in a tone that's something of a cross between an extreme sports broadcaster and a Walter Cronkite monologue, sets up the scenario:

> At the top of the world, there's a job only a few would dare. Last season, the dash for the cash was fought on the smooth playing field of Canada's Arctic ice. This season, two old pros join four of America's bravest truckers to tackle the tundra's deadliest ice passage. Just when you thought extreme trucking couldn't get more dangerous, ice road truckers take on Alaska. These are the truckers who make their living on thin ice.

The affect evoked by the music, the narration, the powerful trucks, and the extreme weather is an admiration for those willing to "live on the edge" of "thin ice."

The cast is made up primarily of men, with the exception of Lisa Kelly, a young female trucker with a penchant for dirt bike racing. As with most of the working-class hero shows, these workers exhibit all the stereotypical traits of the working classes—including lots of *bleeped* profanity (especially from Art), baseball caps, and plaid. They speak in an exaggerated 'countrified' dialect with frequent ritual displays of bravado and an abundance of colloquialisms ("It's colder than a well-digger's ass in a Texas snowstorm"). About half of the truckers are overweight which, according to Leistyna and Alper (2005), is one of the most common factors attributed to the working class in media. Issues of body size are fodder for crude jokes and for the scenes of the men shopping for warm clothing as the camera zooms in on the 4X labels. According to Fleras and Dixon (2011), these types of 'working-class hero' shows, "in their attempts to valorize the working-class heroic by escaping into fantasy—gloss over too much of the men's working lives" (p. 593). They do little to give viewers a realistic portrayal of working-class struggles or "to contextualize deprivation, risk-taking, or ill health, much less to explain the causes of these hardships in structural rather than individualistic terms" (p. 593). They go on to point out that

> [h]eroicizing workers in risky occupations has had the effect of flattening their humanity, with the result that they are elevated to the status of mythic creatures—noble, virtuous, manly—whose sacrifices ensure a comfortable standard of living for the population at large. This worker as unsung hero also performs ideological work insofar as the mythology conceals how the blue-collar working class as professional risk-takers generate wealth for those who own or control.
>
> (p. 594)

Whether it's the youngest member of the *Great Lake Warriors* cleaning out the toilets on a boat and describing how the waste gets in his mouth, an *Ax Man* explaining that "working over, working weekends—it's all just part of the job," or even an *Ax Man* star dying after crashing a helicopter while attempting to lift logs (heli-logging) (Associated Press, 2013), there is no attempt by RTV producers to explore the rampant structural oppressions that forces workers into such high-risk, dangerous, and 'dirty' jobs. Instead, the various workers are depicted as *choosing* to 'adhere to tradition,' despite the risks and the lack of monetary rewards. They are repeatedly filmed espousing the almost utopian nature of their jobs. A parallel can be drawn with the images of, for example, Sambo, in the late 1800s and early 1900s. This happy, contented servant "was seen as proof that the old plantation system was a benign and benevolent institution" (Mellinger, 1992, p. 13). Corporate America would have viewers perceive laborers in much the same way.

Throughout these programs, the stars' speech denotes a lack of education (even when that is not the reality, as in the case of *Duck Dynasty* stars), and facial hair is abundant and unkempt. Working-class labor is romanticized, mythologized, and set to classic rock. Viewers observe that working long hours in dangerous conditions for moderate pay is a chosen lifestyle, not the result of neoliberalism's inequitable economic structures, institutionalized class, race, and gender oppression, and unregulated corporate greed.

Buy, Bargain, and Barter

While the working-class hero trope leaves viewers amazed by the risks some jobs require, this group of programs appeal to everyone who enjoys browsing a garage sale or thrift store in hopes of finding a lost treasure. These shows depict lives that are built around small businesses engaged in buying, bargaining, and bartering. These small-scale capitalist ventures are portrayed as fun and, while not lucrative, they provide a comfortable working-class lifestyle. This group includes shows like *American Pickers*, *Pawn Stars*, *Down East Dickering*, *Duck Dynasty*, and *Storage Wars*. These programs are extremely popular with merchandising campaigns, 24-hour marathons, and seriously committed fans.

According to Leistyna (2008), "Research clearly shows that TV's representations have worked to perpetuate the myth of a classless society, where upward mobility is simply a question of individual virtue" (p. 148), desire, work ethic, and innate ability. These programs represent various rungs on that ladder of upward mobility and, in each space, the reality personalities, like those working-class heroes discussed above, are shown to be perfectly content. This group is made up primarily of White men, who self-describe as 'rednecks.' Many are small business owners, often working long hours and seven-day weeks in order to enjoy middle-class privileges. Their businesses, however, are usually dependent on their working-class and poor customers (who are often shown in a less than positive light). These are the people who have become prosperous from selling to or buying from working-class people—many times profiting from the misfortune of others.

Counted among the most popular RTV shows, these are examples of capitalism at its most basic and rewarding—the hard-working and personable reality stars and their offspring are 'living the American Dream' as several claim in their opening narrations. While a few of the small enterprises are service oriented, like *Bad Ink*, which is about a tattoo parlor, and *American Hoggers*, which depicts the exploits of wild boar removal experts, most are focused on the acquisition of and selling of 'stuff,' and the lifestyle afforded those working-class rednecks who excel at such commerce.

At the top of the economic spectrum are shows like *Duck Dynasty* and *Country Buck$*. Both are situated in Louisiana and feature families with rags-to-riches patriarchs who have turned 'redneck' into multi-million dollar businesses. Both programs depict White men who have 'proven' that social mobility is possible, if you have the right stuff. The preponderance of the programing centers, not on the business, but on hunting, fishing, off-road four-wheeling, camping, and other leisure pursuits. One is left to wonder how much of the reality of the business is being depicted when so little work is being done—but, clearly, making it big is fun.

Duck Dynasty, for example, features the Robertson family of West Monroe, Louisiana, who turned their father's invention of a superior duck call (a wooden whistle-like instrument that calls ducks to hunters) into a multi-million dollar company headed by CEO Willie Robertson. He employs the other male members of the family, his father, Phil, three brothers, Jase, Alan, and Jep, and his uncle, Si, plus a handful of other men.

All are long-haired, long-bearded, camouflage-wearing good-ol'-Southern-boys who work as little as possible and spend an inordinate amount of time hunting frogs and squirrels, catching catfish, and camping out. Clearly, the message is that if they can build a financial empire, anyone can—and those who don't are simply not trying.

Somewhat lower on the economic spectrum of working-class success stories are the smaller business owners featured in programs like *American Pickers*, *Pawn Stars*, *Storage Wars*, and *God, Guns, and Automobiles*. There are numerous shows in this category, and their major theme is that capitalism is wonderful, small businesses are fun, success is a matter of persistence, and taking advantage of others' misfortune is just good practice. *Storage Wars*, for example, is about the tens of thousands of storage units abandoned by people who cannot pay the storage fees, so the contents are auctioned off to the highest bidder. Serpe (2013) asserts that these shows represent a "coming out for a number of predatory business practices" and a "heartwarming" tribute to "bootstrapping" (p. 18). While this is the message enacted by the 'stars,' the people whose possessions they acquire are either absent, or they provide examples of those who do not embody the 'correct' spirit of capitalism. Poniewozik (2011) observed that, "it's as if cable TV has entered the postapocalypse, half its denizens scrounging the ruins of a once rich civilization, the other half carting off their goods for appraisal" (p. 59).

American Pickers, for example, is a wildly popular show about two likeable guys who turned their childhood passions for collecting things into a business. Mike Wolfe, owner of a shop called Antique Archaeology, in LeClaire, Iowa and Frank Fritz, who sells in Mike's shop, travel the country together "picking" things—buying stuff from people with the hopes of reselling for a profit. While Mike and Frank are articulate and well-groomed, the people they "pick" from often sport shaggy beards, are socially awkward, and represent those who have been unsuccessful in their pursuit of the American dream.

While many of the people Mike and Frank visit on their treks are other pickers or sophisticated middle-class collectors, the best "picks" are places where people have hoarded items intended for a business they never opened or from one that failed. Telling stories of dashed hopes and bemoaning unfulfilled dreams these sellers invariably struggle to let go of plans to make a fortune on their hoard "someday." The result is piles of decaying, rusting, dust-covered "stuff," and it's Mike and Frank's job to pick through the debris for any surviving treasures. Often, owners are emotionally attached to their "junk," and Mike and Frank have difficulty convincing them to sell. These working-class dreamers sometimes insist that their items are worth much more than they actually are, revealing ignorance of their possessions' true value and making it clear to viewers *why* they have not achieved the neoliberal dream of self-employment and financial independence. These less savvy consumers and failed capitalists enact sketches intended to validate a culture built upon an ethos of social Darwinism. RTV isn't "just about winners and losers, but strivers and failures, the bold and the broken. In this universe there are simply some people on the right side of the asymmetrical information divide, and others born to be conned" (Serpe, 2013, p. 18).

Redneck "Bidness"

The last RTV subset depicts people who have created subsistence economies rejecting traditional employment while personifying the capitalist ideal of the rugged, independent individual. This group is made up of the lower echelons of the working class and poor people who live on the edge of poverty. They have relatively few middle-class comforts and securities and spend most of their time trying to 'do a deal' that will enable them to survive until the next deal. Examples include *Appalachian Outlaws*, *Swamp People*, *Mountain Men*, and *No Man's Land*. These shows feature, again, mostly bearded, White men who live off the land and/or their wits.

Swamp People opens with the explanation that the life these men lead— making a living by hunting and killing alligators—"goes back 300 years" and implies that nothing has changed for the hunters. Tommy, a young swamper, describes himself in the first episode as, "coon-ass. I live off the land. I rely on the land to make my money." With a similar theme, *Mountain Men* features men who live off the grid, hunting and foraging to eke out an existence in various mountain ranges. *Mountain Men*'s theme song is Lynyrd Skynyrd's "Simple Kind of Man," and each week the featured mountaineers seem to find themselves near death in their attempt to survive without the benefit of corporate America. These luddites are portrayed as heroic figures who have rejected modern life with all its 'complications' (middle-class consumer society) in order to risk their lives every day just to survive, trap enough animals, sell enough fur, etc. to make it till the next time—an extreme version of living paycheck-to-paycheck. Yet, they make it clear that, for them, they have achieved their American Dream—independence and self-reliance. They are not asked what they would do if a family member became seriously ill, or how they will survive when they're aged, since they pay no social security. Like the 'working class heroes' these macho men are portrayed as having chosen the life they lead as if all other socio-economic possibilities were open to them.

Down East Dickering opens with scenes of long-haired, bearded White men, four-wheeling and enjoying the outdoors, with a voiceover pro-claiming, "Welcome to the good life. Around here we don't answer to anyone. No bosses, no rules and the best of everything." The "good life" is a fairly meager existence where survival depends on the next deal. Using a weekly print publication of classified ads, *Uncle Henry's Weekly*, these rural Maine residents will buy, sell, barter, and do just about anything to turn a profit. In the pilot episode, Yummy, a featured dickerer, proudly exclaims, "As long as I don't have to punch a clock and have someone telling me what I got to do, I'm happy . . . I've traded around for goats, pigs, chickens, I even sold a guy a bucket of moose shit one time." These "redneck hillbillies" as they call themselves, earn just enough to survive and spend the rest of their time pursuing recreational activities. They epitomize many of the negative stereotypes associated with the poor and working classes. There is no mention of the effects of no healthcare, no retirement, no social security or no recourse if a deal they are depending on for food, shelter, and heat falls through.

The production of programs about "swamp people" or "mountain men" serves to objectify class "by detaching persons from the set of relations that make up their experience of the world" (Skeggs, 2009, p. 637). For example, shows like *Appalachian Outlaws* often

> depict Appalachian whites as ignorant, lazy, barefoot and pregnant, toothless, and moonshiners while ignoring more positive characteristics of the region's people. Such portrayals mask serious economic, social, and health issues Appalachian whites frequently confront. Perpetuation of the poor white stereotype permits dominant culture, as represented by the mass media, to justify the marginalization of this sub-group while validating its own status.
>
> (Cooke-Johnson & Hansen, 2008, p. 184)

Appalachian Outlaws follows bearded, White men as they search the Appalachian mountains for ginseng or "seng," which they sell to buyers who ship primarily to Asian markets. Since over-harvesting has caused states to regulate the gathering and selling of ginseng, restricting when and where it can be dug up, those who depend on its sale for their livelihood become "outlaws" in order to survive. They are the modern-day equivalent of moonshiners.

RTV viewers are presented the neoliberal argument against social programs intended to help those in these poverty-laden areas like Appalachia. The producers of these shows construct poor and blue-collar people not only as the other, but as a proud and content other to the same effect as the 'happy darkey' propaganda pervasive in early twentieth century popular culture (Mellinger, 1992; Domke, 2001). As the number of poor living below the poverty line increases, representations of 'happy poor'—a carefree, juvenile working class—have exploded on RTV. The emphasis on the inordinate amount of time spent at play is not accidental. As Mellinger (1992) found, the 'happy darkey' propaganda often manifested in images of African American children or adults in childish activities (Uncle Remus, Sambo, etc.). Positioning the "other-as-child" worked well to justify racist treatment of African Americans and to frame slavery "as paternalistic rather than a profit-oriented system of labor" (p. 16). Mellinger illustrates how portrayals of African Americans as lazy, primarily interested in leisure activities, and content with inequitable economic structures provided justification for a history of slavery and continued discriminatory institutions and practices in the minds of Whites. In the industrial economy, "White cultural practitioners rearticulated the pre-existing slave ideology for the new form of capitalism" (p. 16) through depictions of happy, child-like African Americans. As we shift from manufacturing to a knowledge economy, I contend, RTV about poor and blue-collar Whites serves the same purpose. As the majority of working class and working poor continue to struggle while those at the top of the economic spectrum enjoy a robust 'economic recovery' and exponential growth of wealth, everyone has to be convinced that the fault is not structural inequalities in the free-market system, but in the individuals and their othered group.

Disney's New Song of the South

I could not, as a child, understand my mother's objections to the *Beverly Hillbillies*. I enjoyed watching the pasquinading characters and laughing at their hilarious predicaments. But as I view the RTV discussed in this chapter, I remember that incident with comprehension and dismay. The majority of RTV programing presents working-class people, primarily in the southern US, as immature, ignorant, socially inept and uncouth hicks. Schaffer (2014) dubbed these shows "hicksploitation." The overarching message running through these representations of the heroic worker, savvy (and ruthless) wheeler-dealer, and independent survivalist, is that the US as a meritocracy *is reality* rather than myth, capitalism is a just system of economic rewards, and the poor are poor because of individual failure, choice, or lack of ambition. None of the series examines the *reality* of working-class lives.

Current Disney CEO Roger Iger earns $34 million a year before stock options, sits on the board of Apple, and was appointed by President Obama to the Export Council, which advises the President on the promotion of exports, jobs, and growth. The average ride operator in one of Disney's theme parks, by contrast, makes $9 an hour (The Walt Disney Company, n.d.; Glassdoor, 2014). One can only imagine how little the women and girls working long hours to make Disney products around the globe are paid. After all, the neoliberal view is that the market should be free from civic responsibilities. No safeguard or safety net should prevent stockholders and CEOs from increasing profits. Reality TV "bolster[s] neoliberalism's goals by encouraging individuals to focus on self-resilience, on constructing and reconstructing a marketable self" (Woodstock, 2014, p. 782).

The focus of each RTV program is on how people construct lives in a capitalist, consumer society. Using techniques similar to those used by industrial age propagandists to justify racial inequality, the owners of capital in this knowledge economy promote these images of White, working men (and sometimes women), as appropriately placed along the economic continuum. Their grooming habits, hobbies, language, and excessive tattooing are shown to be examples of working-class, 'redneck,' cultural taste. Scarborough and McCoy (2014) contend that RTV turns cultural taste into "moral condemnation," and when cultural taste is "linked to moral position, then a strong symbolic boundary can be formed that reinforces real-world boundaries amongst social groups" (p. 1), boundaries that perpetuate class inequalities. They naturalize an "unforgiving social landscape, where taking risks at others' expense is the way to get ahead" (Serpe, 2013, p. 17). RTV recreates the myths of the American Dream and the meritocracy of capitalism in half-hour blocks, 24 hours a day. The neoliberal ethos of individual responsibility permeates RTV programming postponing "a systemic critique of capitalism" (Eddy, 2014, p. 4). Rather, such programming idealizes "a recuperative blue-collar masculinity that attenuates the putative losses suffered by working class men under the postindustrial service economy" (Carroll, 2008, p. 263). The actual stories of the working class and poor are not part of the 'reality' of reality TV. Disney's cable networks no longer broadcast the history, arts, and entertainment their channel titles imply, but are suffused with RTV programing that reinforces classist stereotypes in order to support a neoliberal agenda with constant representations of a fantasy wherein the working-class and the poor are (1) content, even happy, to be poor; (2) proud of their ignorance, their poverty, and their 'White trash' social standing; and (3) undeserving of socialistic government programs that might provide opportunities for advancement, authentic education, a robust social safety net, and a possibility of movement into the middle class. In effect, RTV programs overtly create and support a fantasy of a utopian status quo in the aftermath of the deepest economic decline for the working class since the Great Depression. Length restrictions for this chapter preclude an additional exploration of gender, race, and privilege in RTV, but those analyses need to be done and disseminated. Educators, activists and citizens working to expose structural inequalities and institutionalized discriminations that underpin the stories RTV tells must expose the burlesqued depiction of working-class lives that is 'reality' television.

Note

1   It is important to note here that Disney rarely produces RTV featuring African Americans. While some of the other five media giants do have African American centered RTV, those programs feature celebrity, not working-class culture. The only African American celebrity RTV program on a Disney-owned or affiliated channel was the short-lived *The Jacksons—A Family Dynasty* (2009–2010) on A&E. This fact clearly indicates the audience Disney is targeting with its RTV programming and with the messages discussed in this chapter. The dearth of African Americans in the worlds displayed in these shows (and on Disney media in general) supports other criticisms of Disney as creating worlds that portray US culture in racist, classist, and sexist ways (Giroux & Pollock, 2010; Lugo-Lugo & Bloodsworth-Lugo, 2008).

References

Associated Press. (2013, September 18). William Bart Colantuono, *Ax Men* pilot, killed in helicopter crash. *People.com*. Retrieved from: http://www.people.com/people/article/0,,20736383,00.html

Boggs, C. (2010). The imperial system in media culture. In B. Frymer, T. Kashani, A. J. Nocella, & R. Van Heertum (Eds.), *Hollywood's exploited: Public pedagogy, corporate movies, and cultural crisis* (pp. 13–28). New York: Palgrave MacMillan.

Bourdieu, P., & Passeron, J. C. (1977). *Reproduction in education, society, and culture.* London: Sage.

Carroll, H. (2008). Men's soaps, automotive television programming and contemporary working-class masculinities. *Television New Media, 9*(4), 263–283. doi: 10.1177/1527476408315495

Cooke-Jackson, A., & Hansen, E. K. (2008). Appalachian culture and reality TV: The ethical dilemma of stereotyping others. *Journal of Mass Media Ethics, 23*(3), 183–200. doi:10.1080/08900520802221946

Domke, D. (2001). The press, race relations, and social change. *Journal of Communication, 51*(2), 317.

Eddy, C. (2014). The art of consumption: Capitalist excess and individual psychosis in *Hoarders. Canadian Journal of Communication, 44*(1), 1–24.

Fleras, A., & Dixon, S. (2011). Cutting, driving, digging, and harvesting: Re-masculinizing the working-class heroic. *Canadian Journal of Communication, 36*(4), 579–597.

Giroux, H. A. (2000). Public pedagogy as cultural politics: Stuart Hall and the "crisis" of culture. *Cultural Studies, 14*(2), 341–360.

Giroux, H. A. (2010). Stealing of childhood innocence: Disney and the politics of casino capitalism: A tribute to Joe Kincheloe. *Cultural Studies <=> Critical Methodologies, 10*(5), 413–416. doi: 10.1177/1532708610379834

Giroux, H. A., & Pollock, G. (2010). *The mouse that roared: Disney and the end of innocence.* Lanham, MD: Rowman and Littlefield.

Glassdoor (2014). Disney parks & resorts. Retrieved from: http://www.glassdoor.com/Hourly-Pay/Disney-Parks-and-Resorts-Ride-Operator-Hourly-Pay-E13843_D_KO25,38.htm

Goffman, E. (1963). *Stigma: Notes on the management of spoiled identity.* Englewood Cliffs, NJ: Prentice-Hall.

Hoppenstand, G. (2010). Editorial: Truth in advertising. *The Journal of Popular Culture, 43*(4), 669–679.

Iger, R. (2014). The Walt Disney Company fiscal year 2014 annual financial report and shareholder letter. Anaheim, CA: The Walt Disney Company. Retrieved from: http://thewaltdisneycompany.com/sites/default/files/reports/10k-wrap-2014_1.pdf

Leistyna, P. (2008). Working hard to entertain you: The Discovery Channel looks at labor. *New Labor Forum, 17*(1), 148–153. doi:10.1080/10957960701834431

Leistyna, P., & Alper, L. (Co-writers & Producers). (2005). *Class dismissed: How TV frames the working class* [Documentary]. Northampton, MA: Media Education Foundation.

Lugo-Lugo, C. R., & Bloodsworth-Lugo, M. K. (2008). "Look out new world, here we come"?: Race, racialization, and sexuality in four children's animated films by Disney, Pixar, and DreamWorks. *Cultural Studies <=> Critical Methodologies, 9*(2), 166–178. doi: 10.1177/1532708608325937

Mellinger, W. M. (1992). Representing Blackness in the White imagination: Images of "happy darkeys" in popular culture, 1893–1917. *Visual Studies, 7*(2), 3–21. doi: http://dx.doi.org/10.1080/14725869208583700

Miller, T. (2010). *Television studies: The basics.* London: Routledge.

Mirrlees, T. (2013). *Global entertainment media: Between cultural imperialism and cultural globalization.* New York: Routledge.

Moore, R. (2007). Friends don't let friends listen to corporate rock: Punk as a field of cultural production. *Journal of Contemporary Ethnography, 36,* 438–474.

Poniewozik, J. (2011). Trash TV. *Time, 178*(7), 58–59.

Rose, R. L., & Wood, S. L. (2005). Paradox and the consumption of authenticity through reality television. *Journal of Consumer Research, 32*(2): 284–296.

Scarborough, R. C., & McCoy, C. A. (2014). Moral reactions to reality TV: Television viewers' endogenous and exogenous loci of morality. *Journal of Consumer Culture,* 1–28. doi: 10.1177/1469540514521078

Schaffer, G. (2014). Hillbilly nation. *Outside, 39*(3), 30.

Serpe, N. (2013). Reality pawns: The new money TV. *Dissent, 60*(Summer), 13–18. http://search.proquest.com/docview/1372739652?accountid=13158

Skeggs, B. (2009). The moral economy of person production: The class relations of self-performance on 'reality' television. *Sociological Review, 57*(4), 626–644. doi:10.1111/j.1467–954X.2009.01865.x

The Walt Disney Company. (n.d.) Company overview. Retrieved from: https://thewaltdisneycompany.com/about-disney/company-overview

The Walt Disney Company. (n.d.). *Robert A. Iger.* Retrieved from: http://thewaltdisneycompany.com/about-disney/leadership/ceo/robert-iger

Wood, H., & Skeggs, B. (2011). Introduction. In H. Wood & B. Skeggs (Eds.), *Reality television and class* (pp. 1–29). London: BFI/Palgrave Macmillan.

Woodstock, L. (2014). Tattoo therapy: Storying the self on reality TV in neoliberal times. *Journal of Popular Culture, 47*(4), 780–799. doi:10.1111/j.1540–5931.2011.00814.x

9 Deliriumland

Disney and the Simulation of Utopia

Jason J. Wallin

Baudrillard's (1995) *Simulacra and Simulation* advances a wholly original if not hallucinatory speculation on the symbolic world of Disney that commences with the rather moot assertion that Disney functions as a site of simulation, that is, as a reality without referent or actuality. As fans and connoisseurs might very well attest, the magic purveyed by Disney is intimate to its production of fantasy and the ostensible escape from reality that fantasy might afford. Reenchanting the world via simulation,[1] the 'Disney experience'—from the illusory utopias of Disney's theme parks to the nostalgic revisionist worlds of the company's animated productions—aims at the realization of dreams bracketed from the encumbrances and indignities of contemporary life. Such a scenario requires first the division of imagination from reality, or rather, the production of a distance capable of separating Disney's virtual utopia from the hard truth of actuality. As it did with the 2015 Disneyland measles outbreak, Disney quarantines the invasive character of reality. This is all to suggest that Disney functions as a derealized space predicated on the suspension of reality. In this conceptualization, the difference between Disney as a simulation and reality itself is evident.

Questioning this conceptualization, however, Baudrillard (2002) speculates that this distinction of reality and imagination perpetrated by Disney constitutes an alibi occluding the disappearance of reality itself. Herein, Disney is an indexical case for what Baudrillard dubs the third order of simulacra. Where the first order of simulacra emerges in the Early Modern period in the form of counterfeits and the second order of simulacra in the Industrial period via mass serialization, the third order of simulacra extends from the present order in which reality disappears into codes and models (DNA, opinion polls, news media, cloning), or rather, into simulations that prefigure reality. Across these phases of simulation, Baudrillard detects a seismic shift in our relation to reality. That is, wherein the first two orders of simulacra it remains possible to distinguish the original or prototype from its facsimiles, in our present order of media saturation the two have collapsed. In the third order of simulacra, for example, it is no longer possible to distinguish between reality and imagination because reality has become anticipated and prefigured by the simulacrum, or rather, the more real than real idealization of reality. Thus, what Disney preserves is the idea of a real world when no such world exists, masking in this way the disappearance of reality into simulation.[2] This is not to suggest the existence of a true reality perverted by simulation nor one that might be revealed through the magic of analysis. Rather, it is to speculate on the reality of the simulacrum, or rather, the fact that reality is both regulated and informed by simulation. Herein, Disney does not represent the actualization of American ideology—rather, America *is* Disney. It is not, for example, that Disney allows you to be a child, but that Disney masks the perpetuation of childishness and immaturity everywhere (Baudrillard, 1995).[3] This is all to say that the clear-cut distinction between imagination and reality is now short circuited, and by extension, that the simulated universe of Disney obfuscates the fact that reality itself is now disappeared into simulation, produced from models, information, and signs. As Baudrillard (1993) infamously portends, reality neither precedes the model nor survives it. The territory is prefigured by the map.

In the Maw of the Cannibal Mouse

By absorbing the world into its synthetic universe of reference, The Walt Disney Company performs what Baudrillard (2002) dubs a "reality transfusion" (p. 151). That is, Disney's takeover of public space, its canni-balistic subsumption of cultural sign systems, and capture of the collective imaginary metamorphose reality into the "bloodless universe of the virtual" (ibid.). Herein, the passive consumer becomes both casualty of leisure and fully integrated *extra* within Disney's ubiquitous virtual reality universe. As a consequence of such integration, the modicum of agency ascribed to the act of consumption becomes as disappeared as the concept of consumer alienation. From the takeover of the Western imaginary and the fantasy universes of *Star Wars*, *Marvel*, *The Muppets*, and *Pixar Studios*, to the tran-substantiation of real bodies into its synthetic world,[4] Disney renders the subject a fully interactive servomechanism within its imaginary universe (Baudrillard, 2002). Inverting a hypothesis of critical theory, then, Disney will not be revealed as an exploitative parasite of labor power (that much has already occurred); rather, the revelation is that humans are already the meat puppets of a hyperreal Disneyish order to which our identities and self-understandings are inherent (Fisher, 2014). Such "attractive cannibalism" is symptomatic of the New World Order figured elsewhere through our *willing* technological integration within systems of digital and algorithmic disembodiment (social networking, market tracking, technological surveill-ance) that anticipates vectors of social engagement and self-identification[5] (Baudrillard, 2002, p. 152). That the reality transfusion perpetrated by Disney arouses little beyond moral denouncement and academic condem-nation might indicate that the world has *already* undergone transubstantiation into simulation. Reality becomes a special effect that is no longer linked to imagination at all, but rather, to the viral power of virtual reality and its "cancerous proliferation" across the real (Baudrillard, 1993, p. 7).

The White Glove of Liberation

Frequently academically maligned as a vehicle of homogenization, Disney is paradoxically enjoined to forces of liberation. That is, Disney's juncture with modernity coincides with the liberation of childhood from children, of art from reality, and the unconscious from superego repression, or more generally, the freeing of signs and images from their pre-modern pre-constituted relations (Baudrillard, 1993). In the wake of modernity's explosion into all social spheres and its upheaval of pre-modern fixed social relations, every avenue in the overproduction of "signs, messages, ideologies, and satisfactions" has now been pursued (Baudrillard, 1993, p. 2). Signs,[6] forms, and desires become liberated from their reflection of a natural order (their direct connection to the natural world via use-value) and decon-textualized first according to their exchange-value (where signs become equivalent to money) and then for their value as signs (where signs circulate in reference to other signs), where the control and regulation of sign systems becomes paramount. As Virilio (2002) develops, the aim of corporations like Disney is for a "monopoly on the market in appearances; capitalists no longer rushing for gold, but for the totality of the world's images" (p. 59). Baudrillard's (2008) tripartite order of value (use, exchange, and sign) aside, the "orgy of the real" by which the liberatory impulse of modernity is charac-terized is concomitant with the motors of capitalist deterritorialization, or rather, the liberation of relations from the highly regulated territories of meaning, access, and exchange intimate to the pre-modern State (p. 2). The juncture of modernity and capitalism herein functions as a revolutionary force that unbinds fixed social arrangements (the fixity of use-value) into complexity, uncertainty, and productive crisis. Yet, as Baudrillard (2008) develops, the ultimate event of liberation has transpired, having already culminated with modernity's emancipation of every sign, form, and desire. *After the orgy*, where all forms of liberation have *already* been anticipated through over-representation and production, freedom becomes pursued today via *simulation*. So it is with the fantasy brokerage of Disney, which simulates freedom in its myriad forms—from the theme-park liberation of childhood for adults, the filmic freeing of history from historical referent, the suspension of repressive forces in infantile regression, and the Cinderella-story of bourgeois utopianism emancipated from fixed social relations and status. Disney thus functions as the specter of an already transpired revolu-tion, where cultural sign systems emancipated from fixed social relations have been projected into an orbit of circulatory exchange and interminable commutation, no longer bearing any reference to reality whatsoever (Baudrillard, 1995).

Disney figures as a symptom of liberation's disappearance into simulation, where what remains is but the interminable re-run of "ideals, phantasies, images and dreams . . . now behind us, yet which we . . . continue in a sort of inescapable indifference" (Baudrillard, 1993, p. 4). Having already realized the actual and potential liberation of childhood, the imagination and the unconscious for instance, Disney today functions as a vehicle of liberation's repetition through *simulation*. As though it had not already occurred, Disney portends a utopia toward which we continue to accelerate. We might take as an index of this assertion the simulation of utopic happy endings throughout Disney's filmic oeuvre, where those characters we are called to care about are freed from their negative passions, radical differences, and resentments. Elsewhere, Disney perpetuates an aseptic utopianism emptied of its potential for inversion in annihilation or implosion, setting into motion the hyperreal quality of utopia in its literal meaning of *no place*. The forms of liberation intimate to Disney's utopia are interminably replayed against the backdrop of their *a priori* overrepresentation. Accelerating the *mise-en-scène* of liberation, Disney advances upon a void (Baudrillard, 1993). That is, where the moments of both real and potential liberation have already passed into circuits of over-representation and exchange, what remains are the obsessive *hyper-real* pursuit of liberation and utopia via the third order simulations of Disney's *Main Street,* the hyper-real town *Celebration,* the desire for a decelerated return to the good old days that were themselves simulated, and the re-casting of all ethnic, national, and sexual relative to its fabulated utopia.

The Disney Contagion

In a proposition as delirious at the contemporary moment, Baudrillard (2002) speculates that Disney no longer functions through conventional or heavy modes of power, but rather, by dint of molecular contagion and proliferation throughout the social sphere. As Baudrillard (2002) contends, contemporary reality is remade via the kind of proliferative logic perpetuated by Disney, the imaginary universe of which extends as if by contagion into all pre-existing semiotic systems and material arrangements. As an inadequately brief sampling, Disney's power of contagion ranges from the emplacement of Disney princesses in seminal horror movie moments, the correlation of Disney princesses and 'real' historical referents, the revision of male subjects as princesses, Disney character personality quizzes, ethnically revised princesses, Disney/ *Star Wars*/ *Sailor Moon* crossovers, and Disneyish inspired makeovers. Such examples of viral infection go on *ad infinitum*. This viral proliferation breaks from critical descriptions of Disney as either a spectacle or producer of spectacles. Rather, the tentacular extension of Disney into every corridor of the social obliterates the spectacle by absorbing the outside and performing the generalized capture and metastases of our mental and material universe (Baudrillard, 2002). "We no longer live in the society of the spectacle," Baudrillard (2002) writes in relation to Disney's universal takeover, for it is no longer that mass media alters reality, but rather, that reality is already a special effect of the viral and virtual (p. 152). Here, Disney redeems everything via its utopian simulacrum (Baudrillard, 2002, p. 151). Baudrillard (2002) notes, for example, how such events as the Red Army Choir performance at Euro Disney are normalized within its enchanted dreamworld of possibility. Exemplified in that ostensibly benign redemption, Disney's simulated liberation extends to the absorption of pornography and war, those aspects of the social apparently antithetical to a bourgeois happy curriculum that evacuates the negative from The Walt Disney Company's synthetic universe. This posed, the very notion of 'antithesis' has become facile, for it is increasingly difficult to think of anything antithetical to our Disneyish New World Order, the very logic of which is predicated on the freeing of all signs, forms, and desires into utopian simulacra. In this mode of liberatory contagion, Disney's synthetic world circulates and exchanges with all others in a manner that demonstrates both its actual and potential investment everywhere (Baudrillard, 2007). Through the extent of its orbital diffusion across the whole of reality, Disney's center of gravity is now impossible to locate, rendering the critical notion of power or the analysis of Disney in terms of power obsolete. That is, insofar as critiques levied at Disney aim at an analysis of power at macro or structuralist levels, they fail to grapple with the fact that its logic is corpuscular and already molecularly diffused throughout the Western imaginary.

Simulation and Disney's Human Centipede

While power becomes disappeared through Disney's simulation of power relations errantly assumed to mirror the 'truth' of reality, we might yet speculate on the particular ways in which the synthetic world of Disney has become fetishized and an invested part of the contemporary libidinal economy[7] (Lyotard, 2014). Where critics of Disney often misrecognize its *simulation* of power as a mirror of real social production, this is to overlook a libidinal investment in the *simulacrum* that has already transpired. Herein, Baudrillard's speculation on the eternal re-run of the *simulacrum* enjoins to a form of *jouissance* (unbearable pleasure) that Lyotard (2014) ascribes to the schizophrenic libidinal investment of contemporary labor. For while life's condemnation to simulation forecasts the extermination of life in representational and literal ways, Lyotard (2014) speculates on the jouissance of labor intimate to "the repetition of the same in work, the same gesture, the same comings and goings . . . the same parts of the body used [and] made use of" (p. 215). What bourgeoisie political intellectuals purporting to the liberation of the proletariat will not admit, Lyotard contends, is that one can *enjoy* swallowing the shit of capital without either suffering or disgust (p. 218). Herein, we might connect Lyotard's argument on the pleasure of repetition to Disney's investment in the "capitalist libidinal infrastructure"

(Fisher, 2014, p. 339). For what the contemporary fetishization of Disney might portend is not the false consciousness of the masses, but rather, a libidinal investment in the repeatable universe of the simulacrum and the delirious disappearance of reality in repetition and overrepresentation. As a corollary to the repetitive acts of contemporary labor, Disney's viral repetition of forms, desires, and satisfactions invests libidinal enjoyment in the *repetition of the same*. For example, despite the effervescent differences throughout Disney's filmic productions, it is generally observable that they draw from a genetic metaphysical and narrative model through which they are observably self-same—a quality that ostensibly attracts rather than repels Disney's viewership.

Coextensive to what Lyotard describes as the jouissance of the body's decomposition through factory routine, the synthetic universe of Disney performs a corollary disintegration where reality is disappeared via the hyper-repetition of forms, desires, and satisfactions. Its facile tinkering with semiotic difference aside, Disney remains a cloning technology redoubling the liberation of signs within its simulated utopia, which long having lost any 'real' point of reference, constitutes a hyperreality destined to outpace and overtake the real.[8] Yet, Disney's exhaustion of the real is far from dismal, signaling instead a joyous affirmation of reality's obliteration—the interminable re-run of reality already having been represented in every possible configuration. Herein, the fetishization of Disney might enjoin with the jouissance of annihilation advanced by Lyotard (2014), where things and individuals achieve enjoyment through accelerative delirium and disappearance. Simply put, Disney's dispersion of reality is enjoyable precisely because of its capacity for the delirious destruction of things and individuals dislocated and recast as freeze-dried extras within Disney's interactive virtual reality show (Baudrillard, 2002). Herein, Lyotard's argument on the jouissance of disintegration ostensibly affirms Baudrillard's (1993) speculation that the fate of things and individuals is today connected to an "urge to be rid of their ideas, their own essences, so as to be able to proliferate everywhere, to transport themselves simultaneously to every point on the compass" (p. 7).

As an index of this urge for diffusion, Disney functions as a vehicle that proliferates the subject across both space and time, from the imaginary *anywhere-whatsoever* of Disneyland's *Main Street* or Disney World's *Epcot Theme Park*, to the synchronization of all historical periods in simultaneous virtual accessibility. Such disintegration occurs equally via Disney's cinematic nostalgic neo-Medievalism, Renaissance, and tribal romanticisms, which, while purporting the ideal of authenticity redeemable from under the yoke of oppression, are *already* invested in those "cinematic proto-VR [technologies]" that make them possible *in the first place* (Fisher, 2014, p. 339). As Fisher argues, it is highly doubtful that anyone truly wants to return to the kinds of pre-capitalist territories imagined by Disney. Rather, Disney is illustrative of a double denial particular to the contemporary moment, for one can only be seduced by the images of subjective authenticity, unadulterated morality, and inner primitivism through immersion in the libidinal economy of capitalism, its technologies of spectral derealization, and plastic dream worlds (Fisher, 2014). This is to say that the dream of deceleration, that is, of a simpler and more naïve time intimate to Disney's nostalgic neo-realization of reality, is possible only via its accelerative technologies of liberation through which all signs becomes available and enveloped in the Disney universe.

The Horror of Dreaming

The *enjoyment* of annihilation is as much a symptom that one can be invested in Disney's libidinal economy without despair as it is that such investment relieves the individual from having to dream, to wish, or imagine on their own. This is not to suggest that people *want to be told what to want*, but rather, that there exists among the masses a general reversal of the impetus to revolt or subvert (Baudrillard, 2007). The revolutionary events of May 1968 and the theories of power and revolution developed in its wake having proved largely inconsequential,[9] the masses are today involved in a "gigantic devolution from unwanted liberty" (p. 100). Into such devolution, Disney figures as a vehicle for offloading responsibility, "turning power back to its fantasies, knowledge to its obsessions, will to its illusions" (Lotringer, 2007, p. 100). The investment of the subject within Disney's libidinal economy might herein be thought as a means for the individual to jettison both the horror and banality of the human imagination, or rather, the burden to dream when the expanse of imaginary potential has already been anticipated in the media, advertising, and the delirious sign exchange of information networks.

Disney not only prefigures all imaginary options in advance through its synchronization of time and space, but, having rendered its synthetic universe weightless, divests it from the burden of meaning. As the proliferation of Disneyish images across the mental universe of the West suggests, Disney has already eclipsed its relation to reality, operating at the level of ecstatic exchange with all other signifying universes, with which it readily assembles and absorbs. It is thus no longer adequate to critique Disney at the level of its meanings, for Disney's derealization of reality is already intimate to its liberation from reference. In a similar way, we might speculate that investment in Disney's libidinal economy of dreams, desires, and satisfactions becomes a means to flee from meaning, or otherwise, from the banality and burden to make meaning in the face of its inconsequence to social change. Disney's self-same universe herein defers the unwanted liberty to dream and wish, insofar as all dreams and wishes have already been fulfilled and reconstructed within Disney's utopian virtual reality. Such automatic fulfillment is exemplified in the Disney slogan "Where Dreams Come True," which signals the theme park as a dream brokerage and guarantor of wish fulfillment. Since all dreams of utopian liberation have already transpired into simulation, Disney relieves the horrific impossibility to *dream further* by dreaming utopian liberation on infinite repeat.

Perpetual Utopia or the Death of Death

The accelerative utopia of Disney is emblematic of a moment in which the prospect of death becomes non-normal. That is, insofar as the fate of things is enjoined to the interminable *simulation* of an already realized utopia in which *nothing ever dies,* the prospect of death today figures as a monstrous inversion of repetition and proliferation. Now even death has been captured in terms of its market value. While seemingly counterintuitive, Larsen (2010) argues that the contemporary moment is not one obsessed with death, but rather, with its demise via overrepresentation. *Nothing dies.* In a scenario anticipated by the dark proselytization of Baudrillard (2002), the dead live on, necromantically parasited as data, market research, media fodder, and so on. As with the body of Walt Disney,[10] things simply enter into temporary cryo-statis for their inevitable exhumation and recirculation. Such vaunted films as *Maleficent* figure as a rerun of Disney's semiotic corpus subjected to interpretive excavation and the multiple perspectives of forensic analysis where nothing is beyond redemption as nostalgia, pastiche, recapitulation, and information (Fisher, 2014). Herein, Disney's *simulacrum* establishes in confluence with the liberatory impulse of capitalism the conditions for the *death of death,* or rather, the liberation of all signs from circulatory entropy.

Within Disney's universe of euphoric circulation, Baudrillard (1993) argues, suffering is not born of repetition, but rather, of an "excess of positivity" perpetrated therein (p. 49). For what Disney cannot absorb into its utopian simulacrum, Baudrillard suggests, are the resources of the negative—violence, hatred, and frustration. Even the villains of the Disney universe fall short of the intensity of negativity Baudrillard evokes insofar as they are always offset by their comedic bumblings, hapless lackeys, and their overcoding by a higher, more noble impetus. Here, Baudrillard develops, the Disneyish universe we inhabit relies upon a form of cosmetic surgery, or rather, on a state of contemporary affairs in which the whole of reality is "lit from all angles, overexposed and defenseless" from the forensic power of technology, screens, images and information (p. 49). What we thought would be the near future unmasking of Capital in all its monstrosity, Fisher (2014) argues, turned out to reveal the opposite—the "New Sincerity" and "kitschy-cutesy pop" of a Disneyish reality, or rather, of reality exhausted of negativity and bound to simulated utopian retrospection (p. 344). It is in this forensic mode that Disney now absorbs the outside thought of its villains, rehabilitating them into its moral and just universe. As with the critically acclaimed *Maleficent,* Disney forensically reconstructs the cause of villainy in a manner that ultimately liberates its villains as such, hence relieving them of their distance and difference via Disney's redemptive utopianism.

In plumbing its dark and edgy villains, Disney obliterates its outside. The consequence of such overrepresentation and forensic excavation of reality constitutes for Baudrillard (1993) a moment in which we are doomed to "complete aseptic whiteness" (p. 50). Submitted to the virulence of images, information, and the synchronization of space-time, all social relations, bodies, and histories undergo a form of cosmetic surgery through which their negative traits are evacuated. Disney already constitutes something of an index for this process, having long since excised the radically negative qualities of misanthropy, hatred, and extreme violence from its synthetic universe. Even in the case of the critically acclaimed *Maleficent*, it is the liberation from radical difference that is the film's ultimate gesture. From the transubstantiation of actual laborers into its bloodless imaginary universe, to its infantile simulation of reality evacuated of violent excess, Disney's 'white glove' remodels the imagination into ideal forms, palpating the *more beautiful than beautiful* via simulation (Baudrillard, 1993). Not only is death averted in this ecstatic scenario, but so too the reversibility of a Disneyish utopianism via negativity. Today, such a scenario pertains not only to Disney, but also to the metastases of a Disneyish mentality wherein both happiness and hope function as "a normal [and legitimate] form of delirium" (Cioran, 1998, p. 167). This delirium persists across the whole of reality, where the repetition of hopefulness and the happy curriculum of the bourgeoisie insist despite the fact that Disney has long given up on any 'actual' future, it long since having disappeared into the ecstasy of utopian simulation (Fisher, 2014).

Expelling negativity from its synthetic universe, Disney concomitantly performs a kind of "otherness surgery" (Baudrillard, 2002, p. 51). Where the forensic excavation of reality has led to the discovery and exploration of all representational dimensions, Baudrillard (1993) asks, "what became of otherness?" (p. 141). As reality is cosmetically overexposed and subsumed into representation, otherness is recast as the 'degree zero' of difference. Such otherness surgery is intimate to the utopian simulacrum of Disney, which recasts throughout its oeuvre the immediate accessibility of all worlds, from romanticized 'natives' to the anthropomorphization of animal and nonhuman life surgically rerendered human. As Baudrillard (1993) argues, the other no longer insists as a force of reversal or danger, but instead as a thing "to be understood, liberated, coddled, recognized" (p. 142). Such otherness surgery is indexical to our Disneyish universe, where the over-representation of reality perpetrates the disappearance of an 'outside.' Herein, Disney's universal harmonization extends not only to the absorption and remodeling of difference, but also to the representational categorization and annexing of reality such that no difference remains. From Disney's *Main Street* to the University lecture hall,[11] the whole of reality is today made over as an already identifiable object, the very act of which signals the dispossession of the *other*. As Baudrillard (2002) argues, this scenario marks our doom, for where alienation is annihilated in simulation and the other disappeared virtually, we are condemned to our image, our identities, desires, and satisfactions. This is a thoroughly Disneyish condemnation, for where Disney harmonizes reality within its utopian simulacrum, we encounter a form of reconciliation tantamount to the extermination of all that is alien, negative, and radically evil.

Fatal Strategies

The Disneyish enchantment of reality that proliferates throughout the mental universe of the West signals a curious fate of civilization in its divestment from the *future of the future,* or rather, a future not already prefigured in simulation. That the libidinal economy of the masses remains invested in such simulation, however, suggests a more complex relation to our Disneyish reality. Such a relation, it might be speculated, is marked less by an investment in Disney's effervescent images than its logic of otherness surgery and repetition of the liberatory *mise-en-scène*. Everything about this Disneyish order corresponds to the happy curriculum of the Western subject, for whom everything is possible through hope. It is this thoroughly Disneyish delirium that has become virulent throughout the mental universe of the West, desperate as it is for the kind of infantile security and promise of infinite utopia proffered by Disney—a world now impossible to extract from 'reality' proper. If not in image then by its virulent strategies, Disney's permeation into and takeover of reality renders both critical reliance on counter/anti-narratives and strategies of resistance obsolete. That is, where Disney has already remodeled reality within its virtual universe, there is nothing that cannot be redeemed, liberated, or remodeled into its utopia. Likewise, where our Disneyish universe is already disappeared into simulation, there is nothing to resist. Its gravitational center long jettisoned into orbit, to critique Disney is akin to "barking at an artificial satellite" (Baudrillard, 2002, p. 57).

That the "power of the virtual is merely virtual," Baudrillard (2002) contends, "is no reason to bend the knee" to its supremacy (pp. 60–61). To evade the servitude of the virtual will require new resources, first among which would involve the divestment of the libidinal economy from a Disneyish universe, its forms, desires, and satisfactions. More specifically, it would involve rejoining the libidinal economy to the forces of the negative and its impulses of non-reconciliation (Baudrillard, 2008; Fisher, 2014). Jettisoning the naïve decelerative impulse for a simpler time, we today require the mobilization of strategies that ride Disney's liberatory impulse to their fatal terminus, or rather, that "deepen negative conditions until they flip" (Pettman, 2008, p. 15). The stakes herein are immense, for as Pettman elides, "from a 'fatal' perspective, we are all hostages, stripped of our symbolic connection to death and destiny" (p. 16). It is here that Disney studies might be recommended against the critical proclivity for interpretive meaning making insofar as such an approach keeps all its imaginary resources in circulation. In lieu of forensic analysis, we might mobilize *fatal strategies* capable of accelerating and reversing the very logic of our Disneyish universe: the inversion of Disney's surgical remodeling by pushing the ideal to the point of its hideous inversion (the more ideal than ideal); the reversal of Disney's whitewash by pushing happiness into delirium (the happier than happy); the reversal of utopian liberation to the horrific moment in which death is refused you (the more liberatory than liberatory). The list goes on. While far from constituting methods, what is crucial is that each of these strategies entail a spiraling up of Disney's logic rather than adherence to conventional forms of deep reading and interpretation that preserve Disney's forensic logic of discovery and mapping. Bordering on science fiction or speculative theory, fatal strategies foster imagination, or rather, they stymie the Disneyish scenario in which the simulacrum imagines *for us*. Here, such diabolical techniques aim to accelerate those tendencies already at work within Disney's synthetic universe, but for the purpose of harnessing the positive feedback of its excess. In doing so, we might be flung from its orbit and into the void beyond, where we might once again look ahead divested of remedies for the trouble of living.

Notes

1   For Baudrillard (1993), contemporary culture is no longer entwined to the Platonic model and its copy. With post-industrialization and the rise of consumer culture, the status of the model as a transcendent ontological substance is disappeared (Baudrillard, 2002). Signs are detached from their symbolic obligations to 'float' in a sea of ambient consumerism.

2   A key case here pertains to those who, upon seeing footage of the 9/11 attacks on the world trade center, believed it to be footage from a Hollywood action-disaster film. In the case of Disney, Baudrillard speculates on a time when the replication of historical epochs at *Disneyland* and *Disney World* (the *Roman* period, for example) will be confused for the actual thing.

3   In another instance, Disney's production of an imaginary universe for offloading subjective responsibility masks the ubiquitous deferment of power to fantasy and will to illusion endemic to contemporary Western culture (Lotringer, 2007, p. 100). Elsewhere, ideals of goodness, sincerity, and truth preserved in Disney circulate in dominant cultural predilections for the nostalgic restoration of human wholeness. Likewise, Disney's repetition of a hyperreal history without referent masks a cultural fetishization for recapitulation, pastiche, and deceleration already intimate to Western life (Fisher, 2014).

4   Baudrillard (2002) remarks here on Disney's purchase of New York's 42nd Street 'red light district' and its transfiguration as a pornographic amusement zone absorbing prostitutes, johns, and pornographers into its enterprise.

5   There exists a compelling relationship to this conceptualization and Deleuze's (1992) speculations on the *societies of control*.

6   Quite generally, 'signs' can be taken here as a shorthand for the binding of words and mental images, and further, as the ambient relationship between signs, where for example, one sign (Mickey Mouse) evokes another (childhood or purity).

7   Libidinal economy might herein be thought in terms of one's investment of desire within particular social relations, processes, and objects.

8   As Disney's critics inadvertently demonstrate, we can no longer tell the difference between 'reality' and simulation.

9   This is an allusion to Baudrillard's criticism of the May 1968 student revolutions as ineffectual.

10   This is, of course, to play on the urban legend of Walt Disney's cryogenic internment as a corollary to Disney's general logic of cryogenic utopianism and frozen futurism.

11   Critical close readings of Disney often illustrate the frenzy to explain, attribute, and footnote everything—a logic intimate to Disney's own overmultiplication of representational qualities.

References

Baudrillard, J. (1993). *The transparency of evil: Essays on extreme phenomena*. New York: Verso.

Baudrillard, J. (1995). *Simulacra and simulation*. Ann Arbor, MI: University of Michigan Press.

Baudrillard, J. (2002). *Screened out*. New York: Verso.

Baudrillard, J. (2007). *Forget Foucault*. Cambridge, MA: MIT Press.

Baudrillard, J. (2008). *Fatal strategies*. Cambridge, MA: MIT Press.

Cioran, E. M. (1998). *Drawn and quartered* (trans. R. Howard). New York: Arcade Publishing.

Deleuze, G. (1992). Postscript on the societies of control. *October,* 59(Winter), 3–7.

Fisher, M. (2014). Terminator vs. Avatar. In R. Mackay & A. Avanessian (Eds.), *#Accelerate#: The accelerationist reader* (pp. 335–346). Falmouth, UK: Urbanomic Media.

Larsen, L. B. (2010). Zombies of immaterial labor: The modern monster and the death of death. Retrieved from: http://www.e-flux.com/journal/zombies-of-immaterial-labor-the-modern-monster-and-the-death-of-death/

Lotringer, S. (2007). Postface: Forget Baudrillard. In J. Baudrillard, *Forget Foucault* (pp. 71–125). Cambridge, MA: MIT Press.

Lyotard, J. F. (2014). Every political economy is libidinal. In R. Mackay & A. Avanessian (Eds.), *#Accelerate#: The accelerationist reader* (pp. 211–221). Falmouth, UK: Urbanomic Media.

Pettman, D. (2008). Introduction: A belated introduction to the orgy. In J. Baudrillard, *Fatal strategies* (pp. 7–24). Cambridge, MA: MIT Press.

Virilio, P. (2002). *Ground zero*. New York: Verso.

10 Camp Disney

Consuming Queer Subjectivities, Commodifying the Normative

Will Letts

Gay subtexts within Disney's animated films, whether explicit or implied, have received much attention and critical analysis over the past two decades (e.g., Griffin, 2000; Roth, 1996; Towbin, Haddock, Zimmerman, Lund, & Tanner, 2004). As Halperin (2012) insists, "[g]ay culture, after all, is not something you have to be gay to enjoy—or to comprehend" (p. 16). In this chapter I explore Halperin's ideas "about the relation between sexuality, on the one hand, and cultural forms, styles of feeling, and genres of discourse, on the other" (p. 14) to see where they might productively lead us. I am interested in how Disney commodifies, caricatures, and capitalizes upon 'camp' sensibilities and enactments, seemingly as sources of humor, in order to entertain, and to educate. Unlike other aspects of Disney films, where [gay] audiences need to "queer heteronormative culture . . . to decode heterosexual cultural artifacts and recode them with gay meanings" (Halperin, 2012, p. 18) or where gay audiences "find the 'hidden message' aimed at the homosexual reader" (Griffin, 2010, p. 193) within Disney advertisements, this project starts with already-queer camp moments in these films. As I use it here, camp is "an in-group word which denote[s] specifically homosexual humor" (Newton, 1979, p. xx).

I explore 'camp' Disney with reference to five iconic Disney villains—Ursula, Jafar, Scar, Governor Ratcliffe, and Hades—from films released over eight years, both as points of departure for my inquiries and as analytics that help exhume ways in which the curriculum of popular culture teaches and is learned. Though "[s]uch films appear to be wholesome vehicles of amusement, a highly regarded and sought after source of fun and joy for children" (Giroux & Pollock, 2010, p. 91), my analysis intends to depict them otherwise. That is, by analysing the depictions of these characters' camp subjectivities I explore what these films have the possibility to teach. Because these animated texts are sites for the production and affirmation of children's cultures, they are useful cultural products to explore the impact that Disney has on the consumption of commodities like heteropatriarchal normativity. In this way, consumers (even critical consumers) of this popular culture are not just consuming material goods but also ideologies that ultimately have material consequences.

Halperin's (2012) important distinction that male homosexuality is "not only a set of specific sexual practices but also an assortment of character-istic social and cultural practices" (p. 10) holds the key to why such an interrogation of camp is of cultural and educational importance, "for gay male cultural practices often consist in mobilizing the figural potential of seemingly unassuming, taken-for-granted objects" (p. 37) such as a show tune, a wig, or anything phallic. And while my interest here is the 'un-assuming' objects of Disney animated films, and more specifically some of Disney's camp villains, this is not a project of queering Disney, but rather a recuperative reading of these camp characters in order to excavate the 'already queer' and to insist on other ways of understanding these texts. So where they're villianized, mocked, or ridiculed in the films or by audiences, I also read the characters in a fashion in order to recover what they might teach us about camp sensibilities. In the next section I canvas some of the theoretical and conceptual terrain identified as camp, and illustrate this landscape with examples from the five focus villains.

Camp Sensibilities and Enactments

Camp, both in its theorizations and its enactments, has a history marked by debate and diverse characterizations. I am drawing on the school of thought about camp that envisions it "not only [as] a mode of cultural appropriation, a way of recycling bits of mainstream culture; it is also productive, a creative impulse in its own right, a strategy for dealing with social domination" (Halperin, 2012, p. 203). As such, camp satirizes mainstream culture while also affording both its practitioners and viewers a critique of dominant social and cultural relations. As Newton (1979) wryly observed, "Camp is not a thing. More broadly it signifies a *relationship between* things, people, and activities or qualities, and homosexuality" (p. 105). Camp is thus quite a useful frame in my analysis here "insofar as it enables us to identify and to understand the peculiar features of gay male discourse, its unique pragmatics" (Halperin, 2012, p. 201), and to counterpoise them with the more normative sex, gender, and sexuality representations that saturate each of these animated films. For instance,

> [m]asculine-feminine juxtapositions are, or course, the most charac-teristic kind of camp, but any very incongruous contrast can be campy. For instance, juxtapositions of high and low status, youth and old age, profane and sacred functions or symbols, cheap and expensive articles are frequently used for camp purposes. Objects or people are often said to be campy, but the camp inheres not in the person or thing itself, but in the tension between that person or thing and the context or association.
>
> (Newton, 1979, p. 107)

Such a rendering of camp honors its relational nature as being more than a label for people, things, or performances, and instead characterizes it as contextually-situated "incongruous contrasts" between cultural polarities such as rich and poor, gay and straight, and man and woman, whereby humor is derived through the interplay of these dominant and subjugated subject positions.

Because camp "emerges as a specifically gay parody possessing cultural and ideological analytic potential" (Meyer, 2010, p. 42), it holds tremendous potential for assisting in this project of critically examining camp manifestations through the cultural juxtapositions in these films and for demonstrating what we can learn from them. Meyer (2010) locates this incongruous representation squarely as "the process for the social signification of gayness" (p. 4) which "allows creative free play with cultural referents" (p. 5). That camp has been inextricably linked, through its history, with homosexuality is significant in that it was a prevailing form of cultural critique arising *from below*, rather than from dominant or mainstream cultures. Newton (1979) explains that, "While camp is in the eye of the homosexual beholder," there is an "underlying unity of perspective among homosexuals" about what makes a particular thing "campy" (p. 106). Newton outlined three recurrent themes that could characterize a particular campy thing: incongruity, theatricality, and humor. She notes that, "incongruity is the subject matter of camp, theatricality is its style, and humor its strategy" (Newton, 1979, p. 106). This is quite a different project from the one that emerged out of the school of thought that envisioned objects being camp, that is, in and of themselves having a camp identity. This school of thought derived from Sontag's (1964/1983) work in which she codifies 58 theses about camp, including some people, items, places, and events that she labels as camp. Instead, as its historical origins are documented here, camp is fundamentally "a set of strategies and tactics that exist within the collective memories (the performance repertoire) of gay men" (Meyer, 2010, p. 2). In fact, Meyer delimits his definition of camp as "the production of gay social visibility, i.e., the process for the social signification of gayness" (p. 1). This relational view of camp is important because it illuminates how camp has been co-opted in these films to serve purposes quite distant in many ways from the project of gay cultural visibility, which works to identify which characters are or may be gay, for instance, all the while still [perhaps unwittingly] referencing those gay origins.

Halperin (2012) depicts this notion of camp existing *in relationship*, noting that, "the distinctive nature and operations of camp, it turns out, make particular sense when they are brought into relation with the long-standing gay male cultural habit of refusing to exempt oneself from social condemnation, as well as the practice of laughing at situations that are horrifying or tragic" (pp. 201–202). Writing about the person who embodies camp as 'the camp,' Halperin (2012) notes, "The camp's function is defined in opposition to the beauty's and vice versa" (p. 208) because "[i]t is a subjectivity formed in dichotomy" (p. 209)—the camp and the beauty are set in opposition to one another. We see this tension in all of the films referred to in this chapter—the 'beauty,' often the film's title character, and the campy villain who offsets this beauty and plays counterfoil to her or him.

In the end, "Camp's favouring of exaggeration and artifice highlights its 'in between' border status: it is part of popular culture, yet its affiliation with queer culture ensures that it hovers on the margins of the dominant culture" (Mallan & McGillis, 2005, p. 4), making it a very useful analytic device for exploring the roles that these villainous characters play in their films in order to illuminate new possibilities for representation and new subject positions that are part of the educative project of critically viewing these movies. Therefore, allowing that homosexuality is "an assortment of characteristic social and cultural practices" (Halperin, 2012, p. 10), as opposed to an essentialized identity or a genetically-determined orientation, I read these camp characters both with and against the grain—as both referencing and drawing upon, and yet repudiating, queer sensibilities. Meyer (2010) notes a similar tension as he writes, "Camp appears, on the one hand, to offer a transgressive vehicle yet, on the other, simultaneously invokes the specter of dominant ideology within its practice, appearing, in many instances, to actually reinforce the dominant order" (p. 43). Flipping that order, I contend that what is foregrounded is Disney's commercial interest in using camp to help delimit and sharpen our focus on the dominant ideology of heteropatriarchy, and in this project I attempt to exhume the transgressive potentials in reading camp Disney otherwise. In the sections that follow, I investigate how camp subjectivities are manifest and deployed as a foil to normative, culturally dominant, and desirable subjectivities, and then explore how these queerly configured subjectivities commodify heteropatriarchy, packaging it for ready consumption. I conclude the chapter by refuting and refusing such normative characterizations and by insisting that we take queer subjectivities seriously, rather than tolerate them or treat them as an afterthought.

Interrogating How Difference is Rendered Normative

The camp subjectivities of the five iconic Disney villains at the center of my inquiry announce themselves to the viewer through physical characteristics, personality traits, and dialogue, both through content and affectation. Drag queen-esque Ursula, the sea witch in *The Little Mermaid* (Musker, Ashman, & Clements, 1989), intones, "The little tramp, she's better than I thought!" while instructing Ariel to use her feminine charms to lure men; her campy lamentation "highlights the fraudulence of her [Ursula's] purportedly natural feminine performance" (Mallan & McGillis, 2005, p, 15). Ursula's curvy, even obese body is punctuated with her butch, Divine-inspired face and hair. In *Aladdin* (Clements & Musker, 1992), the Grand Vizier Jafar's "gothic-styled clothes, theatrical mannerisms, exaggerated facial features, arched eyebrows, neatly curled goatee beard, and precise lisping speech and bitchy asides are hallmarks of a camp sensibility" (Mallan & McGillis, 2005, p. 12). He is an evil sorcerer who swaps "effortlessly between simpering sycophant and conniving usurper" (p. 12).

Scar, the patronizing presumptive heir in *The Lion King* (Hahn, Allers, & Minkoff, 1994) is "a physically weak male who makes up for his lack of sheer strength with catty remarks and invidious plotting" (Griffin, 2000, p. 211). His witty, acerbic quips and catty sensibility are occasionally accompanied by "a fey smile and a raised pinkie in his claw" (Griffin, 2000, p. 194). He's a "villainous uncle . . . [who] masterfully voices scheming and betrayal using a British accent that contrasts with the all-American intonation of the ruddy-maned hero, Simba" (Giroux & Pollock, 2010, p. 102). When Simba says, "You're so weird," Scar looks him directly in the eyes and replies wryly, "You have *nooo* idea . . . " By contrast, Governor Ratcliffe, in *Pocahontas* (Pentecost, Gabriel, & Goldberg, 1995), is fashioned, though perhaps only very loosely, on the eponymous character from history. He sings *Dig for Virginia* to a legion of burly sweating men in his pink and purple outfit, pink hair bows and high-heeled boots, and ironically notes "the ladies of court will be all a-twitter!" when he returns home with mountains of gold from the new world. He finishes his big number, spent singing and dancing with a troop of sweaty, working men, with a self-satisfied smirk, eyes narrowed, denoting the mischief embedded in his plans, and the pleasure he derives from it. He is "a foppish gay stereotype (wearing pink outfits with ribbons in his hair) with hardly any personality whatsoever" (Griffin, 2000, p. 210). Finally, Hades, the likeable and funny camp villain from *Hercules* (Dewey, Musker, & Clements, 1997) sings in "My Town," "the Parthenon, that crowning jewel, could use my flair for urban renewal" when one of the Muses asks incredulously, "What?" and Hades replies, " . . . .I'm just kidding, I wouldn't change a thing. I'm serious!" He is flaming, literally (!), as evidenced by the blue flames for hair (which turn orange-red when he gets angry) and his finger-snap lighter. He's full of sardonic quips like, "Meg, my sweet, my flower, my little *nut* Meg."

To scrutinize these portrayals of normative subjectivities, I marshal Ahmed's (2006) work on queer phenomenology in order excavate queer conceptualizations of subjectivities (Kumashiro, 2002; Rasmussen, 2006) and what this might mean for the educative project of engaging with popular culture (DePalma & Atkinson, 2009; Giroux & Pollock, 2010; Halberstam, 2011). My analysis of how these five characters seem to understand themselves and are understood illustrates how a presumed 'normalisation' of such camp sensibilities actually functions as a pedagogy to commodify heterosexuality and heteropatriarchy, thus reinscribing the very practices such camp sensibilities and instantiations emerged to militate against. This understanding of camp enables me to better "understand the larger relations between sexuality and culture, between kinds of desire and conventions of feeling," and to capture "the extent to which social practices and cultural forms are both gendered and sexualized" (Halperin, 2012, p. 15). This is important because the camp subjectivities imbued in these villains are gendered and sexualized in ways that are an affront to dominant cultural narratives and norms. In such a queer turn of events, [hetero]normative masculinities and femininities are valorized at the expense of [figuratively and often literally] non-normative subjectivities.

For instance, these sensibilities are evident in Ursula's sarcastic groan, "I'm wasting away to nothing," playing off the corporeal reality of her hefty, larger-than-life size as she launches into her cabaret-style performance of "Poor Unfortunate Souls." Although Ursula seems to be female, "her octopus-like lower half further renders her gender ambiguous: the first view of her tentacles emerging from the darkness is played up for shock value" (Roth, 1996, para. 33). "She might move like Rita Hayworth and have the body of Mae West, but she *looks* like a drag queen" (Mallan & McGillis, 2005, p. 14), and a 'real' one at that, as it is reported that she was styled after the uber-queen Divine (Sells, 1995). She's a husky-voiced parody of a woman who gives a young girl advice about using her feminine charms to lure a mate. Her own life stands in stark opposition to the heteropatriarchal one for which she's grooming Ariel. Her persona seems to challenge heteropatriarchy, but her advice to Ariel about ensnaring a man, and the beauty she transforms into when she steals Ariel's voice exemplify an adherence and advocacy of it.

Likewise, in his disdain for the heteronormative privilege exemplified in the film's carnivalesque opening musical montage "Circle of Life," "Scar's unforgivable sin seems to be his refusal to support the heterosexual patriarchy that Simba and his father represent" (Griffin, 2000, p. 212). His bachelorhood is read as an active and intentional refusal of the hetero-familial expectations that not only allow but in fact drive the circle of life to keep cycling. And when chastised by Mufasa for calling Simba a 'hairball', Scar "dons a mockingly prissy graciousness as he responds, 'Oh! I shall practice my curtsy!'" (Griffin, 2000, p. 211).

Hades, in his show tune "My Town," belts out, "the Parthenon, that crowning jewel, could use my flair for urban renewal . . . I'm just kidding, I wouldn't change a thing!" This song references both his vaunted penchant for design and decorating, and also the shock of the mainstream society, as represented by the five Muses who narrate the story, at the thought that something so treasured and enduring can be tampered with or destroyed. His God of the underworld persona sits incongruously with the role of a designer/decorator, making the juxtaposition quite a queer one. Hades almost proved a threat to the status quo, but it turns out, like a good camp, he was just kidding. But also like a good camp there was a biting truth to his assertion that he'd raze the Parthenon, and that the town needs some work, delivered in a sassy, effeminate manner that is familiar to us.

Jafar's "deliciously evil and sinister actions, measured enunciation, and sarcastic retorts . . . elicit a perverted kind of humour" (Mallan & McGillis, 2005, p. 13), making him an archetypal camp villain. His meticulous personal grooming and fastidiousness is matched only by his acerbic tongue. In an ironic twist, one of his big musical numbers is "You're Only Second Rate." But, although well-groomed, he pales in comparison (despite, or perhaps because of, his swarthy complexion) to the film's beautiful hero Aladdin. Jafar and Ursula are both well-groomed villains, but in an exaggerated manner reminiscent of a drag show. They're not pretty like the heroines, and especially like the heroes, of the movies in which they star.

The irony of Governor Ratcliffe's refrain "the ladies of court will be all a-twitter!" is not lost on the audience as this corpulent despot twirls around the dance floor. They may be laughing at him rather than with him at the thought that he could ignite women's passions. As with villains like Scar, Governor Ratcliffe is voiced by a British actor, and his prissiness shines through in his effeminate, fashionable persona. Characters like Ratcliffe embody a camp sensibility in part because a "feminine item [e.g., pink hair bows] stands out so glaringly by incongruity that it 'undermines' the masculine system and proclaims that the inner identification is feminine" (Newton, 1979, p. 101).

In contrast to the comely heroes and heroines whose names often appear as the titles of Disney movies, "in some ways the camp is an alternative for those who are not pretty" for "camp depends on inventiveness and wit rather than on physical beauty" (Newton, 1979, p. 105). As illustrated above, camp serves as a notable valance of difference, but one that is de-valued as it works to reaffirm and reassert heterosexual patriarchy. These films need the camp characters to stand in contradistinction to and to reiterate heteropatriarchy, offering the 'not' to what it is and should be—heteronormativity. Camp in this context unwittingly authorizes the sanitized, palatable, and normalized, while de-authorizing its very origins and roots. Further, as Allen (2014) notes, "Disney's queer-coded male characters [to which I am adding Ursula] tend to be feminized in order to make them seem even more evil."

Commodifying Heteropatriarchy

Historically, as Tinkcom (2002) deftly illustrates, camp "arose as a way of producing critical awareness of capital" (p. 191) and "as a philosophy in its own right, one that offers explanations of how the relation between labor and the commodity is lived in the day-to-day by dissident sexual subjects who arrive at their own strategies for critique *and* pleasure" (p. 4). But these historical origins, however, are far from evident in the ways we see camp marshalled in these Disney films. Instead, the camp characters are foils to the 'main' characters, creating the tensions and conflict necessary to propel the narrative forward. And this is heightened in the instances of these five characters because they also (perhaps not coincidentally) serve as villains in these films—camp embodiments of evil. In making sense of these camp characters and their roles in the movie, "the concept of connotation allows straight culture to use queerness for pleasure and profit in mass culture without admitting to it" (Doty, 1993, pp. xi–xii). To illustrate, as Roth (1996) writes, "Ursula eventually pulls off a drag queen's coup. She takes on the appearance of a svelte brunette, speaks with the Little Mermaid's stolen voice (solving a chronic problem for female impersonators), and seduces the virile young prince into marrying her" (para. 33). But in so doing, she commodifies heteropatriarchy by aspiring to it and promoting it.

Although "the complexity and volatility of mass culture production and reception-consumption often make any attempt to attribute queerness to only (or mostly) producers, texts, or audiences seem false and limiting" (Doty, 1993, p. xiii), I am interested in the ways these camp characters help to reinscribe heteropatriarchal storylines, and how they serve as examples in opposition to the desired, normative, normal state of the social and cultural order. To illustrate, it is not only Scar's refusal to participate in the circle of life by not marrying or fathering offspring, but his active attempts to disrupt and sabotage this cycle by killing his brother and trying to kill his nephew, that epitomizes how villainous it is to eschew heterosexualized patriarchy. This task is about examining the reception of these characters embedded in the contexts in which they are presented, acknowledging how those contexts may delimit one's viewing/reading and restrict what is seen as possible.

"Devising novel ways to entertain children goes hand in hand with the desire by corporate culture to expand children's consumer clout" (Mallan & McGillis, 2005, p. 16), which in this case would not just include the myriad of collateral ways to consume the products of these films, but also to consume the heteropatriarchal privilege they peddle, prop up, and work to preserve. Working to these ends, "camp becomes a designation of the pleasures unleashed in the sphere of consumption of popular culture that seem unwarranted by it" (Tinkcom, 2002, p. 13). We can see in the characters and films examined here how a marshalling of camp sensibilities and embodiment works to commodify traditional, rather narrowly defined acceptable gender roles and gendered embodiment for the consumption of those who view these films—or encounter their advertising, or buy from their extensive product line of movie collaterals. Think about the feminine fashion affectations of Governor Ratcliffe, the sarcastic, queeny asides of Jafar, or the androgynous appearance of Ursula, for instance, to understand how these characters accomplish this commodification. As Doty (1993) explains, these movies "implicitly set up straight men and straight women as the ultimate reference points for their analysis of gender because their authors don't seriously consider the possibility that the gayness, lesbianism, and bisexuality . . . might be crucial to that destabilization of gender roles" (p. 85).

Newton's (1979) analysis of the dynamics of camp proves a useful metaphor for (re)considering (re)readings/(re)viewings of these camp Disney characters and their place in these narratives by framing up the interrelations between *camps* and *beauties*, juxtaposing these two polarities. Newton (1979) noted the contrast between the "competing, yet often complementary" figures of the highly attractive and sexually desirable gay man and the "'campiest,' most dramatic most verbally entertaining queen" (p. 56). As Newton further explains, "The camp, both on and off the stage, tends to be a person who is, by group criteria, less sexually attractive, whether by virtue of advancing age or fewer physical charms or, frequently, both" (p. 56). Because "[t]he camp's function is defined in opposition to the beauty's and vice versa" (Halperin, 2012, p. 208), Disney's camp characters serve necessarily as unpalatable, if not still amusing, non-alternatives to dominant cultural representations. To illustrate, Ursula provides advice and advocates for Ariel's dream of finding a perfect human husband—the beauty and the camp mutually define one another. Who would want to be as bitter and twisted, as lonely and loathed, as prissy and preened, and frankly as queer as these characters? Thus, the presence of these characters buttresses heteropatriarchal normativity, making it seem even more desirable, and perhaps even inevitable, without ever needing to name it. Heteropatriarchy is the 'is' to queer camp's 'not.'

But camp can be quite fun too. Camp can astound and delight, for all of its unlikely referents, cheeky and acerbic wordplay, and incongruous cultural juxtapositions. As Tinkcom (2002) reminds us, "one way of locating camp in the sphere of production is by finding the repeated incidents of narrative filmmaking that seem to depart from the more usual expectations of visual and acoustic form" (p. 28). In fact, "the affectively necessary labor of camp resides in the occasions where one senses that the film image has diverged from *narrative* expectations, both in ways such as the visual excess [such as the large musical numbers] . . . or the playful corporeality that might easily be dismissed by even the most engaged of viewers as so much 'fluff' or 'bad taste'" (such as the hallmark camp plumpness of Governor Radcliffe or Ursula) (Tinkcom, 2002, p. 28). But lest this devolve into a game of 'find the camp,' the reason to search it out is to take it up as an object of analysis, to interrogate how it both arises from and contributes to a project of gay cultural visibility, and to think deeply about what the consequences of manifestations might be, as I do in the next section.

Refusing Normative Readings, Insisting on Queer Subjectivities

Reclaiming such instantiations of camp, and re-reading and reg(u)arding these sensibilities and the subjectivities they both afford *and negate*, can help us to re-fashion a pedagogy of engagement with these films that may never have been intended, but which yields a robust curriculum about not only social and cultural norms, but also viable and valued subjectivities. To that end, camp sensibilities and embodiments can serve, when read against the grain, to challenge and even upend the very normative ideologies discussed in the previous section. Because "pleasure is one of the defining principles of what Disney produces, and children are both its subjects and objects" (Giroux & Pollock, 2010, p. 97), this work is important—we must broaden what constitutes pleasure, and how pleasure is read and interpreted. As noted by Giroux and Pollock (2010), we must resist surrendering pleasure to the realm of the uncritical, for not only can pleasure be critical, but we can derive a great deal of pleasure from acting critically to excavate silences and blind spots. They explain that "it must be made clear that there are other ways to engage popular forms than merely through the realm of pleasurable consumption," arguing that it is "crucial to address not just the pleasure created by the object but the pleasure created by learning and critical engagement" (p. 127).

What if we used these Disney films to teach and learn about queer subjectivities? What if, instead of remaining the abject other, or the alternative necessary only to understand the default dominant subject position, these subjectivities were named, explored, and critiqued? What, too, if we named straight subjectivities instead of leaving them as the unnamed, default, normative and therefore normal subject position? In a campy outcry I can't resist for its head-on confrontation of the notion that queer reading practices depict alternative readings, Doty (1993) croons, "I've got news for straight culture: your readings of texts are usually 'alternative' ones for me, and they often seem like desperate attempts to deny the queerness that is so clearly a part of mass culture" (p. xii). Other reading/viewing practices that deviate from prevailing practices do not constitute 'alternative' practices, with the connotation of inferiority an afterthought. Instead, we must take up a stance as a producer and consumer of texts to contribute to the proliferation of a diversity of reading/viewing practices, analyzing what's foregrounded and what's left invisible in each, and working to make sense of those disparities.

We could certainly recruit many other characters—such as the Genie, Timon, and Pumbaa, as well as Gaston, Ratigan, Terkina, Captain Hook, Prince John, and Shang—to assist in this educative project. Because "the queerness of most mass culture texts is less an essential, waiting-to-be-discovered property than the result of acts of production or reception" (Doty, 1993, p. xi), we would not be asking if these characters are queer or not, but rather *in what ways* are they queer, upending and challenging dominant representational narratives of what is acceptable and who has a voice. Concomitantly, we would explore in what perhaps unintended ways their queerness may be working to buttress the status quo, as illustrated here with the five villains.

A close reading of these five movie characters leads me to ponder how, by reclaiming such instantiations of camp, by re-reading and reg(u)arding these sensibilities and the subjectivities they both afford and negate, we can think differently. As discussed above, even playful representations of camp can serve to commodify dominant and normative sex, gender, and sexuality constructions, packaging them for mass consumption. And only through reading these narratives and these sensibilities against the grain are we able to make the most of their full potential. For although, as Hayward (1994) cautions, "Disney's moral hierarchy has implications which are damaging for all of us who lie outside the 'mainstream'" (p. 16), there are recuperative readings we can offer these characters and storylines that explicitly name how they commodify heteropatriarchy. As Mallan and McGillis (2005) note, "Whether or not audiences (child or adult) pick up on the camp signifiers, which may lurk as a queer subtext or an overtly queer supratext, is immaterial as camp functions between spaces: between a performance and a viewer, between a playful wink and a knowing nod, between a frock and a hard place" (p. 16).

Meyer (2010) suggests that "Camp is not simply a 'style' or 'sensibility' as is conventionally accepted. Rather what emerges is a suppressed and oppositional critique embodied in the signifying practices that processually constitute gay identities . . . Camp embodies a specifically gay cultural critique" (p. 39). As such, camp is

> the total body of performative practices used to enact gay identity, with enactment defined as the production of social visibility. Gay identity is performative, discontinuous, and processually constituted by repetitive and stylized acts marked by the deployment of specific signifying codes, the sum of which I am calling Camp.
>
> (p. 52)

This means that the "suppressed and oppositional critique" is there for us to explicitly identify and engage with, should we go looking for it. And we should. For we might find value in Scar's eschewing of marriage and reproducing, in Jafar's bitchy wit and fastidious appearance, or in Ursula's androgynous look and drag queen stylings that allow us to re-view what we take away from these films. Reading camp as critique, and identifying how these characters are deployed and to what ends in these films, we might read in multiple, sometimes contradictory ways. In light of normative readings/viewings we need to reclaim, or reanimate camp because

> value production is the prerogative of the dominant order, dominant precisely because it controls signification and which is represented by the privilege of nominating its own codes as the 'original' . . . parody becomes the process whereby the marginalized and disenfranchised advance their own interests by entering alternative signifying codes into discourse by attaching them to existing structures of signification.
>
> (pp. 42–43)

In order to make space for varied, alternative readings, we must 'advance our own interests' and refuse to only accept readings from over-privileged, normative subject positions.

Halperin (2012) offers us a productive, educative, and recuperative way forward, noting that "Dominant social roles and meanings cannot be destroyed, any more than can the power of beauty, but they can be undercut and derealized: we can learn how not to take them straight" (p. 218). Not only is it gleeful to ponder the ways in which a Disney animated film *is already* a queer party (!) with the features that Halperin chronicles above, but as Tinkcom (2002) writes, "camp forms a critique of capital's assertions of value" (p. 189). Multiple readings, some of which originate from below and some originating from the very critique that camp constitutes, will diversify what is seen to constitute cultural capital. The hope is that such work will aid in the project of "removing mass culture queerness from the shadowy realm of connotation to which much of it has been relegated" (Doty, 1993, p. xi) by opening up and revealing new subject positions to viewers/consumers of these movies. An analysis of these camp characters and their place within these films makes explicit the ways they function to render dominant ideologies as commodities for cultural consumption, which in turn might fuel the creation of viewing strategies to keep these issues at the surface, rather than submerged. The camp characters help draw explicit attention to how "sexual orientation comes to be understood as integral to the subject, as a matter of its identity" (Ahmed, 2006, p. 69), something that would likely go unnoticed with an all 'non-queer' cast who are presumed to be neutral and natural. Further, such a turn to elucidating and valuing queer subjectivities could allow us "to recapture and reassert a militant sense of difference that views the erotically 'marginal' as both (to use bell hooks' words) a consciously chosen 'site of resistance' and a 'location of radical openness and possibility'" (Doty, 1993, p. 3). And you can't get much more camp than that!

References

Ahmed, S. (2006). *Queer phenomenology: Orientations, objects, others.* Durham, NC: Duke University Press.

Allen, S. (2014, September 25). What Disney movies taught me about being gay. *The Daily Dot.* Retrieved from: http://www.dailydot.com/opinion/ursula-little-mermaid-disney-movies-lesbian/

Clements, R., & Musker, J. (Producers/Directors). (1992). *Aladdin* [Motion picture]. United States: Walt Disney Pictures.

DePalma, R., & Atkinson, E. (Eds.) (2009). *Interrogating heteronormativity in primary schools: The No Outsiders project.* Stoke on Trent, UK: Trentham Books.

Dewey, A. (Producer), Musker, J., & Clements, R. (Producers/Directors). (1997). *Hercules* [Motion picture]. United States: Walt Disney Pictures.

Doty, A. (1993). *Making things perfectly queer: Interpreting mass culture.* Minneapolis: University of Minnesota Press.

Giroux, H. A., & Pollock, G. (2010). *The mouse that roared: Disney and the end of innocence.* Lanham, MD: Rowman & Littlefield.

Griffin, S. P. (2000). *Tinker belles and evil queens: The Walt Disney Company from the inside out.* New York: NYU Press.

Hahn, D. (Producer), Allers, R., & Minkoff, R. (Directors). (1994). *The lion king* [Motion picture]. United States: Walt Disney Pictures.

Halberstam, J. (2011). *The queer art of failure.* Durham, NC: Duke University Press.

Halperin, D. (2012). *How to be gay.* Cambridge, MA: Harvard University Press.

Hayward, T. (1994, September 21). The lyin' king. *Planet Homo, 69,* 16–17.

Kumashiro, K. (2002). *Troubling education: Queer activism and antiopprerssive pedagogy.* New York: RoutledgeFalmer.

Mallan, K., & McGillis, R. (2005). Between a frock and a hard place: Camp aesthetics and children's culture. *Canadian Review of American Studies, 35*(1), 1–19.

Meyer, M. (2010). *An archaeology of posing: Essays on camp, drag, and sexuality.* Madison, WI: Macater Press.

Musker, J. (Producer/Director), Ashman, H. (Producer), & Clements, R. (Director). (1989). *The little mermaid* [Motion picture]. United States: Walt Disney Pictures.

Newton, E. (1979). *Mother camp: Female impersonators in America.* Chicago: University of Chicago Press.

Pentecost, J. (Producer), Gabriel, M., & Goldberg, E. (Directors). (1995). *Pocahontas* [Motion picture]. United States: Walt Disney Pictures.

Rasmussen, M. L. (2006). *Becoming subjects: Sexualities and secondary schooling.* New York: Routledge.

Roth, M. (1996). The Lion King: A short history of Disney-fascism. *Jump Cut: A Review of Contemporary Media, 40,* 15–20.

Sells, L. (1995). "Where do the mermaids stand?" Voice and body in *The Little Mermaid.* In E. Bell, L. Haas, & L. Sells (Eds.), *From mouse to mermaid: The politics of film, gender, and culture* (pp. 175–192). Bloomington: Indiana University Press.

Sontag, S. (1983). Notes on camp. In *A Susan Sontag Reader* (pp. 105–119). New York: Vintage. (Original work published in 1964.)

Tinkcom, M. (2002). *Working like a homosexual: Camp, capital, cinema.* Durham, NC: Duke University Press.

Towbin, M. A., Haddock, S. A., Zimmerman, T. S., Lund, L. K., & Tanner, L. R. (2004). Images of gender, race, age, and sexual orientation in Disney feature-length animated films. *Journal of Feminist Family Therapy, 15*(4), 19–44.

11 Black Feminist Thought and Disney's Paradoxical Representation of Black Girlhood in *Doc McStuffins*

Rachel Alicia Griffin

Doc McStuffins (2012–) debuted on Disney Jr. in 2012 as the first preschool cartoon to center on an African American main character since *Little Bill* (1999–2004) (Peck, 2012). Targeting children ages two to seven (Ayot, 2013), six-year-old Dottie "Doc" McStuffins emulates her mother, a medical doctor, by tending to injured toys and stuffed animals with her magical stethoscope. According to Disney (n.d.), "Doc's backyard playhouse becomes her clinic where she uses her special ability to communicate with toy friends to help them when they have physical or emotional bangs and bruises" (para. 1). Via cheerful sing-along lyrics, Doc also offers valuable lessons on health, hygiene, and happiness. As a biracial (Black and White) Black female critical scholar who teaches a course entitled "Walt Disney: The Man, The Empire, and The Politics of Popular Culture," I am drawn to deconstruct Dottie "Doc" McStuffins as a representation of Black femininity. My interest in doing so is rooted in the rarity of Black female protagonists in Disney productions (Barnes, 2009; Lester, 2010), and Disney's longstanding repro- duction of problematic raced and gendered stereotypes (Buescher & Ono, 1996; Lester, 2010; Moffitt & Harris, 2014). Moreover, the considerable absence of representations of Black girlhood in contemporary popular culture necessitates being attentive to how Black girlhood is portrayed on the rare occasion that Black girls are centered.

Of significance is that Disney chose to depict Doc McStuffins as a Black girl even though the show's creator, Chris Nee, pitched the character as a White girl (Barnes, 2012). In a rare public acknowledgment of Disney's pedagogical power, Gary Marsh, the President and Chief Creative Officer of Disney Channels Worldwide, says, "What we put on TV can change how kids see the world ... By showcasing different role models and different kinds of families we can positively influence sociological dynamics for the next 20 years" (Barnes, 2012, para. 13).

From a critical stance, Marsh's willingness to acknowledge Disney's corporate, pedagogical influence while praising Disney for showcasing racial diversity via *Doc McStuffins* is marred by convenience. When Disney has faced criticism for oppressive representations of diversity (e.g., race, gender, ability, etc.) their corporate response has customarily been to ignore the criticism, negotiate modifications to their benefit and liking, and/or underscore the company's commitment to mere entertainment rather than education (Giroux & Pollock, 2010; Norden, 2013; Sun & Picker, 2001; *The New York Times*, 1993). Therefore, I critically interpret the acknowledgement of Disney's corporate, pedagogical influence amid praise, and the intentional portrayal of Doc as a Black girl, as an indication of the company's capitalistic desire to appear inclusive while further tapping into Black children and their parents as a market. Thus, Disney's focus on diversity and inclusion "only 'celebrates' difference in order to exploit multiculturalism for its economic value" (K_ra, 2014). Nonetheless, engaging with *Doc McStuffins* as a site of "public pedagogy," defined as "the education provided by popular culture" (Giroux, 2000; Sandlin, 2007, p. 76), is essential. Quite demonstrative of the show's pedagogical reach as a representation of Black girlhood is its current status as "the top-rated cable TV show for preschoolers" and its viewership of approximately two million (Palmeri, 2012, para. 1).

In this chapter, I examine *Doc McStuffins* as paradoxical public pedagogy that is simultaneously 'inclusive' and exploitative. I begin by describing the considerable absence of Black girls in popular culture and academic scholarship as the context in which the show emerges. Then, I couple US American Black feminist thought (Collins, 2009) as theory with textual analysis as method (McKee, 2003) to reveal Doc as a paradoxical representation of Black girlhood. Via my analysis, I argue that while *Doc McStuffins* importantly functions as a site of progressive empowerment for Black girls, the show also deracializes Doc as a girl of color and fuels 'post-' logics, supports the commercialized commodification of Black girlhood, and strengthens the racist and sexist naturalization of Black females as caretakers. Finally, I conclude with an apprehensive yet optimistic discussion of Disney's redeeming qualities as a media empire that can choose to be more progressive and inclusive, if, of course, the price and profit are right.

Black Femininity, Media Representation, and the Invisibility of Black Girlhood

Representations of Black females in popular culture most often cater to negative, stereotypical interpretations of who we are regarding personality, character, values, and potential (Coleman, 2011; Griffin, 2012; Lindsey, 2013; Smith-Shomade, 2002). Termed "controlling images" by Collins (2009, p. 76), mediated allegiances to representations of Black femininity in alignment with the mammy, jezebel, sapphire, and/or welfare queen sacrifice diversity and endorse dehumanized understandings of Black female children, adolescents, and adults as inferior, unintelligent, hopeless, hypersexual, and/or contemptible (Coleman, 2011; Griffin, 2014; Lindsey, 2013; Smith-Shomade, 2002; West, 2009). According to Boylorn (2008), "counterstereotypical" (p. 415) representations of Black femininity are desperately needed. Amid the largely unrealized potential of popular culture to engage in liberatory praxis, there is a substantial absence of positive and gratifying representations of Black femininity for Black female spectators of all ages to identify with, enjoy, and celebrate.

Mirroring the widespread availability of representations of Black womanhood confined to controlling imagery, most scholarship addressing portrayals of Black femininity centers Black women to expose the intricacies of racism and sexism (e.g., Boylorn, 2008; Griffin, 2014; hooks, 1992). Such works importantly challenge the reduction of Black women into presumptive logics that situate us as disrespectful, whorish, and ignorant, poor public charges. In comparison to Black womanhood, much less scholarly attention has focused on representations of Black female adolescents and children (Lindsey, 2013). More pointedly, although mediated discourse about and pertaining to Black girls surely circulates (e.g., Malia and Sasha Obama, Gabby Douglas, Quvenzhané Wallis, Mo'ne Davis, etc.) and past shows such as *The Cosby Show* (1984–1992), *Family Matters* (1989–1998), *That's So Raven* (2003–2007), and *True Jackson, VP* (2008–2011) featured Black female children and adolescents, scholarly works that deconstruct representations of Black girlhood rarely emerge. To be clear, Black girls are indeed implicated by representations of Black womanhood. However, at the intersections of race, gender, and age, representations of Black girlhood are important to deconstruct to more fully theorize how Black femininity is negatively and/or positively scripted via popular culture.

Quite unique given their focus on representations of Black girlhood are Hopson's (2009) critique of bell hooks' *Happy to Be Nappy* and McNair and Brooks' (2012) critique of a transitional chapter book series starring Dyamonde Daniel, Nikki and Deja, and Willimena Thomas. Hopson (2009) interprets *Happy to Be Nappy* as a children's book that champions Black feminism's commitment to self-expression and self-love, while resisting dominant discourses that situate 'nappy' (i.e., Black) hair as 'bad' hair. Similarly, McNair and Brooks (2012) highlight how each book series aligns with Black feminism's emphasis on intersectionality, while supportively affirming Black girlhood via resistant storylines. Building upon the analyses of representations of Black girlhood in literature, the nuance of this chapter is rooted in my focus on Doc McStuffins as a representation of Black girlhood on television. In the following section, I establish Black feminist thought as theory and textual analysis as method to critically interpret *Doc McStuffins'* public pedagogy.

Black Feminist Thought as Theory and Textual Analysis as Method

With regard to media critique, Black feminist scholars are deeply concerned with controlling images. In contrast, imagery that situates Black females beyond stereotypical restraints challenges oppressive representations and functions as a site of resistant empowerment. To analyze controlling imagery, Black feminist thought (BFT) theoretically necessitates a commitment to: intersectionality as an assertion that identities are multiplicative; self-definition and self-determination as means to empowerment; and the challenging of, at minimum, racist and sexist marginalization (Collins, 1986, 2009, 2013; Crenshaw, 1993; Griffin, 2012). To deconstruct *Doc McStuffins*, I couple BFT with textual analysis. Defining textual analysis as a means of revelatory sense-making, McKee (2003) describes this method as an "attempt to understand the likely interpretations of texts made by people who consume them" (p. 2). To critique *Doc McStuffins*, I employ textual analysis as a deconstructive tool to expose the show's public pedagogy and approach the characters, dialogue, plotlines, and sing-a-long jingles, asking: "How does *Doc McStuffins* function paradoxically (i.e., both positively and problematically) as a representation of Black girlhood?"

In total, I watched 15 episodes via three DVD collections: *Doc McStuffins: Friendship is the Best Medicine* (2012), *Doc McStuffins: Time for Your Checkup* (2013), and *Doc McStuffins: Mobile Clinic* (2014). Each episode contains two individually titled programs that are approximately 12 minutes long. Altogether, the DVD collections offer nearly six hours of viewing time. To foster a nuanced critique, I watched each episode twice, and frequently revisited scenes that emerged as key illustrations of how Black girlhood is portrayed. Through the process of watching and re-watching episodes and scenes, four overarching themes solidified: (1) The Power of Doc as a Departure from Oppressive Norms, (2) The Significance of Doc as Self-Defined and Self-Determined, (3) The Deracialization of Doc as Commodified Black Girlhood, and (4) The Nurturing Nature of Doc as Mammified Black Girlhood. Taken together, these themes illuminate Doc McStuffins as a paradoxical representation of Black girlhood.

The Power of Doc as a Departure from Oppressive Norms

Doc McStuffins can be interpreted as a departure from the omnipresent controlling images of Black femininity in US American culture. At the intersections of race, gender, and age, Doc embodies a range of praiseworthy attributes including creativity, kindness, and curiosity. Equally important is the emphasis on her intellect rather than her physicality. Not only is *Doc McStuffins* predicated on Doc's intelligence as an aspiring medical doctor, but every episode showcases her brainpower. For example, in "Gulpy, Gulpy Gators!" (Nee, 2013), when Doc's little brother Donny is saddened by his broken game, Doc becomes a problem solver who investigates why Gustave the green gator is unable to gulp marbles. Settling on a diagnosis of "Stuffedfulliosis" (Nee, 2013), Doc chronicles the illness in her Big

Book of Boos Boos, a colorfully illustrated record of each ailment she treats. Then Doc cures the overstuffed gator by emptying his stomach, and her success is accompanied by the lesson to stop eating when full.

Depicting Doc as an admirable and intellectual Black girl contradicts racist and sexist reductions of Black femininity. Although Doc is not verbally scripted to overtly oppose oppression, her embodiment of creativity, kindness, curiosity, and intelligence functions as a counterstereotypical representation. Worth noting is that negative representations of Black femininity are not the only problem; equally problematic is the lack of competing images. This is where Doc's significance in our mediated landscape shines brightly in that she offers a representation of Black femininity that challenges US American culture's parade of negative imagery. Emphasizing Doc as a uniquely positive representation, Ayot (2013) says *Doc McStuffins* depicts "a little Black girl aspiring to be a doctor. Not a singer. Not a reality TV star. Not a princess. But a doctor" (para. 3).

Alongside Doc's admirable characteristics, it is important to highlight her being celebrated as an esteemed character on the show. As the show's protagonist, Doc, and Kiara Muhammad as the Black female adolescent who voices her (Lewis, 2012), is centered in every episode. Therefore, *Doc McStuffins* can be understood as a television show that shifts Black girlhood from the margins of mediated representation to the center of attention. The cultural significance of Disney's intentional decision to do so more clearly emerges via a comparison between Doc's role and Tiana's role in *The Princess and The Frog* (Del Vecho, Lasseter, Clements, & Musker, 2009). Amid the excitement that surrounded Tiana as Disney's first Black princess, Moffitt and Harris (2014) highlight how Tiana, as the film's 'main' protagonist, was circumvented by Charlotte La Bouff's omnipresence in the storyline as Tiana's White female counterpart. Charlotte's character can be theorized as a lucrative sidekick and racist safety net that communicates the at worst actual, and at best perceived, inability of a Disney film featuring a Black princess to generate profit among Disney's predominantly White consumer base. In this context, albeit imperfect given the show's exploitive commodification of Black girlhood and the omnipresence of controlling imagery, *Doc McStuffins* can be understood as a means for Disney to redress past offenses by centering a Black girl as a protagonist unencumbered by a White female counterpart competing for the spotlight.

Doc is also celebrated by multiple characters in each episode and mainstay jingles that forecast and document her success. For instance, each episode begins with the show's theme song which conveys confidence in Doc's competence via the lyrics, "It's okay/Don't be afraid/the Doc really knows her stuff!" and "The Doc is going to help you feel better!" (Nee, 2012). Additionally, the jingle that is sung in every episode communicates that Doc is both capable and trustworthy. Her patients, joined by her close-knit toy community, appreciatively declare:

I feel better, so much better.
Thank you Doc for taking all the ouches away!
I didn't feel so good til you fixed me like I knew that you would.
And I feel better, so much better, now!

(Nee, 2012)

Watching these gleeful sing-a-long scenes, awash in bright colors and jovial dancing, Doc portrays Black girlhood as a cerebral site of enjoyment, compassion, and affection. Her being depicted in this way unequivocally opposes the dominant norm to represent Black females as inferior, unintelligent, and unworthy of care. Amplifying my argument that Doc functions as a progressive departure from how Black femininity is typically scripted, next I highlight how Doc radiates Black feminism's commitment to self-definition and self-determination.

The Significance of Doc as Self-Defined and Self-Determined

Black feminist scholars emphasize self-definition and self-determination as essential (Collins, 1986, 2009). The enactment of self-definition calls for Black females to "replace controlling images with self-defined knowledge deemed personally important" (Collins, 2009, p. 111). By comparison, the enactment of self-determination requires that Black females empower ourselves by shaping the trajectory of our lives (Collins, 2009; King, 1988). Extending BFT's emphasis on self-actualization into the realm of Black girlhood, Lindsey (2013) says, "Although full autonomy is not a primary or age-appropriate element of a black girlhood discourse of empowerment, the formation of a sense of self-determination and relative autonomy is significant in the development of black girls and adolescents" (pp. 28–29). Aligning with Lindsey (2013), Doc can be understood as a representation of the significance of self-definition and self-determination in the lives of Black girls.

In each episode, Doc defines and embodies Black girlhood as a site of confidence, potential, and agency and it is clear via her thoughts, actions, and interactions that Doc is committed to self-actualization. For example, Doc makes the faithful assertion, "I don't know, but I won't give up until we figure it out!" when she is unsure of a diagnosis for Lenny the fire truck, who keeps running out of water in "Engine Nine, Feelin' Fine!" (Nee, 2012). Underscoring her embodiment of Black girlhood as a site of agency is Doc's use of her magical stethoscope to bring the toys to life. Not only is Doc entrusted with the magical stethoscope, she also keeps the secret of her personified toy community safe by ordering the toys to "Go Stuffed!" (Nee, 2012) if someone appears. Therefore, Doc's Black girlhood is characterized by special talents that she uses responsibly to sharpen her knowledge, share her experiences, and embody team-oriented leadership. For instance, in "Caught Blue Handed" (Nee, 2012) Doc creates an illustration of how the "Mystery Pox" (i.e., blue dots) are spreading like germs among the toys. Then, she and Hallie jointly teach the toys, and the audience, how germs work and the importance of hand-washing. Taken together, Doc, and those who affirm her, validate "the strong belief that to be Black and female is valuable and worthy of respect" (Collins, 2009, p. 132).

Given the show's impetus to reduce children's fears about doctor visits (Barnes, 2012), Doc often encounters patients who are scared and reluctant to be examined and/or fixed. While their fearful reluctance could inhibit Doc's ability to self-define and self-determine by sparking insecurity, Doc skillfully soothes her patients' fears and garners their cooperation. For instance, when Suzy Sunshine is diagnosed with "Eyeswiditis" (i.e., her eyes are stuck open and she is unable to sleep) in "Tea Party Tantrum" (Nee, 2013), Doc empathetically shares that being sleep deprived can lead to being "spacey" and "cranky" (Nee, 2013). Then, Doc and her close-knit toy community sing Suzy Sunshine to sleep after Doc has cured her by removing a sticky substance from her eyelids. Overall, Doc never doubts her ambition or abilities in accordance with how Black females are typically defined by dominant societal discourses.

Quite symbolic of Doc's enactment of self-definition and self-determination are the medical artifacts she surrounds herself with. Doc wears a white doctor's coat with her magical stethoscope around her neck, carries a medical satchel, and her playhouse clinic mirrors a doctor's office. She also asks her patients exploratory questions, notes their responses, and maintains her Big Book of Boo Boos—which jointly signal her vision of becoming a doctor. We can further interpret Doc's playhouse clinic as a site of empowerment where she practices the skills that she will eventually need. For example, in "Starry, Starry Night" (Nee, 2013) Doc works diligently under pressure to fix Aurora the telescope in time for the meteor shower. Affirming Doc's self-perception as an equipped, capable, and resourceful doctor is her reputation for fixing toys. In "Arcade Escapade" (Nee, 2013), Doc is so renowned that toys in the arcade's toy claw machine beckon her over to help Gabby—a ripped, stuffed giraffe. Exuding confidence, and open to the challenge of winning Gabby to repair her, Doc declares "Doctors don't ever give up on their patients! Besides, I'm pretty good at games!" (Nee, 2013). Coupled with her self-confidence, Doc's strong reputation signals that her family, peers, and toy community see her as she sees herself—which is a testament to Doc's liberation from stereotypical assumptions about Black females.

Self-determination also manifests in *Doc McStuffins* layered representation of the medical profession as a career trajectory chosen by Black females. More specifically, Doc and her mother, Dr. Myiesha McStuffins, render being and becoming a medical doctor real and imaginable. Their representational presence is especially significant given the reality that most US American Black females will never encounter a Black female physician, since they represent less than 2 percent of doctors in the United States (Elber, 2012). Reflecting on the show's significance, Dr. Myiesha Taylor, the Texas Regional Medical Center emergency room doctor that Doc's mother is named after, says "It's so important that television provides alternative depictions of Black women . . . You simply don't see enough women represented in STEM (science, technology, engineering, and math) fields on screen" (Issa, 2014, para. 8). Signifying the power of Doc's mediated presence, 131 Black female doctors contributed their photos to a collage with a caption that reads, "We Are Doc McStuffins!" (Coily Embrace, 2012).

Also relevant to the representation of the medical profession is Hallie the purple hippo. Voiced by actor Loretta Devine, Hallie is linguistically scripted as a southern Black female who serves as Doc's clinic receptionist and nurse. Together, Doc, Dr. McStuffins, and Hallie jointly render the medical profession accessible to Black females, and do so as recipients of each other's support. For example in "Ben/Anna Split!," Ben the huggy monkey is diagnosed with "Huggypatchotis" (Nee, 2012) after his Velcro patch is ripped off. During Doc's evening rounds to check on Ben, Hallie describes Doc as "the best doctor in the whole wide world" and Doc describes Hallie as "a pretty fantastic nurse" (Nee, 2012). Likewise, similar to Mr. McStuffins, Doc's mother consistently supports her daughter's dreams. To see Black girls and women actively supporting each other is spectacular—and shamefully rare in popular culture.

Doc McStuffins as paradoxical popular culture functions positively and problematically with regard to representations of Black femininity. While Doc's departure from normativity and her embodiment of self-definition and self-determination are significant, especially amid US American culture's bleak-with-regard-to-Black-girlhood media landscape, the show is also oppressive, as I discuss in the following sections. More pointedly, *Doc McStuffins* deracializes Doc as a girl of color, fuels 'post-' logics, and commercially commodifies Black girlhood. Additionally, the show strengthens the racist and sexist naturalization of Black females as caretakers.

The Deracialization of Doc as Commodified Black Girlhood

With regard to deracialization, similar to *The Cosby Show* (1984–1992), *Doc McStuffins* likens a Black middle-class family and Black girlhood to White middle-class families and White girlhood which deracializes (i.e., Whitens) representations of Black culture. Mediated deracialization includes the minimization of race and racism, an endorsement of race neutrality that mimics colorblindness, and the sanitized representation of people of color in accordance with Whiteness (Miller, 1988; Sieving, 1998). According to Miller (1988), "By insisting that blacks and whites are entirely alike, television denies the cultural barriers that slavery necessarily created; barriers that have hardened over years and years, and that still exist" (p. 140). Challenging the deracialization of *The Cosby Show*, in an argument that extends to *Doc McStuffins*, Leonard (2013) says,

[T]he black middle class has not transcended race; it has not secured entry into a post-racial reality where racism and stereotypes no longer affect life's opportunities. Whether dealing with police brutality, the legacy of institutionalized racism, or housing segregation, racism still plays through the lives of the black middle class.

(p. 119)

Given the intended preschool audience of *Doc McStuffins*, it is unreasonable to expect explicit references to how systemic oppression influences Black middle-class families. However, a Black feminist lens illuminates the absence of Doc's Black femininity as a site and source of identity and empowerment. Similar to Lindsey's (2013) interpretation of *That's So Raven* and *True Jackson, VP* as shows that forefront Black female protagonists but largely neglect addressing racial stereotyping and incorporating elements of Black culture, *Doc McStuffins* fails to offer a specifically raced and gendered model of empowered Black girlhood. In all three shows, the protagonists merely 'happen' to be Black and female. In reference to Doc specifically, the only aspects of her that are explicitly indicative of Black femininity are linked to her physicality (e.g., skin color and hair texture) rather than her intellect, personality, and/or worldview.

By feeding into 'post-' discourses that antiquate racism, sexism, and classism despite their contemporary relevance in the Black community, *Doc McStuffins* implies that Black Americans can and have achieved the American Dream. While successful Black middle-class families do of course exist, circulating antiquated 'post-' assertions is problematic because they expunge the gravely disproportionate, systemized impact of unemployment, under-employment, inadequate education, poverty, incarceration, etc. on Black families in pursuit of the US American Dream. Therefore, *Doc McStuffins*, like *The Cosby Show*, partakes in the falsification of economic success as equally feasible for people of color and women of color. In essence, the "peculiar racial logic" of "if Cliff Huxtable/Bill Cosby could succeed, then racial barriers to economic and social success have disappeared" (Squires, 2009, p. 229) is newly extended at the intersections of race, gender, and class to imply that, if Doc McStuffins/Dr. McStuffins/Dr. Myiesha Taylor can succeed, then barriers to the medical profession for Black women have been eradicated. Hence, *Doc McStuffins* can be critically interpreted as a show hinged upon the fallacy of widespread social consciousness, or what Teasley and Ikard (2010) term "Obama-Inspired Optimism" (p. 413).

As a Black feminist, my concerns about *Doc McStuffins* are amplified by the use of Doc as a means to commodify Black girlhood. Since Disney is famous for the commercialization of childhood via character licensing (Giroux & Pollock, 2010), a cursory Google search for "Doc McStuffins products" expectedly reveals Disney's candid commitment to profit via an aggressive commodification of Black girlhood. A modicum of the products available include: bedding, bikes, books, cars, clothing, costumes, dishes, dolls, first aid kits, furniture, games, jewelry, luggage, posters, stationary, and shoes. Termed "conspicuous consumption" (Ott & Mack, 2010, p. 137), each product fuels capitalist logics that attaining happiness and satisfaction is possible via the acquisition of material goods reserved for those with middle-to-upper class status. Moreover, because Doc is a Black girl, the implicit message to Disney's predominantly White consumer base is that the consumption of *Doc McStuffins* products offers an opportunity to experience diversity, i.e., Black girlhood. Returning to deracialization as a vehicle for 'post-' logics, Black feminism exposes the implicit message as mythical given the show's decided erasure of Black culture (i.e., history, art, vernacular, etc.).

The Nurturing Nature of Doc as Mammified Black Girlhood

Of great importance to interrogate is how Disney relies on "mammification" (Omolade, 1994, p. 54) to commercialize and strengthen the naturalization of Black females as caretakers via the medical profession. Characterized by self-sacrificial servitude, the mammy as a controlling image problematically relegates Black females to caretaking professions—even middle-to-upper class caretaking professions—and naturalizes our willingness to care for others (Collins, 2009; Omolade, 1994). Although the trajectory into the medical profession that Doc, Dr. McStuffins, and Hallie representationally widen is valuable, the continuity of selflessness that characterizes their roles coupled with the scant depiction of self-care is troubling. Equally disconcerting is the absence of any counterstereotypical hobbies, interests, etc. that are un-related to their work, alongside the stereotypical portrayal of Dr. McStuffin's and Hallie's size and shape. Taken together, each aforementioned exemplar signifies the mammification of Doc, Dr. McStuffins, and Hallie, which reflects the domination and reduction of Black femininity.

Utilizing Doc as an example of self-sacrificial mammification, in "That's Just Claw-ful" (Nee, 2012), Doc skips snack time to coordinate her team's search for Hermie the crab and, in "One Note Wonder" (Nee, 2013), Doc skips lunch to treat her friend Alma's ladybug shaped xylophone. For Doc, her selfless nature incites malnutrition and isolates her from human company because she has to work privately for her magical stethoscope to work. Consequently, Doc is often limited to the company of the toys she serves, and she is always available for emergencies. As such, Doc's Black girlhood aligns with mammification given the omnipresence of selfless service to others and work in her daily life. Additionally, Doc embodies her selflessness in "Doctoring the Doc" at the expense of her health when she goes to work at the clinic, despite Hallie describing her as "draggy and saggy" (Nee, 2013). While her toy friends do eventually convince Doc to let them care for her, of importance to note is that Doc's first impulse is to sacrifice her health for her patients rather than take a necessary day off from work. Mirroring Hallie's resistance to medical care in "Hallie Gets an Earful" (Nee, 2012), both Black female medical professionals diminish and dismiss their personal need for medical attention.

Also problematic is Doc's mammification according to rigid gender normativity; her bedroom, apparel, clinic, and medical instruments are doused in bright pinks and purples rather than the teals and blues typically associated with the medical profession. Returning to "Arcade Escapade" (Nee, 2013) as an episode in which Doc's self-definition and self-determination are on rich display, it is also important to note that she went to the arcade—clad in her typical purple striped shirt and pink skirt, leggings, shoes, and stethoscope—with her dad and brother to have fun. Yet soon after their arrival, Doc was beckoned to help Gabby. Embodying obligation as a toy doctor, Doc responded without hesitation and an opportunity for her to have fun, apart from work, morphed into an opportunity for her to selflessly spend her tokens to rescue her patient.

Further illuminating the presence of mammification in the show, the depiction of Dr. McStuffins as a Black woman with visibly ample thighs and buttocks is concerning. Quinlan, Bates, and Webb (2012) align the public's focus on First Lady Obama's size and buttocks with mammification. Extending their insight to Dr. McStuffins we can understand her size and shape as formulaic and in sync with controlling imagery. Similarly, as a hippo, Hallie is depicted as a southern Black female of size whose preoccupation with food is stereotypical at the intersections of race, gender, region, and size. A smattering of Hallie's constant references to food include "It's hotter than a hippo dipped in hot sauce out here!," "Your breath could strip the grease off a griddle," and her repetitive reference to patients as "Sugar" (Nee, 2013). Hallie's continual references to food manifest as an indication that she is too fat to control her own body. For example, in "Hallie Gets an Earful" (Nee, 2012) Hallie gets stuck under the exam table, and in "One Note Wonder" (Nee, 2013) she accidentally squishes Squeakers. From my perspective, Disney's portrayal of Dr. McStuffins and Hallie both as women of size reductively represents the sizes and shapes of Black women's bodies. While Doc is absent the curves embodied by her mother and Hallie, the absence is more reasonably interpreted as an indication of her age as opposed to Disney espousing a critically conscious outlook that not all Black females are robust akin to Mammy in 1939's *Gone with the Wind* (Selznick & Fleming 2009).

Conclusion

Referencing *The Cosby Show's* "unprecedented success in depicting the lives of affluent blacks" in 1989 (para. 5), Henry Louis Gates Jr. made an assertion that sadly remains accurate today. According to Gates (1989),

> [t]here is very little connection between the social status of black Americans and the fabricated images of black people that Americans consume each day. Moreover, the representations of blacks on TV is a very poor index to our social advancement or political progress.
>
> (para. 4)

While *The Cosby Show* and *Doc McStuffins* positively portray middle-class Black families and professionals, their mediated influence—albeit decades apart—foundationally supports 'post-' logics that decry the realness of contemporary systemic oppressions. However, purporting 'post-' logics and deracialization in exchange for popularity and profitability among White audiences does not entirely nullify Doc's visual presence in millions of homes as an intelligent and compassionate Black girl who dreams of becoming a doctor.

The omnipresent dominant practice of confining Black femininity to reductive, controlling images is redundant, disrespectful, and just plain wrong amid the rich contributions of Black girls, adolescents, and women globally (Collins, 2009; Griffin, 2012; Smith-Shomade, 2002). Offering guidance on how to delineate between the need to deconstruct oppressive representations and the need for Black females to imagine and see themselves apart from oppressive representations, bell hooks (1992) says, "Loving ourselves begins with understanding the forces that have produced whatever hostility toward blackness and femaleness that is felt, but it also means learning new ways to think about ourselves" (p. 58). From this vantage point, *Doc McStuffins* emerges as a tool in the arsenal of every little Black girl who needs to see herself characterized (seemingly) apart from dominant culture. However, consumers should not be so optimistic as to believe that Disney has a vested interest in resisting the dehumanizing reduction of Black femininity or in progressively transforming how US American society perceives Black girls. Rather, *Doc McStuffins* is productive on both fronts only because a paradoxical representation of Black girlhood marked an (ironic) opportunity for Disney to center a Black girl and 'celebrate' racial diversity through a covert and profitable erasure of Blackness. Despite sincere distaste for Disney's corporatized motivations and practices, Doc's visibility as an imaginative/self-defined/self-determined dark-skinned Black girl chasing and achieving her dreams *matters*.

References

Ayot, H. (2013, February 6). Disney celebrates Black history month with "We Are Doc McStuffins." *Ebony Magazine*. Retrieved from: http://www.ebony.com/entertainment-culture/disney-celebrates-black-history-month-with-we-are-doc-mcstuffins-305#axzz2zIMHEN4L

Barnes, B. (2009, May 31). Her prince has come. Critics too. *The New York Times*. Retrieved from: http://www.nytimes.com/2009/05/31/fashion/31disney.html

Barnes, B. (2012, July 30). Disney finds a cure for the common stereotype with "Doc McStuffins." *The New York Times*. Retrieved from: http://www.nytimes.com/2012/07/31/arts/television/disneys-doc-mcstuffins-connects-with-black-viewers.html

Boylorn, R. M. (2008). As seen on TV: An autoethnographic reflection on race and reality television. *Critical Studies in Media Communication, 25*(4), 413–433.

Buescher, D., & Ono, K. (1996). Civilized colonialism: Pocahontas as neocolonial rhetoric. *Women's Studies in Communication, 19*(2), 127–153.

Coily Embrace. (2012, May 29). 131 African American women physicians from around the world join together to express thanks and support for Disney's groundbreaking children's TV show Doc McStuffins. Retrieved from: http://www.coilyembrace.com/coily-blogs/coily-news/505-131-african-american-women-physicians-from-around-the-world-join-together-to-express-thanks-and-support-for-disneys-groundbreaking-childrens-tv-show-doc-mcstuffins

Coleman, R. R. M. (2011). "ROLL UP YOUR SLEEVES!": Black women, Black feminism in *Feminist Media Studies*. *Feminist Media Studies, 11*(1), 35–41.

Collins, P. H. (1986). Learning from the outsider within: The sociological significance of Black feminist thought. *Social Problems, 33*(6), S14–S32.

Collins, P. H. (2009). *Black feminist thought: Knowledge, consciousness, and the politics of empowerment* (3rd ed.). New York: Routledge.

Collins, P. H. (2013). *On intellectual activism*. Philadelphia: Temple Press.

Crenshaw, K. (1993). Demarginalizing the intersection of race and sex: A Black feminist critique of antidiscrimination doctrine, feminist theory, and antiracist politics. In D. K. Weisberg (Ed.), *Feminist legal foundations* (pp. 383–397). Philadelphia: Temple University Press.

Del Vecho, P., Lasseter, J. (Producers), Clements, R., & Musker, J. (Directors). (2009). *The princess and the frog* [Motion picture]. United States: Walt Disney Pictures.

Disney. (n.d.). Doc McStuffins Products. Retrieved from: http://movies.disney.com/doc-mcstuffins

Elber, L. (2012, June 12). "Doc McStuffins" TV show gives Black girls, aspiring doctors hope. HUFF POST. Retrieved from: http://www.huffingtonpost.com/2012/06/12/doc-mcstuffins-tv-show-give-black-doctors-hope_n_1590683.html

Gates, H. L. Jr. (1989, November 12). TV's Black world turns—But stays unreal. *The New York Times*. Retrieved from: http://www.nytimes.com/1989/11/12/arts/tv-s-black-world-turns-but-stays-unreal.html

Giroux, H. A. (2000). Public pedagogy as cultural politics: Stuart Hall and the "crisis" of culture. *Cultural Studies, 14*(2), 341–360.

Giroux, H. A., & Pollock, G. (2010). *The mouse that roared: Disney and the end of innocence* (2nd ed.). Lanham, MD: Rowman & Littlefield.

Griffin, R. A. (2012). I AM an angry Black woman: Black feminist autoethnography, voice, and resistance. *Women's Studies in Communication, 35*(2), 138–157.

Griffin, R. A. (2014). *Pushing* into *Precious*: Black women, media representation, and the glare of the White gaze. *Critical Studies in Media Communication, 31*(3), 182–197.

hooks, b. (1992). *Black looks: Race and representation.* Boston: South End Press.

Hopson, M. (2009). Language and girlhood: Conceptualizing Black feminist thought in "*Happy to be Nappy.*" *Women and Language, 32*(1), 31–35.

Issa, E. S. (2014, January 8). Disney's "Doc McStuffins" honors Dr. Myiesha Taylor. *Jet Magazine*. Retrieved from: http://www.jetmag.com/life/disneys-doc-mcstuffins-honors-dr-myiesha-taylor/

King, D. K. (1988). Multiple jeopardy, multiple consciousness: The context of a Black feminist ideology. *Signs, 14*(1), 42–72.

K_ra. (2014). How to uphold White supremacy by focusing on diversity and inclusion. *Model View Culture*. Retrieved from: https://modelviewculture.com/pieces/how-to-uphold-white-supremacy-by-focusing-on-diversity-and-inclusion

Leonard, D. J. (2013). Post-racial, post-civil rights: *The Cosby Show* and the national imagination. In D. J. Leonard & L. A. Guerrero (Eds.), *African Americans on television: Race-ing for ratings* (pp. 114–140). Santa Barbara, CA: Praeger.

Lester, N. A. (2010). Disney's *The Princess and the Frog:* The pride, the pressure, and the politics of being a first. *The Journal of American Culture, 33*(4), 294–308.

Lewis, T. (2012, August 7). New and next: Meet Kiara Muhammad, the voice of Disney's newest animated character, "Doc McStuffins."*Essence Magazine*. Retrieved from: http://www.essence.com/2012/08/07/new-and-next-meet-kiara-muhammad-the-voice-of-disneys-newest-animated-star-doc-mcstuffins/

Lindsey, T. B. (2013). "One Time for My Girls": African-American girlhood, empowerment, and popular visual culture. *Journal of African American Studies, 17*, 22–34.

McKee, A. (2003). *Textual analysis: A beginner's guide.* Los Angeles: Sage.

McNair, J. C., & Brooks, W. M. (2012). Transitional chapter books: Representations of African American girlhood. *The Reading Teacher, 65*(8), 567–577.

Miller, M. C. (1988). *Boxed in: The culture of TV.* Evanston, IL: Northwestern University Press.

Moffitt, K. R., & Harris, H. E. (2014). Of negation, princesses, beauty, and work: Black mothers reflect on Disney's the *Princess and the Frog. Howard Journal of Communications, 25*(1), 56–76.

Nee, C. (Executive Producer). (2012). *Doc McStuffins: Friendship is the best medicine* [Television series]. Burbank, CA: Buena Vista Home Entertainment.

Nee, C. (Executive Producer). (2013). *Doc McStuffins: Time for your checkup* [Television series]. Burbank, CA: Buena Vista Home Entertainment.

Nee, C. (Executive Producer). (2014). *Doc McStuffins: Mobile clinic* [Television series]. Burbank, CA: Buena Vista Home Entertainment.

Norden, M. F. (2013). "You're a Surprise from Every Angle": Disability, identity, and otherness in *The Hunchback of Notre Dame*. In J. Cheu (Ed.), *Diversity in Disney films: Critical essays on race, ethnicity, gender, sexuality, and disability* (pp. 163–178). Jefferson, NC: McFarland & Co.

Omolade, B. (1994). *The rising song of African American women.* New York: Routledge.

Ott, B. L., & Mack, R. L. (2010). *Critical media studies: An introduction.* Malden, MA: Wiley-Blackwell.

Palmeri, C. (2012, November 27). Disney's "McStuffins" overtakes "Dora" on preschool TV. *Business Week*. Retrieved from: http://www.businessweek.com/news/2012-11-27/disney-s-mcstuffins-overtakes-dora-on-preschool-tv

Peck, P. (2012, July 31). Disney takes a worthwhile risk in Doc McStuffins cartoon. *Black Entertainment Television.* Retrieved from: http://www.bet.com/news/national/2012/07/31/disney-s-doc-mcstuffins.html

Quinlan, M. M., Bates, B. R., Webb, J. B. (2012). Michelle Obama "Got Back": (Re)Defining (Counter)stereotypes of Black females. *Women & Language, 35*(1), 119–126. http://www.bet.com/news/national/2012/07/31/disney-s-doc-mcstuffins.html

Sandlin, J. A. (2007). Popular culture, cultural resistance, and anticonsumption activism: An explanation of culture jamming as critical adult education. *New Directions for Adult and Continuing Adult Education, 115,* 73–82.

Selznick, D. O. (Producer), & Fleming, V. (Director). (2009). *Gone with the wind* (70th anniversary edition) [Motion picture]. United States: Selznick International.

Sieving, C. (1998). Cop Out? The media, "Cop Killer," and the deracialization of Black rage. *Journal of Communication Inquiry, 22*(4), 334–353.

Smith-Shomade, B. E. (2002). *SHADED LIVES: African-American women and television.* New Brunswick, NJ: Rutgers University Press.

Squires, C. (2009). *African Americans and the media.* Malden, MA: Polity Press.

Sun, C. F. (Producer), & Picker, M. (Director). (2001). *Mickey Mouse monopoly: Disney, childhood, and corporate power* [Motion picture]. United States: Media Education Foundation.

Teasley, M., & Ikard, D. (2010). Barack Obama and the politics of race: The myth of postracism in America. *Journal of Black Studies, 40*(3), 411–425.

The New York Times. (1993, July 11). Accused of Arab slur, 'Aladdin' is edited. Retrieved from: http://www.nytimes.com/1993/07/11/us/accused-of-arab-slur-aladdin-is-edited.html

West, C. M. (2009). Still on the auction block: The (s)exploitation of Black adolescent girls in rape(e) music and hip-hop culture. In S. Olfman (Ed.), *The sexualization of childhood* (pp. 89–102). Westport, CT: Praeger.

Part III

Being Disney

Freedom, Participation, and Control

12 On the Count of Three

Magic, New Knowledge, and Learning at Walt Disney World

George J. Bey, III

Walt Disney theme parks are, more than anything else, teaching tools. They provide a vast yet carefully integrated set of lessons and 'new knowledge' designed to shape a particular set of norms and values (Bryman, 2004; Fjellman, 1992; Hermanson, 2005). In fact much of the pleasure derived from the Disney theme park experience as well as the success of the parks is due to the teaching that goes on in them and our desire to be taught by Disney. This relationship between teaching and pleasure helps explain why we are willing to pay such a high price to participate in the theme park experience. By the time Walt Disney decided to build Disneyland in the middle of the twentieth century he had begun to recognize not only the teaching power of the theme park experience as a way to help shape values and norms, but also the most effective ways to do so. His work in animation and propaganda, particularly during World War II and immediately afterward, taught him how his products could be tools for shaping attitudes and perceptions. After the early 1950s Disney's interests shifted from just providing his audience animated entertainment to focusing film and television products to explicitly teach his corporate curriculum about nature, science, history, cultures, and gender, subjects that ultimately allow for the definition of what it means to be a good person and a good citizen. Sammond (2005) argues that after the mid-1950s "the term educational may have referred to a common . . . perception (or Disney's hope) that everything they [The Walt Disney Company] produced was educational" (p. 313).

Because of the close relationship The Walt Disney Company built with Americans early on through its eponymous theme parks, consumers in the United States (and eventually the world) learned to believe that Disney could "balance an honest desire for profit with the public service of entertaining and educating" (Sammond, 2005, p. 321). Theme park guests learned to overlook the high cost of a Disney 'vacation' because of its value, which is largely tied up in the educating of the vacationer. At Walt Disney World, which emerged in the 1970s out of Walt's efforts to create a utopian model of socio-economic organization, we find the most complete envisioning and enactment of Disney's educational narrative. Much has been written about the lessons offered in the various parks, from the environmental consciousness of Disney's Animal Kingdom, to the tall-tales of the old west in Frontier Land, to the construction of the other in EPCOT's World Showcase (Fjellman, 1992; Hermanson, 2005), yet these lessons constitute only part of the curriculum. What brings all of these lessons together is 'Disney Magic.' Saving the tigers of Africa, listening to President Obama, learning about how Hollywood stunts are created, or shopping in the bazaar in Morocco in World Showcase are all pieces of the Disney lesson plan for teaching us particular understandings of nature, history, science, and more. As this chapter argues, Walt Disney World uses the idea of Disney Magic to link these attractions, shows and activities at a higher, more integrated level. By doing so, Disney Magic and what it means becomes the overarching curriculum for visitors to Walt Disney World. In other words, Disney Magic is the strategic plan or mission statement of the institution, and is used to define and give meaning to all the rest of the curriculum. In this chapter, through my field work at Walt Disney World, particularly as regards various sound and light shows, and the use of internet websites associated with different aspects of Walt Disney World, I explore what Disney Magic is, how it operates within Walt Disney World, and what is being taught to visitors about the way they should interpret 'the world.'

It has long been recognized how Walt Disney World functions as a pilgrimage center, hidden behind a wall of forest, lakes, and landscaped berms designed to keep guests inside a self-contained 'world' in order to remain focused on their experience (Fjellman, 1992). Walt made it clear with the Magic Kingdom that visitors would enter a different reality, and even posted this statement on a plaque at its entrance: "Here you leave Today and enter a world of Yesterday, Tomorrow and Fantasy." Within this bubble Walt Disney World uses a formula developed over three-quarters of a century to teach us that Disney Magic is the source of all possibilities and structures the fabric of reality, or at least a Disney reality. Taking a set of ideas from films and combining them with the company's groundbreaking work in the use of propaganda as way to entertain and educate, Disney produced an ideology of magic that is not about the effects of waving a wand nor about the 'magic of Hollywood' (though both are important at Walt Disney World), but about an intellectual and emotional state of awareness. It teaches us that magic is a power that resides within each of us and that, in order to achieve an understanding of what is important about the lessons offered at Walt Disney World, we need to acknowledge and allow this magic to become real, which also involves accepting and enacting Disney's particular moral positions and dispositions.

This chapter examines how this idea of Disney Magic is taught; how it is embodied in a host of shows, objects, characters, music, foods, places, and moments at Walt Disney World designed to help us learn what Disney Magic is; how to use it; and what we learn both about the rest of Disney's curriculum and about the very idea of being a whole healthy learner by doing so. The ideology of magic taught within Walt Disney World, though simple on its surface, is one of the most powerful examples of pedagogy in the arsenal of this vast and amazingly complex organization and perhaps in all of contemporary American society.

A Brief History of the Development of the Ideology of Disney Magic

The centralizing ideological message about magic was developed both consciously and unconsciously by a wide variety of individuals and groups within the Disney organization and for a wide variety of purposes. Completely wrapped in a capitalist-consumptive mantel, Disney's ideological system is designed to teach people how to enjoy and interpret what they are experiencing at Walt Disney World as they consume it. At the parks, Mickey Mouse becomes the main 'teacher' of these lessons. Mickey has been interpreted since his origin as a go-getting All-American, an everyman type of figure, and as a stand in for Walt Disney (the man) (Gabler, 2006), thus it is easy to see why he is the perfect 'person' to teach us how to enter a magical state. Mickey appeared as a magician in animated films as early as 1937 and by 1940 he had assumed one of his defining roles, the Sorcerer's Apprentice in *Fantasia* (Disney et al., 1940). We can find him in both of these roles at Walt Disney World today and visitors can even meet and greet Mickey as a magician at the Main Street Theatre in the Magic Kingdom. In Walt Disney World however, the Sorcerer Mickey is no longer an apprentice but is in control of the power of Disney Magic and serves as our teacher and the conqueror of evil dreams.

In 1940, Jiminy Cricket (voiced by Cliff Edwards) sang "When You Wish Upon a Star" during the opening credits and in the final scene of *Pinocchio* (Disney, Sharpsteen, & Luske, 1940). This song contains most of the ideological elements found in the Disney Magic lectures at Walt Disney World, which I will describe below; it won the Oscar for best original song in 1940 (the first Disney song to do so) and is the highest ranked Disney animated film song (seventh) in the American Film Institute's 100 Greatest Songs in Film History. If Mickey Mouse is the ultimate representative of Disney then "When You Wish Upon a Star" is the ultimate song of Disney. In the 1950s the song began to be used in the opening sequence of the Walt Disney television show and since the 1980s it has been the music in the opening logos of all Walt Disney Pictures. With this song, the idea of all of us having the power to take a wish from our hearts and make our dreams come true is crystalized in the Disney universe. This idea was further elaborated in the 1950 film *Cinderella* (Disney, Geronimi, Jackson, & Luske) with the song "A Dream is a Wish Your Heart Makes." The song literally chants the ideological message we see in the Disney lectures, repeating it in slightly varied forms:

When you can dream then you can start
A dream is a wish you make with your heart
When you can dream then you can start
A dream is a wish you make with your heart

In 1953, Tinker Bell, introduced in the film *Peter Pan* (Disney, Geronimi, Jackson, Luske, & Kinney, 1953), was added as another Disney icon representing the magic of Disney. Since 1954 she has been highlighted in Disney television programming, beginning with her introducing Disneyland through a haze of pixie dust during the period that Disneyland the park and Disneyland the TV show were one and the same (Marling, 1994). Her role is to fly around sprinkling pixie dust, which can help people achieve a state of magical being when combined with happy thoughts. As this brief history reveals, the pieces of the Disney ideological lectures offered today in Walt Disney World, which I explore below, were in place before Disneyland even opened in 1955. They have had over half a century to simmer and blend into the seamless lessons offered to millions in Walt Disney World every year as a teaching tool for how to experience the parks.

Lectures on the Ideology of Disney Magic

The ideology composing Disney Magic is simple, which makes it easy to teach, assimilate, and use. Visitors to Walt Disney World, and its axis mundi the Magic Kingdom, know it as 'the most magical place on earth.' Living in the United States (and increasingly in much of the world), one can hardly avoid hearing about Walt Disney World, and for the most part visitors have learned to associate Disney (in all of its facets, but especially its films) with magic prior to arriving at the parks. In fact, the association of Disney with magic is so well known that we are likely to not even recognize the parts composing Disney Magic and how it operates as an ideology directing us to experience the parks in a particular way.

The primary and most fully developed and articulated way Walt Disney World teaches visitors how Disney Magic works and what it means is through a series of lectures or sermons, which take the form of shows offered in the Magic Kingdom, Disney's Hollywood Studios, and EPCOT. These include "Dream Along with Mickey" and "Wishes" in the Magic Kingdom, "Fantasmic" in Disney's Hollywood Studios, and "IllumiNations: Reflections of Earth" in the World Showcase section of EPCOT. In "Dream Along with Mickey" and "Fantasmic," Mickey Mouse is our teacher. The lack of a similar lecture in Disney's Animal Kingdom is currently being rectified, as the Imagineers prepare a new nighttime show called "Rivers of Light" (opening in 2016). The Magic Kingdom and Hollywood Studio shows are similar in content and focus on three central ideas: dreams, wishes, and magic. The shows illustrate how we have the power to generate magic through dreams and wishes in a very specific way. In this chapter I will examine the content and message of "Dream Along with Mickey," "Fantasmic," and "Wishes."

"Dream Along with Mickey"

"Dream Along with Mickey" is presented several times a day directly in front of Cinderella's castle (the axis mundi for both the Magic Kingdom and Walt Disney World). It begins with Minnie Mouse informing us that we are invited to a magical occasion, a castle party, where Mickey is going to show up with a big surprise. A chorus tells us:

> Come join the party, a castle party. You're all invited to come and join the fun. So let's get started, so much to do. Come join the party where dreams really do come true!
> Get ready for the magic, a spectacle beyond compare. There's romance and adventure, there's laughter and much more with our imagination. Imagine what's in store!
> Welcome to a kingdom of dreams where enchantment never ends. Where every day's a magic day.
> Any dream is possible, wishes do come true. You can reach the stars if you just believe.
> Share the magic in your heart, there's nothing you can't do. Anything is possible so find a dream inside of you.

In the song, the castle party is a metaphor inviting us to assume an alternative position from which to see the world. By joining the castle party our dreams can come true and our day can be transformed from normal into magical. The chorus also lays out the primary formula for Disney Magic: Magic is found in one's heart, where it takes the form of a dream one has, and can be released by wishing. This formula is, very simply, the core of the Disney lecture and the only path to experiencing Walt Disney World correctly. The castle party is open to all of us, as it teaches us how to use our ability to imagine and thus to learn how to make our dreams come true. That is, we will learn how to use Disney Magic as way to alter the nature of our everyday experience—Disney Magic is proposed as an alternate positive reality, and not as magic per se.

At this point Mickey arrives and begins to describe how the party works. He explains that his surprise is to get his special guests to "dream along with us." He further explains how magic is made real when he states that, "everyone believes in dreams. You see, that is the only way dreams can come true." Making dreams come true becomes a communal affair that requires all of us, and thus Mickey implores guests to:

> Just reach down, deep inside, and find the magic in your heart. Then on the count of three we'll all wish together real loud by saying

"Dreams come true!" . . . Concentrate, everybody. Are you ready now? One, Two, Three!

Mickey serves as the teacher who leads us in the process of making magic manifest, as the magic located in our hearts is released by wishing together as a community. We dream the wishes in our heart to become our reality, and this reality is Disney Magic.

While "Dream Along with Disney" teaches us that making dreams come true is as easy as "One, Two, Three!," we also learn from two different characters that dreaming should not be taken for granted. First, Donald Duck, the skeptic, exclaims, "Ah, phooey, nobody believes in dreams anymore." Donald represents the jaded modern individual whose experiences have led him to deny the existence of magic, particularly Disney Magic. However, Donald's mild skepticism pales in comparison to the dark desires of the wicked fairy Maleficent, who represents the idea that there is evil in the world seeking to squelch magic, a theme that is consistent throughout all three of the major Disney Magic lectures explored in this chapter. Maleficent wishes to "change this place to a place where nightmares come true." We are not exactly sure what this nightmare looks like, but it is presented as a threat to our ability to create Disney Magic. Luckily, Mickey easily dispatches Maleficent, but she warns us that she is always going to be lurking and waiting and, if we falter in our ability to dream Disney Magic into existence, she will be there to provide an alternative nightmare scenario.

"Fantasmic"

Maleficent and her nightmares also appear in "Fantasmic," usually performed twice nightly in the Hollywood Hills Amphitheater in Disney's Hollywood Studios. According to the Walt Disney World website, the show features "Pyrotechnics, laser lights and one million gallons of dancing water [that] make the dream come alive" (Walt Disney World, n.d.). Although Disney does not give out the number of people the theatre actually holds, various Disney websites list the number at somewhere around 10,000, including 7,900 seats and standing room for several thousand more. Assuming these numbers are close to accurate and the show is typically performed twice nightly (weather permitting), anywhere between 110,600 and 140,000 people a week receive this elaborate lecture on how Disney Magic is created and what it means. "Fantasmic" begins with a montage of visual elements from Disney's animated films, which are presented in conjunction with a song entitled "Imagination." The images highlight and focus the message of the song so that they become the representation of a single message. The song tells us to "use your imagination" to "dream a fantastic dream." Here, imagination exists in our minds and can be used to dream any dream we want. The film images displayed on walls of water provide us with the range of dreams that are within us. We are asked—even though we have been taught that dreams are make believe—"could they [not] all come true?" And the answer provided is "Yes!" The song teaches us that our minds hold our imaginations, where dreams can be made, and we are taught that the process by which dreams come true is magic: "In your imagination," the chorus sings, "deep in your mind, it's magic you'll find."

Jiminy Cricket appears at the end of this montage and explains to us that the magic we create from our dreams is a powerful reality that needs to be guided by a moral compass. To reinforce this idea we are introduced to Sorcerer Mickey, who serves as our example of the magical dreamer made real. All of what we have seen represents Mickey's dream, but as in "Dream Along with Mickey," this dream has the potential to become a nightmare, as we are shown via a fantastic light and sound display how "all the forces of evil have the power to control his mind." During the montage of evil, each villainous Disney character morphs into the next to suggest a unified continuum, a single idea of evil dreams creating nightmares as reality. Eventually Sorcerer Mickey fights back and finds himself facing Maleficent again. As Mickey demonstrates, defeating evil is about controlling yourself and letting your conscience be your guide. He tells evil, "You may think you are so powerful, but this is my dream," and then proceeds to destroy evil by freeing the sword in the stone, a symbol of righteousness and the legitimate moral right to rule. At this point, Tinkerbell arrives on the scene, as a symbol of magic made real. With her pixie dust, she calls forth a string of giant barges filled with every Disney character you can imagine— symbolizing Disney Magic made real. Here, imagination has triumphed, generating our dreams along with the dreams of Mickey, the magical everyman.

"Wishes"

Based on the seating and number of performances, "Fantasmic" may offers its ideological message to more than 5.7 million people annually, but even more Disney visitors are exposed to the nighttime fireworks display lecture known as "Wishes," which is presented each evening, 365 days a year. Wishes is best viewed in front of the castle in an area known as the hub, or along and up Mainstreet USA, but it also can be viewed from a number of the hotels that face the Magic Kingdom as well as many other parts of the park. Visitors can also hire a private boat and view the show from the Seven Seas Lagoon. In 2014, 18.6 million people visited the Magic Kingdom, and though there are no numbers available from Disney, it is likely the majority of them, in order to get their money's worth, stayed to see "Wishes" at some point during their vacation. "Wishes" is positioned by many Disney visitors and fans as a necessary part of a Disney vacation that helps visitors comprehend the nature of magic at Walt Disney World, as seen in the language used to describe the show in this quote from the popular fan-run Mouse Hints website:

Your Disney vacation is never complete until you get a chance to see the Wishes Nighttime Spectacular Fireworks Show! This show truly captures the "magic of Disney". We've known of people who didn't really understand why people made such a big deal about Disney World, as they began their day touring the Magic Kingdom. But then when the lights went out, the parade and fireworks began, and *their eyes were opened*! [my italics]

(Mouse Hints, 2015, para. 1)

What makes "Wishes" perhaps the most powerful of all the Disney lectures is its directness. The message is delivered simply through voices, song, and exploding fireworks. The powerful audio component of the show, which is synchronized to the visual presentation, makes for a mesmerizing effect beyond a typical fireworks display. Again, along with the other shows, these special effects deliver the primary ideological message that wishes can come true, in this case by wishing on a star. We are taught that dreamers are wish makers who have the ability to make all their wishes come true. We learn that this power is in all of us regardless of race, class or gender, because, as the song lyrics tell us, it "makes no difference who you are." Also, as in "Dream Along with Mickey" and "Fantasmic," "Wishes" negates the false belief that dreams are not real or cannot come true, as Jiminy Cricket (symbolizing conscience and consciousness) explains how he did not first believe, but learned how wishing can work. Tinker Bell, who actually flies across the night sky (the one live actor in the show), is used to symbolically open the doorway to considering these positive ideas, which starts, we are told, with the need to realize "your heart is in your dreams." Tinker Bell is a Disney icon recognized for her ability to help people achieve a magical state of being. Once more, the basic fact being taught is that our greatest dreams reside in our bodies, our hearts, or our minds. The important point is that we hold this power within us—it does not come from an outside force.

Like the other shows, "Wishes" features a montage of princesses and associated characters that illustrate a range of dreams (going to a ball, getting your prince, being part of the larger world, going to Neverland, being a real boy, being free). Providing a montage of characters from many different films that represent various dreams is a repeated part of the ideological message. As the characters are removed from the original contexts of their respective films and reconfigured to illustrate dreams that transcend those individual films, they come to represent archetypical dreams—our dreams. And, as in the other lectures, Jiminy Cricket indicates that there is a price to freeing these dreams. One needs "a little courage, to set it free" and an ability to love. "Fate is kind, she brings to those who love, the sweet fulfillment of their secret longing . . . . Fate steps in and sees you through."

In each show we are reminded that we need to let our conscience be our guide, or, in other words, that the state of dreaming and wishing is only achieved through a proper moral and cultural stance. Scholars recognize that Disney, through its films, "increasingly educates on moral behavior" and that Disney films act "as tools for defining and encouraging morality"— almost as a "competitor to religion for moral authority" (Ward, 2002, p. 128). Although Walt Disney himself tended to play down the relationship between his products and morality (making a point of having no church on Main Street USA, for example), he nonetheless stated in a 1962 article in the religious monthly magazine *Guideposts* that, the "important thing is to teach a child that good can always triumph over evil" (Pinsky, 2004, p. 2). It is in these outdoor lectures at Walt Disney World where we see the connection between being the right kind of person and getting your dreams to come true made most explicit. The Evil Queen is used to highlight the danger involved in having the wrong moral stance, as she also has wishes, albeit bad ones. As Jiminy Cricket points out, wishing is powerful, so be careful what you wish for, as it can create "an awful mess." However, with the help of the Blue Fairy we are able to "put our hearts together and make a wish come true," and Jiminy Cricket reminds us of the magic we each possess:

> You see, it's just like I told ya.
> Wishes can come true, if you believe in them with all your heart.
> And the best part is, you'll never run out of wishes.
> They're shining deep down inside of you.
> 'Cause that my friends is where the magic lives.

These powerful lectures, presented in the form of engaging, elaborate shows and performed daily to tens of thousands of visitors, all provide the same ideological message: Magic is real, and it is created by us through a process whereby we tap into our innate ability to dream. This ability lies within all of us and allows us to make our dreams come true. The culmination of all our dreams coming true is a state where Disney Magic is not a metaphor but a reality, a state of being that can only be generated through an act performed by a moral community. It makes no difference who you are, but you must be careful of two threats: the failure to believe in dreaming, and bad dreams that are the source of chaos and nightmares.

Disney Magic Defined

As these descriptions illustrate, the shows at Walt Disney World are designed to teach guests how they can create magic. However, we are still left with the questions of just exactly what is Disney Magic and what are we supposed to do with it once we occupy this state of consciousness? Part of the answer lies in reflecting further on what Disney Magic is not. Disney Magic stands in sharp contrast to a traditional idea of magic in which there are supernatural forces that can be controlled through the use of specific language, symbols, actions, or rituals (Glucklich, 1997). This magic sees the world as natural and supernatural, and as something that is accessed by a limited set of trained practitioners. In the current world of theme park magic this traditional approach to magic is best illustrated in the Wizarding World of Harry Potter at Universal Studios Orlando. Here J. K. Rowling's world of magic is meticulously recreated as a theme park experience in two distinct areas (Hogsmeade and Diagon Alley), which bring to life the magical world of the Harry Potter novels. This world is composed of those possessing access to magic and the rest of us, the muggles, people stuck in the mundane world of non-magic. It is a world of them and us, of the natural and the supernatural. We love Harry Potter because we want to be part of that world while recognizing that we are muggles or magical wanna-bes.

Disney Magic is very much the opposite of a Harry Potter sort of magic. It is based on all of us creating it (what we might call the "makes no differ-ence who you are" principle) so that we all have the ability to make the world magical. In fact, Disney Magic is predicated on the fact that we all *have* to participate in generating it. In this way it is more like a form of what anthropologists call magical thinking (Glucklich, 1997), wherein a causal relationship exists between actions (dreaming, wishing) and events (creating magic) which cannot be justified by reason and observation (Donald's "phooey, no one believes in dreams anymore"). The major difference between the traditional definition of magical thinking and Disney Magic is that the process taught to us in what I argue is the central pedagogy of Walt Disney World is not to *do* something magical, but to *make* the world a magic place, *to make reality a magic state of being*. Ultimately what Disney Magic tries to do is put us in a particular position from which to interpret the world around us, providing us a lens through which to properly see and understand everything Walt Disney World offers us as members of this community. We are taught Disney Magic not to *use* it but *to be within it*, to exist in a magical state of awareness. Disney Magic is not about the supernatural, but about making a new form of natural wherein a more accurate or truthful understanding of history, nature, gender, etc. can be found. It is not a fantasy state but as is plainly stated in Splash Mountain's theme song "Zip-a-Dee-Doo-Dah"—"It's the truth, its actual, everything is satisfactual."

The Reality of Disney Magic

This brings us finally to ask, what does teaching to see the world through the lens of Disney Magic do for its students? Again, although very powerful, like any good methodological approach to learning, the lesson is simple. While the Disney experience is often described as hyper-realistic, or a simulacrum, or realism being replaced by idealism or fantasy, or sanitized and simplified—what is now commonly discussed as Disneyfication (Bryman,

2004; Schickel, 1968)—Disney Magic teaches us to fight back or see beyond this. By learning to use magic we are able to see the experiences offered at Disney in the form of themed parks, attractions, shows, etc. not as sanitized, simplified, and saccharine interpretations of reality but as valid truths, and to recognize this truth as natural. The truth, according to the narratives of Disney Magic, is that knowledge and experience as presented by Walt Disney World represents reality—the essential and most important form of reality for us as citizens (both US and global). Fantasyland is not a fantasy, but an important set of moral lessons that are real. Scholars have outlined these moral lessons to include "individualism, advancement through self-help, strict adherence to the work ethic, and the supreme optimism in the possibility of the ultimate improvement of society through the progressive improvement in humankind" (Taxel, 1982, p. 14). Wasko (2001), in her literature review, also states that Disney's moral themes and values include "individualism and optimism" (p. 117), "escape, fantasy, magic, imagination" (ibid.), "inno-cence" (p. 118), "romance and happiness" (ibid.), and "good triumphing over evil" (p. 119). These themes are enacted not only in Classic Disney films, but also throughout Walt Disney World. For example, we see these themes through the stories of Fantasyland (from Peter Pan to the Seven Dwarfs Mine Train), narratives teaching us that "we can fly" or that we should "whistle while we work" even if it is in a mine! Everything we enjoy at the parks can become a metaphor for a complete and fulfilling life, accord-ing to Disney Magic. The Kilimanjaro Safari at Disney's Animal Kingdom is not a ride through a make-believe ecosystem, it is a lesson in what Africa has to offer us as citizens of the world and our responsibility both to Africa and the idea of nature. The Hall of Presidents in Liberty Square is not simply a set of animatronic figures mouthing platitudes, but a lesson in the greatness of America and what it means to be a true American. Through the lens of Disney Magic we can accept these and all the other lessons in the parks without Donald Duck skepticism or the nightmarish chaos of a world that rejects this dream outright. The ideology of Disney Magic connects the total array of Walt Disney World experiences, from hotels to attractions to restaurants to transportation, into one large seamless entity.

This is how the message offered in Disney's shows and attractions becomes the moral and real way we should think and see nature, history, gender, sexuality, patriotism, race and ethnicity, culture, consumption, and work. With a highly developed ideology and a sophisticated system to deliver its message, it teaches us to see everything around us in 'the world' through a lens of Disney Magic. As we move through the park, experiencing attractions, attending shows, consuming foods and branded products, we are bombarded with literally millions of mnemonic devices that work to reinforce the reality we have been taught to occupy. We only need to see or hear or taste or smell a part to recognize the whole. Mickey Ears; a Tinker Bell Wand; a Lion King stuffed animal; the words Magic, Wish, and Dream on a sign; a pre-recorded spiel; a fragment of a particular music number or a catch phrase—all of these things serve to reinforce Disney Magic. Each character becomes a metaphor for the ideological message we are taught.

In the face of this bombardment, the visitor or student has a limited chance of resisting the lesson and many visitors strive to learn the lesson and 'have their eyes opened' so they can fully enjoy and understand their expensive experiences and patterns of consumption within 'the world.' They want to learn to see cultures, history, nature, adventure, fantasy, progress, and media as the reality Disney Magic offers. They want to have the entire experience integrated into the larger lesson of Disney Magic. For these visitors, the most magical place on earth becomes the most real place on earth. These trained Disney students are not content to randomly come into contact with these icons of Disney Magic. They search out these images, looking for 'hidden mickeys' and the smallest details in rides and buildings, and by doing so further establish their devotion and special status and understanding of why Disney is so magical.

Is it therefore any wonder that many of my students who spend a semester critically analyzing the Walt Disney Company and its impact on American culture from every possible academic voice I can offer completely lose their ability to critically experience Disney World and succumb to the magic within a day after passing beneath that famous entrance sign that tells every visitor that this is "Where Dreams Come True"? It helps us understand why people become so devoted to Disney Magic that they argue daily in online communities about each word, phrase, building permit, change, new construction, and renovation as if they were talking about the proper interpretation of passages from the Bible. And, it should come as no surprise that guests complain about experiencing varying states of depression and anxiety after leaving Walt Disney World, with a commonly offered cure being to immediately start planning the next vacation there.

Taking Disney Magic Home

The lectures on using Disney Magic as a way to fully understand Walt Disney World are found in various forms at Disney parks all over the world, including Disneyland, Tokyo Disney, Disneyland Paris, Hong Kong Disneyland, and Shanghai Disney. And although the same ideological messages discussed above have been transmitted through film and television over the decades to a wider audience than theme park visitors, the experience of being taught within the parks about Disney Magic and its utility in the interpretation of the entire theme park experience is qualitatively different than any other form of Disney teaching. "Dream Along with Mickey," "Fantasmic," and "Wishes" are live lectures performed communally to millions of people in specially designed settings making for particularly intense experiences that include all the senses. The lectures, designed to 'open one's eyes' can then be immediately applied throughout the various parks as a way to help understand the messages people receive from the attractions, shows, etc. As a result, the communal set of experiences focused and given meaning by the use of Disney Magic is one of the most powerful social experiences available to us today.

The visitors to these parks, learning the lessons of Disney Magic and able to apply them to understanding the whole of the Disney experience, can then take this understanding with them outside the parks, back to their homes and communities, where they can be replicated and reinforced by further exposure to Disney films, television, music or the objects they purchase. People can tattoo their bodies with Disney imagery, they can design a room or an entire house around Disney attractions, they can even buy scents that reproduce the smells of Walt Disney World, like the water smell of Pirates of the Caribbean.

It is difficult to judge how much of the Magic is actually carried home from the parks and how much or quickly it decays once the visitor is outside the controlled environment of the parks, but it is safe to say Disney Magic learned in the theme parks is an ideological message that does influence millions of people in their daily lives around the world. To what degree does it condition the way people see 'reality' and their system of values and norms is a subject worthy of further study.

References

Bryman, A. (2004). *The Disneyization of society*. London: SAGE.

Disney, W. (Producer), Geronimi, C., Jackson, W., & Luske, H. (Directors). (1950). *Cinderella* [Motion picture]. United States: Walt Disney Productions.

Disney, W. (Producer), Geronimi, C., Jackson, W., Luske, H., & Kinney, J. (Directors). (1953). *Peter Pan* [Motion picture]. United States: Walt Disney Productions.

Disney, W. (Producer), Sharpsteen, B. (Producer/Director), Armstrong, S., Algar, J., Roberts, B., Satterfield, P., Hand, D. D., Luske, H., Handley, J., Beebe, F., Hee, T., Ferguson, N., & Jackson, W. (Directors). (1940). *Fantasia* [Motion picture]. United States: Walt Disney Productions.

Disney, W. (Producer), Sharpsteen, B., & Luske, H. (Directors). (1940). *Pinnochio* [Motion picture]. United States: Walt Disney Productions.

Fjellman, S. M. (1992). *Vinyl leaves: Walt Disney World and America*. Boulder, CO: Westview Press.

Gabler, N. (2006). *Walt Disney: The triumph of the American imagination*. New York: Knopf.

Glucklich, A. (1997). *The end of magic*. New York: Oxford University Press.

Hermanson, S. (2005). Truer than life: Disney's Animal Kingdom. In M. Budd & M. H. Kirsch (Eds.), *Rethinking Disney: Private control, public dimensions* (pp. 199–227). Middletown, CT: Wesleyan University Press.

Marling, K. A. (1994). *As seen on TV: The visual culture of everyday life in the 1950s*. Cambridge, MA: Harvard University Press.

Mouse Hints. (2015). "Wishes" nighttime spectacular fireworks show. *Mouse Hints Website*. Retrieved from: http://mousehints.com/disneys-magic-kingdom-park/entertainment/wishes-nighttime-spectacular-fireworks-show/

Pinsky, M. I. (2004). *The gospel according to Disney: Faith, trust and pixie dust.* Louisville, KY, and London: John Knox Press.

Sammond, N. (2005). *Babes in Tomorrowland: Walt Disney and the making of the American child, 1930–1960.* Durham, NC: Duke University Press.

Schickel, R. (1968). *The Disney version: The life, times, art, and commerce of Walt Disney.* New York: Simon and Schuster.

Taxel, J. (1982). *A literature review of the impact of Walt Disney Productions, Inc. on American Popular Culture and Children's Literature.* University of Georgia, Department of Language Education. ERIC Document 213648.

Walt Disney World. (n.d.). Fantasmic! Retrieved from: https://disneyworld.disney.go.com/entertainment/hollywood-studios/fantasmic/

Ward, A. R. (2002). *Mouse morality: The rhetoric of Disney animated film.* Austin: University of Texas Press.

Wasko, J. (2001). *Understanding Disney.* Malden, MA: Polity.

13 Disneyfied/ized Participation in the Art Museum

Nadine M. Kalin

Art museums have adopted a number of Disney theme park features as strategies for survival at a time of dwindling resources for cultural institutions. Within museum education departments, visitors are increasingly considered customers and museums are adapting to please consumers by embracing entertainment in their programming. In order to compete in the experience economy, museum participation is now a commodity to consume for those with leisure time. Moreover, the modes through which visitors are being asked to engage with museums through processes and strategies long-employed by The Walt Disney Company entices visitors towards the consumption of themed experiences, entertainment, and products, thereby sanitizing and de-politicizing public participation. This entertainment-as-participation standing in for political activity furthers the current post-political landscape where political issues are concealed, neglected, parodied, and/or quickly forgotten while continuing on unchallenged and unchanged.

In order to better understand these claims about the shifting nature of participation in contemporary art museums, in this chapter I take up an exploration of the concepts of both *Disneyization* (Bryman, 1999, 2004), which refers to how characteristics of Disney theme parks are increasingly at work in broader social, labor, and corporate practices, and *Disneyfication* (Schickel, 1986; Walz, 1998), which focuses on how an object or phenomenon is stripped of unpleasantness and complexity as it is transformed into a more agreeable and palatable Disney product. Using these concepts, I present a case study—the Walker Art Center's "Discourse and Discord" to illustrate Disneyfied/ized participation. Finally, drawing upon the theoretical offerings of Jodi Dean and Zygmunt Bauman, I discuss more deeply these new modes of participation and their implications. In particular, I explore how Disneyfied participationism in the art museum exacerbates the depoliticization of civil issues under neoliberalism.

Disneyized Art Museums

Museums today have a public function as outlined in their individual mission statements and educational programming that goes beyond the preservation and exhibition of objects towards providing broader cultural and educational programming that meets the needs of and engages with the communities within which they are embedded. Since the 1970s, museums have been accused of bowing to the influence of Disney (Ballard, 1970/1990) in their attempts to attract more visitors and compete with theme parks for the public's free time. Other scholars have claimed since the 1990s that the public art museum is primarily a vehicle for entertainment (Newhouse, 1998/2006) or *edutainment* (Hooper-Greenhill, 2007, p. 33). As less public funding is allotted to the arts and their institutions, museums have had to adapt modes of entertainment and participation in order to fight the perception of their own irrelevance and economic viability in a world of distracting entertainment and media options vying for individuals' attention. Common examples of the adapted modes of entertainment and participation include weekly themed events and the integration of technology and social media within the museum experience, as well as an increased range of programming from flower arranging inspired by master still-life paintings to cat video contests.

Marrying exhibition content with strategies from the experience economy (Pine & Gilmore, 1999), the range of interactive choices within art museums counters the impersonal nature of large art institutions and their apparent didacticism and/or objectivity through fostering greater audience participation. Today the consumption of culture has become synonymous with consumer demands for pleasure, social exchange, sensuous experience, and interaction. Under a post-Fordist cultural economy, visitors consume culture as they would any commodity wherein they increasingly enjoy enhanced customer choice and customization of experience through greater varieties of programming (Phillips, 2011). Here the visitor is

> brought into the loop, made less passive and contemplative, more participating and responsive. Rather than remaining inward-turned, museums began to circulate information outward, and also to solicit input, not only speaking to visitors but spurring them to speak back, to become loquacious.
>
> (Relyea, 2013, p. 176)

In turn, visitors are rewarded through the validation and acknowledgement of their own knowledge and agency to make choices about their own museum participation. This participatory art museum model of education (Simon, 2010) is positioned by the institution as benefiting the public good towards social transformation, when in actuality it might be complicit in the curtailment of democracy by adopting a Disneyfied/ized participatory model that offers a potential replacement for engaged social action. To illustrate how Disneyfied/ized participation in the art museum works against social action, I first describe, following Bryman's concept of Disneyization, four features of Disney theme parks that are being enacted within art museums. To accomplish this, I focus on the Walker Art Center's "Discourse and Discord," which I analyze through the features and procedures associated with Disney theme parks. "Discourse and Discord" then becomes the backdrop for further analysis into these modes of participation and their implications.

Bryman (1999) describes Disneyization as "the process by which *the principles* of the Disney theme parks are coming to dominate more and more sectors of American society as well as the rest of the world" (p. 26, original italics). Hancock (2005) argues that Disneyization is essentially a theory "about consumption and the proposition that the global organisation of consumption is increasingly conforming to a template provided by the practices and principles of the Disney theme parks" (p. 545). The principles of Disney parks captured by the concept of Disneyization include theming, hybrid consumption, merchandising, and performative labor, the maintenance and success of which depend upon the existence of control and surveillance (Bryman, 2004). These principles have also become globally diffused to dominate the organization of other parts of cultural, societal, and economic systems beyond the actual brand of Disney. Moreover, the organization of consumption through Disneyization increasingly conforms to the Disney theme park template wherein consumers' access to and choice among a diversity of pleasurable activities is expected. For decades now, museums have not only competed with theme parks such as Disney for the public's leisure time, but they have also gradually succumbed to Disneyization.

The first dimension of Disneyization, the *theming* of economic life, is apparent within Disney theme parks and other associated venues, and has grown more prevalent under the experience economy. According to Hancock (2005), theming is a "mechanism directed at infusing objects with meaning above and beyond their immediate use or exchange value and, in doing so, creating experiential dimensions rather than simply consumer outlets" (p. 545). Thus, theming occurs when a business or company creates physical spaces that constitute distinct worlds through the use of focal narratives that distinguish those sites of consumption from other locations or experiences; examples include restaurants such as Rainforest Cafe and outdoor stores such as Bass Pro Shops. As museums undergo branding wherein an institution's mission aligns with its exhibition and education mandates, they are attempting to carve out a type of coherence distinct from other institutional and consumer offerings. Much like a theme park or attraction within Disney, museums, through theming, aim to maximize their allure to visitor/consumers as they advertise and present every new attraction as an experiential destination that promises to immerse visitors through art works, products, technologies, spaces, time periods, etc. The device of theming encompasses the lucid display of art works within a space either chronologically, conceptually, culturally, according to medium, or otherwise depending on curatorial priorities. Theming provides immersion within the atmosphere of the museum so that visitors anticipate types of engagement, behaviors, merchandise, and entertainment. Visitors might even describe a certain feeling as they enter a museum space. Theming is implemented not only through the objects on display, but also through the didactics, modes of engagement, and demarcation of particular spaces. This immersion is further enhanced by the selling of themed products that invite visitors to take with them a piece of their experience that can be purchased either in a central gift shop or at a kiosk adjacent to the specific exhibition itself. Additionally, any particular theme can be accompanied by further programming that provides a variety of experiences for visitors to partake in apart from a specific exhibition such as workshops, contests, lectures, and symposia.

According to Bryman (2004), *hybrid consumption* denotes the "general trend whereby the forms of consumption associated with different institutional spheres become interlocked with each other and increasingly difficult to distinguish" (p. 33). Through the process of hybrid consumption, multiple consumer attractions blend together and thus create larger, more entertaining consumer destinations, which results in visitors wanting to stay longer, buy more, and return again; examples include casinos, zoos, and sports stadiums. Within one Disney park, for example, guests can visit attractions, dine, shop, and be entertained through a variety of live shows. As museums collapse previous boundaries between viewing, shopping, interpreting, and eating into one destination of fused activity, they must now compete against other sites of hybrid consumption. As art museums increasingly embrace hybrid consumption, they seek to maximize the use of visitors' leisure time by offering more consumptive activities in a limited space. As museums offer a wider variety of edutainment opportunities, they increase their desirability within the experience economy under post-Fordism where consumer choice and variety reigns supreme (Bryman, 2004, p. 5). The dedifferentiation of consumption enables visitors to consume "while actually giving the impression that they are doing something else" (Bryman, 1999, p. 43) such as partaking in wholesome family time or civic engagement beyond cultural consumption.

A third characteristic of Disneyization is *merchandising*. Bryman (1999) explains that merchandising encompasses the promotion of goods and products bearing copyrighted images and branded logos. Merchandising works through and is driven by synergy, which involves the "mutual reinforcement of commodity visibility across product ranges as diverse as movies, fast foods, stationary and toiletries" (Hancock, 2005, p. 546), branded products that would otherwise be indistinguishable. Disney theme parks participate in merchandising by providing strategically placed sites at which a vast array of general Disney merchandise can be sold, while also offering products that are specific to the particular park in which the retail sites are located (for example, one can buy all manner of Disney Princess merchandise at any Disney park, as well as site-specific merchandise branded with EPCOT, Disney World, or Disneyland images and logos, along with general Disney characters such as Mickey Mouse in site-specific scenarios such as French Mickey gear available at the French Pavilion at EPCOT). Similarly, museums participate in merchandising by selling branded products including their own merchandise based on collections and traveling exhibitions, or one-time events. Some museums even have mascots (such as Arturo, the parrot mascot of the Dallas Museum of Art) similar to Disney characters, that are attached to children's programming just for that museum and found on promotional materials, websites, in-person meet-and-greets, and goods and products for sale at the gift shop.

Finally, Bryman (2004) describes *performative labor* (he explains that this is a combination of emotional and aesthetic labor) as indicative of the "growing tendency for frontline service work to be viewed as a performance, especially one in which the deliberate display of a certain mood is seen as part of the labour involved in service work" (p. 2). Disney employees are controlled and scrutinized for their abilities to remain highly committed to the company while performing to script and providing customer care on a daily basis as they embody the brand. Disney employees are known for their friendly, happy, helpful dispositions and are expected to maintain this emotional performance at all times. Bryman (2004) explains that

> the ever-smiling Disney theme park employee has become a stereotype of modern culture. Their demeanor coupled with the distinctive Disney language is designed among other things to convey the impression that the employees are having fun, too, and therefore not engaging in real work.
>
> (p. 107)

Within art museums, education departments are largely fulfilling the service role of these institutions' missions to their clients/visitors/members. Furthermore, educational workers are the human face of the museum, on display to enhance the customer experience of an exhibition, while making visitors feel welcomed. Museum educators also perform a similar kind of emotional labor, often improvising from a curatorial script or sanctioned content connected to a particular exhibition, the role of tour leader, otherwise known as docent. Educators also facilitate programming objectives with the public, cultivating customer satisfaction in inviting and non-threatening ways. As education departments are integral in providing enjoyable experiences with a smile for visitors so they might come back, the ability to provoke, question, critique, and mobilize may be tempered through a de-intellectualizing of this labor within a convivial museum under the experience economy—especially when these *jobs* are traditionally unpaid or low-paying internships, temporary posts, or volunteer gigs (Kalin, 2015). This precarity places limits on how educational labor in museums will behave and, in turn, constrains the participatory forms visitors will be invited to engage in. As museums compete on the experience economy market, they want to entice visitors to spend their free time in the museum instead of engaging in other leisure activities, such as a trip to the movie theater or zoo, venues that also employ performative labor.

Discourse, Discord, and Disneyization

I now turn to an exploration of how these facets of Disneyization played out in one program at the Walker Art Center which is, like many large art museums in the United States, attempting to bridge several currents within the experience economy, and with dwindling resources. At this writing, a brief browse of the Walker's offerings highlight its third annual Internet Cat Video Festival and the weekly Target® Free Thursday Nights, among many other options. Here, I focus on a three-day symposium held in the spring of 2012 titled "Discourse and Discord: Architecture of Agonism from the Kitchen Table to the City Street" (henceforth referred to as D&D). This symposium focused on how agonism—which is characterized as relations of respect and struggle between antagonism and consensus (Bielak & Duffalo, 2012)—functions in the public sphere.

Agonism is a requirement for a democracy that asks people to not shy away from or ignore differences of opinion and ideology. Instead of claiming that politics and religion are not discussed in polite society, agonism seeks out a diversity of perspectives so that alternative views can be heard and respected. This requires that the individuals that make up a democracy participate in dialogues with those outside of their current communities of consensus. Here, there is room for negotiated points of connection among equal, but different points of view that then may be developed and mobilized towards a more just society. In the United States we tend to interact more with people who are already similar to us while avoiding contact with those who do not share our views. This holds us in a less democratic antagonism of opposition and stagnation. One only needs to think of the current United States Congress for an example.

Programming for the D&D symposium included a collection of talks, workshops, actions, and experiments all with the intention of bringing together people from different viewpoints for debate in order to see "what happens when you move beyond agreeing to disagree" (Walker Art Center, 2013, para. 3). To explore this theme, a choir performed song lyrics interpreted from tweets compiled in response to the symposium, and artist Steve Shada created a Pro+agonist Playlist that included *Smokey and the Bandit* by Waylon Jennings, *Eye of the Tiger* by Survivor, and *The Gambler* by Kenny Rogers. The D&D website displayed a yellow poster designed by Carl Di Salvo that stated, "YOUR DEMOCRACY IS NOT WORKING AND NEVER WILL." Workshops provided opportunities to test out certain productive possibilities of agonism through a variety of themes, including Embodying Agonism, Harmony from Discord, Discourse Karaoke, and Engaging the Avenue: Agonistic Tactics for Social Design. At a subsequent event for Pro+agonist at the School of Art of The Cooper Union, audience members were invited to "Come wearing black and blue, the colors of a good bruise" (Studio REV, n.d., para. 4), promising an evening "rife with pleasurable and productive friction" (Pro+agonist, n.d., para. 1).

The D&D symposium was augmented with the publication of a book titled *Pro+agonist: The Art of Opposition*, which brought together writings by "interdisciplinary thinkers, artists, scientists, CEOs, crackpots, war strategists, psychotherapists, and philosophers who raise questions about the importance of political dissent, the function of discord in discourse, the rules of escalating conflict, the roles of parasites within systems, and more" (Walker Art Center, 2013, para. 5). The volume includes a chapter authored by Belgian political theorist Chantal Mouffe, who has proposed a radical-ization of modern democracy called "agonistic pluralism." This was accom-panied by a deck of agonism playing cards created by Marisa Jahn. Both of these resources were rendered in blue and black like bruising after conflict; as their creators explain, "There's a half-inch hole running through the center of both the book and the playing cards so that you can peek through, frame the Other, and keep them with you as you read along" (Studio REV, n.d., para. 1).

Using Bryman's framework of Disneyization, we can see that the Walker Art Center's D&D offers a rich example of theming within the art museum. The symposium aims to immerse its visitors within a theme through a wide array of experiences that transform the institution into a kind of amusement park or themed land within a Disney park. In this instance, the programming was not attached to an art exhibition, but certainly the concept of agonism is found within current art movements, and gaining a richer understanding of agonism through partaking in the Walker's offerings will likely be useful as an interpretive framework for art museum visitors and art enthusiasts. This theme, overlaying the museum, transforms the less flexible exhibition timetable and space into another world of experience, making the museum a destination and morphing the theme of agonism into an attraction.

Exemplifying hybrid consumption, D&D synthesized a number of experiences within one three-day event. In the museum, the symposium acted as both a conduit and context for the selling of goods and mementos, intimately entwined with the consumption of experiences. One could choose from an array of participatory modes of engagement with the concept of agonism from karaoke to social design, among other options. This effec-tively exchanged "the mundane blandness of homogenized consumption experiences with frequently spectacular experiences" (Bryman, 2004, p. 4), so that while attendees were participating in discourse and discord associated with agonism, they were simultaneously engaged in choosing how to spend their money and leisure time within the museum through consuming experience.

Merchandising was apparent in conjunction with this symposium. D&D's playing cards and the book *Pro+agonist: The Art of Opposition* furthers the commercialization of the museum as a niche, limited-time-only experience. While individuals participated in the symposium experiences held at the Walker, they could also visit the gift shop and purchase products associated with the museum, its collection, and exhibitions. The gift shop sells branded merchandise such as chocolate bars, coffee, gift wrap, scarves, tote bags, greeting cards, and bumper stickers, all of which would be largely indistinguishable from products sold by other retailers except for the presence of the Walker brand. These products both act as mementos marking visitor experience, and also further the reach of the Walker brand beyond the physical institution.

Performative labor as service work at the Walker attempted to make agonistic confrontation an inviting experience. While attendees were invited to wear black and blue to emulate bruising to attend a book launch for D&D's Pro+agonist (Studio REV, n.d., para. 4), museum employees enacted a more convivial performative labor, which, along with the diversity of activities for the Walker symposium, side-stepped a more combative version of conflict for a more inoffensive one. In line with the strategy of performative labor, museum educators at the Walker acting as facilitators of experience had to strike a delicate balance in order to interface with their publics in ways that would engage the topic of agonism as inviting and approachable, while moving attendees outside of a more comfortable, passive role as viewer.

Disneyfication in the Art Museum

A second framework, that of Disneyfication, is also helpful to understand how museums have employed Disney strategies. Whereas Disneyization (Bryman, 2004) refers to the spread of Disney principles into social, cultural, and economic life, the concept of Disneyfication focuses more on how Disney bowdlerizes history, culture, myth, and literature into streamlined, charming, and predigested forms devoid of content that might be considered noxious or offensive to the consumer of Disney products and images (Walz, 1998). In what follows I explore how Disneyfication operated through the D&D symposium in relation to the theme of agonism, which illuminates the changing nature of participation in museums.

Apart from selling and theming devices to enable a specific market niche, museum content itself may undergo processes of Disneyfication (Walz, 1998). Museums are institutions that, like Disney theme parks, have a history of trivializing culture, inequality, and conflict in representational practices that, by their very nature, involve simplification of or disregard for the complexities of the past and/or the present. This process has been termed Disneyfication (see Schickel, 1986; Walz, 1998) wherein an object or concept is Disneyfied of disagreeableness as it is turned into a more agreeable Disney product. In the case of D&D, the symposium claimed an agonistic perspective as essential to democratic politics in current times, implying that through participating in conflict we can bring about structural and social change. Certainly those who attended this symposium would represent the museum's publics with some level of diversity, albeit limited to those groups that have leisure time and expendable income to devote to such scheduled programming, thereby also limiting ideological diversity. Moreover, through focusing on fun, entertainment value, and variety of experience, the Walker brought to life agonism in a simulated, short-term, convivial, and bastardized form as Disneyfied edutainment palatable, and not too uncomfortable, to its attendees (as well as its management and board, presumably). We might consider that the Walker, through its presentation of agonism and the ways in which it invited visitors to participate, controlled for resistance and offense, sanitizing the representation and enactment of conflict within the museum, a process parallel to Disney's creation of agreeable experiences and products. Below, I will further explore how a Disneyfied agonism was conceptualized and programmed within D&D.

According to Mouffe (2013), democracy requires agonism—a politics of disagreement—in order to flourish. D&D aimed to address agonism by

> looking at how it works on the ground and what kind of "architectures" —whether the built environment, online technologies, songs, or even recipes—can draw people together for genuine dialogue and debate. It also reinforces the notion that democracy thrives on and even requires an agonistic foundation: the friction between people of different minds, views, and beliefs.
>
> (Bielak & Duffalo, 2012, para. 2)

D&D's programming for dissensual-participation-as-edutainment co-opts discord while putting the fun back into the pain of disagreement by offering therapeutic strategies for enduring differences of opinion as a type of game (Bielak & Duffalo, 2012; Duffalo, 2012). In my reading of Mouffe (2013), this is a misuse of her version of agonism enacted as *faux* participation (jagodzinski, 2013) or *participationism* (Dean, 2009; Not An Alternative, 2014) that reduces its political potential to entertainment for citizen consumers craving novel experiences. As Mouffe (2013) herself notes, this sort of museum programming abandons its "original function of educating citizens about the dominant culture" thereby reducing Disneyfied museums "to sites of entertainment for a public of consumers" that embrace visitor participation as consumerism, thereby actively contributing "to the commercialization and depoliticization of the cultural field" (p. 101).

Further, Disneyfication employs Disney-speak, a language game wherein one term stands in for another in order to influence perception (Bryman,

2004); for example, a Disney theme park customer or visitor is re-termed 'guest' in Disney-speak (p. 11). Mouffe (2008) refers to this as a post-Fordist process of discursive re-articulation that uses existing discourses and practices for other purposes so that language, such as agonism, that is challenging to an existing order is repurposed, redefined, and neutralized from its subversive possibility. In its Disneyfied re-articulation, D&D overtly embraces conflict in its very name, while purging it of objectionable characteristics within its programming for attendees' consumption and entertainment. The sanitizing of agonism to a few catchphrases in a poetry slam and agonism-themed playlist, trivializes the potential of this concept and its political implications for mobilization against the status quo. This programming effectively neutralized the subversive potential of agonism as substantive public debate moving into sustainable civic action, thereby replacing the democratic citizen with the consumer and hollowing out the public sphere of its democratic potential. This form of participation enacts an ideology of passive consumerism instead of social responsibility, wherein "commercial culture replaces public culture, the language of the market becomes a substitute for the language of democracy; at the same time, the primacy of commercial culture has an eroding effect on civil society" (Giroux & Pollock, 2010, p. 211).

Museums, like art, are always already in a compromised position standing in an engaged autonomous relation to capitalism, both complicit with and in potential opposition to it through embracing democratic deviance (Esche, 2004). Yet, Mouffe (2013) contends,

> In the case of museums, my view is that, far from being condemned to playing the role of conservative institutions dedicated to the main-tenance and reproduction of the existing hegemony, museums and art institutions can contribute to subverting the ideological framework of consumer society. Indeed, they could be transformed into agonistic public spaces where this hegemony is openly contested.
>
> (p. 100)

In this light, the Walker's D&D appears to have missed an opportunity in not turning the tables on itself as a space of discord and resistance where power is exercised even through the embracing of participation. In not examining how the Walker is complicit with the hegemony of capitalism, for example, it is endorsing the perpetuation of this complicity and thus its attempts at dissensus become no more than a populist foil of participationism aimed at neutralizing the museum from its political and economic priorities under neoliberal capitalism. In the end, D&D provides an example of how critical practices such as agonism and participation are coopted, commer-cialized, consumed, and seamlessly integrated into the very neoliberal institutions they are intending to problematize.

Disneyfied/ized Participation

Whereas visitors may be lured into museums via niche theming and the desire for entertainment facilitated by performative labor in the form of convivial educational staff, more and more museums also provide a participatory mode of edutainment that adds to their hybrid consumption of experience and culture, not to mention associated merchandise, at the museum. Moreover, potentially uncomfortable themes, such as social justice, inclusion, or agonism, are turned into participatory games through a form of Disneyfied expurgation. All of this soothes visitors into a Disneyfied participationism wherein visitors are engaged in the enjoyment of participating in a museum experience related to agonism, for instance, that stands in as a fetish for actual participation (political or otherwise). As outlined throughout this chapter, D&D provides one example where agonism and conflict are Disneyfied into convivial participation for visitors, cultivated within an art museum industry that is increasingly embracing Disneyized principles. This form of Disneyfied participation is censored of the rough edges and purged of any prolonged struggles associated with agonism within democratic societal transformation such as those associated with activist modes of social change.

Apart from the Walker's D&D, museums embracing a participatory approach to education increasingly employ Disneyfied/ized practices in order to compete within the experience economy. Whether offering participation in programming focused on agonism, social justice, or inclusion, museums exhibit aspects of Disneyfication and Disneyization while sanitizing public participation. This intensifying tendency is transforming how the public perceives of and activates participation both inside and outside of the museum experience. Participation in the art museum effectively takes participation out of its real world contexts and deprives it of its political use, while exalting participation as a radical end in and of itself. As D&D illustrates, the Disneyfied/ized art museum resigns participation to this lack, effectively leaving "behind the time-consuming, incremental, and risky efforts of politics" (Dean, 2009, p. 47), which is a form of participation within the real world. Barney (2010) uses the term "participatory ontology" to describe this proliferation of participatory media and cultural sites offering alluring opportunities to participate (p. 142).

Art museums have embraced activities with social tagging projects, conversational dialogues in front of artworks, response boards in exhibitions, and spaces that offer drop-in activities. D&D provided various workshop options (each for a $10 fee) beyond just listening to a series of lectures on the importance of political dissent in the public sphere. Attendees were invited to take part in a workshop promising the embodiment of agonism through moving chairs (among other activities), collaboration with others in the creation and performance of an original song as a manifestation of consensus, and participation in tactics employing radical imagination and hands-on political design within agonistic interventions. These offerings reflect an impressive diversity of edutainment for a three-day symposium. Nevertheless, D&D privileges diluted and pleasurable forms of participation that are not equal to other forms of democratic mobilization and agonistic relations (Foster, 2004/2006, p. 195).

The works of political theorist Jodi Dean (2005, 2009) articulate the fantasy of participation's steady hold on the political imaginary propagated by finance- and consumption-driven entertainment culture found in art museums and Disney theme parks. Herein, participation works as a fetish. Participants believe they are active while that activity is passively embodied in a fetish preventing action from occurring—contributions of opinion and affect may be linked and shared, narrated or displayed, rapped or acted out, but they are nonetheless passive, failing to coalesce in any substantial manner towards change. Participants *believe* their contributions matter and mean something in a broader context. Participants feel like their entertainment is their political activity—temporary relief from enduring the status quo, which amounts to Disneyfied instead of actual participation towards sustained political and structural change through political activity, activism, protest, and/or policy development.

As Dean (2009) shares, "[c]ontributing to the information stream . . . has a subjective registration effect detached from any actual impact or efficacy" (p. 31). The *registration effect*, wherein participants deliver up thoughts, opinions, activities, leisure time, narratives, creative works, paths of movement, and so on, generates an intensity of affect in participatory museum experiences that make them compelling and imbue them with significance beyond mere registration. The more visitors use the museum, the less and less attention individual contributions demand, so that participants are caught up in increasingly meaningless or valueless contributions without utility. Dissenting voices are registered without a response, as in museum response boards, short-term interventions, karaoke performances, and the like so that alternative viewpoints are subsumed by participationism into a politically ineffectual consensus (Dean, 2009). Essentially, participationism reduces and captures potential political energies that perpetually circulate information and entertainment without end or response (Dean, 2009).

Through the fetish of Disneyfied participationism, museum visitors contribute, circulate, and network without coalescing or fully connecting through sustained debate. Instead, this circulation of communication is depoliticizing, foreclosing participation, and protecting official politics from collective resistance (Dean, 2005). Coincidentally, museums are filling the gap of dwindling opportunities for political efficacy in society through the empty promise of participation on which participants project fantasies for political efficacy. Museums, not unlike online experiences or visits to Disney theme parks, allow us to escape the complexities of the actual world into a controlled and safe environment of individuals making choices within the experience economy. This amounts to a distancing effect into a depoliticization that limits the public's ability to sustain a coherent politics in collective structures. Bauman (2001) refers to this dilemma as individual life politics, as opposed to actual politics within the public sphere, wherein the public exists in a rat race, believing individual efforts alone matter in improving the system as a whole. Here, I am not lamenting a previous time when museums were models of meaningful participation, but, rather, I am pointing out that museums such as the Walker are embracing and even making claims towards political potentials that are only further neglected and fetishized through Disneyfication. Again, D&D provides an example of how politicized versions of agonism are negated for more short-term, easy, therapeutic, and pleasurable forms of agonism-lite within a Disneyized museum experience. In this, Disneyfied participationism acts in line with Adorno's (1941) distraction thesis, wherein participation-as-entertainment and relaxation distracts us from other forms of activist participation, thereby maintaining the interests of capitalism.

The illusion of participation with museum visitors perpetuates a consensual post-politics—referring to the current state in politics under neoliberalism that increasingly forecloses disagreements and conflicts through consensual processes such as convivial, public participation (Žižek, 1999). Participation's investment in focused and busy activity perpetuates a post-political landscape where political issues are concealed, glossed-over, neglected, parodied, and/or quickly forgotten while continuing on unchallenged and unchanged. In this sense, "participationism plagues us. More than dismantling or distributing power, we've invisibilized and extended it" (Not An Alternative, 2010, para. 5). In this way, participation has become synonymous with depoliticization that disempowers the public as individually responsible citizens while depoliticizing civil issues. For example, to delve into the politics of the art museum would risk losing visitors (who prefer to be entertained rather than educated), which is considered worse than the loss of the public sphere.

Just as Disney has seamlessly merged entertainment with education, museums have also taken up corporate culture's subordination of critical consciousness and democratic potential in the name of consumerism. While Disney might work overtime to provide escape from negative life issues, the Walker's D&D did not ignore or edit out conflict in this specific example of programming. It embraced it. Such programming supports the view that art museums can contribute to the public good and civil society. Nevertheless, the Walker sanitized the political potential of agonism opting instead for a form of participation that provided a soft approach to social issues while diverting attention from the structural causes and difficult solutions necessary to transform society (Merli, 2002). In the end, participation as an experience to consume and purchase a memento may increase visitor numbers, but does not do much for political participation within or outside of museums. The Walker presented an oversimplification of agonism as entertaining participationism that at once commercialized it through the selling of products and the serving up of experiences while simultaneously constricting its democratic potential and responsibility to the public good through its very reliance on a commercial logic. Disneyfied/ized modes of participation help perpetuate a post-political society and keep the public entertained, while other more political, complex, and long-term modes of public participation languish.

References

Adorno, T. (1941). On popular music. *Studies in Philosophy and Social Sciences, 9*(1), 17–18.
Ballard, J. G. (1990). *The atrocity exhibition* (2nd ed.). San Francisco: RE/Search Publications. (Original work published in 1970).
Barney, D. (2010). "Excuse us if we don't give a fuck": The (anti-)political career of participation. *Jeunesse: Young People, Texts, Cultures, 2*(2), 138–146.
Bauman, Z. (2001). *The individualized society.* Malden, MA: Polity Press.
Bielak, S., & Duffalo, A. (2012, April 10). Agonizing over "agonism": Exploring how difference can fuel democracy. Retrieved from: http://www.walkerart.org/magazine/2012/agonism-politics-consensus-art-democracy
Bryman, A. (1999). The Disneyization of society. *The Sociological Review, 47*(1), 25–47.
Bryman, A. (2004). *The Disneyization of society.* London: Sage.
Dean, J. (2005). Communicative capitalism: Circulation and the foreclosure of politics. *Cultural Politics, 1*(1), 51–74.
Dean, J. (2009). *Democracy and other neoliberal fantasies: Communicative capitalism and left politics.* Durham, NC: Duke University Press.
Duffalo, A. (2012, October, 10). The ballad of black and blue [Web log post]. Retrieved from: http://blogs.walkerart.org/ecp/2012/10/10/the-ballad-of-black-and-blue/
Esche, C. (2004, April). What's the point of art centres anyway?—Possibility, art and democratic deviance [Blog post]. Retrieved from: http://republicart.net/disc/institution/esche01_en.pdf
Foster, H. (2006). Chat rooms. In C. Bishop (Ed.) *Participation* (pp. 190–195). Cambridge, MA: MIT Press. (Original work published in 2004).
Giroux, H. A., & Pollock, G. (2010). *The mouse that roared: Disney and the end of innocence* (2nd ed.). Lanham, MD: Rowman & Littlefield.
Hancock, P. (2005). Disneyfying Disneyization. *ephemera, 5*(3), 545–550.
Hooper-Greenhill, E. (2007). *Museums and education: Purpose, pedagogy and performance.* New York: Routledge.
jagodzinski, j. (2013). Anonymous: The Occupy Movement and the failure of representational democracy. *The Journal of Social Theory in Art Education, 33*, 21–37.
Kalin, N. M. (2015). The occupation of art museum educator in the time of Occupy Museums. *International Journal of Education Through Art, 11*(2), 299–309.
Merli, P. (2002). Evaluating the social impact of participation in arts activities: A critical review of François Matarasso's "Use or Ornament?" *International Journal of Cultural Policy, 8*(1), 107–18.
Mouffe, C. (2008). Critique as counter-hegemonic intervention. *eipcp* (European Institute for Progressive Cultural Policies). Retrieved from: http://eipcp.net/transversal/0808/mouffe/en/print
Mouffe, C. (2013). *Agonistics: Thinking the world politically.* New York: Verso.
Newhouse, V. (2006). *Towards a new museum* (expanded ed.). New York: Monacelli Press. (Original work published in 1998).

Not An Alternative. (2010). *Limits of participation.* Retrieved from: http://www. booki.cc/collaborativefutures/interlude-the-limits-of-participation/

Not An Alternative. (2014). Counter power as common power. *The Journal of Aesthetics and Protest, 9.* Retrieved from: http://www.joaap.org/issue9/notanalternative.htm

Phillips, A. (2011). A short plan for art institutions post-participation. In N.V. Kolowratnik & M. Miessen (Eds.), *Waking up from the nightmare of participation* (pp. 268–73). Utrecht, The Netherlands: Expothesis.

Pine, J., & Gilmore, J. (1999). *The experience economy,* Boston: Harvard Business School Press.

Pro+agonist: The Art of Opposition. (n.d.). Retrieved from: http://cooper.edu/events-and-exhibitions/events/protagonist

Relyea, L. (2013). *Your everyday art world.* Cambridge, MA: MIT Press.

Schickel, R. (1986). *The Disney version: The life, times, art and commerce of Walt Disney* (revised ed.). London: Pavilion.

Simon, N. (2010). *The participatory museum.* Santa Cruz, CA: Museum 2.0. Retrieved from: http://www.participatorymuseum.org/read/

Studio REV. (n.d.). Pro+agonist: The Art of Opposition. Retrieved from: http://www. studiorev.org/p_proagonist.html

Walker Art Center. (2013). Discourse and Discord Architecture of Agonism. Retrieved from: http://www.walkerart.org/calendar/2012/discourse-and-discord-architecture-of-agonism

Walz, G. (1998). Charlie Thorson and the temporary Disneyfication of Warner Bros. cartoons. In K. S. Sandler (Ed.), *Reading the rabbit: Explorations in Warner Bros. animation* (pp. 49–66). New Brunswick, NJ: Rutgers University Press.

Žižek, S. (1999). *The ticklish subject—The absent centre of political ontology.* London: Verso.

14 The Corseted Curriculum

Four Feminist Readings of a Strong Disney Princess

Annette Furo, Nichole E. Grant, Pamela Rogers, and Kelsey Catherine Schmitz

Once upon a time there were four feminists and a Disney princess. The princess, Merida, was "independent and brave," a "princess by birth and an adventurer by spirit" (The Walt Disney Company, 2014). Indeed, Merida was born of the 2012 Disney franchise *Brave*, a trailblazer in the portrayal of strong royal heroines. Described as an "impulsive young lady" who defies "age-old tradition and sacred customs" Princess Merida is determined to "carve out her own path in life" (The Walt Disney Company, n.d.). Her red curly hair epitomizes her rebellious and adventurous spirit; unwilling to be pulled in and tamed, it remains an unruly mass around her pale face. She is also a skilled archer, an unprincess-like attribute according to her mother Queen Elinor, but the secret pride of her father King Fergis. The four feminists were intrigued. "Could Merida really be a 'new' type of Disney princess?" they asked. They wanted to embrace a new type of Disney heroine but knew that despite years of criticism for the gendered portrayal of females in Disney films and marketing (Do Rozario, 2004; Dundes, 2001; Giroux & Pollock, 2010; Peterson & Lach, 1990), Disney princesses continued to be one of the company's most iconic and lucrative cultural symbols.

A Disney princess has become, in the words Do Rozario (2004), the "princess of all princesses," who influences contemporary notions of what it means to be a princess, conjures the nostalgia of childhood fairytales that take place within the reassuring order of patriarchal realms. Part of the appeal of a Disney princess is her timelessness, which spans generations. Appearing in films from the 1930s to the 1950s came the classic Disney princesses of *Snow White and the Seven Dwarfs* (Disney et al., 1937), *Cinderella* (Disney, Geronimi, Jackson, & Luske, 1950), and *Sleeping Beauty* (Disney, Geronimi, Clark, Larson, & Reitherman, 1959). Through the 1980s and 1990s princesses were revived in *The Little Mermaid* (Musker, Ashman, & Clements, 1989), *Beauty and the Beast* (Hahn, Trousdale, & Wise, 1991), *Aladdin* (Clements & Musker, 1992), *Pocahontas* (Pentecost, Gabriel, & Goldberg, 1995) and *Mulan* (Coats, Bancroft, & Cook, 1998). More recently Disney has sought to usher in a new generation of princesses who appear in such films as *The Princess and the Frog* (Del Vecho, Lasseter, Clements, & Musker,

2009), *Tangled* (Conli, Lasseter, Keane, Greno, & Howard, 2010), and, the subject of our current study, *Brave* (Sarafian, Andrews, & Chapman, 2012). The princesses of these films have never been more lucrative than they are today. Since 2001, when Disney began marketing their princesses together, the Disney Princess brand has increased ten-fold in revenues to the tune of $3 billion in merchandise sales worldwide (Orenstein, 2006), and has risen as the top selling entertainment product in the United States (Goudreau, 2011). It is in the context of this legacy and marketing windfall that we find Princess Merida.

In this chapter, each feminist/author presents a critical reading that focuses on a different aspect of Princess Merida. While some of her most defining characteristics (i.e., bravery, independence) diverge from the traditionally feminine princess (i.e., obedient, dependent), her story, her image, and Disney's marketing products are as bound to female gender roles and stereotypes as her corset is bound to her torso. The critical readings expose four separate, yet interrelated, ways the public pedagogy of Merida as a Disney princess molds her within a 'corseted curriculum': through her physical appearance, the structure of the fairy tale story, the heteronormative narratives in which she is situated, and the marketing of her as a Disney princess.

Situating Merida: A Critical Framework

To situate the four readings of Merida as a Disney princess, we look to understandings of the gendered body, the notion of a curriculum as a lived experience of meaning making, and the power of public pedagogy. Each reading takes up these elements in different ways, with different emphases in order to more fully grasp the complex interrelated contexts that surround the making, telling, displaying, and selling of Merida as a Disney princess.

What the gendered body can do is limited by the ways obedience and delinquency are defined (Foucault, 1979). What makes a character 'brave' and willful, for example, stands against what is normative behavior. Disney relies upon, and reaffirms that such definitions are part of the audience's common sense. As such, female heroines, especially those within the Disney Princess franchise, perform a constricted notion of gender (Butler, 1990) within static, gendered standards of good conduct, polite behavior, and marriage expectations. Butler asks, "If there is no recourse to a 'person', a 'sex' or a 'sexuality' that escapes the matrix of power and discursive relations that effectively produce and regulate the intelligibility of those concepts for us, what constitutes the possibility of effective inversion, subversion, or displacement within the terms of constructed identity?" (p. 44). Rebellion against these gender norms is a subversive act but ultimately the heroine's existence never strays outside of these narratives. As we will see, even Merida's 'new' princess identity is bound to narrow gender norms through a contradictory language of free will and empowerment.

Shaping Merida: A Curriculum of Gender Performance for Disney Princesses

The first critical reading considers Merida's female body as a curriculum of gender performance. Taken broadly, curriculum is a landscape of multiple meanings that work through and between people, shaping their tastes and experiences (Aoki, 2005). These multiple meanings hold underlying assumptions, interests, values, and perspectives that have the effect of emphasizing certain ideas and knowledges over others. In this sense, the gendered curriculum circulated through the Disney Princess brand, whether in physical attributes, media and advertising, or 'real life' experiences at Disney parks, is never a neutral practice (Aoki, 2005; Pinar, 2011).

Merida, a young woman who enjoys horseback riding, archery, and exploring the woods around her home, has a problem: she is a princess in a world where young women are expected to behave according to their gender and rank, and to broker no argument. Though Merida may think she has only her family and her clan to answer to, she is also subject to the curriculum of gender performance for Disney princesses. No matter that she bucks the expectations for a royal daughter, a princess's performance of gender dictates that Merida fit into the assigned role regardless of her attempts at subversion. Even off-screen once the movie ends, Merida continues a performance of princess as marketers seek to pretty her up, feminize her, and transform her body to one of traditional femininity and grace. Merida is never free of the Disney curriculum of gender performance, and the limits of possibility within this gender performance constitute the first dimension of a corseted curriculum.

What does it mean to perform gender? And can our bodies be sites of performances projected by others? Butler (1990) suggests that "gender is the repeated stylization of the body, a set of repeated acts within a highly rigid regulatory frame that congeal over time to produce the appearance of substance, of a natural sort of being" (p. 45). As the storyline unfolds, Merida's bodily representation moves from a wild haired, dirt smudged, warrior girl-child, to a properly attired and crowned princess. Merida is never released from the performance of princess, as it would first appear. In a way, her own corseted princess body is a curriculum she cannot escape.

As she struggles within the cultural confines of gender that the script of the movie binds her to, Merida's gender performance, her taming, and the image of her body teach viewers of all ages what it means to be a 'brave' young woman in her world: there is no (permanent) escape from the performance of princess. De Beauvoir (1949) reasons that, within the gendered discourse, the category 'woman' is meaningful only when it is situated with/in a social and historical context. As she put it, "One is not born, but rather becomes, a woman" (p. 267). That is to say, women acquire and perform (Butler, 1990) gender through interactions with the society we grow within, from our parents and schools, and from the images and media we consume. Butler (1990) asks us further to consider de Beauvoir's point, "If gender is always there, delimiting in advance what qualifies as the human, how can we speak of a human who becomes its gender, as if gender were a postscript or a cultural afterthought?" (p. 151). One becomes a woman, Butler (1990) contends, a constructed and reinvented entity that has neither a start nor a finish. In becoming a woman, Merida is placed in an uncertain gendered place where, as de Beauvoir (1949) and Butler (1990) articulate, her identity is both a social construction imposed from without (via society/cultural/institutional influence) as well as a self-made concept articulated from within.

When examining the performance of gender in Merida's context, we are presented with a dichotomy of gender: on one hand, we have a young, rebellious woman whose personal values and skills conflict greatly with her societal worth. On the other hand, we have a specific set of rules Merida must eventually come to terms with by the end of the film. The choice (not to marry) is hers, but it comes with a compromise: her gendered body and her tomboy behavior are returned to the mold of princess and beloved daughter. In reading the ways Merida's body is used to subvert the initial messages of difference and rebellion we see her woman's body returned to the confines of the corset: her weapons are removed (absence of bow), and attributes of her physical body such as womanly hips and perfect makeup, are devoid of her tomboy bravery. Frasca (2003) suggests that narratives are based on semiotic representation. When we read the text of Merida's princess body, the narrative 'it is best to look like a traditional princess' is driven home. According to Hall (1997), "all cultural objects convey meaning, and all cultural practices depend on meaning, [thus] they must make use of signs" (p. 36). If this is so, then the cultural object in question, the Princess Merida, conveys a representation of real-world culture blended with fictional storylines and fantasy role-playing. When given the opportunity to subvert the performance of the gender roles of past Disney princesses, Disney fails to recognize Merida's strengths, bravery, or ambitions, forcing the strictures of gender representation back into a corset instead. Instead of seizing the opportunity for Merida to perform a different kind of role, and allowing her different notion of gender responsibility to blossom, her body is used to signify 'Disney Princesses', and is thus a site of the corseted curriculum.

Destined to Be a Princess: The Restrictive Structure of the Tale

Not only is Merida constricted by her performance of gender and Disney's continuation of her female role as normative and valuable, the story in which she finds herself—a Disney fairy tale—controls her will and her very ability to be the 'brave' new Disney princess. Ahmed (2011) relates that "one form

212 *Annette Furo et al.*

of will seems to involve the rending of other wills as willful; one form of will assumes the right to eliminate the others" (p. 240). The will of the corseted curriculum—for this particular reading, the will of the story's structure as a fairy tale—reins in the story in a way that makes it seem as if it must be bound and controlled in the first place. The will of the corseted curriculum binds the plot and characters, tightening and contouring, shaping the characters the way a corset shapes the female form to the will of its boning. In this way Merida's will is structured and defined by the bounds of the plot, limiting her development to a set, prescribed formula.

In an analysis of fairy tales, Propp (1968/2009) creates a schematic structure of the fairy tale plot, broken down into 31 possible functions or events, where each function of the tale is designated with a symbol to create a formula for the combined set of functions for any one fairy tale. Some functions have several 'varieties' designated with a super or subscript, yet the general schema of the tale follows with a preparatory part including what Propp calls an interdiction and its violation. This stage is followed by the function of villainy and the effects of villainy ending with a wedding or promise of wedding. Within this schema the hero character has little agency in the functions of the plot and is more a product of what Propp calls "picturesqueness and color" (p. 8). This is not to say that all readings of *Brave* (2012) need to follow this type of analysis, but simply that the film follows the general sequence of events typical of a folk tale or fairy tale and in so doing the very structure of the tale itself binds the possibility of the plot and Merida's character development. At the same time, Merida's strong willful character seems to struggle against the typical plot structure of a fairy tale: she refuses to be wed through an arrangement, she is adventurous and daring, and rebels against the 'fate' of being a princess and the duties and qualities that traditionally entails. In such a reading, Merida seems to come close to the 'progressive' and liberatory character she is professed to be in the popular press (Emme, 2014; Kishon, 2014). However, what her character *does* or is able to do is restricted to the structure of the tale itself, which trumps the potential for Merida to be a 'new' type of Disney princess. The functions of the plot and its sequence are in this way independent of Merida as a character (Propp, 1968/2009).

After the initial situation (α), where the hero and their family are introduced, Propp (1968/2009) explains that the hero of the plot (Merida) follows the paired plot functions of *interdiction* (y^1) and *violation* (δ): Merida is given an order (her mother tells her to 'act like a princess' and consequently accept her fate as such), which she violates by participating in an archery competition and ripping her dress. Merida's violation is understood as willful, an attribution of getting in the way of an intention; she is considered "obstinate or perverse" because she is "not persuaded by the reasoning of others" (Ahmed, 2014b, p. 18). Willfulness can however be a style of politics within feminism, a purposeful rebellion against the designation of being willful as a dismissal (Ahmed, 2014b) or an assertion of a feminist identity (Braidotti, 1994). Merida's willfulness is resistant only to err from the right and good will and stand in the way of the fate to which she is destined. Willfulness is then a 'swerve' or a bend away from the good will, a selfish deviation from the right path that is the moral will. Willfulness thus requires 'straightening' or a bending back to the right path, the good will. In this way Merida's rebellion is not allowed its potential positioning as a politics of feminist resistance but rather "becomes 'yet another' symptom of willfulness; and being heard as such is dismissed as such" (Ahmed, 2014b, p. 90). Merida's willfulness is consequently villainized and made to be the character flaw that leads her astray from the will of her family—the right and good will. This positioning sets up willfulness as the metaphorical 'villain' within the story itself.

Typical of the fairy tale plot structure Propp describes, Merida next commits an act of *villainy* (A). By deceitfully enticing her victim (A^8) to eat magical cake, and casting a spell on the victim (A^{11}), Merida violates her mother's interdiction to follow her willfulness to 'change her fate': "Change my mother, change my fate". The victim in this case is her mother, Queen Elinor, who metaphorically embodies Merida's good will. Here, Queen Elinor personifies the right (good) will, the willingness to be willed toward the appropriate destiny. By contrast, willfulness is personified through a mythic bear prince who succumbs to his own willful character and does not follow the right (good) will. It is no accident that Elinor is then turned into a bear by Merida's willful determination to change her own fate. Merida's act of villainy is directly juxtaposed to the bear king as the embodiment of willfulness, the bent selfish will, and therefore willfulness itself is positioned as a negative attribution. The will then comes to be personified within the story, split between the right (good) will, and the bent (or willful) will— the will that is not willing.

Throughout the remainder of the story Merida learns a valuable lesson about her willful determination and the powerful binding of a gendered, plot-driven fate. Following the functions of the plot outlined by Propp, she uses her necklace (not accidently a representation of her position as a wealthy royal) to buy a magic cake that will change her fate (F^4_3) by changing her mother. Queen Elinor is transformed into a bear (a personification of Merida's willfulness). Realizing that her desires have consequences, Merida embarks on a desperate quest (G^3) to restore her mother back to a human, literally reversing her willful 'change my mother, change my fate' assertion. Upon direct combat with the bear king (H^2) (a metaphor for Merida's own willfulness), Merida 'bends back' to the right good will by fighting the bear king and bonding with her mother. This 'bending back' comes to a head as Merida must decipher the witch's riddle (M)—"Fate be changed, look inside, mend the bond torn by pride"—and consequently must mend her torn bond of fate and return to the right good path (N—resolving the task) by forsaking her willfulness. In the process she kills the villainous willfulness within her, and the bear king who personifies it (U), acquiescing to her fate as a princess in the process.

Merida's willfulness then is not emancipatory or liberatory for her, but rather leads to a moment of being 'bent back' to the right will. For her efforts she simply delays the inevitable marriage and is 'straightened' to the will 'on the way' (Ahmed, 2014a), the will of being and becoming a princess. It is of note that Propp considers ascension to the throne (W↓) with or without marriage as part of the story structure and the final function of the tale. Though Merida does not marry in the tale directly, there is an assumption of marriage to come and her ascension to her right place in the order of the kingdom. The plot structure shapes the outline of the corseted curriculum: the happiness assumed, the prince at the end, the happily ever after to which, despite her moments of willfulness, in the end Merida is forced to conform.

Bonded Fates: Policing the Heteronormative Social Fabric

Intertwined with the production of gendered knowledge and restrictive plotline, the third critical reading of *Brave* examines how heteronormative policing provides the illusion of choice in whom to marry, while continuing to bind Merida to the social norm of marriage without the choice of remaining single. The signification of Merida and the plot itself constrict the readings and meanings of this Disney princess, yet in her tightly laced gown and free flowing mane, Merida defies the age-old social tradition of the clans by "winning her own hand in marriage" through an unprecedented act of courageous rebellion. With her bow and arrow in tow, she rips open the back of her restrictive dress, exposing the corset beneath for all to see, and shoots arrows into the center of three targets, defeating all three male suitors in an archery contest. Merida's act of defiance symbolizes her unwillingness, or as Ahmed (2014b) notes, the absence of good will, to be bound to the strictly enforced gender and (hetero)sexual norms of the clan system, consequently attempting to change her fate, and in turn, setting in motion the unraveling of the entire social fabric through her 'selfish' actions of independence.

Juxtaposing her unruly character is Merida's mother, who embodies the right/proper will of femininity as a refined, eloquent, powerful woman with the ability to tame unruly men and young boys, all the while remaining graceful, composed, and beautiful. Her performance of gendered femininity is lost on Merida, who remains in constant conflict against the barrage of attempts to sculpt the princess into a respectable future wife. Similar to a process of social knowledge construction Giroux (2004) calls public pedagogy, Queen Elinor both advances and enforces these knowledges of femininity and grace through a strict policing of performances and practices considered to be masculine. Merida is reminded daily that real princesses do not exhibit, or perform, the same masculine behaviors such as archery, stuffing her mouth with food, and going on adventures into the wilderness alone. Through this continual feedback loop of (negative) gender reinforcement, her mother not only is the gold standard for Merida to live up to, but she is the lone enforcer of the heteronormative social contract, through her public pedagogy of gendered performances.

Merida's character often acts 'unladylike,' differing from Disney princesses of the past. However, the rest of the plotline remains undeniably heteronormative, with assumptions that she will be married to a male partner, as the possibility of remaining single is not an option. Heteronormative sexualities are acts of embodied performances, like gender, and as such are policed through processes of monitoring and regulation, in order to correct gendered patterns of desire that could fall outside of what is considered 'normal' (Butler, 1990; Foucault, 1978, 1979). Ongoing surveillance includes repeated insistence that women will fulfill obligations of marriage and reproduction, which are seen as their sole functions in the fabric of society. Mothers, in particular, have the duty to tame and police young girls' wills in order to reproduce heteronormative social contracts, as illustrated in a split scene where Merida and Elinor are discussing their feelings about potential suitors, although not directly to one another. Elinor reveals that she would not want all of Merida's so-called training to go to waste, and asks if she is willing to "pay the price that her freedom will cost." Simultaneously, Merida proclaims that she "doesn't want her life to be over." While Merida sees marriage as limiting her freedom and her life, her mother cautions against acting upon selfish desires of independence, which she alludes will lead to the destruction of society itself.

Although Merida succeeds in renegotiating the rules of engagement among the clans and prolongs her inevitable marriage until a later date, she cannot escape the social bond of marriage. As a curriculum of normalizing messages, Disney's strong-willed princess learns that her rebellion has given her choice in whom to marry, but her destiny, the marriage plot, and the strictly adhered to gendered and heterosexist norms, do not evolve. Symbolic of her act of rebellion, she rips open a layer in her princess gown, exposing unfair and outdated gendered social norms by evoking change, but underneath the external layer of gendered performance lays the exposed corset, silent and steadfastly tied. In this way the corset represents heteronormative sexuality, with its assumed neutrality, yet binding to the woman's body and restricting its movement just as social pressures to conform bind to Merida's will. As a popular fairy tale, *Brave* propagates the notion that women's lives function as the gatekeepers of social order, through the policing of gendered performance of their children. Through this, *Brave* demonstrates the restrictive nature of heteronormative desires and gendered norms on Merida's narrative, which simultaneously recast her as an idealized hetero-feminine subject and limit her agency in choosing her own path.

Marketing Merida: Consuming a Corseted Curriculum

The fourth critical reading will explore how the marketing of Princess Merida adds another important dimension to the corseted curriculum. Already shaped against the confines of the plot structure and the pressure to conform to heteronormative values, Princess Merida is wedged literally and meta-phorically into a corset. Adoring little girls, however, do not have to wear a corset in order to play dress up as Merida, or rather, they do not have to *literally* wear a corset in order to be metaphorically bound by one. The desire to dress or shoot a bow like Merida can be easily achieved through acts of consumption, such as buying Disney Princess products and engaging in rituals of imitation and dress up. Pedagogies of consumption help us understand how marketing Merida is a key aspect of the corseted curriculum, which cultivates a desire to idolize her gendered body and her sexually normative experience, and to submit willingly to one's own gendered binding. Consumption is tied to learning and identity through an ideology of consumerism, which we enact "in almost every aspect of our lives" (Sandlin & McLaren, 2010, p. 2). When embedded in everyday life, acts of consumption are more than a matter of economics and also part of larger socio-cultural processes bound to notions of image, identity, and desire. Through consumption children learn to create identities in relation to fashion, advertising, and media. As a series of cultural objects, it is worth considering how the Disney Princess brand has the ability to influence what it means to be a girl, and how the brand merchandise encourages certain rituals of consumption.

A decade of Disney Princess brand success has worked to rebrand 'girlhood' at the intersection of gender roles and consumption (England, Descartes, & Collier-Meek, 2011). As Stover (2013) notes, advertising and merchandise become "a vehicle for selling empowerment as commodity to the empowered female consumer" (p. 6), meaning that the sense of female agency channeled into purchasing power is derived from a rhetoric of autonomy and is in fact still associated with outward appearance. To see how Stover's point resonates with *Brave*, we can consider some of the Princess Merida merchandise that is available in Disney's online store and at major retailers in the United States. Merida becomes Disney-fied through an assortment of eye-catching gowns, gold shoes, and crowns adorned with feminine embellishments like lace, gemstones, and bright colors. The selection of items seems to send the message that a Princess must have a wand, tiara, and hair tamed into voluminous spirals in order to be admitted to the 'court of Disney.' Mattel's Merida 'fashion doll', for example, has enlarged eyes, a tiny waist, ballerina fingertips, coiffed hair, and a special painting wand for hair highlights. The doll not only bears little resemblance to Merida as we see her in the film, it also ascribes to her 'feminine' interests in beauty and grace, which as the first critical reading explained, bind her to a princess's performance of gender. Yet in *Brave*, Merida begrudges every minute she must spend primping and polishing at her mother's behest. She wears a long green dress that is quite plain by comparison. She does not have a wand, nor does she wear a crown or jewel-encrusted shoes or gowns.

There is a contradiction between the adventurous and free spirited Merida from the film and the refined, traditionally feminine Merida of the merchandise. Just imagine Merida the fashion doll reenacting a scene where Merida hops on her horse, Angus, and goes charging off into the forest. Her gold tiara would fly off, her hair would be utterly ruined, and the glittery corseted bodice of her dress would be so impractical for a night of adventure! Such exciting escapades are rather beyond the fashion doll's intended purpose. This is important because it not only limits the scope of play that girls can engage in, but it guides them toward activities (e.g., hair high-lighting) that work to cultivate a consumer-dependent image of outer beauty. Buying into this type of brand merchandise is, in a way, like buying oneself a corset. It is a corset of fixed meanings about femininity which reinscribe Merida with narrowly defined gender roles, ideals of beauty that fail to be 'brave', and narratives that remain at odds with the notion of women's empowerment. Merida's character from the film disrupts traditional Disney princess femininity as quickly as marketing her to young girls seeks to re-fix it. Through a pedagogy of consumption the corset is a curriculum that encourages young girls to desire and effectively purchase their own gendered binding. Of course a young girl can be adventurous and independent and still want to play 'princess' some of the time. It is not an either/or choice to be like Merida from the film or Merida from the merchandise. A young girl may subvert the intended meanings of the traditionally feminine princess doll and take her on a fantastical adventure. However, as we saw in the preceding critical readings, the overarching Merida narratives from which a young girl could draw are already confined along gendered and heteronormative lines. After the film is over and the dolls fly off store shelves, Merida's destiny is up to the impressionable imaginations of young girls as she lives on eternally as a princess in the 'court of Disney.'

Conclusion

The laces of the corset have been pulled ever tighter and these four feminists are discouraged. Even when accounting for the non-traditional aspects of this Disney princess the corseted curriculum restrains Merida contorting her image, her spirit, and her rebellious and willful potential. The surface-level personality traits of bravery and adventure are an obvious choice for proclaiming Merida a different kind of princess, but the narratives in which she is situated and the processes of signification that imbue her body with meaning prevent her from truly departing from the traditionally feminine Disney princess. As public pedagogy, the corseted curriculum ensnares Merida and the possibility for her to exist outside the age-old schema of a willful girl's struggle. The plot structure and heteronormative discourses restrain her rebellion, while the consumerist pedagogy of the Disney Princess franchise literally reshapes her image to conform to the gendered fantasies of the 'court of Disney.' Merida continues to wear and be constricted by the corset, a restrictive and contorted understanding of gender, sexuality and freedom perpetuated by a multibillion dollar industry, a curriculum of great power and influence that these four feminists are continually attempting to unknot, untie and unravel.

References

Ahmed, S. (2011). Willful part: Problem characters or the problem character. *New Literary History, 42*(2), 231–253.

Ahmed, S. (2014a, March 19). Willfulness: A feminist history. *Shirley Greenberg Annual lecture in Women's Studies.* Conducted from the Institute of Women's Studies, University of Ottawa, Ottawa, ON.

Ahmed, S. (2014b). *Willful subjects.* Durham, NC: Duke University Press.

Aoki, T. (2005). *Curriculum in a new key: The collected works of Ted T. Aoki.* W. Pinar & R. Irwin (Eds.). New York: Routledge.

de Beauvoir, S. (1949). *The second sex.* New York: Knopf.

Braidotti, R. (1994). *Nomadic subjects: Embodiment and sexual difference in contemporary feminist theory.* New York: Columbia University Press.

Butler, J. (1990). *Gender trouble: Feminism and the subversion of identity.* New York: Routledge.

Clements, R., & Musker, J. (Producers/Directors). (1992). *Aladdin* [Motion picture]. United States: Walt Disney Pictures.

Coats, P. (Producer), Bancroft, T., & Cook, B. (Directors). (1998). *Mulan* [Motion picture]. United States: Walt Disney Pictures.

Conli, R., Lasseter, J., Keane, G. (Producers), Greno, N., & Howard, B. (Directors). (2010). *Tangled* [Motion picture]. United States: Walt Disney Pictures.

Del Vecho, P., Lasseter, J. (Producers), Clements, R., & Musker, J. (Directors). (2009). *The princess and the frog* [Motion picture]. United States: Walt Disney Pictures.

Disney, W. (Producer), Geronimi, C., Clark, L., Larson, E., & Reitherman (Directors). (1959). *Sleeping beauty* [Motion picture]. United States: Walt Disney Productions.

Disney, W. (Producer), Geronimi, C., Jackson, W., & Luske, H. (Directors). (1950). *Cinderella* [Motion picture]. United States: Walt Disney Productions.

Disney, W. (Producer), Cottrell W., Hand, D., Jackson, W., Morey, L., Pearce, P., & Sharpsteen, B. (Directors). (1937). *Snow White and the seven dwarfs* [Motion picture]. United States: Walt Disney Productions.

Do Rozario, R. C. (2004). The princess and the magic kingdom: Beyond nostalgia, the function of the Disney princess. *Women's Studies in Communication, 27*(1), 34–59.

Dundes, L. (2001). Disney's modern heroine Pocahontas: Revealing age-old gender stereotypes and discontinuity under a façade of liberation. *Social Science Journal 38*(1), 353–365.

Emme. (2014, February 6). Princess shape-up at Disney. *Huffington Post.* Retrieved from: http://www.huffingtonpost.com/emme/princess-shapeup-at-disne_b_4734135.html

England, D. E., Descartes, L., & Collier-Meek, M. A. (2011). Gender role portrayal and the Disney princesses. *Sex Roles, 64*(7–8), 555–567.

Foucault, M. (1978). *The history of sexuality, volume 1: An introduction* (trans. R. Hurley). New York: Vintage.

Foucault, M. (1979). *Discipline and punish: The birth of the prison.* New York: Vintage Books.

Frasca, G. (2003). Videogames of the oppressed. In P. Harrigan & N. Wardrip-Fruin (Eds.), *First person: New media as story, performance and game* (pp. 85–94). Cambridge, MA: MIT press.

Giroux, H. A. (2004). Cultural studies, public pedagogy, and the responsibility of intellectuals. *Communication and Critical/Cultural Studies, 1*(1), 59–79.

Giroux, H. A., & Pollock, G. (2010). *The mouse that roared: Disney and the end of innocence* (2nd ed.). Lanham, MA: Rowman & Littlefield.

Goudreau, J. (2011). Disney Princess tops list of the 20 best-selling entertainment products. *Forbes Magazine.* Retrieved from: http://www.forbes.com/sites/jenna goudreau/2012/09/17/disney-princess-tops-list-of-the-20-best-selling-entertainment-products/

Hahn, D. (Producer), Trousdale, G., & Wise, K. (Directors). (1991). *Beauty and the beast* [Motion picture]. United States: Walt Disney Pictures.

Hall, S. (1997). The work of representation. In S. Hall (Ed.), *Representation: Cultural representations and signifying practices* (pp. 1–74). London: Sage

Kishon, A. (2014, March 31). Frozen, Tangled, Brave and other Disney epics. *Liberty Voice.* Retrieved from: http://guardianlv.com/2014/03/frozen-tangled-brave-and-other-disney-epics/

Musker, J. (Producer/Director), Ashman, H. (Producer), & Clements, R. (Director). (1989). *The little mermaid* [Motion picture]. United States: Walt Disney Pictures.

Orenstein, P. (2006, December 24). What's wrong with Cinderella? *The New York Times.* Retrieved from: http://www.nytimes.com/2006/12/24/magazine/24princess.t.html

Pentecost, J. (Producer), Gabriel, M., & Goldberg, E. (Directors). (1995). *Pocahontas* [Motion picture]. United States: Walt Disney Pictures.

Peterson, S. B., & Lach, M. A. (1990). Gender stereotypes in children's books: Their prevalence and influence on cognitive and affective development. *Gender and Education, 2*(2), 185–197.

Pinar, W. (2011). *The character of curriculum studies.* New York: Palgrave Macmillan.

Propp, V. (2009). *The morphology of the folktale* (trans. L. Scott). Austin: University of Texas Press. (Original work published in 1968).

Sandlin, J. A., & McLaren, P. (2010). *Critical pedagogies of consumption.* New York: Routledge.

Sarafian, K. (Producer), Andrews, M., & Chapman, B. (Directors). (2012). *Brave* [Motion picture]. United States: Walt Disney Pictures & Pixar Animation Studios.

Stover, C. (2013). Damsels and heroines: The conundrum of the post-feminist Disney princess. *LUX: A Journal of Transdisciplinary Writing and Research from Claremont Graduate University, 2*(1), Article 29.

The Walt Disney Company. (n.d.). *Brave.* Retrieved from: http://movies.disney.com/brave

The Walt Disney Company. (2014). *Meet Merida.* Retrieved from: http://princess.disney.com/merida

15 A New Dimension of Disney Magic

MyMagic+ and Controlled Leisure

Gabriel S. Huddleston, Julie C. Garlen, and Jennifer A. Sandlin

In 2013, after spending one billion dollars designing and testing new guest services, The Walt Disney Company began implementing "MyMagic+" (Garcia, 2013), a new set of technologies that were conceived by Disney CEO Bob Iger as a way to "overhaul the digital infrastructure of Disney's theme parks, which would upend how they operated and connected with consumers" (Carr, 2015, para. 3). MyMagic+, which is driven by radio frequency identification technology (RFID), is a complex digital system that involves several interactive components, including the My Disney Experience mobile application and website, which allow visitors to plan, manage, and share the details of their vacation; the MagicBand, which acts as a waterproof ticketing system, a hotel door key, a digital form of payment, and a fashion accessory that can be customized with charms; the Disney FastPass+ service, which enables advance reservations for attractions; and the PhotoPass Memory Maker, which allows guests to take unlimited photos while in the park and download them later. According to the Walt Disney World website, these new services enhance the guest experience by unlocking "a *new dimension* of Disney Magic" and offering "unprecedented control" of one's vacation. The website further asserts that "MyMagic+ takes your Walt Disney World vacation to an all-new level, making it uniquely yours, so you can enjoy every moment with family and friends" (Walt Disney World, 2015). In using these services before, during, and after their trip, visitors are encouraged to construct scripted excursions in which all moments are carefully planned to insure a 'magical' experience. Thus, the 'fun' of a trip to Walt Disney World is not guaranteed with park admission but must be carefully planned for and achieved by visitors within the limits imposed by the use of customized consumer services. In other words, Walt Disney World offers its guests *controlled leisure* as a means to guarantee, through the guest's own diligence, research, and organization, the experience of a lifetime.

In this chapter, we argue that MyMagic+ operates as both a regulatory device and a mechanism of surveillance to construct theme park experiences in a particular way that both appeals to the desires of consumers and serves Disney's corporate interests. Drawing on Bryman's (1999, 2004) concept of Disneyization along with Deleuzean notions of societies of control and post-panoptic surveillance, we explore how Walt Disney World, through services like MyMagic+, operates as a society of control. Next, we explore how the controlled leisure of Disney's control society is expanded into new realms through the practices of the new MyMagic+ technologies. Finally, we examine how, through engaging with MyMagic+, visitors to Disney parks take up the role of prosumer (Ritzer, 2014, 2015; Ritzer & Jurgenson, 2010) as they engage in the exploitative immaterial labor (Arvidsson, 2005; Lazzarato, 1997) that benefits The Walt Disney Company. As prosumers— productive consumers—we willingly participate in the Disney experience and become productive in ways that feel participatory but are in fact also providing free labor for the brand. Understanding how controlled leisure operates through MyMagic+ provides a lens through which we can examine how Walt Disney World's curriculum of control shapes our buying decisions within the theme park and beyond.

Walt Disney World as a Society of Control

Scholars have long focused on control as a major theme in their analyses of Disney theme parks, as numerous Disney studies scholars have examined the ways that The Walt Disney Company enacts control. Most of these scholars start with the premise that popular culture plays a large role in the shaping of society itself, as reflected in the theoretical foundations of cultural studies (Fiske, 1989; Hall, 2009). Within and, increasingly, beyond the United States The Walt Disney Company is pervasive within popular culture and, as such, wields significant influence. Disney's attempt to codify its products as markers of childhood represents the center from which most of its influence resonates (Giroux & Pollock, 2010). As Giroux and Pollock argue, Disney attempts to exert ideological control by shaping what childhood, and thus, parenting, means through its marketing of television shows, movies, and merchandise that influence the buying decisions of parents and children alike. Disney has been further analyzed by scholars as a site of ideological control in regards to gender (Griffin, 2000; Henke, Umble, & Smith, 1996), history (Edgerton & Jackson, 1996), culture (Lacroix, 2004; Van Maanen, 1992), business (Allerton, 1997), and family (Wynns & Rosenfeld, 2003)

Among the various analyses of Disney principles and discourses, Bryman's concept of Disneyization offers significant insight toward understanding how control operates within Disney theme parks. Disneyization, as a theory about how consumption works in late capitalism, posits that "the global organisation of consumption is increasingly conforming to a template provided by the practices and principles of the Disney theme parks" (Hancock, 2005, p. 545). The principles through which Disney theme parks are organized and that thus make up the process of Disneyization are theming, hybrid consumption, merchandising, and emotional or performative labor; according to Bryman, these principles are practiced not only in Disney parks but also have spread beyond Disney to dominate current business practices in late capitalist modernity. Bryman (2004) explains that the success and maintenance of these principles cannot be achieved without the exertion of control and surveillance. In fact, Bryman (1995) suggests that the concept of control was foundational to the vision of Walt Disney himself, with his fixation on the "control of people's movement and their experience of the park, of the behaviour of employees, and of the parks' boundaries with the outside world" (p. 98). As Sehlinger and Testa (2015), in *The Unofficial Guide to Walt Disney World,* explain: "Disney's theme parks are the quintessential system, the ultimate in mass-produced entertainment, the most planned and programmed environment anywhere" (p. 5). Control is enacted within the parks through the parks' actual physical design as well as through the emotional control of guests and park employees.

Mechanisms of control are embedded in the very design of the park to such an extent that they are mostly hidden to the visitor (Borrie, 1999; Shearing & Stenning, 1992). Such mechanisms include "weenies," which are visual icons or events used to attract guests' attention and move them toward specific locations. As Gennawey (2014) explains, weenies were named for the hot dogs Walt Disney used to direct the movement of his pet dog. Similarly, shooting fountains are used to stop guests' movement and redirect them to other areas of the park. Even less visible to guests is the underground network of "utilidors," tunnels that connect the parks and hide from guests' sight the movement of employees, water and gas pipes, electrical wiring, computer cables, and other technologies and processes that would ruin the fantasy of the parks operating by 'magic' (Telotte, 2008). The landscapes are also meticulously monitored and controlled. Each night after the visitors leave, the theme parks go through a high level of cleaning using power washers. Simultaneously, dying and dead plants are removed throughout the park. Combined with other cosmetic improvements made overnight, the overall effect is that the parks seem clean and new for the next day's visitors (Borrie, 1999).

Another element of the planned and programmed design of Walt Disney World that directly involves surveillance is an electronic nerve center located under Cinderella Castle that uses video cameras, computer programs and digital park maps to monitor the length of lines at park attractions so that immediate measures can be taken to reduce wait time. The underground command center also allows park engineers to monitor traffic flow in restaurants and redistribute visitors in crowded areas by dispatching characters and mini-parades in less populated areas of the park. The center also operates in tandem with elements of the new MyMagic+ system, including

MyMagic+ wristbands, smartphone applications, and digital kiosks to track the movement of bodies and collect data on visitor behavior, including spending patterns. As Barnes (2010) notes, "the primary goal of the command center, as stated by Disney, is to make guests happier—because to increase revenue in its $10.7 billion theme park business, which includes resorts in Paris and Hong Kong, Disney needs its current customers to return more often" (para. 12). It is also important to note that, because functional MagicBands are only provided for free to guests staying in expensive Disney hotels (other guests must purchase them), they operate to control which kinds of guests will return to the park, perpetuating the company's long-held association with middle-class customers, which has historically differentiated Disney parks "from the more working-class overtones and clientele of the older amusement parks like those at Coney Island" (Bryman, 1995, p. 73).

The control embedded within the design of the park itself extends to employees and the ways in which they interact with visitors. To begin, they are not referred to as employees at all, but rather as "cast members" (Allerton, 1997). The use of this stage term is to fuel the perception that Walt Disney World is not a business, but rather a place of entertainment where employees are actors in a production (Borrie, 1999; Shearing & Stenning, 1992). Relying on the utilidor system, cast members are rarely seen out of their work clothes (referred to as costumes) to keep up the illusion of a staged production. Strict rules dictate that Disney cast members who play 'face' and 'mask' characters stay in character at all times when interacting with guests (Wickstrom, 2005). Stories of characters vomiting in their heads while 'onstage' and not being able to remove their heads until reaching a 'backstage' area illustrate the lengths to which Disney goes to control the illusion of fantasy at the parks. Exemplifying what Bryman (1999, 2004) refers to as performative or emotional labor, cast members are trained to be forever upbeat and positive. Every interaction with guests is executed with a smile and positive disposition as guests are directed to wait in lines, park their strollers in designated areas, board rides at directed times, and move out of the street when a parade is starting (Shearing & Stenning, 1992). Indeed, when cast members are trained at Disney University, the second directive they are given is to "create happiness" (Allerton, 1997). Consequently, guests are struck by the pleasant, friendly nature of the interaction rather than the fact they are being controlled. In the end, guests are more willing to submit because those in charge are exceedingly friendly and cheery. Cast members themselves must be highly self-regulated while exerting control over guests. Indeed, Bryman (2004) quotes a Disney cast member as saying, "We have to smile at a guest no matter what he does. It's really a way of controlling what you're really feeling" (p. 152).

All of these mechanisms of control and surveillance add up to a park experience for the visitor that is pleasurable because it is predictable. As Ritzer and Liska (1997) observe, "Disney World is highly predictable . . . . Indeed,

Disney theme parks work to be sure that the visitor experiences no surprises at all" (p. 115). Disney delivers a controlled, safe, and predictable environment to meet the expectations of its guests—expectations that the company has worked hard to instill and solidify in terms of what a theme park vacation entails. Williams (2013) describes the appeal of this orderly, enclosed environment where "everything you need in a given day, from food to bathrooms to medical care, is available at a moment's notice" (p. 173). Williams writes that "it's easy to feel the seductive ideological pull of the 'Disney moment,'" and yet, "Disney World is also a place of control, simulation, reactionary conservatism, corporate branding, and surveillance" (p. 173). In another context, consumers might hesitate to submit themselves to such manipulation, but the promise of pleasurable conveniences makes the sacrifice of privacy more palatable.

The happiness that Walt Disney World provides thus comes at the cost of privacy, and, to a large extent, choice, despite the apparent freedom to choose one's vacation, which amounts to choosing among the options provided by the company. This conflict between apparent freedom and expanded control marks the theme park as what Deleuze (1992) termed a society of control. Unlike Foucault's disciplinary society, characterized by the Panopticon with its centralized point from which activity is surveilled, a society of control features an expansive matrix through which information is gathered, tracked, encoded, and interpreted into patterns, which are deemed either acceptable or unacceptable. Poster (1996) explains this expansion on disciplinary control using the example of databases, or superpanopticons, which collect personal information through multiple mechanisms and create transportable identities. Unlike Foucault's disciplinary society, in which observation is hierarchical and explicitly normalizing, in the database, the observed becomes a willing participant:

> The one being surveilled provides the information necessary for the surveillance. No carefully designed edifice is needed, no science such as criminology is employed, no complex administrative apparatus is invoked, no bureaucratic organization need be formed . . . A gigantic, sleek operation is effected whose political force of surveillance is occluded in the willing participation of the victim.
>
> (Poster, 1996, p. 184)

As Fjellman (1992) notes in his discussion of the underpinnings of the design of Walt Disney World—imbued with Walt Disney's own desire to create not only a perfect theme park, but a perfect society—the willingness of citizens to participate in self-control was essential in the march towards a utopia. As we will discuss further below, we posit that MagicBands are the material representation of willing participation of the theme park guest in the mechanisms of control. As Bogost (2014) aptly observes, the experience of utilizing MagicBands is "uncanny" (para. 22) in that "we don't just tolerate surveillance but openly embrace it as fashion" (para. 23). In fact, as Bogost (2014) notes,

> the MagicBands are treated like precious tiaras. Upon booking, each member of your family selects a color. Weeks before your scheduled Disney deployment, a box arrives. In it: each band, inserted carefully into a foam cutout sized expressly for it, like a James Bond weapon surreptitiously hidden in a briefcase. The forename of its owner is imprinted before it in the packaging, as well as on the inside of the band itself. Even before arriving, one can practice what it feels like to be a transmitter of one's own unique ID.
>
> (para. 23)

This willingness to embrace surveillance is further evidenced by the community of self-proclaimed Walt Disney World fanatics that spend a great deal of their time discussing the necessary planning and organization it takes to visit Walt Disney World. The desire to plan excessively before a trip to Walt Disney World is not something the company has manufactured out of whole cloth—it is demonstrated independently from the company in the various books, podcasts, and websites/blogs dedicated to planning a trip there. While there are many to choose from, there are a few that typify the various examples: *The Unofficial Guide to Walt Disney World* (Sehlinger & Testa, 2015), its companion website, http://www.touringplans.com, and the Walt Disney World Today Podcast (Hochberg, Newell, Scopa, & Testa, 2014).

   The Unofficial Guide to Walt Disney World provides an exhaustive list of everything one could possibly imagine about a visit to Walt Disney World. Tourist books are nothing new, but treating a theme park as a foreign country is certainly a concept worth considering. They equate a visit to Walt Disney World as a dance, one that you must prepare and practice for. While planning for a vacation implies work done before the trip, MyMagic+ requires the planning to continue throughout the trip and, to some extent, after it is over. This process begins with the booking of the trip itself, but one's work is not done after booking hotel rooms, flights, and theme park tickets. As Deleuze (1992) notes about societies of control, "one is never finished with anything" (p. 5).

MyMagic+: Calculability as A New Dimension of Controlled Leisure

As revealed by our brief review of how control has long operated in Disney parks, controlled leisure—which is time spent away from business, work, school, and domestic chores that is highly regulated by a corporate entity—is remarkably ordinary because it has been a long-standing hallmark of the Walt Disney experience. As detailed above, the idea that control is a major element of the Disney theme park experience is not new; Bryman (1995) wrote at length about how control operates in a variety of ways, "at the fairly mundane level of how the visitor is handled while in the parks to the way in which the parks relate to their immediate environment" (p. 78). As Bryman (1995) further notes, "the theme of predictability is closely linked to that of control since one of the functions of controlling things is to render outcomes relating to them more predictable" (p. 92). Bryman related his analysis of Disney theme parks to Ritzer's (2013) concept of McDonaldization, which is "the process by which the principles of the fast-food restaurant are coming to dominate more and more sectors of American society as well as the rest of the world" (Ritzer, 2013, p. 1). Bryman noted that, of the three factors of McDonaldization described by Ritzer—efficiency, calculability, predictability, and control—three of the attributes were consistent with the Disney worldview, while Disney parks were less symptomatic in terms of *calculability*, which Ritzer (2013) describes as "an emphasis on the quantitative aspects of products sold (portion size, cost) and service offered (the time it takes to get the product)" (p. 14).

With the introduction of MyMagic+, however, Disney can now more fully embrace calculability, and can thus infuse its manufacture of controlled leisure with new manifestations of control. MyMagic+, with its capability for data gathering, presents a new opportunity to analyze and act on the quantitative aspects of the theme park experience and lends itself to the application of standardized, even automated processes that are initiated in response to statistical data, all while promising more freedom and fun for the visitor. For example, despite the many ways in which control has long operated in and through Disney parks, before the introduction of MyMagic+, some aspects of visitor experiences were still left to chance—most notably, crowd and attraction wait time. While this kind of data had been circulating for years on the Internet, the information was speculative at best, and visitors were still subject to the fluctuations that could result in long lines and crowding. However, by controlling for those fluctuations through advance planning, attraction reservations, and ongoing digital tracking, Disney's MyMagic+ seeks to reassure Walt Disney World guests that that their theme park vacation will be predictable, and therefore, more fun. In other words, MyMagic+ expands the controlling reach of Disney while further teaching visitors into a form of leisure that is based on control. The Disney website sells this idea of freedom through control, as it positions the service as a way for guests to "feel confident knowing that some of your must-do attractions and entertainment are all set. If your plans change, you can update your FastPass+ selections on the go!" (Walt Disney World, 2015). Guests can make reservations as early as 60 days before their vacation, so this "confident" feeling can begin far in advance of the trip itself. However, the visitor has limited control over the actual scheduling of attractions as guests cannot reserve the specific times they want; instead, the website and app give a list of times from which to choose so that Walt Disney World ultimately retains control. Thus, while the themes of control and predictability have long been a hallmark of the Walt Disney World Resort, the kind of controlled leisure offered in MyMagic+ constructs a new dimension of the theme park experience that Bogost (2014) calls "data tourism," in which calculability is enhanced by increased access to information. Through these new technologies, then, Walt Disney World exploits visitors' desires for predictability and convenience as a means to obtain valuable data that enhance the company's ability to control and monitor every aspect of guests' visits to the park.

As outlined above, societies of control do not operate through a central panopticon; rather, surveillance takes place via expansive matrices and with the willing help of those being surveilled (Deleuze, 1992; Poster, 1996). As Disney seeks to redefine controlled leisure through the new MyMagic+ technologies, surveillance is one of its primary mechanisms of control over guests (Ritzer & Liska, 1997). The RFID technology in the MagicBands, which are free for guests who stay at an onsite Disney hotel or available for anyone else to purchase for $12.95, allows for a constant tracking of the wearer not only in the theme park, but also throughout the various other shops and hotels within the Walt Disney World resort area. RFID tracking also allows digital cameras positioned throughout the park to take photographs of MagicBand wearing visitors, capturing, often unbeknownst to the guests, candid memories that can be viewed and purchased at the end of their vacation. This technology is clearly invasive. Rosen (2013) of Alternet.com, for example, explores in an article on Salon.com how the RFID tracking technology in MyMagic+ bands enables "the company to monitor, track and analyze" visitors' every activity and raises concerns about the growing corporate practices of personal data collection and personal surveillance. However, consumers seem willing to accept the intrusive tracking capabilities of these devices in exchange for safety, convenience, and predictability. Wait time at the entrance of the parks, for example, has been reduced by 30% since the introduction of MyMagic+ bands (Carr, 2015). For example, when visiting the Be Our Guest restaurant in the Magic Kingdom, guests order food on a computer kiosk and scan their MagicBands. They are then instructed to find seats somewhere in one of the restaurant's three large sections, and assured that their food will be brought out to them. Minutes later, the meal appears, as if by magic, as a server delivers a glass enclosed food cart directly to the table. In exchange for such conveniences, guests readily accept the invasive surveillance made possible by the MagicBands.

MyMagic+, Immaterial Labor, and Prosumption

As visitors to Disney parks participate in their own surveillance and control through the consumptive experience that constitutes a Disney vacation, they are at the same time producing the social relations "within which goods can make sense" (Arvidsson, 2005, p. 241). Rethinking the historical separation between consumption and production, Arvidsson (2005) argues that consumers are not the "passive victims of producer interests," but, rather, they actively participate in "the social construction of the value of consumer goods" and thus are part of the "very productive dynamic that has driven capitalist development" (p. 242). While Ritzer (2014) contends that, on some level, prosumption—the "interrelated process of production and consumption" (p. 3)—has always been a "primal and/or evolutionary element" (p. 1), there is currently a new form, where proconsumers "are doing things, performing tasks (e.g., using kiosks to check in at hotels and airports), that they rarely, if ever, did before. That is, most of these tasks were performed for consumers by paid employees" (p. 6). The productive labor provided by Disney theme park guests is similar to other examples of presumption that Ritzer (2014) discusses, from building one's own IKEA furniture to buying and using one's own medical equipment to monitor vital health statistics. Ritzer (2014) outlines a new form of prosumption that occurs through the use of technology as companies encourage consumers to aid in the creation of the product itself. The kind of prosumption exemplified by such services as MyMagic+, in which the primary forms of currency are not only money, but personal information and productive labor, is normalized through the promise of pleasurable predictability.

In the case of Disney parks, for example, in booking FastPass+ reservations, visitors often invest a great deal of time weighing the pros and cons of booking one attraction over another, choosing the correct times, and deciding in which order on what days to visit the various parks. Guests are also encouraged to use online tools such as those offered by www. touringplans.com. Using the website's crowd calendar and touring plans, which provide guidelines regarding the most time-efficient paths through the parks, guests perform the labor it takes to plan their 'perfect' vacation. While the MyMagic+ technology offers the promise of a predictably pleasurable vacation experience, the potential of that promise ultimately depends on the extent to which the guest effectively uses the vacation planning tools. In other words, the 'fun' of the vacation depends on the quality of the free labor performed by the consumer—how well they execute their 'job' in using the tools, and thus enhance the control exercised over them, particularly for those consumers using the MyMagic+ services. Once inside the park, guests can use the MyDisneyExperience application on a smartphone to check for times of shows, make restaurant reservations, and change existing and make new FastPass+ reservations. This constant self-monitoring through the use of controlling technology feeds the willingness of the guest to be controlled—solidifying her or him as the Walt Disney World 'guest'— part tourist, part collected data, and always controlled. As Bogost (2014) asserts, "the MagicBand lays bare the process by which we produce data— not all on our lonesome, but as the result of implicit and explicit pacts with organizations, most often corporations" (para. 24).

Thus, through the ways in which visitors participate in using the MyMagic+ services, including their enthusiasm to generate and publicly circulate data via blogs and other social media about how to best navigate wait times and attractions at the park, as well as to adopt MagicBands+ as a fashion statement and as a way to show and publicize (both at the parks and through social media) their excitement and fan loyalty to Disney, Disney visitors engage in both material and immaterial labor (Lazzarato, 1997) that benefits The Walt Disney Company, as it attempts to coopt free labor on the part of the consumer in the production of Disney products, experiences, or the Disney brand itself. The labor invested by visitors is labor that the Disney Company does not have to perform nor compensate, but that benefits the Company because it helps guests have more pleasurable experiences and thus increases guest satisfaction with the Disney brand. Arvidsson (2005) argues that brands thus exploit consumers through harnessing and appropriating this productive immaterial labor in the service of the brand and ultimately of capital. Through their immaterial labor, consumers create what Arvidsson (2005) calls "ethical surplus," which contributes positively to "the form of life that the brand embodies" (p. 250). The immaterial labor of consumers, which they are not compensated for, increases the positive reputation of brands, and thus increases the market and economic value particular goods and services as well as the value of brands, as measured in reduced marketing costs and increased product sales (Arvidsson, 2005; Freishtat & Sandlin, 2010). Arvidsson (2005) further argues that this exploitation is directly related to an even more fundamental issue that undergirds practices of democracy. When the "productive sociality of consumers" (p. 251) is constructed and limited by brand management, "the very real productive potential of contemporary social relations" is squelched (p. 252).

Walt Disney World and the Curriculum of Control

While control and predictability have long been central to the Walt Disney World experience, MyMagic+ takes controlled leisure to new heights with its capability for invasive surveillance and data mining and its unprecedented erosion of personal privacy within the theme park. These services also reflect a new emphasis on calculability in that they maximize opportunities for visitors to consume goods and services and quantify consumer behaviors in order to sell more products and attract more visitors to the park. Furthermore, the particular brand of controlled leisure offered by MyMagic+ reflects the increasing responsibility of the consumer to participate in consumption through (unpaid) productive labor. While commentators such as Rosen (2013) raise grave concerns about how this technology violates personal privacy, millions of customers do not seem to care—if recent revenue reports are any indication, controlled leisure sells.

According to one report, MagicBands are now being used by about half of the guests who visit Walt Disney World, and, according to Chief Operating Office Tom Staggs, consumer responses to the service have been "overwhelmingly positive" (quoted Pedicini, 2015, para. 10). On January 30, 2015, Thomas Smith, Social Media Director for Disney Parks, announced that as of that date, 10 million ("and counting") MagicBands had been distributed (Smith, 2015). However, Walt Disney World's approach to controlled leisure should not be construed as a fait accompli for theme park marketing since Disney's chief competitor in the theme park business, Universal Studios, recently invested over a billion dollars in building more attractions, betting that consumers would rather go on new rides than scan a wristband to ride old ones (Garcia, 2013). Still, the early success of MyMagic+ suggests that today's consumers are increasingly willing not only to sacrifice privacy for the chance at pleasurable predictability, but to celebrate and publicly acknowledge that sacrifice by embracing and promoting, through various enactments of immaterial labor, MagicBands— tangible, visible symbols of their own complicity.

Such eagerness on the part of consumers to participate in corporate control at the expense of personal privacy raises serious questions about the ways that The Walt Disney Company is teaching us into certain ways of being and buying. As Rosen (2013) points out, we do not know what is happening to the personal data that is being collected, including how long it is stored and how it is used once we have left the park. And yet, those concerns seem secondary to our desire for a vacation that is free of the worries and concerns of everyday life, even if we have to contribute considerable time and effort toward utilizing the services that promise to deliver the perfect theme park experience. While guests are of course free to resist mechanisms of control in a number of ways, including choosing offsite lodging, using cash instead of RFID payment devices, or using non-sanctioned insider guides to subverting traditional traffic patterns, Bryman (2004) notes that "Resistance is not easy for visitors at Disney theme parks" because it "will often result in censure, not just from security guards, but also from fellow guests who have come to the happiest place on earth to have a good time a la Disney" (p. 150). Furthermore, resisting mechanisms of control outside Disney theme parks is increasingly difficult as the kind of invasive pro-sumerism represented by MyMagic+ becomes embedded in the structures of contemporary consumption. While we acknowledge that the increased participation of the consumer in customizing their own goods and services can be read as a form of agency, and while we recognize that there are still some ways that consumers can choose not to provide the personal inform-ation required to enable corporate surveillance and data mining, the popularity of MyMagic+ and Disney's ever-multiplying revenue suggests that Walt Disney World visitors are increasingly willing and even eager to relinquish personal privacy for the conveniences of controlled leisure.

References

Allerton, H. (1997). Professional development the Disney way. *Training & Development, 51*(5), 50.

Arvidsson, A. (2005). Brands: A critical perspective. *Journal of Consumer Culture, 5*(2), 235–258.

Barnes, B. (2010, December 27). Disney tackles major theme park problem: Lines. *The New York Times.* Retrieved from: http://www.nytimes.com/2010/12/28/business/media/28disney.html

Bogost, I. (2014). Welcome to dataland: Design fiction at the most magical place on earth. *reform.* Retrieved from: https://medium.com/re-form/welcome-to-dataland-d8c06a5f3bc6

Borrie, W. T. (1999). Disneyland and Disney World: Designing and prescribing the recreational experience. *Loisir et societe/Society and Leisure, 22*(1), 71–82.

Bryman, A. (1995). *Disney and his worlds.* New York: Routledge.

Bryman, A. (1999). The Disneyization of society. *The Sociological Review, 47*(1), 25–47.

Bryman, A. (2004). *The Disneyization of society.* Thousand Oaks, CA: Sage.

Carr, A. (2015, April 15). The messy business of reinventing happiness. *FastCompany.* Retrieved from: http://www.fastcompany.com/3044283/the-messy-business-of-reinventing-happiness

Deleuze, G. (1992). Postscript on the socieites of control. *October, 59*(Winter), 3–7.

Edgerton, G., & Jackson, K. M. (1996). Redesigning Pocahontas: Disney, the "White man's Indian," and the marketing of dreams. *Journal of Popular Film and Television, 24*(2), 90–98.

Fiske, J. (1989). *Reading the popular.* Boston: Unwin Hyman.

Fjellman, S. M. (1992). *Vinyl leaves : Walt Disney World and America.* Boulder, CO: Westview Press.

Freishtat, R. L., & Sandlin, J. A. (2010). *Facebook* as public pedagogy: A critical examination of learning, community, and consumption. In T. T. Kidd (Ed.), *Adult learning in the digital age: Perspectives on online technologies and outcomes* (pp. 148–162). Hershey, PA: IGI Global.

Garcia, J. (2013, August 18). Disney's $1 billion wristband project is most expensive in theme park history. *Skift.* Retrieved from: http://skift.com/2013/08/18/disneys-1-billion-wristband-project-is-most-expensive-in-theme-park-history/

Gennawey, S. (2014). *The Disneyland story: The unofficial guide to the evolution of Walt Disney's dream.* Birmingham, AL: Keen Communications.

Giroux, H. A., & Pollock, G. (2010). *The mouse that roared : Disney and the end of innocence.* Lanham, MD: Rowman & Littlefield.

Griffin, S. (2000). *Tinker Belles and evil queens: The Walt Disney Company from the inside out.* New York: NYU Press.

Hall, S. (2009). Notes on deconstructing "the popular". In J. Storey (Ed.), *Cultural theory and popular culture: A reader* (pp. 508–518). Harlow, UK: Pearson Education.

Hancock, P. (2005). Disneyfying Disneyization. *ephemera, 5*(3), 545–550.

Henke, J. B., Umble, D. Z., & Smith, N. J. (1996). Construction of the female self: Feminist readings of the Disney heroine. *Women's Studies in Communication, 19*(2), 229–249.

Hochberg, M., Newell, M., Scopa, M., & Testa, L. (Producer). (2014, November 4). *Walt Disney World Today.* Retrieved from: http://www.wdwtoday.com/article.php?story=20141104185332815

Lacroix, C. (2004). Images of animated others: The orientalization of Disney's cartoon heroines from *The Little Mermaid* to *The Hunchback of Notre Dame*. *Popular Communication, 2*(4), 213–229.

Lazzarato, M. (1997). *Lavoro immateriale*. Verona, Italy: Ombre Corte.

Pedicini, S. (2015, May 5). Disney earnings: 2nd quarter profit, revenue increase. *Orlando Sentinel*. Retrieved from: http://www.orlandosentinel.com/business/os-disney-earnings-report-20150505-story.html

Poster, M. (1996). Databases as discourse; or, electronic interpellations. In D. Lyon, & E. Zureik (Eds.), *Computers, surveillance, and privacy* (pp. 175–192). Minneapolis: University of Minnesota Press.

Ritzer, G. (2013). *The McDonaldization of society* (20th anniversary ed.). Los Angeles: Sage.

Ritzer, G. (2014). Prosumption: Evolution, revolution, or eternal return of the same? *Journal of Consumer Culture, 14*(1), 3–24.

Ritzer, G. (2015). The "new" world of prosumption: Evolution, "return of the same," or revolution? *Sociological Forum, 30*(1), 1–17. doi: 10.1111/socf.12142

Ritzer, G., & Jurgenson, N. (2010). Production, consumption, prosumption: The nature of capitalism in the age of the digital "prosumer." *Journal of Consumer Culture, 10*(1), 13–36.

Ritzer, G., & Liska, A. (1997). McDisneyization and post-tourism: Complementary perspectives on contemporary tourism. In C. Rojek & J. Urry (Eds.), *Touring cultures: Transformations of travel and theory* (pp. 96–109). London: Routledge.

Rosen, D. (2013, January 17). Disney is spying on you! *Salon*. Retrieved from: http://www.salon.com/2013/01/17/disney_is_spying_on_you/

Sehlinger, B., & Testa, L. (2015). *The unofficial guide to Walt Disney World*. Birmingham, AL: Keen Communications.

Shearing, C. D., & Stenning, P. C. (1992). From the panopticon to Disney World: The development of discipline. In R. V. G. Clarke (Ed.), *Situational crime prevention: Successful case studies* (pp. 300–304). New York: Harrow and Heston.

Smith, T. (2015, January 30). 10 million and counting: MagicBands a hit with Walt Disney World Resort guests. *Disney Parks Blog*. Retrieved from: http://disney parks.disney.go.com/blog/2015/01/10-million-counting-magicbands-a-hit-with-walt-disney-world-resort-guests/

Telotte, J. P. (2008). *The mouse machine: Disney and technology*. Urbana: University of Illinois Press.

Van Maanen, J. (1992). Displacing Disney: Some notes on the flow of culture. *Qualitative Sociology, 15*(1), 5–35.

Walt Disney World. (2015). Unlock a new dimension of Disney Magic with MyMagic+. *Walt Disney World*. Retrieved from: https://disneyworld.disney.go.com/plan/my-disney-experience/my-magic-plus/

Wickstrom, M. (2005). The Lion King, mimesis, and Disney's magical capitalism. In M. Budd & M. H. Kirsch (Eds.), *Rethinking Disney: Private control, public dimensions* (pp. 99–121). Middletown, CT: Wesleyan University Press.

Williams, B. T. (2013). Control and the classroom in the digital university: The affect of course management systems on pedagogy. In R. Goodfellow & M. R. Lea (Eds.), *Literacy and the digital university: Critical perspectives on learning, scholarship and technology* (pp. 173–184). London: Routledge.

Wynns, S. L., & Rosenfeld, L. B. (2003). Father–daughter relationships in Disney's animated films. *Southern Journal of Communication, 68*(2), 91–106.

16 Consuming Innocence

Disney's Corporate Stranglehold on Youth in the Digital Age

Henry A. Giroux

While the "empire of consumption" has been around for a long time (Cohen, 2003), American society in the last 30 years has undergone a sea change in the daily lives of children—one marked by a major transition from a culture of innocence and social protection, however imperfect, to a culture of commodification. Youth are now assaulted by a never-ending proliferation of marketing strategies that colonize their consciousness and daily lives. Under the tutelage of Disney and other megacorporations, kids have become an audience captive not only to traditional forms of media such as film, television, and print, but even more so to more readily accessible forms of digital media. The information, entertainment and cultural pedagogy disseminated by massive multimedia corporations have become central in shaping and influencing every waking moment of children's daily lives—all toward a lifetime of constant, unthinking consumption. Consumer culture in the United States and increasingly across the globe, does more than undermine the ideals of a secure and happy childhood: it exhibits the bad faith of a society in which, for children, "there can be only one kind of value, market value; one kind of success, profit; one kind of existence, commodities; and one kind of social relationship, markets" (Grossberg, 2005, p. 264). But corporate-controlled culture not only exploits and distorts the hopes and desires of individuals: it is fundamentally driven toward exploiting public goods for private gain, if it does not also more boldly seek to privatize everything in the public realm. Among US multimedia megacorporations, Disney appears one of the least daunted in attempting to dominate public discourse and undermine the critical and political capacities necessary for the next generation of young people to sustain even the most basic institutions of democracy.

The impact of now ubiquitous electronic technologies as teaching machines can be seen in some rather astounding statistics. It is estimated that the average American child (ages 8 to 10) spends almost eight hours a day watching video-based entertainment and, while older children and teenagers spend more than 11 hours per day (American Academy of Pediatrics, 2013). For the last two decades, the combined hours "spent in front of a television or video screen" has been "the single biggest chunk of time in the waking life of an American child" (American Medical Association, cited in Hazen & Winokur, 1997, p. 64; see also American Academy of Pediatrics, 2013). Such statistics warrant grave concern, given that the messages provided through such programming are shaped largely by a massive US advertising industry (Bryce, 2005) that sells not only its products, but also values, images and identities largely aimed at teaching young people to be consumers. A virtual army of marketers, psychologists and corporate executives are currently engaged in what Linn (2004) calls a "hostile takeover of childhood" (p. 8), seeking in the new media environment to take advantage of the growing economic power wielded by children and teens. Figures on direct spending by young people and their influence on parental spending estimate that children ages 9 to 13 are responsible for $200 billion in sales per year, $43 billion of which is their own money (Smith, 2013). Because of their value as consumers and their ability to influence spending, young people have become major targets of an advertising and marketing industry that spends over $17 billion a year on shaping children's identities and desires (Golin, 2007; see also Smith, 2013).

Exposed to a marketing machinery eager and ready to transform them into full-fledged members of consumer society, children's time is conscripted by a commercial world defined by The Walt Disney Company and a few other corporations, and the amount of time spent in this world is as breathtaking as it is disturbing. One Nielsen study found that children ages 2 to 11 see over 25,000 ads a year on television alone (Common Sense Media, 2014). Quart (2003) reports on another study conducted by Nickelodeon that found the average 10 year old has memorized 300 to 400 brands. There was a time when a family traveling in a car might entertain itself by singing or playing games. Now, however, many children have their own laptops or cell phones and many family vehicles come equipped with DVD players or capabilities to stream media via onboard Wi-Fi or satellite (Rideout, Foehr, & Roberts, 2010). Family members need not look to each other or the outside world for entertainment when a constant stream of media sources is at their fingertips. Today, children have more money to spend and more electronic toys to play with, but, increasingly, they are left on their own to navigate the virtual and visual worlds created by US media corporations.

In what has become the most "consumer-oriented society in the world," Schor (2004) observes that kids and teens have taken center stage as "the epicenter of American consumer culture" (p. 9). The tragic result is that youth now inhabit a cultural landscape in which, increasingly, they can only recognize themselves in terms preferred by the market. Multi-billion-dollar media corporations, with a commanding role over commodity markets as well as support from the highest reaches of government, have become the primary educational and cultural force in shaping, if not hijacking, how youth define their interests, values and relations to others.

Given its powerful role among media-driven modes of communication, The Walt Disney Company exercises a highly disproportionate concentration of control over the means of producing, circulating and exchanging information, especially to kids. Once a company that catered primarily to a three- to eight-year-old crowd with its animated films, theme parks and television shows, Disney in the new millennium has been at the forefront of the multimedia conglomerates now aggressively marketing products for infants, toddlers and tweens (kids ages 8 to 12).[1] Web sites, video games, computer-generated animation, Disney TV and pop music, are now accessible online with the touch of a button and are sustaining Disney fans into their teenage and young adult years. Allied with multimedia giant Apple, Inc. and the cutting-edge animation studio Pixar, Disney is beyond doubt a powerful example of the new megacorporate media.

Disney not only represents "one of the best-known symbols of capitalist consumerism," (Lyne, 2004) but also claims to offer consumers a stable, known quantity in its brand-name products. Understanding Disney's cultural role is neither a simple nor a trivial task. Like many other megacorporations, it focuses on popular culture and continually expands its products and services to reach every available media platform. What is unique about Disney, however, is its titanium-clad brand image—synonymous with a notion of childhood innocence and wholesome entertainment—that manages to deflect, if not completely trounce, criticism at every turn. As an icon of American culture and middle-class family values, Disney actively appeals to both conscientious parents and youthful fantasies as it works hard to transform every child into a lifetime consumer of Disney products and ideas. Put the Disney Corporation under scrutiny, however, and a contradiction quickly appears between a Disney culture that presents itself as the paragon of virtue and childlike innocence and the reality of the company's cutthroat commercial ethos.

Disney, like many corporations, trades in sound bites; the result is that the choices, exclusions and values that inform its narratives about joy, pleasure, living and survival in a global world are often difficult to discern. Disney needs to be addressed within a widening circle of awareness, so we can place the history, meaning and influence of the Disney empire outside of its own narrow interpretive frameworks that often shut down critical assessments of how Disney is actually engaged in the commercial carpet-bombing of children and teens. Understanding Disney today requires that we draw attention to the too often hidden or forgotten corporate dimension surrounding the production, distribution and consumption of Disney culture and, in so doing, equip parents, youth, educators, and others with tools that will enable them to critically mediate the ways in which they encounter Disney. In 1999, Disney was a $22 billion profit-making machine (Giroux, 1999). In fiscal year 2014, Iger (2014) reports that the Disney Corporation earned a record $48.8 billion dollars and is continuing to expand the global market for its products in countries such as China, where another park is slated to open in Shanghai in 2016. Now a worldwide distributor of a particular kind of cultural politics, Disney is a teaching machine that not only exerts influence over young people in the United States, but also wages an aggressive campaign to peddle its political and cultural influence overseas. As global capital spreads its influence virtually unchecked by national governments and the international community, citizenship becomes increasingly privatized and youth are educated to become consuming subjects rather than civic-minded and critical citizens. If today's young people are to look ahead to a more rather than less democratic future, it has become imperative for people everywhere to develop a critical language in which notions of the public good, public issues and public life become central to overcoming the privatizing and depoliticizing language of the market.

Disney's Marketing Juggernaut

One measure of the corporate assault on kids can be seen in the reach, acceleration and effectiveness of Disney's marketing and advertising efforts to turn kids into consumers and childhood into a salable commodity. Every child, regardless of how young, is now a potential consumer ripe for being commodified and immersed in a commercial culture defined by brands. The Walt Disney Company spares little expense in generating a coherent brand image and encapsulating its many products and services within the seductive symbolism of childhood innocence and wholesome family fun. The company's approach makes Disney a particularly useful case for understanding corporate strategies directed at youth in the new media environment. At the same time as Disney represents nostalgia and tradition, it has become a global leader in transforming digital technologies into profit-making platforms and developing a consumer-centered discourse that deflects criticism away from, while it softens, what can only be called boldly commercial self-promotion. Disney, with its legion of media holdings, armies of marketers and omnipresent advertisers sets out not just to exploit children and youth for profit: it actually constructs them as commodities while promoting the very concept of childhood as a salable commodity. Childhood ideals increasingly give way to a market-driven politics in which young people are prepared for a life of objectification that will simultaneously drain them of any viable sense of moral and political agency. This is especially true in the current consumer society in which children more than ever mediate their identities and relations to others through the consumption of goods and images. No longer imagined within the language of responsibility and justice, childhood begins with what might be called the scandalous philosophy of money, that is, a corporate logic in which everything, including the worth of young people, is measured through the potentially barbaric calculations of finance, exchange value and profitability.

Disney, perhaps more than any other corporation, has created a marketing powerhouse that uses the pivotal educational force of children's culture in combination with new digital media technologies. Kids can download enormous amounts of media in seconds and carry around such information, images and videos in the palms of their hands. Moreover, "[media] technologies themselves are morphing and merging, forming an ever-expanding presence throughout our daily environment" (Rideout, Roberts, & Foehr, 2005, p. 4). Smartphones have evolved "to include video game platforms, e-mail devices, digital cameras and Internet connections," and support a wide of digital and social media applications, making it easier for marketers and advertisers to reach young people (p. 4). Young consumers are immersed in what the Berkeley Media Studies Group calls "a new 'marketing ecosystem' that encompasses cell phones, mobile music devices, broadband video, instant messaging, video games and virtual three-dimensional worlds," all of which provide the knowledge and information that young people use to navigate their place in families, schools, and communities (Chester & Montgomery, 2008, para. 1). Disney along with its researchers, marketing departments, and purveyors of commerce largely define and control this massive virtual entertainment complex, spending vast amounts of time trying to understand the needs, desires, tastes, preferences, social relations and networks that characterize youth as a potential market.

The disconnect between market values and the ethical responsibility to care for children is on full display in Disney's almost boastful use of research to mine the inner lives and experiences of young children. That Disney's insidious strategies receive front page coverage in *The New York Times* and are presented without so much as a critical comment is a testament to how commercial values have numbed the public's ability to recognize the danger such values often present to children. According to *The New York Times* (Barnes, 2009a), Disney has been at the forefront of finding ways to capitalize on the billions of dollars spent worldwide by young boys between the ages of 6 and 14. As part of such an effort, Disney has sought the advice of educators, anthropologists and even a research consultant with "a background in the casino industry" (para. 2), not only to study all aspects of the culture and intimate lives of young boys, but to do so in a way that allows Disney to produce "emotional hooks" that lure young boys into the wonderful world of corporate Disney in order to turn them into enthusiastic consumers (Barnes, 2009a, para. 8). Disney's recent attempts to "figure out the boys' entertainment market" (para. 13) enlisted the services of Kelly Pena, described as "the kid whisperer" (para. 1), who attempts to uncover what makes young boys tick by using her anthropological skills to convince young boys and their parents to allow her to look into the kids' closets, go shopping with them, and pay them $75 to be interviewed. Ms. Pena, with no irony intended, prides herself on the fact that "Children . . . open up to her" (Barnes, 2009a, para. 16). Given Disney's desire to expand into boys' culture, the company's purchase of Marvel Entertainment Inc. in 2009 came as no surprise. Marvel's comic book empire owns the licenses to approximately 5,000 superhero characters. *The Wall Street Journal* remarked that by "bringing in macho types such as Iron Man, Thor and Captain America, the Marvel deal would expand Disney's audience, adding properties that appeal to boys from their preteen years into young adulthood" (Smith & Schuker, 2009, para. 7).

It is even more disturbing that Disney and a growing number of marketers and advertisers work with child psychologists and other experts, who study young people in order to better understand children's culture so as to develop marketing methods that are more camouflaged, seductive and successful. Disney claims this kind of intensive research pays off in lucrative dividends and reinforces the Disney motto that, in order to be a successful company, "You have to start with the kids themselves" (Barnes, 2009a, para. 23). Several psychologists, especially Allen D. Kanner, have publicly criticized such disingenuous practices.[2] Disney's recent attempt to corner the young male market through the use of sophisticated research models, ethnographic tools and the expertise of academics indicates the degree to which the language of the market has disengaged itself from either moral considerations or the social good. It is clear that Disney's only goal is to win over the hearts and minds of young people so as to deliver them to the market as both loyal consumers and commodities. In such unscrupulous strategies, the contradiction becomes visible between Disney's public relations image as a purveyor of wholesome entertainment and the hidden reality of Disney as a political and economic power that promotes ideology conducive to its own corporate interests, thereby impoverishing the imaginative possibilities of youth and dismantling the public foundations for a thriving civic culture.

Childhood, Inc.

Corporate culture is rewriting the nature of children's culture, a trend that becomes visible in the various ways traditional boundaries once maintained between the spheres of formal education and entertainment are collapsed. According to Grossberg (2005), children are introduced to the world of logos, advertising and the mattering maps of consumerism long before they can speak: Capitalism targets kids as soon as they are old enough to watch commercials, even though they may not be old enough to distinguish programming from commercials or to recognize the effects of branding and product placement. In fact, researchers have found that while children as young as three years old recognize brand logos, not until they are around eight years old do they understand advertising's intention to manipulate their desires (American Psychological Association, 2004; Fischer, Schwartz, Richards, Goldstein, & Rojas, 1991). But this has not stopped corporations from exposing kids from birth to adulthood to a consumer blitz of advertising, marketing, education, and entertainment that has no historical precedent. The last two decades have seen a growing market for multimedia products for toddlers and infants as young as three months old, an area of digital culture into which Disney has increasingly expanded (Molnar & Boninger, 2007).

Disney's expansion into the baby and toddler market has not been without criticism. One notable controversy surrounded Disney's marketing of Baby Einstein videos. In 2000, Disney purchased the Baby Einstein Company from its founder, Julie Aigner-Clark, who had created a line of products and toys that mesmerized these youngest television watchers by displaying, for example, vibrant moving objects while playing a soundtrack of classical music selections. Disney's marketing of these products suggested that parents could purchase toys and videos that would not only enable their children to develop good taste in music, but also make them capable of great intellectual achievements. For example, Disney/Pixar's 2004 film *The Incredibles* plugged the Baby Einstein franchise shamelessly when one character exclaimed, "Mozart makes babies smarter." Despite objections against the marketing of baby videos as educational media by organizations such as the Campaign for a Commercial-Free Childhood, Disney persisted in using clever packaging for the videos that implied they were, at best, beneficial learning tools to be used in a child's most formative years and, at worst, harmless distractions for infant audiences. These marketing strategies seemed to work, as evidenced by a 2007 survey by the Kaiser Family Foundation, which found that 48 percent of parents believed that baby videos have "a positive effect on early childhood development" (Rideout, 2007, p. 7). The news that baby DVDs and videos could actually impair infants' cognitive development broke in 2007 when the University of Washington issued a press release about a study published in the prestigious *Journal of Pediatrics* that concluded infants eight to 16 months old who were exposed to one hour of viewing baby DVDs and videos per day displayed slower language development: those children understood on average six to eight fewer words for every hour of viewing than infants who did not watch the videos (Schwarz, 2007a). Reading to a child once a day, by contrast, produced an observable increase in vocabulary (Zimmerman, Christakis, & Meltzoff, 2007).

How did Disney respond to the researchers' findings? President and CEO Robert Iger demanded that the University of Washington immediately retract its statements on the grounds that the study's assessment methodology was faulty and the publication of the results was "misleading, irresponsible and derogatory."[3] Disney's main objection was that the study did not differentiate between brands when it tested the effects of baby videos on language development. Mark Emmert, president of the University of Washington, refused to comply with Iger's demand for a retraction and instead articulated a need for more "research aimed at helping parents and society enhance the lives of children."[4] While this research was clearly not enough to deter Disney from marketing its Baby Einstein wares as beneficial for babies and toddlers, other researchers have found that one of the greatest costs associated with surrounding very young children with screen media is a reduction in the time they spend engaging in creative, unstructured play. In a 2007 report, the American Academy of Pediatrics lamented, "time for free play has been markedly reduced for some children" (Ginsburg, 2007, p. 183).[5] Yet Disney's message to parents continued to foster the idea that parents should not only accept the ubiquitous presence of screen culture in their babies' lives, but view it as an inevitable fact of life, one pointless to criticize and impossible to change.[6] In an utterly cynical gesture, the Baby Einstein website cited a 2003 finding by the Kaiser Family Foundation that "in a typical day, 68% of all children under two use screen media" (Rideout, Vandewater, & Wartella, 2003, p. 5). This statistic was not presented as something that should alarm concerned parents or encourage different parenting practices; on the contrary, it became simple proof of "the reality of today's parents, families and households" and an indicator of how the American Academy of Pediatrics, which discourages television viewing for children under two years old, was simply stuck in the past.

However, threatened with a class action lawsuit for deceptive marketing, Disney offered refunds for false educational claims and stopped production of the videos, which are now available for free on YouTube. In spite of this controversy, The Walt Disney Company has not been deterred from strategic marketing aimed at infants and toddlers (Barnes, 2011). In 2011, the company embarked on a campaign to market Disney Baby products to new parents in maternity wards through Our365, a company that sells newborn baby pictures. Mothers in 580 maternity hospitals across the United States were visited by representatives who offered them a free Disney Cuddly Bodysuit. The bilingual representatives sold the mothers on the quality of the trademark onesies and encouraged them to sign up for promotional emails from DisneyBaby.com (Barnes, 2011). This direct marketing strategy was combined with a massive retail campaign for a whole new line of Disney Baby products, including apparel, toys, and accessories to be sold through outlets such as Amazon.com, Nordstrom, and Target. At the time of this marketing campaign, Disney executives estimated the North American baby market to be worth $36.3 billion dollars, and planned an expansion of the Disney Baby brand to include a wide range of strollers, clothing, and much more (Barnes, 2011).

Along with the move into the baby retail market, Disney has found new ways to access young consumers through multimedia products and the Internet. The Internet's commercial potential is certainly not lost on Disney, as Steve Wadsworth, former president of the Walt Disney Internet Group, stated, "There is massive opportunity here" (quoted in Barnes, 2007, para. 9). Harnessing the power of virtual space is a strategy that has been openly championed by CEO Robert Iger, whose stated goal has been for the company to establish "clear leadership in the kids and families online virtual worlds space around the globe" (Disney Press Release, 2007, para 1). Disney views online media as an opportunity not so much to enhance children's lives as to make money for shareholders, enjoy low overhead costs and keep the company's film and television franchises profitable. The Disney.com site, redesigned in 2007, includes video games, social networking, customized user content and videos on demand. Internet sites offering cooperative games and social networking to children seem like a relatively innocuous option in a media culture currently exploiting every imaginable angle to populate reality television's competitive worlds of winners and losers. It is far less innocuous, however, that these web sites help Disney collect and use personal information to assail consumer groups with targeted, cross-promotional advertising. Web-based social media not only acculturate children to being constantly bombarded with advertising, but also give them the illusion of control while they are actually being manipulated.

Disney's interest in capturing the attention of very young people through the Internet also involved the acquisition of Club Penguin, a web-based virtual world, in a $700 million deal in 2007. Disney's Club Penguin targets kids ages 6 to 14 and provides each user with an animated penguin avatar that interacts in a snow-covered world, chats with other users and earns virtual money to purchase items such as pets, clothing, and furnishings for an igloo home. Users can play for free, but must pay $7.95 per month for access to certain features of the game. As an interactive and 'immersive environment,' Club Penguin enables Disney to train children in the habits of consumption—products such as sweatshirts, computer sleeves, cell phone cases, and fitness trackers are advertised on the site—while making direct contact with its global consumer base through the online network. Similarly, Disney introduces new online activities including virtual worlds that are timed to coincide with the release of new films and television shows, such as *Pirates of the Caribbean*, and *Cars* (Barnes, 2007). As Barnes (2007) points out in *The New York Times*, these electronic malls are only superficially envisioned by developers as entertainment or educational sites. Their main purpose, he states, is to enable media conglomerates to "deliver quick growth, help keep movie franchises alive and instill brand loyalty in a generation of new customers" (Barnes, 2007, para. 2).

In order to tap further into the youth market, Disney's recent strategy has involved significant monetary investment in video game development. Disney-branded online space included the Internet's first multiplayer game for kids, the now-defunct "Toontown Online." As Grimes (2008) points out, multiplayer online games "construct entire cultural experiences based around beloved characters, fantasy and play [but] entry into these worlds is only possible through a perpetual cycle of consumption" (p. 128). Another product, the video game "Epic Mickey," revamps the character of Mickey Mouse in an alleged effort to make him more appealing to today's generation of youth. The mouse's new design no longer embodied a childlike innocence and generosity, but instead is "cantankerous and cunning" and exhibits "selfish, destructive behavior" (Barnes, 2009c, para. 3). With Mickey's popularity in decline in the United States, Disney's market-driven agenda is visible not only in its willingness to transform the hallowed icon upon which its corporate empire was built, but also in the very way it has transformed Mickey Mouse's character. Although Disney's representatives suggest that this reimagining of Mickey Mouse merely reflects what is currently popular among young people, it seems more aligned with the current ideology of a ruthless economic Darwinism (also evident in reality TV shows) that has little to do with the needs of children and a great deal to do with a survival-of-the-fittest view of the world perpetuated by market-centered culture. The recent moves by The Walt Disney Company to darken the characters it incorporates into its cultural offerings should be seen as less a demystification of the brand image of Disneyfied innocence and more a signal of the company's desire for a growing compatibility between its public pedagogy and a commercial culture's ethos of egocentric narcissism, social aggression and hypermasculinity.

Continuing its expansion into the early childhood market, Disney expanded its programming for children with the launch of Disney Junior in 2011, a new digital cable and satellite television network that offers original television series and movies aimed at children under the age of eight. Since that time Disney has expanded its offerings to include multimedia games and video on demand available online. As of 2015, Disney Junior is available to 74,972,000 households in the United States alone (Seidman, 2015). Interestingly, Disney Junior is marketed with the slogan "Where the Magic Begins," reflecting Disney's desire to increasingly shape the identity and buying behaviors of even the youngest consumers in the digital age.

The issues surrounding Disney culture as a source of identity for young people are complex. Adult existence, according to Zygmunt Bauman (2007), involves "changing one's ego" (p. 107) through "an unending series of self-focused pursuits, each episode lived through as an overture to the next" (p. 109). Whether or not this is a dramatic departure from the way life was lived in the past, it is nevertheless becoming clear that today's youth also are now caught up in negotiating shifting identities through processes that involve a constant engagement with educational sites throughout the culture. How much more challenging, then, will young people who are just embarking on the process of identity development find the navigation of a commercialized culture that appears to offer limitless choice in terms of selfhood, yet, effectively limits the choices that both children and adults can make in extending their sense of personal and collective agency?

One sign of how The Walt Disney Company seeks to intervene in children's lives by shaping their identity narratives was evident in the company's 2010 redesign of over 300 Disney Stores to mirror a theme park design (Disney Press Release, 2015). Based on the prototype called Imagination Park, the renovated stores were networked with interactive technology to create a multisensory recreational experience that encouraged consumer participation and emphasized community through collective activities (Barnes, 2009b). The interactive components include a LED-lit Pixie Dust Trail that guides customers through the store, Magic Trees in which familiar Disney characters appear, a custom silhouetted skyline that lines the perimeter of the store and incorporates local landmarks into a character-filled skyscape, and an expansive video library with media content that guests can watch on large flat screens (Disney Press Release, 2015). The Disney store refurbishment project, which cost approximately $1 million per store, sought "to make children clamor to visit the stores and stay longer" (Barnes, 2009b, para. 3). By enabling visitors to generate a narrative for their own consumption, the stores offer the illusion that kids are the producers of meaning and have the capacity to customize their identities through the stories that are created around Disney products and places. Such power is not necessarily false and it is undoubtedly seductive in a world of narrowing opportunities for agency and expression—perhaps even more so for children and youth for whom such opportunities are few and for whom the spectacular has not yet lost the appeal of novelty. At the same time, it confines the imagination and any corresponding sense of community to the narratives on offer, which ultimately all lead back to immersing the individual in fun, conflict-free processes of consumption designed to generate corporate profits.

It is astounding the ease with which Disney's conventional fantasy formula for young adults—highlighted by the popularity of past films like *High School Musical* and its sequels and current Disney Channel sitcoms such as *Dog With A Blog*, *Jessie*, *Girl Meets World*, and *Liv and Maddie*—reduces unpleasant and contradictory lived experiences to the 'trials and tribulations' of well-off kids who 'just want to fit in,' and can easily do so by participating in consumer culture. Rapping (1995) observes a similar thematic message in the design of Disney World, which, not unlike the world of the *High School Musical* films, is "uniform in its middle-American, asexual, uninflected sameness," all of which works to embody a "sense of classless luxury and unthreatening sameness . . . a synthetic spirit of democracy" that promises a kind of belonging free from the "stress of competition" (p. 36). The Disney celebrity factory has long been masterful at churning out clean-cut teen idols who symbolize these wholesomely bland American values. According to the Disney formula, self-expression is once again reduced to what a young person can afford to buy. And Disney is an expert at reinforcing such cycles of brand promotion by generating relationships between its media offerings and consumer products. As Budd (2005) explains, the company exhibits "highly developed corporate synergy in which every Disney product is both a commodity and an ad for every other Disney commodity" (p. 1).

Disney channel role models should be considered within a context of consumerism and what they teach young people in terms of their identities, values and aspirations. These stars represent the most commodified of role models, severely and insidiously proscribing the imaginative possibilities for a generation of children who are taught that their identities are things to be bought and sold and their emotional and psychological health as best nurtured through consumption. Concepts of self and society are undoubtedly shifting as we witness the "growing interpenetration of the economic and the cultural" (Bryman, 2004, p. 173). Spaces that were once constructed through "forms of public culture," as noted by Zukin (1995), have now become privatized, controlled and framed by corporate culture (p. 77). These spaces, from suburban shopping malls to tourist spots to city centers, encourage leisure while also "priming the young for consumerism" (Bryman, 2004, p. 169). While colonizing multiple cultural spaces, corporations like Disney are increasingly looking to virtual space in order to provide 'enhanced' experiences for a consumer class that wants to maximize its leisure time. Developing virtual online worlds gives Disney, to a greater extent than at any previous point in history, more global corporate control over the "production of subjectivity that is not fixed in identity, but hybrid and modulating" (Hardt & Negri, 2000, p. 331). Paradoxically, though, Disney gains access to children and adults by selling the illusion of fixity. Disney not only represents "one of the best-known symbols of capitalist consumerism" (Lyne, 2004), but also claims to offer consumers a stable, known quantity in its brand-name products. In other words, Disney culture acts as a temporary salve to growing feelings of uncertainty and insecurity produced by economic dislocations and social instability on a national and global scale. It is no small irony that, while offering people the "swindle of fulfillment" promised by rampant consumerism (Ernst Bloch, quoted in Rabinach, 1977, p. 8), multinational corporations such as Disney are one of the globalizing forces largely responsible for the instabilities and upheavals facing contemporary nation states.

Indeed, the sovereignty of national governments is increasingly challenged by the power of multinational corporations and the logic of the marketplace they embody; governments are downsized and their services are privatized or gutted, corporations receive incentives in the form of huge tax breaks or bailouts with taxpayers' money, legislation is passed that further deregulates the market and democratically elected governments fail in their responsibilities to foster a just and equal society. Given these conditions, it is no wonder that individuals find comfort in the stable meanings they can ascribe to Disney and turn to consumption for even the semblance of personal agency. Multinational corporations such as Disney have become "the aristocratic articulations" (Hardt & Negri, 2000, p. 314) of a global monopoly of power and coercion that is imposed from above and that achieves control through circuits that do not reveal themselves because they operate on the "terrain of the production and regulation of subjectivity" itself (p. 321)— that is, in the realm of cultural production and consumption. According to Seabrook (1998), capitalism adapts to local cultures and conditions in ways that secure its profit-making power: "The market does not simply obliterate all earlier traditions. It is opportunistic. It will enhance and concentrate on those features of a society which turn a profit or change them in such a way that they will make money" (para. 9). Consequently, everything potentially becomes a commodity, including and perhaps most especially, identity. Global capitalism manages and controls diversity by commodifying and selling different identity positions, while also encouraging self-commodification—particularly of youth—through various marketing trends and technologies that become increasingly ubiquitous in the lives of adults, teens and the very youngest children alike (Chester & Montgomery, 2007, 2008).

Conclusion

Children are not born with consumer habits. Their identities have to be actively directed to assume the role of consumer. If Disney had its way, kids' culture would become not merely a new market for the accumulation of capital, but a petri dish for producing new commodified subjects. As a group, young people are vulnerable to corporate giants such as Disney, which makes every effort "to expand 'inwardly' into the psyche and emotional life of the individual in order to utilize human potential" in the service of a market society (Rutherford, 2008). Virtually every child is now vulnerable to the many advertisers and entertainment providers who diversify markets through various niches, most recently evident in the use of mobile technologies and online social media. Complicit, wittingly or unwittingly, with a global politics defined by market power, the American public offers little resistance to children's culture being expropriated and colonized by large multimedia conglomerates and Madison Avenue advertisers. Eager to enthrall kids with invented fears and lacks, corporate media culture also entices them with equally unimagined new desires, to prod them into spending money or to influence their parents to spend it in order to fill corporate coffers.

The potential for lucrative profits to be made off the spending habits and economic influence of kids has certainly not been lost on Disney and a number of other multinational corporations, which under the deregulated, privatized, no-holds-barred world of the free market have set out to embed the dynamics of commerce, exchange value and commercial transactions into every aspect of personal and daily life. Wrapping itself up in the discourse of innocence and family-oriented amusement in order to camouflage the mechanisms and deployment of corporate power, Disney uses its various entertainment platforms that cut across all forms of traditional and new media in a relentless search for young customers to incessantly bombard with a pedagogy of commerce. In the broader society, as the culture of the market displaces civic culture, children are no longer prioritized as an important social investment or viewed as a central marker for the moral life of the nation. Instead, childhood ideals linked to the protection and well-being of youth are transformed—decoupled from the "call to conscience [and] civic engagement" (Adatto, 2003, p. 40)—and redefined through what amounts to a culture of excessive individualism and the numbing of public consciousness.

Rather than participate mindlessly in the Disneyfication of culture, we all need to excavate the excluded memories and silenced voices that could challenge the uncomplicated commodified identities offered to young people by Disney in the name of innocence and entertainment. As one of the most influential corporations in the world, Disney does more than provide entertainment: it also shapes in very powerful ways how young people understand themselves, relate to others and experience the larger society. It is not difficult to recognize tragedy in the fact that a combination of entrenched social inequality and a lack of resources means that kids disappear literally into foster care institutions, teachers are overwhelmed in over-crowded classrooms and state services are drained of funds and cannot provide basic food and shelter to growing numbers of kids and their families. Yet, corporations such as Disney have ample funds to hire a battalion of highly educated and specialized experts to infiltrate the most intimate spaces of children and family life—all the better to colonize the fears, aspirations and futures of young people.

Disney's commodification of childhood is neither innocent nor simply a function of entertainment. The values Disney produces as it attempts to commandeer children's desires and hopes may offer us one of the most important clues about the changing nature of our society and the destructive force behind the unchecked economic power wielded by massive cor-porations. Strategies for challenging the corporate power and the consumer culture Disney propagates in the United States and increasingly across the rest of the globe must be aligned with a vision of a democracy that is on the side of children and youth. It must enable the conditions for young people to learn and develop as engaged social actors more alive to their responsibility to future generations than those adults who have presently turned away from the challenge.

Notes

1   For a list of The Walt Disney Company's vast holdings, see the website *Who Owns What*, compiled by Columbia Journalism Review (2013).

2   Allen D. Kanner and some of his colleagues raised the ethical issues with child psychologists helping marketers in a letter to the American Psychological Association (see Kanner, 2005, 2006; Zoll, 2000).

3   A transcript of this letter from Robert A. Iger to Mark A. Emmert, president of the University of Washington, dated August 13, 2007, is available online (see Marco, 2007).

4   Letter from Mark A. Emmert to Robert Iger, dated August 16, 2007, is available online (see Schwarz, 2007b).

5   Additional factors affecting this loss of time include (1) pressure on parents "to produce superachieving children," which leads them to overschedule their kids' time in structured, 'enrichment' activities; and (2) the restructuring of public schools to focus on academic study, which has led to decreased time for recess periods, physical education and creative-arts programming (Ginsburg, 2007, p. 183).

6   For an excellent critique of how parental fears are mobilized as part of a larger effort to professionalize parenting, see Furedi (2008).

References

Adatto, K. (2003, Summer). Selling out childhood. *Hedgehog Review, 5*(2), 24–40. Retrieved from: http://www.iasc-culture.org/THR/archives/Commodification/5.2DAdatto.pdf

American Academy of Pediatrics. (2013). Policy statement: Children, adolescents, and the media. *PEDIATRICS, 132*(5), 958–961. Retrieved from: http://pediatrics.aappublications.org/content/early/2013/10/24/peds.2013-2656.full.pdf

American Psychological Association. (2004, February 23). Television advertising leads to unhealthy habits in children, says APA task force. American Psychological Association press release. Retrieved from: http://www.apa.org/news/press/releases/2004/02/children-ads.aspx

Barnes, B. (2007, December 31). Web playgrounds of the very young. *The New York Times*. Retrieved from: http://www.nytimes.com/2007/12/31/business/31virtual.html

Barnes, B. (2009a, April 13). Disney expert uses science to draw boy viewers. *The New York Times*. Retrieved from: http://www.nytimes.com/2009/04/14/arts/television/14boys.html

Barnes, B. (2009b, October 12). Disney's retail plan is a theme park in its stores. *The New York Times*. Retrieved from: http://www.nytimes.com/2009/10/13/business/media/13disney.html

Barnes, B. (2009c, November 4). After Mickey's makeover, less Mr. Nice Guy. *The New York Times*. Retrieved from: http://www.nytimes.com/2009/11/05/business/media/05mickey.html

Barnes, B. (2011, February 6). Disney looking into cradle for customers. *The New York Times*. Retrieved from: http://www.nytimes.com/2011/02/07/business/media/07disney.html

Bauman, Z. (2007). *Liquid times: Living in an age of uncertainty*. London: Polity.

Bryce, R. (2005, August 22). Click and sell: Marketers shift ad dollars and take advantage of Internet's ability to target potential customers. Austin: The University of Texas at Austin. Retrieved from: https://www.utexas.edu/features/2005/advertising/

Bryman, A. (2004). *The Disneyization of society*. London: Sage.

Budd, M. (2005). Introduction: Private Disney, public Disney. In M. Budd & M. H. Kirsch (Eds.), *Rethinking Disney: Private control, public dimensions* (pp. 1–33). Middletown, CT: Wesleyan University Press.

Chester, J., & Montgomery, K. (2007). Interactive food and beverage marketing: Targeting children in the digital age. Berkeley, CA: Media Studies Group. Retrieved from: http://digitalads.org/documents/digiMarketingFull.pdf

Chester, J., & Montgomery, K. (2008, July/August). No escape: Marketing to kids in the digital age. *Multinational Monitor, 30*(1). Retrieved from: http://www.multinationalmonitor.org/mm2008/072008/chester.html

Cohen, L. (2003). *A consumer's republic: The politics of mass consumption in postwar America*. New York: Vintage.

Columbia Journalism Review. (2013, February 14). *Who owns what*. Retrieved from: http://www.cjr.org/resources/?c=disney

Common Sense Media (2014, Spring). Advertising to children and teens: Current practices. Common Sense Media Research Brief. Retrieved from: https://www.commonsensemedia.org/file/csm-advertisingresearchbrief-20141pdf/download

Disney Press Release. (2007, August 1). The Walt Disney Company acquires Club Penguin. The Walt Disney Company. Retrieved from: http://www.clubpenguin. com/company/news-media/walt-disney-company-acquires-club-penguin

Disney Press Release. (2015, February 27). Disney Store: Disney Store highlights. Anaheim, CA: Walt Disney Company. Retrieved from: https://enterpriseportal. disney.com/gopublish/sitemedia/dcp/Home/Press%20Room/Press%20Kits/us_pr_ press_kit_disney_store_fact_sheet_022715.pdf

Fischer, P. M., Schwartz, M. P., Richards, Jr., J. W., Goldstein, A. O., & Rojas, T. H. (1991). Brand logo recognition by children aged 3 to 6 years: Mickey Mouse and Old Joe the Camel. *Journal of the American Medical Association, 266*(22), 3145–3148.

Furedi, F. (2008). *Paranoid parenting* (2nd ed.). New York: Continuum.

Ginsburg, K. R. (2007, January). The importance of play in promoting healthy child development and maintaining strong parent-child bonds. *PEDIATRICS, 119*(1), 182–191. Retrieved from: www.pediatrics.org/cgi/doi/10.1542/ peds.2006–2697

Giroux, H. A. (1999). *The mouse that roared: Disney and the end of innocence*. Lanham, MD: Rowman & Littlefield.

Golin, J. (2007, August 1). Nation's strongest school commercialism bill advances out of committee. Common Dreams Progressive Newswire. Retrieved from: http:// www.commercialfreechildhood.org/nation's-strongest-school-commercialism-bill- advances-out-committee-ccfc-lauds-joint-committee

Grimes, S. M. (2008, February). Saturday morning cartoons go MMOG. *Media International Australia, 126,* 120–131.

Grossberg, L. (2005). *Caught in the crossfire: Kids, politics, and America's future*. Boulder, CO: Paradigm.

Hardt, M., & Negri, A. (2000). *Empire*. Cambridge, MA: Harvard University Press.

Hazen, D., & Winokur, J. (Eds.). (1997). *We the media*. New York: New Press.

Iger, R. (2014). The Walt Disney Company fiscal year 2014 annual financial report and shareholder letter. Anaheim, CA: The Walt Disney Company. Retrieved from: http://thewaltdisneycompany.com/sites/default/files/reports/10k-wrap-2014_1.pdf

Kanner, A. D. (2005). Globalization and the commercialization of childhood. *Tikkun, 20*(5), 49–51. Retrieved from: http://www.tikkun.org/article.php/Kanner- Globalization

Kanner, A. D. (2006, January/February). The corporatized child. *California Psychologist, 39*(1), 1–2. Retrieved from: http://commercialfreechildhood.org/sites/default/files/ kanner_corporatizedchild.pdf

Linn, S. (2004). *Consuming kids: The hostile takeover of childhood*. New York: New Press.

Lyne, J. (2004, October 10). Hong Kong Disneyland tops out centerpiece structure. *The Site Selection Online Insider*. Retrieved from: http://www.siteselection.com/ ssinsider/snapshot/sf041014.htm

Marco, M. (2007, August 13). Walt Disney demands retraction from University of Washington over Baby Einstein video press release. *The Consumerist*. Retrieved from: http://consumerist.com/2007/08/13/walt-disney-demands-retraction-from-university- of-washington-over-baby-einstein-video-press-release/

Molnar, A., & Boninger, F. (2007). *Adrift: Schools in a total marketing environment: Tenth annual report on schoolhouse commercialism trends 2006–2007*. Tempe: Arizona State University.

Quart, A. (2003). *Branded: The buying and selling of teenagers*. New York: Basic Books.

Rabinach, A. (1977, Spring). Unclaimed heritage: Ernst Bloch's heritage of our times and the theory of fascism. *New German Critique, 11,* 5–21.

Rapping, E. (1995, November). A bad ride at Disney World. *The Progressive, 59*(11), 36–37.

Rideout, V. J. (2007, June). *Parents, children, and media: A Kaiser Family Foundation survey.* Menlo Park, CA: Kaiser Family Foundation. Retrieved from: https://kaiserfamily foundation.files.wordpress.com/2013/01/7638.pdf

Rideout, V. J., Foehr, U. G., & Roberts, D. F. (2010, January). *Generation M2: Media in the lives of 8–18 year-olds.* Menlo Park, CA: The Kaiser Family Foundation. Retrieved from: https://kaiserfamilyfoundation.files.wordpress.com/2013/04/8010. pdf

Rideout, V. J., Roberts, D. F., & Foehr, U. G. (2005, March). *Generation M: Media in the lives of 8–18 year-olds.* Menlo Park, CA: The Kaiser Family Foundation. Retrieved from: https://kaiserfamilyfoundation.files.wordpress.com/2013/01/generation-m-media-in-the-lives-of-8-18-year-olds-report.pdf

Rideout, V. J., Vandewater, E. A., & Wartella, E. A. (2003, Fall). *Zero to six: Electronic media in the lives of infants, toddlers and preschoolers.* Menlo Park, CA: Kaiser Family Foundation. Retrieved from: http://www.dcmp.org/caai/nadh169.pdf

Rutherford, J. (2008, Spring). The culture of capitalism. *Soundings, 38*, 8–18. Retrieved from: https://eprints.mdx.ac.uk/5944/1/02s38rutherford.pdf

Schor, J. B. (2004). *Born to buy: The commercialized child and the new consumer culture.* New York: Scribner.

Schwarz, J. (2007a, August 7). Baby DVDs, videos may hinder, not help, infants' language development. Seattle: University of Washington. Retrieved from: http://www. washington.edu/news/2007/08/07/baby-dvds-videos-may-hinder-not-help-infants-language-development/

Schwarz, J. (2007b, August 16). UW President rejects Disney complaints. *University of Washington News.* Retrieved from: http://www.washington.edu/news/2007/08/16/ uw-president-rejects-disney-complaints/

Seabrook, J. (1998, December). The racketeers of illusion. *New Internationalist, 308.* Retrieved from: http://newint.org/features/1998/12/05/illusion/

Seidman, R. (2015, February 22). List of how many homes each cable network is in as of February 2015. TV by the Numbers, *Zap2it.* Retrieved from: http://tvbythe numbers.zap2it.com/2015/02/22/list-of-how-many-homes-each-cable-network-is-in-as-of-february-2015/366230/

Smith, E., & Schuker, L. A. E. (2009, September 1). Disney nabs Marvel heroes. *Wall Street Journal.* Retrieved from: http://www.wsj.com/articles/SB125172509349072393

Smith, G. (2013, March). Tweens 'R shoppers: A look at the tween market and shopping behaviour. POPAI: The Global Association for Marketing at Retail. Retrieved from: http://www.popai.com/uploads/downloads/POPAIWhitePaper-Tweens-R-Shoppers-2013.pdf

Walker, J. (Producer), & Bird, B. (Director) (2004). *The Incredibles* [Motion picture]. United States: Walt Disney Pictures & Pixar Animation Studios.

Zimmerman, F. J., Christakis, D. A., & Meltzoff, A. N. (2007, October). Associations between media viewing and language development in children under age 2 years. *Journal of Pediatrics, 151*(4), 364–368.

Zoll, M. H. (2000, March 23). Psychologists challenge ethics of marketing to children. *American News Service.* Retrieved from: http://www.berkshirepublishing.com/ans/ HTMView.asp?parItem=S031000377A

Zukin, S. (1995). *The cultures of cities.* Malden, MA: Wiley-Blackwell.

About the Contributors

Tasha Ausman is a PhD candidate in the Faculty of Education at the University of Ottawa. With Master's work in both education and English literature, as well as undergraduate studies in physiology and developmental biology, her research areas include mathematics education, curriculum studies, psychoanalysis, popular, and cultural studies. Tasha's current work uses a psychoanalytic stylistic to understand what might be at stake at the level of subjectivity on account of confronting compulsory mathematics education, and takes into account popular representations of mathematics and mathematicians that people see everyday in film and media. Tasha has published book chapters and conference proceedings, and her articles appear in *Transnational Curriculum Inquiry* and *Multicultural Education Review*.

Sandro R. Barros is an Assistant Professor in the Department of Curriculum, Instruction and Teacher Education at Michigan State University. His research examines how multilingual debates shape and are shaped by national and transnational public discourses, and how these discourses affect the ways in which citizens negotiate the meaning of language and culture. He is the author of *Competing Truths in Latin America: Narrating Otherness and Marginality* (Floricanto Press, 2010).

George J. Bey, III holds the Chisholm Chair in Arts and Sciences at Millsaps College where he also serves as the Associate Dean of International Education. He holds a PhD in anthropology from Tulane University carrying out his fieldwork primarily in Mexico where he studied the ancient Maya. His research interest in the relationships between built environments, ideology, and power both in ancient and modern societies led him to begin studying Disney and in particular Walt Disney World.

Jake Burdick is an Assistant Professor of Curriculum Studies at Purdue University. Jake is the co-editor of the *Handbook of Public Pedagogy* (Routledge, 2012), *Complicated Conversations and Confirmed Commitments: Revitalizing Education for Democracy* (Educators International Press, 2009), and *Problematizing Public Pedagogy* (Routledge, 2014). He has published work in *Qualitative Inquiry, Curriculum Inquiry, Review of Research in Education, Review of Educational Research*, and the *Journal of Curriculum and Pedagogy*. Jake can be contacted at burdics@purdue.edu.

Annette Furo (University of Ottawa) is a PhD candidate and Part-Time Professor, critical pedagogue, and settler Canadian. Her research explores classroom pedagogies of reconciliation, the integration of Indigenous knowledges into the school curriculum, and (de)colonial curricular discourses. Her publications appear in the *Journal of Curriculum Theorizing, Transnational Curriculum Inquiry*, and a number of social justice oriented magazines.

Julie C. Garlen is an Associate Professor of Education in the Department of Teaching and Learning at Georgia Southern University, where she supervises doctoral students in curriculum studies and teaches courses in early childhood education, curriculum, and inquiry. Her co-authored works in cultural curriculum studies have appeared in *Cultural Studies <=> Critical Methodologies, Pedagogy, Cultural, and Society*, and *Journal of Consumer Culture*. She has written extensively on popular culture, critical pedagogy, and curriculum theory, and has served on the review board for a number of regional and national journals.

Henry A. Giroux currently holds a chair for Scholarship in the Public Interest at McMaster University in the English and Cultural Studies Department. He is also the Paulo Freire Distinguished Scholar Chair in Critical pedagogy and holds a Distinguished Visiting Professorship at Ryerson University.

Nichole E. Grant (née Lowe) is a PhD candidate in the Faculty of Education in Society, Culture and Literacies at the University of Ottawa. She researches the intersections of digital culture and antiracism education, including processes of racialization and racialized knowledge production through digital media, discourses of race and racisms, and antiracist methodologies in education.

Rachel Alicia Griffin is an Associate Professor in the Department of Communication Studies at Southern Illinois University (SIU), cross-appointed in Africana Studies and Women, Gender, and Sexuality Studies. As a critical intercultural scholar, her research spans Black feminist thought, critical race theory, popular culture, sport, education, and sexual violence. Dr. Griffin has published in *Women's Studies in Communication, Critical Studies in Media Communication*, the *International Journal of Qualitative Studies in Education, The Howard Journal of Communications*, and the *Journal of International and Intercultural Communication*. She has also delivered well over 100 national and international presentations.

Mark Helmsing is an Assistant Professor of Social Studies Education and affiliate faculty in the Queer Studies Program at the University of Wyoming. His research explores pedagogies of civic virtues and national belonging in figural tropes, such as allegory and myth, and through affective constructs, such as patriotism and heritage. He writes widely on curricular topics in museums and school classrooms as well as objects in popular culture ranging from 9/11 to Walt Disney to horror films and television dramas.

Gabriel S. Huddleston is an Assistant Professor of Curriculum Studies at Texas Christian University. His work utilizes a Cultural Studies theoretical framework within qualitative research to examine intersections between schools and neoliberal education reform. His other research interests include popular culture, spatial theory, new materialism, and postcolonial studies. He recently served as co-guest editor for a special issue of the academic journal *Critical Literacy*, "Spivak and Education" and authored one of its articles, "An Awkward Stance: On Gayatri Spivak and Double Binds." Gabriel is currently Managing Editor of *Journal of Curriculum Theorizing*.

Nadine M. Kalin is an Associate Professor of Art Education at the University of North Texas within the College of Visual Arts and Design. Her work intertwines post-political critique and contemporary art theories with philosophical and arts-based modes of inquiry in the exploration of curriculum, pedagogical ethics, labor, institutional critique, and strategies of dissensus related to visual arts, design, and art museum education under neoliberalism. Nadine graduated from the University of British Columbia in 2007 with a PhD in Curriculum Studies.

Will Letts is the Associate Dean of Courses in the Faculty of Education at Charles Sturt University and a member of the Research Institute for Professional Practice, Learning, and Education. Disney first captured his imagination at the age of six, when he first saw *Bambi* and fell in love with Thumper, and ever since then Disney has provided a host of characters that he could identify with or wanted to count among his friends.

Jorge Lucero is an artist who is currently serving as an assistant professor of art education in the School of Art + Design at the University of Illinois, Urbana-Champaign. Through the permissions of conceptual art Lucero now sees the potential of being in the academy.

Michael Macaluso is a doctoral candidate and Graduate Instructor in Michigan State University's Curriculum, Instruction, and Teacher Education program. His research and teaching focus on critical and postmodern perspectives in English education and young adult and canonical literature.

Linda Radford is a lecturer at the University of Ottawa's Faculty of Education. Her research focuses on social media, changing literacies, and the place of digital technologies in teacher education. Recent and ongoing projects include the empowerment of marginalized youth through engaging literacies in critical ways, the development of an urban education community program, and assessing change practice initiatives through university-ministry partnerships.

Pamela Rogers is a PhD candidate in the Faculty of Education at the University of Ottawa. A former high school social studies teacher and current Part-time Professor in the Faculty of Education at the University of Ottawa and Humber College Department of Liberal Arts, her research interests span policy sociology, social studies education, knowledge production, anti-oppressive pedagogies, and LGBTQ teacher identity formation.

Jennifer A. Sandlin is an Associate Professor in the Justice and Social Inquiry program in the School of Social Transformation at Arizona State University, where she teaches courses focused on consumption and education, public pedagogy, and curriculum theory. Her research focuses on the intersections of education, learning, and consumption, as well as on understanding and theorizing public pedagogy. She recently edited, with Peter McLaren, *Critical Pedagogies of Consumption* (Routledge, 2010); with Brian Schultz and Jake Burdick, *Handbook of Public Pedagogy* (Routledge, 2010); and with Jake Burdick and Michael O'Malley, *Problematizing Public Pedagogy* (Routledge, 2014).

Kelsey Catherine Schmitz (University of Ottawa) is a PhD candidate, Part-Time Professor, and Educational Technologies Consultant. She researches anti-oppressive spaces in digital technologies, with a focus on digital culture, gender, and race. She and Nichole Grant have an upcoming collection titled *Radical Pedagogies: Flipping the Script of the Classroom* which encompasses both their research domains in education.

Shirley R. Steinberg is Research Professor of Youth Studies at the University of Calgary and Director of the Institute for Youth and Community Research at the University of the West of Scotland. She is executive director of the freireproject.org and the author of many books on media literacy, critical pedagogy, urban and youth culture, and cultural studies. Her edited books include: *Critical Youth Studies* (Peter Lang, 2014); *Critical Qualitative Research Reader* (Peter Lang, 2012); and *Kinderculture: The Corporate Construction of Childhood* (Westview Press, 2011).

Caleb Steindam is doctoral candidate in curriculum and instruction and an adjunct instructor of teaching and learning at Loyola University Chicago. Caleb previously worked as an elementary school teacher in Honduras, China, and Sierra Leone, and a high school Spanish teacher in New York City. Caleb's interests as an educator and educational researcher include teaching for social and environmental justice, cultural responsiveness, aesthetic education, social and emotional learning, and community partnerships in P-12 teaching and teacher education.

Jason J. Wallin is Sorcerer's Apprentice at the Ivory Tower, where he teaches courses in the occult works of Chernabog, the politics of object sentience, and critical issues in lycanthrope studies. Previously, Jason studied under Professor Ratigan and Doctor Facilier and was funded by the prestigious Cecaelia Foundation. Jason is perhaps best known for *Fashions of Death: A History of Animal Abuse in the Fashion Industry* (2012) and *Case Studies in Interspecies and Inter-Object Relations* (2013). Jason is currently Assistant Layout Supervisor at *The Pickford Penny Pincher* and is presently researching his third book, which will investigate everyday uses of hedge magic.

Robin Redmon Wright is an Assistant Professor of Adult Education at Penn State, Harrisburg. An award-winning researcher and teacher, her work is framed by critical and feminist theories and focuses on systemic, normalized inequalities, and the ways those discriminatory systems are, or are not, supported and reproduced through popular culture and the creative arts. She is interested in how fans of popular culture internalize or resist its messages, and how they might incorporate that response into their identities and worldviews. She also researches issues of identity, socioeconomic class, gender, and education through autoethnography. She may be contacted at rrw12@psu.edu.

Index

Abowitz, K. K., & Rousmaniere, K. 63, 64
African Americans 125, 131–2; see also Black feminism and girlhood (Doc McStuffins)
agonism 198–9, 200–2, 203–4, 205–6
Ahmed, S. 2, 152, 159, 211–12, 214
American Academy of Pediatrics 233–4, 239–40
American Dream 20, 125, 126, 128, 129, 130, 133, 169
American Pickers 129–30
anthropomorphism 95–6
anti-Semitism 52–3
Appalachian Outlaws 131
Araújo, C. 112–17
Ariel 60, 61, 62, 63, 68–9, 153, 156
art museums: agonism 198–9, 200–2, 203–4, 205–6; democracy/participation 198–9, 201, 202, 203–6; "Discourse and Discord" (D&D) symposium (Walker Art Center) 198–200, 201–2, 203–4, 205–6; Disneyization/Disneyfication 193–8, 200–2
Arvidsson, A. 106–7, 114, 227–8, 229
attachment and identification 62–3
Aurora 40–1, 61, 70–1

Baby Einstein videos 239–40
Bambi 91–2, 95
Barnes, B. 161, 167, 223, 237, 238, 240, 241, 242–3
Baudrillard, J. 117, 124, 136–40, 141, 142, 143–5
Bauman, Z. 205, 242

Beauty and the Beast 38, 68
Belle 38–40
Berlant, L. 62
Berry, W. 93, 96
Bhabha, H. 34, 42, 43
Bielak, S., & Duffalo, A. 198, 201
biophilia, concept of 89
Black feminism and girlhood (Doc McStuffins) 161–2, 164–70; departure from oppressive norms 164–6; deracialization and commodification 168–70; mammification 170–1; media representation 162–3; self-definition and self-determination 166–8; theory and textual analysis method 163–4
blogs: Brazilian 107–11, 112–17; on Disney villains 59, 71; see also waltdisneyconfessions@tumblr
Bogost, I. 224–5, 227, 228
Bourdieu, P. 106; & Passeron, J. 122, 124
boys: research and marketing strategies 237–8
brands 229
Brave see Merida (princess)
Brazil (Disney trip) 105–6; challenging consumption in middle class normativity 108–11; dreaming as commodity 111–17; mapping location of discourse 106–8
Brode, D. 10, 66
Brooks, P. 35, 37–8, 40–1, 43, 44
Brother Bear 91, 94
Bruckner, L. D. 91, 92, 96
Bryman, A. 13–16, 194–5, 196, 197, 199, 200, 221–2, 223, 225–6, 230, 243–4

Budd, M. 1, 5, 6, 8, 10–11, 12–13, 15, 243; & Kirsch, M. H. 7, 10–11
Butler, J. 74, 78–9, 209, 210–11, 215
Byrne, E., & McQuillan, M. 60

camp villains 148–9; camp sensibilities and enactments 149–51; commodifying heteropatriarchy 154–6, 158; difference as normative 151–4; refusing normative readings 156–9
capitalism 10–11, 51, 88–9, 205; Fordist 51, 52, 53–4; libidinal 140–2; and modernity 138; reality television (RTV) 127–30, 132–3; *see also* commodification; consumerism; corporate strategies
Cheu, J. 10
child psychologists 238
childhood: and adult self 113; commodification of *see* corporate strategies
Cinderella 61–2, 66, 68, 181–2
Club Penguin 241
commodification: of childhood *see* corporate strategies; and deracialization 168–70; of dreaming 111–17; of heteropatriarchy 154–6, 158
consumerism: art museums 194, 199; challenges to 108–11; hybrid consumption 196, 199
contagion 139–40
control in theme parks 14–16; *see also* MyMagic+
Cooke-Jackson, A., & Hansen, E. K. 124, 131
corporate agenda of reality television (RTV) 123–5
corporate sponsors 13
corporate strategies 233–6, 245–6; babies and toddlers 238–45; marketing and research 234, 235, 236–8
The Cosby Show 169, 172
cultural hierarchies 5–6
cultural production and reception 81–3

de Beauvoir, S. 210–11
Dean, J. 203, 204
Deleuze, G. 224, 225, 227
democracy/participation 198–9, 201, 202, 203–6
Depression Era 48, 49, 52, 53

deracialization and commodification 168–70
desire: psychoanalytic stylistic method 34–6, 44; spectre of 54–5
discourse: D&D symposium (Walker Art Center) 198–200, 201–2, 203–4, 205–6; middle class Brazilians 106–8; public 84
Disney Baby 240
Disney Junior 242
Disney scholarship 1–5; films 7–11; history of 5–7; theme parks 11–16
Disney Studio strike (1941) 53–4
Disneyfication/Disneyization: of art museums 193–8, 200–2; concept of 16, 194–5, 199, 221–2
diva pedagogues 63–6; diva villains 59–61; queer pedagogues 61–3; transgressive pedagogues 66–9; unhappy endings 70–1
Doc McStuffins see Black feminism and girlhood
Dorfman, A., & Mattelart, A. 10, 11, 117
Doty, A. 63, 155, 157, 159
Down East Dickering 130–1
dreaming: commodification of 111–17; "Dream Along with Mickey" 183–4; horror of 142–3
Duck Dynasty 128–9

Edelman, L. 65–6
Edgerton G., & Jackson, K. M. 10
edutainment 194, 196, 201
Elsa (princess) 73–4, 84; femininity and makeover model 75–7; postfeminist empowerment 77–8; postfeminist ideal 74–5; postfeminist masculinity 80–1; rethinking cultural production and reception 81–3; whiteness 78–80
employees (theme parks) 15, 132, 197, 223
empowerment, postfeminist 77–8
environmentalism 11, 91–2, 97, 179–80

fairy tales 8; plot structure 211–12, 213–14
"Fantasmic" 184–5
fantasy/phantasy 35, 89; nostalgia 47, 54; and repression 55–7
FastPass+ 228

Feldstein, R. 55
feminist perspective 2, 8–9; *see also* Black feminism and girlhood (*Doc McStuffins*); Elsa (princess); Merida (princess)
fetishization of Disney 141
film themes 7–11
Fisher, M. 140–2, 143
Fjellman, S.J. 12, 13, 180, 224
Fleras, A., & Dixon, S. 127
Ford, Henry/Fordism 51, 52, 53–4
Foucault, M. 209, 215
Freud, S. 35, 51, 55
Frozen see Elsa (princess)

Gates Jr., H. L. 172
gay subtexts *see* camp villains; diva villains
gender performance 210–11
Giroux, H. A. 47–8, 81–2, 84, 87, 106, 110, 121–3, 162, 214–15; & Pollock, G. 3, 4, 148, 152, 157, 170, 202, 221
Governor Ratcliffe 152, 154
Griffin, S. 9, 63–4, 148, 152, 153
Grimhilde 64, 65, 68
Grossberg, L. 233, 238

Hades 152, 153
Halperin, D. 148, 149, 150–1, 153, 156, 159
Hancock, P. 195, 196, 221–2
happy/unhappy endings 43, 70–1
Hardt, M., & Negri, A. 114, 244
Harrington, S. J. 48, 49, 50, 53
Harry Potter 188
heteronormative policing 214–15
heteropatriarchy, commodification of 154–6, 158
high and low culture 5–6
hooks, b. 163, 172
humor/parody 149, 150–1
hybrid consumption 196, 199

Ice Road Truckers 126–7
identity/identification 35; and attachment 62–3; influence of corporate culture 242–3, 244, 245; and third space 34, 42, 43–4
Iger, Robert 3, 132, 220, 235–6, 239, 240
Imagination Park 242–3

imagined community 114
Inside Out 54–5, 56
Internet *see* blogs; media technologies; social media; waltdisneyconfessions@tumblr
It's a Small World 56

Jacobson, H. 96
Japan 3
Jhappan, R., & Stasiulis, D. 10
Jiminy Cricket 181, 185, 186, 187
The Jungle Book 91, 92–3, 94

Knight, C. K. 13, 16
Kuenz, J. 15

labor: and anti-Semitism 52–3; Fordism 51, 52, 53–4; immaterial 227–9; and music 49–51, 56; performative 197–8, 200, 223; as pleasure 48–9, 51–2; repression, fantasy, and pedagogy 55–7; spectre of desire 54–5; theme park employees 15, 132, 197, 223; unionization and Disney Studio strike (1941) 53–4; working-class heroes 125–7
Lacan, J. 51, 56
Lady Tremaine 66, 68
language *see* discourse
Leistyna, P. 125–6, 128
Leonard, D. J. 169
liberation 138–9
The Lion King 90; Scar 152, 153, 155
The Little Mermaid (Ariel and Ursula) 60, 61, 62, 63, 68–9, 151–2, 153, 154, 155, 156
lookalike casting 38–40
Luciano, D. 62
Luttrell, G. 75–6
Lyne, J. 235, 244
Lyotard, J. F. 140–1

McCartney, Paul 92
McDonaldization 16, 226
magic 56, 179–81; "auto-magic antibodies" 117–18; defined 187–8; history of ideological development 181–2; lectures on ideology 182–7; reality of 188–90; taking home 190–1; *see also* MyMagic+
MagicBands 224–5, 227, 228, 230

Maleficent 67–8, 70–1, 143–4, 184, 185
Mallan, K., & McGillis, R. 151–2, 153, 154, 155, 158
mammification 170–1
marketing: princess brand 216–17; and research 234, 235, 236–8; theme parks 12–13
Marsh, Gary 161
masculinity, postfeminist 80–1
media technologies 237, 240–3
Mellinger, W.M. 125, 127, 131–2
merchantising 196–7, 200
Merida (princess) 208–9, 217–18; corseted curriculum 216–17; critical framework 209; curriculum of gender performance 210–11; heteronormative policing 214–15; restrictive narrative structure 211–14
Meyer, M. 150, 151, 158
Mickey Mouse 8, 181, 185; "Dream Along with Mickey" 183–4; as ego-ideal 49–50, 51, 56–7; reimagining 241–2
middle class 13; black 169, 172; *see also* Brazil (Disney trip)
Miller, T. 121, 123, 124, 168–9
Moseley, R. 75, 76–7
Mouffe, C. 199, 201–2
music and labor 49–51, 56
MyMagic+ 220–1; calculability of controlled leisure 225–7; curriculum of control 229–30; immaterial labor, and prosumption 227–9; society of control 221–5

narratives: concept of 35; feminist perspective 211–14; *see also* waltdisneyconfessions@tumblr
nature 11, 14–15, 87–8, 97; allure of 88–9; anthropomorphism 95–6; depictions of 89–96; environmentalism 11, 91–2, 97, 179–80; purity 90–2; wildness 92–4
The Nature Conservancy 90, 97
Nee, C. 164, 165–6, 167, 168, 170, 171
neoliberalism 110, 111, 115, 116–17, 132, 133
Newton, E. 148, 149, 150, 154, 156
nostalgia 47, 54

"otherness surgery" 144–5

participation/democracy 198–9, 201, 202, 203–6
performative labor 197–8, 200, 223
Peter Pan 41–2
pilgrimage metaphor 13–14, 180
Poster, M. 224, 227
power: postfeminist empowerment 77–8; simulation of 140
princesses *see* Elsa; Merida
Pro+agonist: The Art of Opposition 199, 200
Propp, V. 211, 213, 214
psychoanalytic perspective 47–8, 49–50, 51, 54–7
psychoanalytic stylistic method 34–6, 44
public discourse 84
public pedagogy 47–8, 106, 162, 214–15, 217–18
purity of nature 90–2

Quasimodo 37–8
queer perspective *see* camp villains; diva villains

race 9–10; African Americans 125, 131–2; postfeminist perspective 78–80; *see also* Black feminism and girlhood (*Doc McStuffins*)
radio frequency identification technology (RFID) 220, 227, 230
Reader, I. 14
reality television (RTV) 120–1; buy, bargain, and barter 127–30; corporate agenda of constructed reality 123–5; Disney-owned networks 121–3; new song of the south 132–3; redneck "bidness" 130–2; working-class heroes 125–7
religious parallels 115–16; pilgrimage metaphor 13–14, 180
Relyea, L. 194
repression and fantasy 55–7
Rideout, V. J. 239; et al. 237, 240
Ritzer, G. 16, 226, 228; & Liska, A. 223–4, 227
Roth, M. 153, 155

Scar 152, 153, 155
Schickel, R. 3, 5–6, 11
Schubert, W.H. 82, 83
Sedgwick, E. 60, 61

Sehlinger, B., & Testa, L. 222, 225
self-definition/self-determination 166–8
Sells, L. 9, 153
Serpe, N. 129, 130, 133
Shortsleeve, K. 49, 52–3
simulation 136–7; contagion 139–40;
   fatal strategies 145–6; horror of
   dreaming 142–3; liberation 138–9; and
   libidinal capitalism 140–2; perpetual
   Utopia or death of death 143–5;
   "reality transfusion" 137–8
Sleeping Beauty 40–1, 63–4, 70–1
Snow White 36–7, 61–2, 64, 65, 88
social media 82–3, 84, 237, 240–1;
   Reddit 76, 78, 79–80, 81; *see also*
   blogs; waltdisneyconfessions@tumblr
society of control 221–5
Sperb, J. 10
Steamboat Willie 48–51, 53
Stefanovic, I. L. 89
Stockton, K. B. 62
Storage Wars 129
surveillance 222–3, 224–5, 227, 229–30
Swamp People 130

Tarzan 93–4, 95
Tasker, Y., & Negra, D. 74, 76, 77, 78,
   80
Taxel, J. 189
technologies: media 237, 240–3; *see also*
   MyMagic+
television *see* Black feminism and
   girlhood (*Doc McStuffins*); reality
   television (RTV)
Telotte, J. P. 15, 222
theme parks 11–16, 179–80, 190–1;
   employees 15, 132, 197, 223;
   Imagination Park 242–3; *see also* Brazil
   (Disney trip); MyMagic+
theming 195–6, 199
third space of identification 34, 42,
   43–4
Thomas, F., & Johnston, O. 95–6

The Three Little Pigs 48–9, 51–3, 56
Tinkcom, M. 154, 156, 159
Tinkerbell 182, 186
transformations 64–5, 75
transgressive pedagogues 66–9
Tumblr *see*
   waltdisneyconfessions@tumblr

Ursula 60, 63, 68–9, 151–2, 153, 154,
   155, 156
utopian simulacrum 143–5

Vargas, V. 108–11
video games 241–2
villainy: fairy tale plot structure 213;
   see also camp villains; diva villains
virtual reality *see* simulation
Vizier Jafar 152, 154
Voloshinov, N. V. et al. 116

Walker Art Center: "Discourse and
   Discord" (D&D) symposium 198–200,
   201–2, 203–4, 205–6
waltdisneyconfessions@tumblr 31–3;
   analysis 42–4; Aurora 40–1; Belle
   38–40; conceptual framework 33–4;
   methodology 34–42; Peter Pan 41–2;
   Quasimodo 37–8; Snow White 36–7
Warner, M. 64
Wasko, J. 1, 5, 6, 7–9, 11–12, 13, 15,
   189
White, C. 79–80
whiteness 78–80
wildness of nature 92–4
willfulness 211–14
Wilson, E.O. 88–9, 93
"Wishes" 185–7
Wolfreys, J. 66–7, 68
Wood, H., & Skeggs, B. 124–5
working class *see* reality television (RTV)
World War II propaganda films 53, 56

Zipes, J. 8, 67